MIYAMOTO
MUSASHI

MIYAMOTO MUSASHI

His Life
and Writings

Kenji Tokitsu

Translated by
Sherab Chödzin Kohn

Art Captions by
Stephen Addiss

SHAMBHALA

BOSTON & LONDON 2004

Shambhala Publications, Inc.
Horticultural Hall
300 Massachusetts Avenue
Boston, Massachusetts 02115
www.shambhala.com

9 8 7 6 5 4 3 2 1

First Shambhala Edition
Printed in the United States of America

⊗ This edition is printed on acid-free paper that meets
the American National Standards Institute z39.48 Standard.

Distributed in the United States by Random House, Inc.,
and in Canada by Random House of Canada Ltd

Tokitsu, Kenji, 1947–
Miyamoto Musashi: his life and writings/Kenji Tokitsu;
translated by Sherab Chödzin Kohn.—1st ed.
p. cm.
Translation of: Miyamoto Musashi: Méolans-Revel [France]:
Editions Desiris, c2000.
ISBN 1–59030–045–9 (hardcover: alk. paper)
1. Miyamoto, Musashi, 1584 - 1645 2. Swordsmen—
Japan—Biography. I. Title.
DS872.M53T65 2004
952'.025—DC22
2003027651

CONTENTS

PART ONE

THE LIFE OF MIYAMOTO MUSASHI

PART THREE

MIYAMOTO MUSASHI AND THE MARTIAL ARTS

INTRODUCTION

A LEGENDARY FIGURE

IN POPULAR JAPANESE CULTURE, Miyamoto Musashi is a legendary figure. This warrior of the seventeenth century, a master of the sword but also a painter, sculptor, and calligrapher, left us a body of written work that has an important place in the history of the Japanese sword. His dense and brief *Gorin no sho,* or "Writings on the Five Elements", popularly known as *The Book of Five Rings,* is a summary of the art of the sword and a treatise on strategy.

Although the painting, sculpture, and calligraphy of Musashi are less well known, they are considered by connoisseurs to be of the first order.

Because of the extension of his art into so many domains and the way in which he explored the limits of the knowledge of his time, Miyamoto Musashi reminds us of Leonardo da Vinci. His personality and his adventurous life have been popularized by a famous novel and many films.

Here I present a completely new and annotated translation of the principal work of Miyamoto Musashi, as well as extensive excerpts from his other works. Because of its concision, the *Gorin no sho* is a hard text for contemporary Japanese people to understand. The misunderstandings can only be greater for Westerners, who might draw the impression from the apparent clarity of the text that they are understanding it when in fact the author's essential ideas are eluding them. For this reason I have accompanied the text with clarifications, some of which are historic, others linguistic, and still others related to the nature of martial arts practice. I undertook this project even though several translations of the *Gorin no sho* already exist. Through carefully rereading the Japanese text, I discovered that these translations contained many errors or misunderstandings.

Translation of this work is a difficult undertaking because of the considerable evolution the Japanese language has undergone since Musashi's time, but even more so because of the major problem connected with the role—at once limited and important—played by verbal explanation in the traditional martial arts. That which is expressed in words is a little like the knot in an obi: only the knot is manifest, visible, but without the continuity of the belt, the whole thing would not hold together. What takes on meaning in the nodal point of the word is the entirety of a shared experience.

The principal mode of transmission of the martial arts was direct teaching. Words played a small role, and writing was confined for the most part to a simple enumeration of technical terms. This approach did not stem from respect for tradition; rather, it was connected with the very considerable difficulty of communicating techniques of the body and mind in writing. In the Scroll of Water, the second section of the *Gorin no sho,* for example, when Musashi explains techniques in words, it is difficult to understand, since the execution of each technique takes only a few seconds. The description in writing of a movement of the body that lasts only a few seconds is very complex—I continually have this experience in my own work. Nevertheless, at certain moments in the course of a student's development, a single word can trigger a profound understanding of the art by creating a new order for the experiences accumulated in the silence of physical practice. Musashi's words have this objective.

One of the big obstacles in translating the work of Musashi lies in this gap between his words and his body. I have attempted to bridge this gap through my own experience of *budo,* for the *Gorin no sho* is one of the books that serve me as a guide in the practice of the way of martial arts. The name and image of Musashi have been familiar to me from earliest childhood through stories, films, and, later, novels.

Musashi reappeared for me in the form of the *Gorin no sho* at a time when, after several years of practicing karate, I began to wonder about the relationship between this art and the tradition of the sword, which I saw as the essence of *budo*. It should be noted that from the cultural and ideological point of view, the tradition of karate is different in some respects from that of *budo*. Karate was a local practice transmitted secretly on the island of Okinawa (in the extreme south of Japan), and it was not included in the framework of *budo* until around 1930. The degree of technical refinement and depth that had been reached by karate at that time was nowhere near that of the Japanese art of the sword. Nonetheless, it quickly emerged, after the presentation of karate to the Japanese public, that this art fit in well with the modern life of the twentieth century and was capable of developing as a contemporary form of *budo*. For this discipline, newly a part of *budo,* the most important reference point was the Japanese art of the sword. By relying on this tradition, and particularly that of kendo and judo, karate found its *budo* form. Hence for Japanese karate practitioners, writings on the art of the sword became the cultural and technical reference points for their art.

As a result, the *Gorin no sho* has been my companion for the last twenty-five of my forty years of practicing *budo*. Of course, the intensity of my practice is not of the same order as Musashi's, but I have tried to bridge the gap between Musashi's words and the body through my own practice, however limited.

The other difficulty encountered in translating the *Gorin no sho* is more classical: How is it possible to bring out the proper sense of a word when the cultures involved are as different as those of the contemporary Western world and Japan of the seventeenth century? I will give just one example: In this work, Musashi very frequently uses the term *kokoro,* which is customarily translated "mind" or "heart." Many sentences, if translated literally, would yield expressions such as "Your mind must be resolute, tight, calm," and so on. Since the English language makes much greater use of expressions in which the person takes on the role of subject, the translation that seems to me to render these Japanese expressions the best is "Be determined, tight, calm," and so on. The idea expressed in Japanese by *kokoro* is included in the English personal form of the subject. In English when you say "Be calm," the underlying idea is that the mind should be calm, the primacy of the mind over the body being implicitly understood. In Japanese this primacy is not assumed in the same way. Musashi wrote: "The mind should not be pulled about by the body; the body should not be pulled about by the mind." This way of distinguishing the mind and body was established within the context of a way of thinking and a language in which the prevailing tendency is to mix the mind and body together nonhierarchically and in which an analytical effort has to be made to distinguish them. A superficial interpretation might see an affirmation of dualistic thinking in such remarks as Musashi's above, whereas, quite to the contrary, we find in such remarks efforts aimed at establishing distinctions that are not taken for granted.

All through this work, proper names have been given in the order customary in Japan, that is, with the patronymic preceding the personal name. For warriors, one or several personal names or names linked to their function may be added (in this society of warriors, the system of names was more complicated than it is in the present day). Patronymics and personal names are variable, being determined by several factors. For example, Musashi, during different periods of his life and in different circumstances, was referred to by the following family names: Hirata, Takemura, Shinmen, Hirao, and Miyamoto. To his personal name (Musashi), which was then a common personal name, he attached a warrior suffix, sometimes Masana, sometimes Masanobu. In addition, when a warrior claimed connection, by distant kinship, with one of the great historical clans, he also put a reference to this in his name. In the *Gorin no sho,* for example, Musashi refers to himself as Shinmen Musashi no kami Fujiwara no Genshin. Shinmen was the name of the lord of whom his family were vassals, and Fujiwara was the name of one of the most important clans starting in the seventh century; finally, Genshin was the personal name chosen by him or his family to designate him within this clan. (Genshin would be the Buddhist name for Musashi. [16, p. 13])

To simplify these very long names, after the second appearance I have designated a historical person by his personal name, since the personal name of a historical person was generally more specific and distinctive than his family name. Thus I have used Musashi rather than Miyamoto, since the name Musashi, for the Japanese, calls to mind most of the time Miyamoto Musashi; but if you write Miyamoto, you are not necessarily referring to Miyamoto Musashi.

Place names in Japanese include specifications such as "village," "island," or "temple." I also preceded the names with these specifications in my translations, in spite of the redundancy, in order to make things easier for those who do not know Japanese.

For dates, the number of the month has been kept, as in the Japanese system. In order to make the chronology clear for those who do not know Japanese, the years are given according to the Western system, despite the risk of some disparity. To be specific, the life of Musashi runs between the twelfth year of the Tensho period, which corresponds on the whole to the year 1584, and the second year of the Shoho period, which in the same way corresponds to the year 1645.

Reference numbers given in parentheses refer to the works listed in the bibliography.

THE STRATEGY OF COMBAT as well as reflection on it constitutes the basic background of Musashi's life and conferred on it several dimensions. It was his constant reaching toward creating an expression of his art in writing that gives a unique quality to Musashi's work.

In his youth, at around the age of twenty-two, Musashi wrote a scroll entitled "Writings on the Sword Technique of the Enmei Ryu" *(Enmei ryu kenpo sho).*[1] *Enmei ryu* was the first name Musashi used to designate his school. *En* means "circle" or "perfection"; *mei* means "light" or "clarity" (*ryu* means "school"). This image is derived from one of the techniques of the school, in which the practitioner holds his two swords in such a way as to call up the image of a circle. This work contains twenty-two instructions having to do exclusively with the art of the sword.

The *Gorin no sho* was preceded by other works that appear to function somewhat as sketches for it. In 1641 Musashi wrote the "Thirty-five Instructions on Strategy" *(Hyoho sanju go kajo),* a work written for Hosokawa Tadatoshi, the lord of Kumamoto on Kyushu, with whom Musashi stayed as a guest during the last period of his life. This scroll, composed of instructions on the art of the sword, is very similar to the *Gorin no sho*. I have translated the parts of it that differ in content from the *Gorin no sho*.

Finally, just before his death, Musashi composed another text, "The Way to Be Followed Alone" *(Dokkodo),* in which he distills his final thoughts.

Most of the time the reflection provoked by the in-depth practice of a martial art is allowed to feed back into the practice itself without being exteriorized, except perhaps in the form of brief aphorisms. As a practitioner of *budo,* I myself feel the difficulty of putting my experience into writing, as though having immersed myself in water, I were immediately to try to turn the pages of a book without getting them wet.

The work of Musashi stands out all the more because very few accomplished practitioners have written on the martial arts, especially during the period when the system of transmission was direct. This exceptional quality is borne out by the limited number of works on the art of the sword written during the two and a half centuries of the Edo period (1603–1867); the number appears very small in view of the large number of practitioners of the art.

There are several reasons why so few texts have been written on the arts of combat.

The Difficulty of Explaining the Practice in Words

Practitioners are generally content to progress on the way of practice without writing about it. Since intensive practice requires a person to immerse himself fully and deeply in his actions, an objective written description is difficult, for it requires one to assume some distance from the practice. If the practitioner has recourse to language, it is usually selectively, in order to bring out an intuition rather than pursue a line of logic.

Moreover, studying the practice of an art of combat in depth is not always compatible with writing about this art, for the process of going into the practice deeply means acquiring a capacity for sensory-motor reactivity that goes beyond the reach of mental reflection. Spontaneous movement and intuitive comprehension are reinforced, and one must avoid increasing the gap between perception and reaction by adding the pitfalls of intellectual speculation. Reflection is a part of *budo,* but it must be self-directed, introspective reflection that is not allowed to intervene in the moment of combat, where the spontaneity of movement is essential. However, as Musashi wrote, combat is not confined to the moment when it is actually taking place.

In Musashi's time, when confrontations were direct, it was enough for the majority of accomplished practitioners to immerse themselves deeply in their practice and limit themselves to a few words, just enough for quasi-subliminal hints intelligible to their students. In the transmission of a school's art, sometimes a language developed that was unintelligible to outsiders, based on a very broad intuitive register and seldom going in the direction of logical development. From that point of view, Musashi's work is exceptional. Nonetheless, looked at from our present point of view, his logic does not always seem coherent, and the meaning of his words is not always precise. If his words had been received directly from him in the flesh, with swords in hand, these verbal inexactitudes and ambiguities would not have been important, because Musashi's body and swords would easily have dispelled the ambiguities. However, three and a half centuries now separate us.

Someone who practices a martial art in depth and trains every day to the point of exhaustion has a tendency to develop a relationship with words that becomes prosaic or perfunctory at the same time as the intuitive aspect of his participation grows; he will tend to distance himself from long-winded objective reflection. He develops an intuition that can find a profound or manifold meaning in a single expression or a single ideogram. The sense of fullness that comes from these intensive physical exercises reduces the amplitude of logical sequences. It is only when the practitioner crosses the threshold of another dimension, where the sensation of fullness is realized through a stable treading of the way, that words will become more tangible. Thus it is no surprise that Musashi wrote his major work just before his death, even though he had been trying to write since his youth.

The Major Importance of the Art of Combat for Japanese Warriors

During Musashi's time, the tradition of a period of war was reflected directly in the way warriors practiced the sword. In the time that followed, with the coming of social stability, the symbolic aspect of the art of combat progressively increased in importance and the link between that art and a warrior's morality became more intimate. At the same time, the schools, now less involved in actual combat, became more dependent on feudal lords. These lords, to build up their prestige, emphasized the secrecy of the teachings of their schools. This secrecy might well have been compromised by the production of writings.

The Relationship between Speech and Action among Japanese Warriors

The proverb "Speech is silver, silence is gold" is found in both the West and Japan, but it is interpreted and experienced in very different ways. The Japanese interpret this phrase as placing absolute value on silence and expressing contempt for eloquence—but this does not suggest contempt for words; on the contrary, it stresses the importance placed on every word. A worthy warrior spoke little, because he knew the importance of words. The word was conceived in terms of the role it might play in a possible chain of cause and effect, even if this were to remain virtual. Like a sword, a word can wound or kill, but as long as one does not touch the blade, the sword is no more than a smooth piece of metal. Someone who knows the qualities of a sword does not play with it, and someone who knows the nature of words does not play with them. Warriors attributed power and effective action to words, especially names. That is why the name of a technique was an important secret for someone seeking to understand the mind behind it. Anonymous transmission of a martial art did not exist, at least for warriors. For them the simple knowledge of how to do something was limited and incomplete. The ultimate transmission was in the name. For this reason the ultimate transmission of a school often took place through communication of the names of all the techniques, of which the practitioner had already for the most part attained mastery. One did not fully acquire the technique of a school until it had been named.

Miyamoto Musashi (1584–1645), a contemporary of René Descartes (1596–1650), lived at a turning point in the history of Japan—at the end of the period of feudal wars, at the moment when Japanese society was beginning to stabilize. Musashi witnessed the advent of the new system of warrior values, which was to be characterized by progressive internalization. Through his thought on strategy, which is pervaded by the philosophy of the period, we gain access to one of the roots of the culture of the Edo period.

The name of Miyamoto Musashi is known to Westerners through translations of the *Gorin no sho* and especially through the translation of the novel by Yoshikawa Eiji entitled *Musashi*. (62) Yoshikawa's novel ends with the famous duel between Musashi and Kojiro at Ganryujima. Musashi was twenty-nine at the time of this fight, which was the period of his youth concerning which we have the least imprecise documentation. The popularity Yoshikawa's image of Musashi has enjoyed over several generations shows that the novelist was able to distill in his character the ideal image of the samurai to which the Japanese people were attached.

Miyamoto Musashi had been renowned in Japan for a long time, but Yoshikawa's novel made him famous on a popular level, with the public as a whole. The author accentuated the introspective side of his personality. People sometimes say "Yoshikawa Musashi" to refer to the image that the Japanese public has of Miyamoto Musashi today. This novel was published as a serial in a daily paper from 1935 to 1939. It is, in a way, an expression of the position Yoshikawa took in the debate over Miyamoto Musashi's true qualities that was going on among Japanese writers at the beginning of the 1930s.

Naoki, a famous writer of samurai novels, triggered the polemic by writing that Musashi did not achieve excellence in the sword until a few years before his death. (21, pp. 39–42) His view is that in his youth Musashi was no more than an expert in publicizing himself and that his strength in the sword was not extraordinary. He takes as his proof

Musashi's duel against Sasaki Kojiro, in which Musashi used a wooden sword so as to have a sword longer than Kojiro's; moreover, he deliberately delayed the time of the fight in order to disconcert his adversary. Naoki adds that although, as Musashi himself wrote, he had had more than sixty duels during his lifetime, most of them were against little-known samurai. This viewpoint is not entirely devoid of truth, but it is primarily based on suppositions.

Another writer attacked this position and defended Musashi's qualities. The debate grew, and Yoshikawa was drawn into the controversy. What was important about this debate is that it touched upon the way the Japanese cultural identity was being presented, a particularly sensitive issue at the moment when Japanese society was preparing for the Second World War.

Since Yoshikawa's book appeared, numerous works have been published on Musashi in Japan. The historical documents concerning Musashi are fragmentary but relatively numerous. They are not rich enough to allow us to construct a precise image of his personality, but they are sufficient to provide food for the imagination. These documents taken together seem to be equivalent to a small fragment of some piece of Greek pottery on the basis of which we might imagine a jar or a vase. Although the image of Musashi is vague, the features that emerge are very potent, strong in odor and color. It is difficult to maintain neutrality in the face of such an image. Either you like it or you do not. It seems to me that it is essentially primal attitudes of this sort that form the main basis for the disparate positions in the assessment of Musashi and his work evinced by contemporary Japanese authors.

The members of one group—for example, Ezaki Shunpei (15) and Naoki (21)—do not like or even detest the image they hold of Musashi. These writers consider him a cunning and accomplished practitioner but a second-class figure in the history of the Japanese martial arts. Some go so far as to characterize him as a paranoiac. In their view, the *Gorin no sho* is a rather mediocre work.

A second group—for example, Shiba Ryotaro (30), Tobe Shinichiro (31), and Saotome Mitsugu (59)—judges the work and martial art of Musashi positively but separates it from their assessment of him personally. In the view of these writers, Musashi was doubtless a great and accomplished artist and practitioner of the martial arts, but his personality is considered unbalanced by some of them and unwholesome by others. They do not like Musashi, but they do appreciate the quality of his accomplishments.

A third group—such as Fukuhara Josen (2), Imai Masayuki (3), Nakanishi Seizo (8), Terayama Danchu (11), Morita Monjuro (20), and Naramoto Tatsuya (58)—assesses both the accomplishments and the personality of Musashi positively. These writers consider his art (both martial and fine) as an overall reflection of his personality. The majority of works on Musashi belong to this category and in many cases display no critical distance.

A fourth group—for example, Takayanagi Mitsutoshi (10) and Watanabe Ichiro (13)—somewhat steps back from its personal appreciation of Musashi. These writers situate his works within their historical period and appreciate them particularly for their originality. Their attitude seems to be the most scientific, but in their method they do not go beyond brief commentaries on the texts. Thus for Takayanagi, the *Gorin no sho* is difficult to understand mainly because of the lack of organization in Musashi's writing, but despite this defect, Musashi's work is admirable when one takes into account the shortcomings of his time, in which the distinction between religion and science was not sufficiently developed.

Though it is perhaps still possible to criticize the swordsmanship of Musashi, since it belongs to the past, by contrast his calligraphies, ink paintings, and sculptures have come down to us. Their artistic quality is undeniable, and they are well known in the history of Japanese art. True, the *Gorin no sho* is difficult to understand, but its style appears relatively clear when compared with the works of Musashi's contemporaries; and as far as the content is concerned, only a great adept of the sword could have written it. As Musashi wrote: "Because I apply the principle of the sword to the other arts, I no longer have a need for a teacher in these other domains." The quality of his work taken overall indicates that he could only have excelled in the art of the sword.

My way of presenting Musashi takes historical research as its point of departure but is somewhat different from the approach of the historians, because I interpret the texts on the basis of my experience in the martial arts and attempt to derive from them teachings applicable to martial arts practice.

How Can We Assess Musashi's Practice of the Sword?

During this period, confrontations with the sword between practitioners of different schools in most cases meant death for one of the participants. The decision to make or accept a challenge demanded the utmost prudence. Mere bravado was not enough to survive a duel to the death. One had to have a level of accomplishment that was equal to that of the adversary. Now, it is undeniable that Musashi never made a mistake in accurately assessing the strength of an adversary—this made it possible for him to avoid fighting an enemy capable of defeating him. The word *mikiri* became the established term for characterizing this particular acuity of Musashi's perception. The origination of this term is attributed to him, but I have been unable to find it in his writings. The literal translation is: *mi,* "look" or "see"; and *kiri,* "cut." This means "to see with cutting minuteness" or "to cut through with a look," which amounts to "discerning the state of situations or things with incisive precision." In my view this precise discernment characterizes the sword of Musashi as well as his aesthetic expressions. If he judged his adversary as potentially his superior, he avoided fighting him. Discernment of incisive precision was, for Musashi, the basis of individual and collective strategy. *Mikiri* distills in one word one of the teachings of Sun Tsu: "If you know yourself and you know your enemy, you will not lose one fight in a hundred."

For Musashi, just being strong individually was not of such great value, because he knew that the strength of a single person is limited and even insignificant in the unfolding of a large battle such as those he participated in several times in the course of his life. He would have preferred to apply his talent fully on a larger scale, because he felt he had discovered a principle applicable to all phenomena of life.

From the end of his adolescence, Musashi began to travel and engage in many duels. The age of thirty marked a change in his life. He continued to travel in order to deepen his art of swordsmanship, but he no longer sought out duels as he had before. At the same time, he was look- ing for a feudal lord who would entrust him with the elaboration of large-scale strategies. However, Musashi's rigor and precision some- times made as disquieting an impression as the blade of his sword. This is something that can also be seen in his works of art. This is without doubt one of the reasons he was not able to obtain the position he was looking for with one of the great feudal lords. I am convinced that Mu- sashi was a very great master of the sword, but I also think that several masters in the history of Japanese swordsmanship attained a level that was equivalent or superior to his.

To reach an accurate evaluation of Musashi's martial art and person- ality, it seems indispensable to situate them within the history of the art of the sword in Japan. This is because—and Musashi's work is an ex- pression of this—his period was the time at which the art of the sword began to pass beyond the sphere of military technique and merge with the practical notion of "the way." The art of the sword was on its way to becoming, both technically and morally, a formative element in the life of the Japanese warrior.

In accordance with the custom of the time, in referring to himself, Musashi used the term *bushi,* "warrior," which means "practitioner of arms." This was a reference to the division of Japanese society into four hierarchical social classes (warrior, peasant, artisan, and merchant), which the Tokugawa government had already firmly institutionalized by Musashi's time. By using the word *bushi,* warriors indicated their place in this hierarchy. This term appeared in the Nara period (eighth century) and progressively supplanted the older term *mononofu,* signifying men who knew how to use weapons and were courageous.

Samurai comes from *saburai,* the substantive form of the verb *sabu- rau,* which means "to serve" or "to remain at the side of someone im- portant" and was itself an evolved form of the older *samurau.* Starting with the Heian period (794–1145), *samurai* designated warriors who were in the service of nobles. Little by little, it came to be used by mem- bers of the other classes to refer to warriors in general. However, within the warrior class itself, it was used to refer to those most highly placed in the hierarchy. For example, the townspeople might call anybody who wore the two swords a samurai, but among warriors, this term was not applied to those who occupied the lower levels of the hierarchy. (106)

The power of the warriors became further established during the Heian period, especially starting with the tenth century, when the power of the government weakened in the provinces. The powerful *go zoku* (regional authority) families began to fight to protect and increase the territory they had acquired. They developed their military capability so they could govern the local peasants by themselves and protect themselves against rival powers as well as the representatives of the state. They built themselves up into larger groups united by ties of blood and also, for those who succeeded in becoming part of it, by a strong consciousness of belonging to the group. These armed groups, called *bushi dan,* developed in the provinces. Their moral values were based largely on the cult of ancestors and on family relations, which were expanded to form a clan hierarchy, as well as on values arising from the personal valor of combatants.

The warrior art to which warriors at first attached their identity was archery. *Yumiyatoru mi,* literally, "he who knows how to shoot a bow," designated men of war during the Kamakura period. *Yumi no ie* designated a family that excelled in the art of archery and thus a family of warriors. Such warriors fought from horseback, mainly with a bow. When the use of the sword on horseback spread, it brought about a modification in swords, which began to take on a curved form. The mode of combat changed progressively, and in the fourteenth and fifteenth centuries, the sword assumed first place among the arts of the warriors and became their emblematic weapon. However, it would be inaccurate to think that the Japanese art of the sword developed in isolation, because the metallurgy connected with it came from China via Korea, and in the wake of this, interaction with these countries increased further (see appendix 3).

During Musashi's time, the art of the sword was dominant, and there were numerous schools teaching sword technique. Thus, in order to gain a clear understanding of the life of Musashi, who founded a school of swordsmanship several branches of which still exist today, it seems essential to situate him within the history of Japanese schools of the sword.

The Main Periods in the History of Japanese Schools of Swordsmanship

The Formative Period (Fifteenth to Sixteenth Centuries)

A decisive period in the formation and evolution of the way of the sword extends from the end of the fourteenth century to the beginning of the seventeenth century. Later this period was to become a point of reference for masters and practitioners of the sword.

Of course, the art of the sword in Japan is much more ancient than this. In the course of the tenth century, the shape of swords was modified, and the curved sword gradually replaced the straight sword. These changes were a reflection of a development of techniques in which the action of slashing became increasingly important. The elevation of the social status of warriors went hand in hand with the evolution of combat techniques. By the eleventh century the change in the form and technique of the Japanese sword was becoming widespread. Before this the military force was overwhelmingly composed of foot soldiers who used the straight sword, mainly for stabbing. With the development of local military groups whose large estates permitted them to keep horses, mounted warriors assumed the primary place. The technique and form of the sword transformed little by little to facilitate the combat of fighters on horseback, for whom slashing is easier than stabbing. Curvature of the sword became important. The curved sword gradually came to be dominant, and slashing techniques were extended to combat on foot. The curved form of the sword stabilized beginning in the twelfth century, and the name *nihon to* (Japanese sword) was used to differentiate this curved sword from the straight sword, which preserved direct Chinese influence. The increase in the number of swords forged shows the dominance the sword was assuming, especially in the period from the twelfth through the fourteenth centuries. The *nihon to,* Japanese swords, made during the six centuries from the end of the tenth to the beginning of the seventeenth (the Keicho era) are classified as ancient swords and called *ko to*. They are of a high quality that has not been equaled since. We know the names of more than fifty-five hundred master smiths of ancient swords. According to Mitsuhashi Shuzo, there were

- 450 sword smiths from the tenth to twelfth centuries (Heian period)
- 1,550 sword smiths from the thirteenth to the middle of the fourteenth century (Kamakura period)
- 3,550 sword smiths from the middle of the fourteenth to the end of the sixteenth century (41, p. 6)

In tandem with the evolution of the form of the sword, there was a remarkable surge in the development of sword technique. However, dependable documents on schools of swordsmanship do not go back beyond the end of the fourteenth century. Despite the fact that most schools like to claim that their roots go back to the Kamakura period (1185–1333) or still further back, the lineages of the main traditional schools of the sword can be traced with certainty only back to the middle of the fifteenth century.

From the last third of the fifteenth century until the end of the sixteenth, Japan was the scene of continual warfare among the feudal lords. It was through experience on the battlefield that the sword masters of that period developed their sword technique as well as their basic attitudes toward swordsmanship. The techniques of that period were relatively simple but forceful, since armor was worn in battle. Combatants used existing techniques but also carried on their own personal search for more effective ones, based on their own experience. While continuing to accept the idea that the true ability to fight comes from actual battlefield experience, some warriors began to attach importance to training, to daily preparation for combat. This included matches that often took place without armor, which resulted in the development of greater subtlety in technique. The practice exercises, called *kumitachi* or *tachi uchi,* consisted in reproducing combat techniques derived from the experience of various masters. These exercises, in which either a real or a wooden sword was used, became standardized.

Miyamoto Musashi lived at the end of this formative period of the classic schools of swordsmanship.

Period of Further Development
(Seventeenth and Eighteenth Centuries)

According to my analysis, we can consider the seventeenth and eighteenth centuries as the birth period of *budo*. This period, in which the art of the sword was developed further, extends from the second half of the seventeenth century to the beginning of the nineteenth century.

The shoguns of the Tokugawa family established and stabilized their power over the whole of Japan between 1600 and 1640. They imposed a strong rule that brought about a long period of peace, which lasted until the middle of the nineteenth century. This meant that warriors had to adjust progressively to a peacetime role.

At the time of the feudal wars, one could have summed up the value of a warrior's swordsmanship by answering the following question: How many heads can he cut off? In time of peace, this simple pragmatism transformed into an effort directed toward advancement in swordsmanship as an art. Since the way of action was closed to them, the sword masters internalized their art—it became a quest for the way, *do*. The level of commitment to this quest was deepened by the fact that the way, *do,* derived a part of its meaning from the relationship between the lord and his vassals.

The objective for the practitioner became finding a means to make progress in the way of the sword without really killing his adversary. From this point on, swordsmen no longer used armor, and sword technique was modified because there was no need for the forceful techniques that made it possible to kill an enemy through his armor. Masters developed subtle techniques that took into account the freedom of movement made possible by town clothes. The art of the sword reached its apex toward the end of this period.

In the middle of the eighteenth century, certain schools began to train with the *shinai* (bamboo sword) and to use armor again. These developments became general by the end of the eighteenth century. These safety measures were conducive to unlimited matches between practitioners, and this encouraged the elaboration of technique within each school. Autonomous trends within schools multiplied. At this point we can enumerate as many as seven hundred schools of the sword.

As the art of the sword became increasingly refined, it became a major vehicle for the energy of warriors within a Japanese society that was becoming closed toward the outside world. Warriors heightened their art while almost never using it in real confrontations. They killed each other every day in practice, but in reality they avoided death. Nevertheless, the idea that combat to the death could become an actuality at any moment remained the basic reference point for the warriors' state of mind. At the same time, through the elaboration of technique, the idea of harmony began to infiltrate deeper and deeper into the basic antagonism inherent in the use of weapons. The art of the warriors flourished under a variety of names *(bujutsu, bugei, kenjutsu, gekiken, to jutsu, ken po)*. In all these disciplines, the energy of antagonistic confrontation remained dominant, symbolized by the wearing of the warrior's sword. The sword that accompanied a warrior everywhere still represented the fundamental idea of "kill or be killed."

The Flowering of the Art of the Sword (Nineteenth Century)

The third period of the history of schools of the sword encompasses most of the nineteenth century. The art of the sword flowered at the time when its power became a major factor in putting an end to the feudal period, which had been the period of the sword's dominance.

At the beginning of the nineteenth century, swordsmanship passed through a brief period of decadence, for as the period of wars became more remote, the sword became dissociated from the reality of combat, and the position of warriors became uncertain. But then, quickly, the threat represented by Westerners provided warriors with a renewed consciousness of their role. In the course of the second half of the century, Japan passed through a succession of troubles connected with the threat of invasion by Western powers. This was the time when the Japanese began to become aware of the power of the Westerners and to look for the most effective means of opposing them. This attitude and a new awareness of society as a whole was reflected in the manner in which warriors practiced swordsmanship. The art of the sword had reached a high point during the preceding period, but in becoming dissociated from the reality of combat it entered a decadent phase. The conflicts that pervaded Japanese society produced new needs, and the art of the sword then reached a level of fruition in which it produced sparks of steel between the two parties into which warriors were now divided— one defending the shogunate, the others seeking to oust this system of government.

The reign of the shoguns came to an end in 1867, and the new regime, as part of its plan to set up a modern military and industrial power, abolished the privileges of the warriors. In spite of these difficulties, some of those who had survived the confrontations of the period of transition continued the tradition and practice of the sword. They had to put up with the prohibition against carrying a sword and come to grips with the then prevailing tendency to discredit traditional culture, which was the support of their identity. The sword of the warrior disappeared at the end of the nineteenth century with the death of those who had lived through the last period of actual sword combat.

The notion of *budo* was born at the moment in which the class of warriors disappeared and the values of feudal society began to dissolve into the depths of modern society. (126) Even though *budo* takes tradition as its basis, it is a modern notion. It defines a practice that takes shape around a kind of dilemma. Arms are fundamentally offensive, but *budo*'s striving for quality in the art of arms contains within it an impulse directed toward the evolution of human beings as such, and this in turn implies a seeking for harmony, an element that is in apparent conflict with the objectives of combat. The ideal goal of *budo* is combat in which aggressive energy is perfectly balanced by its opposite component, harmony—as we shall see in chapter 12, "The Relationship between Adversaries."

Kendo (Nineteenth and Twentieth Centuries)

The conception and practice of kendo developed and took on definitive form toward the end of the Meiji period (1868–1912), in the latter part of the nineteenth century and the first half of the twentieth. The name itself dates from this period. Kendo is a modern reformulation of the warriors' art of the sword, in which combat is practiced mainly with *shinai* and armor. Thus the kendo of today is not exactly the same art practiced by the sword masters of old.

Although this period was short, it was important because of the intermediary role it played between the kendo that was a continuation of the historical warriors' practice and modern kendo.

From 1945 to the Present

The destruction in Japan in 1945 was major, and in the shock of defeat, Japanese society as a whole was challenged. After the war, Japan was occupied, the pressure exercised by the Allies was heavy, and the practice of the martial arts was forbidden. Practitioners of karate were the first to get permission to resume their discipline, which they presented as a form of boxing. This comparison to Western boxing allowed them to put karate in the category of a sport. This did not work for kendo, for even when practiced with bamboo swords, it continued to evoke the strange barbarity of wartime Japan. Kendo practitioners tried to perpetuate kendo under the name *shinai kyogi,* "gamelike competition with *shinai,*" by transforming the techniques of kendo to make it resemble a sportlike activity that would be acceptable in the eyes of the occupiers. To this end, they glossed over as much as possible the traditional aspect of the discipline, with its costumes and customs, and followed the model of European fencing. This experience continued to be one of the shaping factors in the transformations that led to contemporary kendo. Indeed, when kendo was able to resume in 1952, it was in the context of a society that had changed, and the spirit of the practice had been changed by integrating into it the modern idea of a combat sport.

In parallel with all this, a certain number of ancient schools of the sword continued, and continue down to the present day, to transmit their techniques in the traditional form but with a very limited number of practitioners.

Let us summarize the main lines of this history.

In the beginning, the nature of the sword was obvious. The blade was the main thing—it killed in a bloody way. Spirituality had little place in the practice of the sword.

In the next phase, the sword continued to be there, but it was in a scabbard. It killed less frequently, almost not at all. Sword practice was more a matter of technique, and it coexisted with spirituality. The notion of *do* developed in association with the consciousness of one's duty toward the ruler.

With the disappearance of the class of warriors and the prohibition against carrying a sword, the *shinai* supplanted the sword in the practice of the art, and a new conception of the way *(do)* was formed in connection with the idea of *budo*. This was a modern reforging of tradition that proposed as its overall objective the training of the human being as such in conformity with the expectations of nineteenth-century society.

Chronology of Musashi's Life

Certain contradictions exist among the documents relating to Miyamoto Musashi's life. I give a detailed analysis of this in the first part of this book. I have put together the following chronology by selecting the most plausible ones among the currently accepted hypotheses concerning the events of Musashi's life in view of the elements actually known to us (see part 1, "The Life of Miyamoto Musashi").

According to the ancient system, a person is considered to be one year old during the course of the year following his birth. For example, according to the *Gorin no sho,* Musashi fought at the age of thirteen, but according to the modern system currently in use, this corresponds to the age of twelve. In references to Musashi's age in the following chronology, I have used the modern system. (For the dating method, see appendix 1.)

1578

Birth of Jirota, older brother of Musashi, who died in 1660.

Musashi also seems to have had two sisters.

1584

Birth of the child who was to be known as Miyamoto Musashi, during the third month, in the village of Miyamoto-Sanomo (Mimasaka region). He received the name of Bennosuke. His father's name was Hirata Munisai and his mother's was Omasa. His mother died on the fourth day of the third month. Munisai then married the young Yoshiko, who would act as Bennosuke's mother.

1587 (three years old)

Around this time, Yoshiko divorced Hirata Munisai and left for the village of Hirafuku with Bennosuke. Her family having been scattered by war, she was taken in by the adoptive son of her uncle, Tasumi Masahisa. Later he would marry her. He already had two sons by his first marriage.

Yoshiko, being uneasy about Bennosuke's future, placed him under the care of her uncle Dorin, who was a monk in the temple of Shoreian. Bennosuke received his education from Dorin and Tasumi.

1589 (five years old)

On the orders of his lord, Shinmen Iganokami, Munisai killed Honiden Gekinosuke (twenty-seven years old), who was one of his disciples in the study of strategy.

1592 (eight years old)

Certain documents record that Munisai died this year, but this is contradicted by other documents. It is probable that the person who died at this time was Hirata Takehito, not Hirata Munisai.

1596 (twelve years old)

Bennosuke fought a duel with Arima Kihei of the Shinto ryu (school). The fight took place in the village of Hirafuku-mura.

1599 (fifteen years old)

Bennosuke left the region. He visited his sister Ogin and her husband, Hirao Yoemon, who lived in the village of Miyamoto, and gave them the family possessions: weapons, furniture, the family genealogy, and so on.

In one of the documents of the village of Miyamoto, we find the following passage: "Musashi left this village ninety years ago. . . . He was accompanied by his friend Moriiwa Hikobei. At the time of their separation, the latter received from Musashi a *bokken* made of black wood. Musashi then went to the village of Hirafuku-mura to take leave of his mother Yoshiko and his stepfather Tasumi. He traveled to Tajima [Hyogo], where he fought a duel with a martial arts practitioner adept named Akiyama." (8, p. 43)

1600 *(sixteen years old)*

In the battle of Sekigahara, Musashi was part of the army of the West.

During the seventh month, he took part in an attack on Fushimi castle (his first battle).

During the eighth month, he took part in the defense of Gifu castle.

On the fifteenth of the ninth month, he took part in the battle of Sekigahara. The West lost in a few hours. Musashi was in the battalion of Lord Ukita, who was the liege lord of Lord Shinmen, of whom Musashi's family were vassals. Following this defeat, Shinmen Sokan took refuge on Kyushu. Musashi perhaps also traveled in the direction of Kyushu. One legend tells us that he trained on Mount Hikosan during his stay on Kyushu.

1604 *(twenty years old)*

On the eighth of the third month, Musashi engaged in a victorious duel with Yoshioka Seijuro in the hamlet of Rendaino on the outskirts of Kyoto.

Victorious duel against Yoshioka Denshichiro, younger brother of Seijuro, who had then challenged him.

Combat against the clan and dojo of Yoshioka at Ichijoji (Kyoto). Musashi won the victory and killed Matashichiro, the nominal head of the Yoshioka, aged twelve or thirteen.

According to certain documents, it was after these fights that Musashi went to Hozoin in Nara to engage in combat with the monks there, who were experts with the lance.

After Nara, Musashi went to Banshu (Hyogo) and stayed at Enkoji temple. The monk in charge of Enkoji liked the martial arts and had turned a part of the temple into a martial arts dojo. The monk's brother, Tada Hanzaburo, received teachings from Musashi in this temple. At this time Musashi called his school Enmei ryu, and Tada Hanzaburo received the certificate of transmission of this school from Musashi.

Later, Tada Genzaemon, the grandson of Hanzaburo, founded the Ensu ryu on the basis of the Enmei ryu and the art of swordsmanship called *mizuno iai jutsu* (the art of drawing the sword).

Musashi traveled in various regions of western Japan, using Enkoji as a base.

1605 (twenty-two years old)

One of the first certificates of transmission written by Musashi is dated this year. It ends as follows:

> the one and only under the sky
> Miyamoto Musashi no kami
> Fujiwara Yoshitsune [signature] [hand-executed seal]
> To Mr. Ochiai Tadaemon,
> the auspicious day of the eleventh year of the Keicho era [1606].

1607 (twenty-three years old)

A certificate of transmission written by Musashi's father, Miyamoto Munisai, for his disciple Tomooka Kanjuro, is dated the fifth of the ninth month, 1607, which proves that he was still living that year.

Musashi went to Edo, passing by way of Nara and Yagyu. He fought a duel with Shishido Baiken, an expert with the *kusari gama* (a sickle to which a chain with a steel weight on the end is attached).

1607–1611 (twenty-three to twenty-seven years old)

Having arrived in Edo, Musashi fought a duel with two advanced practitioners of the Yagyu school, Oseto and Tsujikaze. In Edo he also fought Muso Gonnosuke, an expert in the art of the staff, whom he defeated without killing him. On the basis of his experience with Musashi, Muso developed his school of the art of the staff, the Shinto Muso ryu.

Musashi remained in Edo three or four years, traveling from time to time in the vicinity.

1609 (twenty-five years old)

Musashi participated in the clearing of new fields, working the earth with the peasants of Gyotoku in Shimousa (Chiba). Another document puts this episode in 1611.

1611 (twenty-seven years old)

Musashi went to Kyoto. He visited the Myoshinji temple, where he practiced *zazen*. According to one document, at this temple he met Nagaoka Sado, a vassal of Lord Hosokawa Tadaoki, who became the lord of northern Kyushu after the battle of Sekigahara. Nagaoka had been a student of Musashi's father, Miyamoto Munisai, who had moved to Kyushu. It is possible that Musashi made Nagaoka's acquaintance when he visited his father on Kyushu. Nagaoka spoke to Musashi about an accomplished martial arts adept named Sasaki Kojiro and proposed that he organize a duel between Kojiro and Musashi. We may surmise that this was a political move against the Sasaki clan and not merely a matter of a duel.

1612 (twenty-eight years old)

Victorious duel against Sasaki Kojiro on the thirteenth of the fourth month, on the island of Funajima, north of Kyushu.

1613 (twenty-nine years old)

Musashi spent a period of time meditating at a temple on Mount Koyasan in Kishu (Wakayama prefecture). He later stayed in Nagoya and trained some disciples, among them Takemura, a practitioner of the art of the *shuriken*.

1614 (thirty years old)

Tenth month: the winter battle of Osaka. This was Musashi's fourth battle. The usual view is that Musashi was part of the Army of the West, but I believe he fought in the Army of the East under Tokugawa Ieyasu.

1615 (thirty-one years old)

Fourth month: summer battle of Osaka. In the course of the fifth month, the Army of the East won a decisive victory.

1616–1617 (thirty-two to thirty-three years old)

Musashi stayed at Akashi at the invitation of Lord Ogasawara. There he taught the sword and the art of the *shuriken*. He also participated in the construction of Akashi castle.

1618–1620 (thirty-four to thirty-six years old)

Musashi adopted a male child who later took the name Miyamoto Mikinosuke.

1621 (thirty-seven years old)

At Himeji, Musashi fought victoriously against Miyake Gunbei and three other adepts of the Togun ryu in the presence of the lord of Himeji. Musashi participated in the development of the plan of the town of Himeji. He also directed the creation of the gardens of several temples there.

1622 (thirty-eight years old)

Musashi's adoptive son Miyamoto Mikinosuke acquired the rank of vassal of the fief of Himeji. Musashi departed again on his travels.

1623 (thirty-nine years old)

Musashi went to Edo.

1624 (forty years old)

Musashi lived in Edo. He established relations with Hayashi Razan, a Confucianist scholar who was part of the shogun's government. Some historians advocate the theory that Hayashi recommended Musashi to the shogun as a sword master. At this time the shogun already had two principal sword masters, Ono Jiroemon and Yagyu Munenori. Musashi's application to the shogun ended in failure.

Musashi departed, traveling in the direction of Oshu (northern Japan). He got as far as Yamagata.

He adopted a second son, to whom he gave the name Miyamoto Iori. He traveled with Iori, passing through Edo, then Hokuriku, Kyoto, Ise, Kishu, finally arriving at Osaka, where he stayed for some time. According to one document, the adoption of Iori took place when he was at Yamagata; other documents indicate that Iori was his nephew and the adoption took place when he returned to the region of Banshu.

1625 (forty-one years old)

Meeting with Mikinosuke in Osaka.

1626 (forty-two years old)

In the course of the fifth month, Miyamoto Mikinosuke ended his life through seppuku, following his lord into death in accordance with tradition.

Miyamoto Iori entered the service of Lord Ogasawara of Akashi, probably in the course of this year.

Musashi again passed through Nagoya, where his attempt to become a vassal of the lord of Owari did not meet with success. This lord belonged to the family of the shogun and was one of its most powerful members. Musashi searched for a lord worthy of his level in strategy.

1633 (forty-nine years old)

Lord Hosokawa Tadatoshi left Kokura for the fief of Kumamoto. Lord Ogasawara Tadasane, coming from Akashi, succeeded him at Kokura. Iori, who was in the service of this lord with the rank of vassal, accompanied him.

According to certain documents, Musashi stayed at Izumo (Shimane), where he fought a duel with a vassal of the lord of Matsumoto castle, Matsudaira Naomasa, and then with this lord himself. The lord became his student. Musashi remained for a time in this fief to teach. According to other documents, Lord Matsudaira established his residence in Izumo in 1638. If this is the case, the dates are in conflict.

1634 (fifty years old)

Musashi returned to Kyushu. He arrived at Kokura, where the lord was now Ogasawara Tadasane, to whom Musashi had taught the sword and the art of the *shuriken*.

Lord Ogasawara organized a duel for Musashi against a famous lance specialist, Takada Matabei. Musashi defeated him.

1637–1638 (fifty-three to fifty-four years old)

During the tenth month of 1637, the Christians of Shimabara (Kyushu) revolted against the regime, and the siege of Shimabara began. Musashi participated in the battles with Iori and directed Ogasawara's troops. Iori became the principal vassal of Lord Ogasawara. This was the sixth and final time Musashi participated in a battle.

A letter from Musashi to Lord Maruoka Yuzaemon dates to this year.

At this time, Nagaoka Sado, principal vassal of Lord Hosokawa, probably began applying to his lord to take on Musashi as a vassal.

1639 (fifty-five years old)

Nagaoka arrived in Kokura, charged with responsibility for the affairs of this fief. He visited Musashi, to whom he directly passed on an invitation from his lord that had already been indicated by letter. The time passed without a decision being made, and Hosokawa continued with his approaches to Musashi and also to Ogasawara.

1640 (fifty-six years old)

Musashi decided to go to Lord Hosokawa. At the end of the first month, he took up residence at Kumamoto.

Correspondence between Musashi and the representatives of Lord Hosokawa.

Lord Hosokawa Tadatoshi organized a duel for Musashi, meant as a means of training, against Ujii Magoshiro, principal martial arts master of this fief. Musashi was victorious.

1641 (fifty-seven years old)

In the course of the second month, Musashi wrote the *Hyoho sanju go kajo* for Lord Hosokawa Tadatoshi and practiced the arts: calligraphy, painting, tea ceremony.

During the third month, Hosokawa Tadatoshi died at the age of fifty-six. His eighteen vassals followed him into death *(junshi)*.

Letter from Musashi recommending his third adoptive son, Hirao Yoemon, to one of the principal vassals of the Owari fief. Hirao Yoemon became Owari master of arms.

1642 (fifty-eight years old)

Musashi fell ill and suffered attacks of neuralgia.

1643 (fifty-nine years old)

Musashi departed for Mount Iwato, located near Kumamoto, where he began living in Reigando cave. He had a low table there, and on the tenth of the tenth month, he began to compose the *Gorin no sho*.

Letter from Musashi to Lord Hosokawa Mitsuhita, dated the eighth of the tenth month.

1645 (sixty-one years old)

Musashi lived at Reigando and composed the *Gorin no sho,* which he completed during the second month. Musashi sensed the approach of death. On the thirteenth of the fourth month, he wrote a letter of farewell to the three principal vassals of Hosokawa, Lords Shikibu, Kenmotsu, and Uemon, with whom he was particularly closely connected.

He dedicated his last work, the *Gorin no sho,* to his disciple Terao Magonojo, and gave the latter's younger brother, Terao Motomenosuke, his own copy of the *Hyoho sanju go kajo*.

On the twelfth of the fifth month, Musashi distributed his possessions among those close to him. During his final days, he wrote the twenty-one articles of the *Dokkodo*. He died on the nineteenth of the fifth month.

We do not know for sure whether Musashi died at his home or in Reigando cave. His hair was buried at Mount Iwato and his body, dressed in warrior's armor, was interred, in accordance with his wishes, near the main road, so that he would be able to greet the Hosokawa lords on their trips in the direction of Edo, where they periodically had to go to visit the shogun.

IT WAS IN A CAVE CALLED Reigando (*rei,* "soul" or "spirit"; *gan,* "rock"; *do,* "cave") where Musashi, at the age of sixty, set himself up to write. He spent the last two years of his life there. This cave had long been considered a sacred place. It was in the most remote part of a group of lands belonging to Iwato-dera temple. It was deep in a mountainous setting, surrounded by rocks with vivid forms, between which water fell in cascades. Near the entrance to the cave, there were several statues of deities. It was an unfrequented spot, reserved for meditation.

Musashi indicated that he began writing the *Gorin no sho* in this place at four o'clock in the morning on the tenth day of the tenth month (of the twentieth year of the Kanei period (1643).

Why did he choose this place and this moment to begin this work? To begin the main written work of his life in this manner says something about Musashi's art of swordsmanship. Beginning this work meant ending his life. And in fact, he died shortly after finishing it. To accomplish his endeavor in just the right way, he had to begin it in this place filled with the mysterious power of the mountain, before the break of day. He had to begin in a deep state of calm, by the light of a lamp, in the cool of the shadows. He welcomed the dawn by writing. This approach was indispensable for his act of writing to become one with the nature of the sacred beings. According to the beliefs of those days, morning is filled with positive yang energy, which is at the origin of creation; thus Musashi was not without reasons for choosing this hour. Through paying homage to heaven and bowing before Kannon and the Buddha, his act of writing became mingled with their presence. Through this it became a sacred act. But when he bowed to these sacred powers, it was not in the manner of a Christian bowing to an altar. In Japanese belief, the sacred takes on many forms that are accessible to human beings. By undertaking his writing in the way he did, Musashi entered the sacred world.

Before his death he wrote: "I respect the Buddha and the gods, but I do not rely on them." This sentence is found in a short text entitled "The Way to Be Followed Alone" *(Dokkodo),* which he wrote after the *Gorin no sho.* These two texts seem to have been written with the last of Musashi's life force, for it was only a week after having added to the end of his manuscript the name of his successor that Musashi died, on the nineteenth day of the fifth month of the second year of Shoho (1645).

Musashi bequeathed the *Gorin no sho* to one of his disciples, Terao

Magonojo Katsunobu. Later this work would be copied by another of Musashi's disciples, who, on the fifth day of the second month of the seventh year of Kanbun (1667), gave this copy to his disciple, Yamamoto Gennosuke. It is through this copy that we know the work. The original of the *Gorin no sho,* written in Musashi's own hand, has never been found.

ONE

THE LIFE OF MIYAMOTO MUSASHI

Introduction to the
Life of Musashi

DOES THE STUDY OF HISTORICAL documents confirm the mythical image of Miyamoto Musashi?

In his novel about Musashi, Yoshikawa Eiji largely took over the deeply rooted popular image of this hero, though he consulted a number of historical documents. He succeeded in crystallizing the values to which the Japanese were attached in the image of Musashi, a warrior treading the way of the martial arts—so much so that at the present time the Japanese have difficulty separating the image of Musashi from that of anyone seeking the way through perfecting the art of the sword. Most people who speak of Musashi, of his art, of his swordsmanship, and of his thought on strategy, identify him with this ideal image.

If you meet a renowned and aged kendo master who speaks to you of Musashi, you might easily get the impression that you are coming in contact with the true Musashi. However, I have frequently observed that what you are actually getting is the personal thought of this master, who has taken a few fragments of Musashi's work as a starting point and meditated on them for a long time. In truth, in Japan Musashi is very popular, but this does not mean that people know him well.

As I read through the historical documents that are available today and the contemporary studies on Musashi, I saw that certain periods in the life of this samurai remain enigmatic. The enigmas begin with his birth and the identity of his parents. But as soon as I came to the parts of his life for which historical data are available, his image became more complex and more human.

Musashi's training seems to be a key to understanding his real personality. The questions to be answered with regard to this are many. How and why did Musashi found his School of Two Swords? Was he really self-taught, as is generally thought? Why did he not become the vassal of some lord, despite the fact that he had the opportunity to do so? What was his fighting level? What abilities did he possess? What sorts of combat did he really engage in?

Is it possible to profit from his teaching today, and in what disciplines and in what way? To what extent has his work been incorporated in the tradition of Japanese swordsmanship and to what extent has it become embodied in a continuity that has come down to us today?

What you can find out about the life of Miyamoto Musashi from the historical documents is very limited. The most reliable evidence is what can be found in his own written work. The principal documents we have are funerary inscriptions, texts inscribed on monuments, chronicles of families and villages, certificates of transmission of schools of swordsmanship, and anecdotal tales about masters of swordsmanship. The major problem one faces is evaluating the comparative reliability of these frequently contradictory sources.

The most controversial part of Musashi's life is his childhood. There are a number of hypotheses concerning the date of his birth, the identity of his parents, and the precise place of his birth. These hypotheses have been propounded by various researchers on the basis of their analysis of many documents that do not agree with each other.

In the *Gorin no sho,* Musashi succinctly tells us what the main turning points in his life were. Focusing on his training and the evolution of his art and personality, I distinguish four major periods.

1. Childhood and Training, from Birth to Age Fifteen (1584–1599)

The first period runs from Musashi's birth to the time he left the region of his birth, at the age of fifteen.[1] For this period I go along with the currently accepted hypothesis that Musashi was born in 1584, but the uncertainties relating to this period as a whole have been the cause of extremely animated controversies among Japanese scholars. They concern the year and place of Musashi's birth and the fate of his father. When Musashi left his village, was his father living or dead?

What was the relationship between the creation of Musashi's school and the transmission of his family's martial arts tradition? Did Musashi learn his father's art? Up to what age did he study with him? Musashi writes that at the age of thirteen he defeated his opponent in his first duel; therefore, by that time he had reached a certain level of swordsmanship.

2. Duels and Wars, Age Fifteen to Thirty-One (1599–1615)

After leaving his village in 1599, Musashi traveled continuously. Before the age of thirty, he had participated in more than sixty duels in which he risked his life. In 1600 he fought in the battle of Sekigahara. In 1614 and 1615 he fought in the battles of Osaka, following which the hegemony of the Tokugawa regime was definitively established.

3. Further Development, Age Thirty-One to Fifty (1615–1634)

There are only a few documents relating to this second period of Musashi's travels. We can surmise that for him this was a period of inner development. His preoccupation was no longer with fighting duels in order to prove his ability or accumulating further experience in combat; rather, it was the search, in all the arts, for a common principle. His talents allowed him to express himself in painting, calligraphy, and various handcrafts, as well as in the art of combat. We can also surmise that during this time he familiarized himself with the practice of Zen.

4. The Accomplishment of the Transmission, Age Fifty to Sixty-One (1634–1645)

Musashi moved to the island of Kyushu. In 1634 he was the guest of Lord Ogasawara of Kokura, whose vassal Musashi's adoptive son was, and starting in 1640 he entered into the service of Lord Hosokawa with the title of Guest of the Lord. There he passed the most peaceful period of his life, devoting himself to various artistic pursuits and the transmission of the art of his school of swordsmanship. He died on the nine-teenth of the fifth month of 1645, shortly after completing the compo-sition of his most important work, the *Gorin no sho*.

The documents on this period are relatively numerous.

||| 1 |||

Childhood and Training

The Birth of Musashi

There are a great number of uncertainties concerning Musashi's origins because the existing documents are frequently contradictory.

It is usually thought, though without certain proof, that he was born in one of two neighboring villages in Sakushu or Banshu in 1584, during the last years of the feudal wars that lasted more than a century and to which Toyotomi Hideyoshi put an end in 1590, when he unified the whole of Japan under his power.

The information we have concerning his family is important in understanding how Musashi's art developed. I find it difficult to believe that Musashi was self-taught, as is generally said, because in the history of the martial arts, when a master founds his personal school, he has generally received adequate systematic training in one or more schools. Musashi's method seems to me to cover an area of technique that is too vast, too well systematized, and too thoroughly elaborated to have been developed through the experience and thought of a single person. My theory is that he received teaching on an already existing art, and that this was the basis for his founding his own school. I will show how certain documents support this view.

Who Were Miyamoto Musashi's Parents?

It is generally agreed that Musashi's father was Hirata Munisai, one of the principal vassals of a petty feudal lord of the mountainous region of Sakushu, west of Kyoto. He was an adept of the sword and the *jitte,* a weapon made of metal and equipped with hooks that can parry a sword blow. Nevertheless, that Hirata Munisai was his father is uncertain, and Musashi may have been adopted.

The name Miyamoto comes from the village of Miyamoto where Musashi was born. Musashi's family was traditionally called Hirata. Hirata Munisai and Hirata Shokan, Musashi's presumed father and grandfather, were vassals of Lord Shinmen.

It is generally thought that Musashi was born in 1584. According to an inscription carved on the tomb of the Hirata family, Hirata Muni (Munisai) died in 1580. Since Musashi could not have been born four years after the death of his father, either this tomb is not that of Musashi's parents or there is an error in the inscription. This is the first enigmatic point.

According to the genealogy handed down in the Miyamoto family, resident today in Kyushu, Musashi's year of birth was 1582.

Four hypotheses have been put forward.

1. Musashi was adopted after the death of Munisai.

According to this view, Munisai died in 1580, leaving behind two children, both daughters. Omasa, Munisai's widow, had the heavy responsibility of seeing to the survival of the Hirata family. Her daughters were still too young to be married. She succeeded in adopting a boy who had just been born in the village of Miyamoto, part of the fief of Banshu. This was the third son of Okamoto Jinemon, a member of the Akamatsu clan, to which the Hirata family also belonged. Thus this boy was adopted after the death of Munisai to be his successor.

This hypothesis fits in with a sentence written by Musashi in the *Gorin no sho:* "I am a warrior from Banshu named Shinmen Musashi Fujiwara Genshin."

2. Musashi is indeed the son of Munisai, and the date carved on the tombstone is mistaken.

A number of researchers advocate this view and think that Munisai lived longer, probably at least until 1590. Two hypotheses then developed concerning the identity of Musashi's mother.

One is that Musashi's mother was Munisai's first wife. The village of Miyamoto is situated in the region of Mimasaka (Sakushu), near its border with the Harima (Banshu) region. The village of Hirafuku is near Miyamoto but in the region of Harima (Banshu). Bessho Shigeharu was the lord to whom the village of Hirafuku owed fealty. In 1578 he lost a battle against Yamanaka Shikanosuke. Many of his vassals perished, but he himself survived and went into hiding in the village of Hirafuku. His daughter Yoshiko married Hirata Munisai and gave birth to Musashi. But for unknown reasons, Munisai and Yoshiko divorced. Yoshiko returned to her father's house in the village of Hirafuku, leaving Musashi with his father. Munisai then married Omasa, the daughter of Lord Shinmen, while Yoshiko remarried in the village of Hirafuku, with Tasumi Masahisa, whose wife had just died, leaving him with two children.

In the genealogy of the Tasumi family, we find the following entry:

The daughter of Bessho Shigeharu first married Hirata Muni and was divorced from him a few years later. After that she married Tasumi Masahisa.

The second wife of Tasumi Masahisa was the mother of Miyamoto Musashi.

Musashi's childhood name was Hirata Den. He later became famous on account of his swordsmanship. During his childhood, he went to Hirafuku to find his real mother. He moved in with the Tasumi family. (12, p. 113)

The second hypothesis is that Musashi's mother was Omasa. According to the inscription on the tomb, Omasa died immediately after giving birth to Musashi, March 4, 1584. Munisai first had Musashi raised by a nurse, then he married again, to a woman named Yoshiko, the daughter of Bessho Shigeharu. They divorced some years later and Yoshiko took Musashi with her. She later married Tasumi Masahisa.

In either of these hypotheses, the kinship between Musashi and Munisai is possible only if there was a mistake in the death date inscribed on his tombstone and if the same mistake was made in the temple registry.

3. Musashi was not born in 1584 but around 1580.

Right at the beginning of the *Gorin no sho,* Musashi wrote: "At the beginning of the tenth month of the twentieth year of Kanei [1643], I came to Mount Iwato . . . to write. . . . My life now adds up to sixty years."

The year of Musashi's birth is calculated on the basis of this sentence. It is therefore deduced, taking into account the way of counting a person's age in use at the time, that Musashi was born in 1584. All the scholars whose works I have consulted base their calculations on this sentence, and when they find other evidence and documents that contradict it, it is the latter that they challenge.

I would like to put forward an entirely different hypothesis here. I agree with these scholars that in order to resolve the contradictions, we must look for errors outside Musashi's text. But my hypothesis is that the text written by Musashi, although it is not in error, is ambiguous.

In the *Gorin no sho* Musashi in effect tells us that in 1643 he was sixty years old, but we must consider that in ancient Japan there was a kind of rhythm to be found in literary style, particularly in Musashi's style. If you read Musashi's phrase *"toshi tsumotte rokuju"* out loud, this rhythm is evident. In this kind of text it is quite natural to write "sixty years" instead of "sixty-three years" or "sixty-four years." Thus when Musashi writes "sixty years," in my view he means "in my sixties" and not the exact figure "sixty." This expression is of the same type as when he writes, to indicate the number of his duels, *"Roku juuyodo made shobu su,"* "My duels number in the sixties." A contemporary example of this manner of speech is the popular expression *"Otoko ippiki goshaku no karada,"* which means, "Me, a man of five *shaku* in height." A *shaku* is about 30 centimeters, so five *shaku* amounts to 1.5 meters, but this rhythmical expression refers to any man of less than 1.8 meters in height; for if you said a man of *"go* (five) *shaku* (30 centimeters) *roku* (six) *sun* (3 centimeters)" or "*go shaku nana* (seven) *sun*," the rhythm would be broken and the phrase would lose its force. We find a great number of comparable expressions in classical Japanese literature. In fixating on an exact figure, the scholars neglected this aspect of the Japanese language.

Using this hypothesis, we may consider that in 1643 Musashi was in his sixties— sixty-four years old or older (and not exactly sixty). In this way the Hirata family genealogy no longer presents a contradiction. This hypothesis strikes me as more acceptable than that of an error—the omission of the figure 10—in the inscription on Munisai's tombstone. Moreover, Munisai's wife was interred in the same tomb as her husband four years later, and the date was inscribed in 1584. She was therefore interred after Munisai, and it is difficult to conceive of such an error in juxtaposed inscriptions at dates so close to each other.

My hypothesis of the kinship between Musashi and Munisai agrees with the Hirata family genealogy, but nevertheless various contradictions remain.

Could Musashi have received the transmission of the family martial arts tradition?

If Munisai died in 1580, just after the birth of Musashi, Musashi could not have received the transmission of the family art, at least not directly from his father. Could Musashi then have received it from students of his father? Or did he never have a chance to learn the family art?

Another hypothesis: Musashi's father was not Hirata Munisai, and he lived at least until his son's adolescence.

4. Musashi's father was Munisai and he died a long time after 1590.
   Here is how Tominaga Kengo puts the story together:

> Hirata Shokan, a vassal of Shinmen Sadashige, was an adept of the sword and of the *jitte*. He was a cultivated man, and his lord held him in such high esteem that he gave him his daughter in marriage. Through this alliance, the Hirata family became closer to the Shinmen family, and it occasionally used Shinmen as its own family name.
>
> Shokan's son was named Muni. He was sometimes called

Muninosuke, sometimes Munisai. He succeeded his father in the arts of the sword and the *jitte*. According to the *Nitenki,* he called his school Tori ryu. He was a valiant warrior and he fought at the side of his lord Shinmen through several wars. In the presence of the shogun Ashikaga Yoshiaki, Munisai fought a famous sword master named Yoshioka. He won two bouts out of three and received from the shogun the title of "best in Japan." That is the reason that when Munisai composed the certificate of transmission of his art, he used the title "best in Japan." This Munisai was the father of Musashi. (1 2)

In this hypothesis there is a problem of chronology that Tominaga Kengo does not mention and that I analyze as follows. According to the registry of the Hirata family temple (1 2), Hirata Shokan, Musashi's grandfather, died in 1 5 0 3 and his wife in 1 5 0 6. Here is the first problem: If Munisai, Musashi's father and the son of Hirata Shokan, died in 1 5 8 0 at the age of fifty-three, he would have been born in 1 5 2 7, twenty-four years after the death of his father. Was Hirata Shokan really Musashi's grandfather?

I believe Hirata Shokan was Munisai's grandfather and thus the great-grandfather of Musashi; I think that Munisai's father simply does not appear in the documents. The absence of any mention of his name can be explained by the troubles of this period of feudal wars.[1]

Whatever the hypotheses concerning Miyamoto Musashi's descent, it is certain that his father, genetic or adoptive, was called Miyamoto Muninosuke or Miyamoto Munisai and was an accomplished practitioner of the art of the sword and the *jitte*. In my view, Musashi certainly received the transmission of the family art during his childhood, and this served as the basis for formation of his School of the Two Swords.

MUSASHI'S CHILDHOOD AND HIS FIRST DUEL

In the following account of Musashi's childhood, I have attempted to determine the most coherent flow of events based on consultation of sometimes contradictory documents. I have filled in the uncertainties by offering a variety of hypotheses.

So, Musashi was born around 1580, and at his birth he was given the name Bennosuke. His father, Hirata Munisai, was already more than fifty years old, and his mother, Omasa, daughter of Lord Shinmen, died in 1584. Munisai married a young woman, Yoshiko, the daughter of Bessho Shigeharu, who was formerly the lord of the neighboring region but, following a defeat in war, was in hiding in the village of Hirafuku. Yoshiko took good care of Bennosuke, who considered her his real mother. Munisai was already almost sixty. Not long after their marriage, Munisai divorced her. Yoshiko returned to the village of Hirafuku with Bennosuke and soon after married Tasumi Masahisa, a member of her clan whose wife had just died, leaving him with two sons.

Little Bennosuke and his mother (who was not his birth mother) lived with his stepfather and his two stepbrothers. He soon became aware of what the situation was and also of the fact that Hirata Munisai, who lived in the village of Miyamoto, twelve kilometers away, was his real father.

He learned that his family belonged to a lineage of martial arts masters. His father, like his great-grandfather Hirata Shokan, was a great adept of the sword and also of the *jitte* who in his youth had received the title "the greatest adept in Japan" from the last shogun of the Ashikaga family.

Bennosuke no doubt asked himself the question: "Why am I not living with my father, who has an excellent reputation and who occupies an important position in the fief? Why do I have to live with a man and his children who are neither my father nor my brothers?"

He became a difficult and violent child, engaging in games of war with the children of the village. Soon his mother, worried about his education, placed him with one of his distant relatives, a monk named Dorin who lived in Shoreian temple in the neighboring village, three kilometers from Hirafuku. From this monk, who was around fifty years old, Bennosuke received his basic education.

In Yoshikawa Eiji's novel, the young Musashi was strongly influenced by the Zen monk Takuan, but this is purely fictional. The monk Takuan did exist, and he wrote an important text on Zen and the art of the sword, but it is not certain that Musashi ever met him in the course of his life.

So Bennosuke lived most of the time at Dorin's temple and from time to time went to visit the house of his stepfather, Tasumi, where he was reunited with his mother, Yoshiko. He also began to go occasionally to the village of Miyamoto to visit his father, Munisai, an austere man who was quick to see the talent of his son for the martial arts.

If the situation was such as I have depicted it here, then from the psychological point of view, Bennosuke's relationships to his family were quite complex.

As he grew up, Bennosuke became more and more interested in the art of his father, who instructed him in the art of the sword and the *jitte,* treating him with particular severity. In the meantime, in 1589, on the order of Shinmen Sokan, Munisai had to kill Honiden Gekinosuke, who was his student in the martial arts. After this event, under pressure from the Honiden family and other vassals, Munisai had to leave the village of Miyamoto and take up residence four kilometers away in the village of Kawakami.

Bennosuke, who was a powerful and precocious lad, made remarkable progress and reached the point of expressing criticism of his father's swordsmanship. Because of the friction between him and his father, Bennosuke stopped visiting his father's house.

The *Tanji Hokin hikki* provides some material on this period of Musashi's life. Before reporting this material, a remark about the credibility of this work: Tachibana Hokin, the fourth-generation lineage successor of Musashi's school in the fief of Fukuoka, wrote down in 1727 what he had heard from his predecessors in the work entitled *Tanji Hokin hikki.* The account was completed and revised in 1782 by Niwa Nobuhide, the seventh successor of the school, who passed the work along under the title *Hyoho senshi denki.* Musashi died in 1645; thus we are dealing with an account that reflects a long oral tradition handed down by Musashi's disciples, with all the embellishments that such an account is liable to have undergone. These texts have been assimilated into several contemporary works, including that of Ozawa Masao, which I now cite:

The master was born in the twelfth year of the Tensho era [1584] in the fief of Banshu. Bennosuke was his childhood name. His father Muninosuke was an adept of the sword. When he was a child, the master often criticized his father's art. One day, when he was nine years old, leaning against a post, he watched his father cutting some toothpicks. As usual, he criticized his father's art. His father lost his temper and threw a knife at him. The master dodged it with a slight movement of his head, and the knife stuck in the post. Muninosuke got still angrier and drove him out of the house. At this time Muninosuke's younger brother was a monk in a temple not far away. The master went there and the monk raised him. The master lived in the temple until the age of thirteen and learned calligraphy there from a master of this art. (9, p. 221)

Even if doubts may be raised concerning the authenticity of this account, it leads us to think that when he was very young, Musashi had already attained a certain level of accomplishment in the martial arts and that he was conscious of it, even though this might have been misplaced juvenile pride.

Four years later, at the age of twelve, Bennosuke fought his first duel.

Musashi's First Duel

Musashi's opponent in his first duel was Arima Kihei, an adept of the Shinto ryu, founded by Tsukahara Bokuden (1489–1571). Bokuden was a master trained in the Kashima school, and it was in reference to him that Musashi wrote in the Scroll of Earth: "Some time ago, the Shinto priests of the Kantori shrine near Kashima . . . founded a school, saying that their art had been transmitted to them by the gods, and they propagated this art in all the provinces."

Bokuden was born into a family of Shinto priests of the Kashima shrine, where, according to legend, the priests had transmitted the martial arts from ancient times. A document of the time tells us that a period of seclusion *(gyo)* of a thousand days in this temple, leading an ascetic life, was required in order to prepare one's mind to perfect one's swords-

manship. Legend reports that at the end of these thousand days of *gyo,*
Bokuden had a divine revelation, and he then named the essence of his art
hitotsu no tachi, "the single sword." Musashi mentions this legend.

Gyo is the ascetic practice through which a spiritual level that could be
called a realization of the way, *do* or *michi,* is sought. It could also be said
that wherever the way, *do* or *michi,* is put into practice, inevitably the
practice of *gyo* takes place. The ideogram *gyo* means "to go" or "to walk."
These ideas are derived from Buddhism, but they were incorporated at a
very early stage into the body of traditional Japanese practices and beliefs
and also into traditional Japanese art. As discussed in appendix 1, Musashi frequently used the word *michi,* which has these connotations.

The duel took place in the village of Hirafuku. Here is the account
given in the *Hyoho senshi denki:*

> In 1596, when the master was thirteen, Arima Kihei, an adept of
> the Shinto ryu, who was traveling in order to perfect his art, came
> to the province of Banshu. He issued a public challenge by putting
> up an announcement on a notice board, in which he wrote: "He
> who wishes to fight me with the sword should write his name and
> the date of the duel on this notice board." The master read this no-
> tice on his way to his calligraphy lesson, and on his way back he
> painted Arima's announcement black and after it wrote his name,
> his address, and the date of the duel. He went back to the temple,
> not saying a word to anyone about this, and picked out among the
> firewood a good hard piece from which to make a wooden sword.
> At this point a messenger arrived. The monk received him him-
> self, wondering why a messenger should have come, given that he
> was not lodging anyone at the little temple. The messenger said:
> "I have come to convey a message from Arima Kihei, who is trav-
> eling to improve his swordsmanship. Would you be kind enough
> to pass on to Mr. Miyamoto Bennosuke that Arima agrees to fight
> him at the exact time he indicated."

> The monk was shocked by this news and said: "This is incon-
> ceivable because Bennosuke is only a child of thirteen. He is in-
> capable of facing an accomplished swordsman." He continued

and pointed out the master, who was sitting off to one side and listening. "We are talking about this little kid here. It is unthinkable for him to fight a duel. Would you be kind enough to go back, please, and ask Mr. Arima to excuse him, given that it was no more than the silly prank of a young kid to dare to mess up his announcement."

The messenger grasped the situation and laughed and said: "I understand. But in my opinion Arima will not be persuaded even if I give this explanation. I would like you to come with me to his inn and explain to him directly and make your excuses to him. Then I think he will accept. Please come with me."

The monk had no choice, and he left with the messenger, murmuring, "What a rotten kid." When he got to Arima's inn, he made excuses to him: "As your messenger has seen, the person in question is no more than a child whom you could only play with. Please have the indulgence to excuse him."

Arima replied: "I understand that carrying on with the duel is out of the question. Since the person in question is a child, it is better just to drop the matter. But I am traveling to various regions and no one will believe that my announcement being painted black when I got to Banshu was only a child's prank. My honor is on the line. I request you to come with Bennosuke to the place of the duel on the appointed day and explain to the public the reason the duel is not taking place. That will clear away my dishonor."

Having no choice, the monk departed having promised to do as Arima asked.

The day of the duel, the monk said to the master: "How annoying you are! Follow me!" And he took him to the place appointed for the duel. Arima, dressed in his walking pants, was sitting on a chair in the dueling enclosure. His disciple was holding his sword and a wooden sword. Spectators surrounded the enclosure. The monk entered the enclosure and said to Arima: "As I explained to you, it was that young boy over there who was so stupid as to spoil your announcement. I ask you to be indulgent and forgive him for it."

While the monk was saying this, the master entered the enclosure carrying his wooden sword and shouted, "Come on, let's fight!" He then attacked Arima. The latter drew his *wakizashi* (short sword) and attacked. The master quickly ducked and Arima's sword cut the air and his hand came down on the master's shoulder. The master dove down and put his hand between his opponent's legs and threw him over his shoulder. The moment Arima tried to get up, the master, who had picked up his wooden sword, struck him hard between the eyes. Arima was stunned and was unable to get up quickly, and during this time the master struck him several blows in a row. Arima died and his disciple ran away. The spectators applauded and shouted out loud, but the monk was extremely upset.

Hearing the news, his father, Muninosuke, tried to get the master to return to his house. But the master did not want to be under anybody's thumb. He continued to immerse himself in training in strategy, and he never even combed his hair. Following this first victory that he had achieved by closing in on his opponent, it seems that he began to give particular heed to closing in on an opponent. (2, 9)

This description probably contains exaggerations, but it conveys certain information about Musashi's training and his techniques. Let us now look at the interpretation of this duel by a contemporary kendo master, Morita Monjuro (1889–1978). This master studied Musashi's texts by applying them to his practice of kendo, to which he devoted his entire life.

To explain how this duel unfolded, Morita Monjuro takes as a reference point a technique described in the Scroll of Water, banging into your opponent:

The moment you get in close to your opponent, you bang into him. You tilt your face slightly to the side, stick out your left shoulder, and bang into his chest. Bang into him filling your entire body with force, relying on a *hyoshi* of concordance with the breath and with a sensation of rebounding. By mastering this technique, you can strike so violently that your opponent will be thrown back a distance of four to six meters and knocked over. This blow can be so strong your opponent dies of it.

Morita thinks that the child Musashi must have employed this technique. He casts doubt on this description in the *Hyoho senshi denki:*

> The latter drew his *wakizashi* (short sword) and attacked. The master quickly ducked and Arima's sword cut the air and his hand came down on the master's shoulder. The master dove down and put his hand between his opponent's legs and threw him over his shoulder. The moment Arima tried to get up, the master, who had picked up his wooden sword, struck him hard between the eyes. (9)

He gives the following analysis:

> For those who have practiced kendo over a long period of time, it is evident that such a throwing technique would be impossible during combat. In my view, Musashi must have first banged into his opponent with his left shoulder, as he describes in the *Gorin no sho.* He had learned this technique from his father. . . . For the *jitte* is a weapon that is used with just one hand, and with this you learn body movements more completely than in kendo; that is why with this [weapon] there are techniques that resemble those of sumo [Japanese wrestling]. (20)

Morita's interpretation merits special attention because the explanations he gives on Musashi's art and on parts of his life are based on his own experience of kendo. Of course, this is not a scientific mode of explanation, but his personal approach is an attempt to fill in gaps that no scientific approach could hope to deal with because of the absence of any objective data.

One consideration is that Miyamoto Munisai was well known among adepts of the sword of that period. Could Arima Kihei have come to the region to challenge him and to heighten his reputation by gaining a victory over his art or his school? If Munisai was alive, why did he not fight him himself? And why did Musashi, a child of twelve, fight him? Did he do so with his father's permission or in defiance of him? Did Arima Kihei's challenge specify the name of a person or a school, or was it indeed addressed to the general public?

Some people think that the young Musashi took on this challenge as a way of making an insolent gesture toward his father and his school. That is why he replied to Arima Kihei by blotching his challenge sign with black ink and announcing that he accepted the duel. The monk, Musashi's uncle, was unaware of his feelings of pride and also of his determination, therefore he asked Arima to cancel the duel. Some put forward the debatable theory that the monk was Musashi's accomplice. According to that hypothesis, Munisai, for an unknown reason, was not able to undertake the duel, and Bennosuke decided to fight despite his young age. The monk then pretended to be unaware of the situation and by requesting that the duel be canceled, he succeeded in causing the adversary to relax his awareness, thus creating an opening for Bennosuke.

We have no means of verifying what the situation surrounding the duel was, but we are certain that Musashi fought and defeated his opponent.

According to the text cited above, we may surmise that the young Musashi had an advantage in the duel against Arima, in that Arima did not realize that the child was determined to fight to the death. By the time he realized that the situation was serious, the initiative in the duel was already held by Musashi. We can say that Arima was killed mainly because he slackened his awareness, and that Musashi, whether intentionally or not, used a trick. It must be said that this situation was very difficult for Arima, because even if he had won, it would have added nothing to his honor and he would have been reproached for having killed a child—whereas Musashi could fight under the shield of indulgence afforded to children. Thus it was not a duel on equal conditions, but that was not of great importance in the combats of this period. The important thing was to win, and even if your error in your assessment of your opponent was slight, you could never make up for it. This was Arima's plight. This situation is entirely different from that of a sports match, however serious it might be. We must try to disengage ourselves from our habitual criteria when we look at Musashi's combats.

We know that after his first duel, Musashi remained in the region for three years. Did he continue to study martial arts under his father's direction and to study art and reading under the direction of the monk Dorin? According to some authors, after this experience, which had given him confidence in himself, Bennosuke went back to his father to continue to receive instruction in the traditional art of his family, the sword and the *jitte*. Others think that Musashi's father was already dead or had left for another fief. Personally, I adopt the hypothesis according to which Munisai was still alive and Musashi continued to receive his teaching. In my view the main import of this duel for Musashi was that it gave him a glimpse of the precariousness of life and how it had to be laid on the line in a combat to the death. He would have felt a complex sensation in which a certain self-confidence mingled with anxiety about engaging in a kind of combat for which he was aware that he had not yet acquired sufficient technique. So this duel would have given him a fresh push toward resuming his training with his father.

During this period a boy was considered to enter adulthood between the ages of twelve and thirteen. This transition was marked by a ceremony called *genpuku,* which took place at different ages, depending upon the overall milieu and social situation. At this time a boy changed his name, his hairstyle, his bearing, and his way of dressing. Thus it came time for Bennosuke to take an adult name. At first he chose the name Takezo; then, shortly afterward, he changed the pronunciation to Musashi, as the same ideograms can also be read. For a family name, he adopted the name of the village of Miyamoto, as his father had done. During this period the family name an individual used for himself varied in accordance with the situation he was in. For example, when Musashi wished to stress his warrior descent, he called himself Shinmen Musashi, Shinmen being the name of the lord to whom Musashi's family had been attached for several generations. Nevertheless, the way in which the transition between Bennosuke and Musashi was made is not certain.

Three years after this duel, Musashi left his native village. His departure is described in the "Text on the Six Regions East of Mimasaka" *(Tosakushi),* a document compiled by Masaki Teruo in 1815 from the *Texts on the Ancient Facts of the Village of Miyamoto,* which the mayor of this village, Jinbei, presented to Lord Mori of Tsuyama in 1689:

> At the time of his departure, Musashi left in the care of his sister's husband, Hirao Yoemon, his furniture, weapons, genealogical papers, and other objects that belonged to him. Later, Kurobei, who had decided to till the soil and had set himself up as a farmer a kilometer away from the village of Miyamoto, inherited these objects. . . . Moriiwa Hikobei, of the same village, possesses a *bokuto* (wooden sword) once carried by Musashi. It is 110 centimeters long. . . . It is made of medlar wood and is blackish in color. At the time of his departure, Musashi was using this *bokuto* as a walking stick. Moriiwa Hikobei accompanied him as far as the pass of Kamasaka in the village of Nakayama. Musashi gave his walking stick to Hikobei as a token of farewell. (8)

The Founding of the School of Two Swords

The *Gorin no sho* tells us that one of the characteristics of Musashi's school was the use of two swords. He did not content himself with merely proclaiming the occasional usefulness of a second sword. He established a new school with a method based on two swords that could be transmitted. This was an entirely innovative approach, for at that time there was no other school that explicitly proclaimed the benefit of using two swords. Musashi explains the reasons for their use, but he does not say why and how he came to practice this way. In my view the hypothesis according to which he received systematic instruction in the school of martial arts founded by his grandfather, or more likely by his great-grandfather, enables us to understand the specific qualities of his art better.

The invention of the art of two swords by Musashi has been explained in three different ways.

The first explanation is that his insight about the simultaneous use of two swords arose in connection with his experience of village life.

In the village of Miyamoto, where Musashi spent a part of his childhood, there was a Shinto shrine called Aramaki daimyojin, most often referred to as Aramaki jinja. When the priest of this shrine said his morning and evening prayers, he beat a large drum with two short sticks, one held in each hand. From his childhood, Musashi had observed the priest's movements. One day, noting that the drum made the same sound whether struck with one hand or the other, he had a moment of intuitive insight. It was this insight that led to his development of the art of two swords.

According to Yoshida Seiken, a kendo practitioner of the School of Two Swords, this is no more than a mere legend. He writes: "There is no connection whatever between the mind of the School of Two Swords and the fact that the sounds made by a drum are the same whether you strike it with one hand or the other. . . . There is nothing to link the School of Two Swords with the manipulation of two sticks to beat a drum." (35, p. 39)

Taking the opposite point of view, Morita Monjuro, also a kendo practitioner, writes: "The two drumsticks are big and long. In using them you put forward first one foot, then the other." (20) And by trying the practice of beating such a drum himself, Morita Monjuro discovered that this action produced within the body, between the upper and lower limbs, two diagonal tensions that crossed at the level of the lower belly (tanden). He noted that this exercise required a high level of flexibility in the pelvic region and that the principle of striking contained in it conforms perfectly to that of the School of Two Swords. According to Morita Monjuro, Musashi worked out his art of two swords by applying the principle he discovered in the course of practicing striking a drum with two sticks, because this principle was close to that involved in the wielding of the jitte, which he had been practicing since childhood.

The second explanation for Musashi's adoption of two swords is connected with a situation in which Musashi was supposed to have fought against some peasants holding a wooden sword in one hand and a stick in the other. It is based on the following anecdote.

During his travels in western Japan, Musashi spent several days in a peasant village. He was staying with the mayor, who was an acquaintance of his. One day he heard the noise of men moving around outside the house.

He asked the mayor, "Is there some problem?"

"Yes, sir. That's what I'd like to talk to you about. We have heard that the people of the neighboring village are preparing to attack us. We are in the midst of getting together some men to defend us. We would be happy if you could give us a hand."

And the major explained that the two villages had come into conflict over a question of dividing up water resources for the rice paddies and the other village was about to attack.

"I agree to give you a hand." For a traveler like Musashi, making his fighting skills available in case of a problem amounted to paying for his room and board. "But," he continued, "I don't want to increase the problems. Tell all your men to go back inside the village, and I will take charge of defending the entrance to the village by myself."

Saying that, Musashi left the house, carrying a *bokuto* (wooden sword). On his way to the village gate, he picked up a broken oar and took it in his left hand. Shortly after his arrival at the gate of the village, where he stood alone, the peasants from the neighboring village arrived, armed with tools. They were bewildered by Musashi's face and strange air, but understanding that he was defending the entrance, they began to attack him. Musashi defended himself spontaneously against the attack of these men armed with sticks and other objects. After having smacked down a few of the men, he realized that he was parrying with the oar he was holding in his left hand and striking immediately afterward with the *bokuto* in his right. This experience is supposed to have furnished the basis for his development of his art of two swords. (30)

The third explanation, which is the one I support, is that his art resulted from a reorganization of existing knowledge of technique.

In the history of the martial arts, from time to time we run across reformers of technique and strategic thought. Musashi was one of these. In most cases, if they end up founding a martial arts school, it is not because they have personally invented all the elements that distinguish their particular art. It is more a matter of reorganizing a heritage of practical know-how whose level of sophistication is already considerable. The transmission of the art takes place through the qualities and talents of the people who contribute to its qualitative transformation.

Karate is an example that is close to us. Karate was originally a local practice on the island of Okinawa, in the extreme south of Japan, practiced and transmitted within limited circles. At the beginning of the twentieth century, this art was presented to a large public. Around 1905 Itosu Anko, a master of classical karate, composed a series of five katas (techniques expressed as standardized sequences of movements), which he called *pinan*. Their purpose was to function as a reference point in teaching this art to the students of Okinawa's primary schools. Because of his creation of the *pinan* katas, his revision of several of the other classic katas, and also his development of a new way of teaching, Itosu Anko is considered the founder of modern karate. However, even the katas that he created were not something he invented but a reorganization by him of the classical art of combat in connection with a new idea of physical education. Thanks to Itosu, karate broke out of the limited framework of special transmission. Following that, this art went through a major expansion. At the same time, we cannot overlook the fact that as a result of Itosu Anko's reform, a certain number of techniques and classical katas were lost. Modern karate is a qualitative evolution of the classical Okinawan art, and this evolution contains both positive and negative elements.

In the history of Japanese swordsmanship, we can consider Musashi's School of Two Swords to be a positive development. For he managed to systematize, and furnish a theoretical basis for, a type of combat that until then had appeared only accidentally and had not been studied. The two anecdotes reported above might have some truth in them, but just by themselves they seem to me insufficient to explain the formation of a new school by Musashi. Instead they should be looked at as indicating possible ways an addition was made to a body of inherited knowledge.

THE TWO SOURCES OF MUSASHI'S ART

On the basis of what heritage did Musashi come to conceive of his art of two swords?

On the Kokura monument, a memorial to Musashi raised nine years after his death, the following inscription appears: "The creation of the art of two swords on the basis of the art of the *jitte* was a development of his family art. Musashi also acquired the ability to throw either a sword or a wooden sword."

The Art of the *Jitte,* a Family Art

Hirata Shokan founded the Tori ryu toward the end of the fifteenth century. In his school he taught the art of the sword and also, more specifically, the *jitte* and jujutsu. It was a period of war, and the martial arts were being directly applied on the field of battle. Thus Hirata Shokan also taught the *naginata,* the lance, and the bow, indispensable weapons for warriors of this period.

Miyamoto Munisai, Musashi's father, was a famous adept of the arts of the *jitte* and the sword. Several documents bear witness to this. In addition he had received the transmission of the family art. Did he receive his training directly from Hirata Shokan, as is generally thought, or were these two separated by a generation, as I have hypothesized for reasons related to consistency of dates. The question remains open.

In any case, it appears certain that Musashi received tutelage in the arts of the *jitte* and sword during his childhood. However, we are uncertain of the duration of his familial training.

Let us look again at the text on the Kokura monument:

His father's name was Shinmen Muni, a master of the traditional art of the *jitte*. Musashi received the family art and developed it further by practicing from morning till night and reflecting profoundly. Then, comparing it with the sword, he realized that the *jitte* had great advantages, even more than the sword.

However, the *jitte* is not a weapon that a samurai carries every day, whereas he is never separated from his two swords. If it were possible to realize the principle of the *jitte* with two swords, the effectiveness of this would be indubitable. The creation of the art of two swords on the basis of the art of the *jitte* was the development of the family art. (17)

The story already cited of Munisai's execution of Gekinosuke corroborates the hypothesis of the existence of a family school of martial arts. We may consider that the monk Nakatsukasa, whose help Munisai asked for in carrying out this execution, was the jujutsu adept who founded the Takeuchi ryu jujutsu, which is still in existence today.[2] Here I put forward the hypothesis that Munisai, with his art of the *jitte,* and Nakatsukasa, with his jujutsu, communicated their knowledge to each other. The principal techniques of the art of the *jitte* are moves intended to immobilize the adversary first by parrying with the *jitte,* then using it to pull the adversary's sword or other weapon from his hand. Thus the use of the *jitte* serves in a certain way as an introduction to jujutsu. Therefore technical exchanges between these two adepts were highly possible.

It should be pointed out that during this period the divisions between the various disciplines of the martial arts were not clear-cut. Munisai must have been in a sense a generalist in the martial arts, specializing in the art of the *jitte*. This absence of boundaries between the disciplines comes out when Musashi talks about the art of the sword in relation to the practice of strategy in general.

What is the *jitte?*

For the Japanese, the word *jitte* evokes the image of a simple weapon, made of a bar of steel with a hook above the handle in the place of a hilt guard (fig. 1). This weapon, which usually measured about fifty centimeters in length, was a defensive arm used during the Edo period by police as a secondary weapon. It served mainly to block a strike by a sword and to immobilize the sword afterward by wedging its blade between the bar and the hook by twisting the wrist. This weapon can be used alone or as a secondary weapon if one has a sword in the other hand.

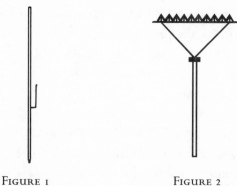

It is most often thought that Musashi's *jitte* was of this form, but according to a work by Imai Masayuki, a contemporary master (tenth generation) of Musashi's school, Musashi's *jitte* was quite different (fig. 2). The hooks were ten in number, and this corresponds to the etymology of the word *jitte,* which means "ten hands." One could much more easily immobilize an opponent's sword with this weapon than with the weapon shown in figure 1. In fact, the form was later simplified to that shown in figure 1, but the original term, *ten hands,* was kept, even after it no longer corresponded to the form. The function of the weapon also remained the same, that is, immobilization of an opponent's sword. (3)

Miyamoto Musashi was an expert in this art and left behind two instructions on the *jitte* in the form of poems:

Know that victory is in your hands
If you hold well the sword of your enemy
With your own *jitte*.

Know that victory is in your hands
If you break the attack of the enemy
By placing your attention on his strongest hand.
In this way your art of the *jitte* will flourish.

The *jitte* was a formidable weapon when an adept of the sword used it on the field of battle because he could be sure of a solid defense with this weapon in one hand while he wielded his sword with the other. During the era of feudal peace, the *jitte* was used principally as a defensive weapon to make an enemy capitulate without killing him. That is why the art of the *jitte* is part of jujutsu, an art of bare-handed combat containing techniques to immobilize and capture an adversary. Most of the time the *jitte* was held in the right hand when used to parry a sword attack. Once you succeed in immobilizing your adversary's sword, you grab his right arm with your left hand in order to disarm him, then you immobilize him with a rope of five and a half meters in length. The greatest level of efficiency is reached when these actions constitute a continuous series of movements. This technique is the same with the simplified *jitte* (fig. 1). During the Edo period, policemen employed similar techniques of immobilization but with the simplified *jitte,* which was easier to carry but more difficult to use than its ancestor.

According to Imai Masayuki, the master of the Hyoho niten ichi ryu, the five techniques for the *jitte* from the school of Miyamoto Munisai are transmitted today under the name Niten ichi ryu jitte jutsu. (3) These five techniques are devised to respond to a particular attack on the part of the adversary:

- when the adversary attacks you horizontally on your side
- when the adversary attacks intending to slash your arm
- when the adversary attacks you on an angle from above your left shoulder
- when the adversary attacks you from above your head
- when the adversary attacks you on an angle from above your right shoulder

Following are the instructions for the execution of each of these techniques.

When the adversary attacks you horizontally on your side
The adversary launches a horizontal attack on your right side immediately after drawing his sword *(nuki uchi).*

Holding the *jitte* in your right hand, you parry this attack and apply pressure on the adversary's sword, downward and to your right. You continue this until the right hand of the adversary comes away from the handle of his sword, beginning with the thumb. With your left hand, you continue to twist his arm, turning your thumb to the left. The adversary will be forced to lower himself, leaning forward until his right shoulder touches the ground. He will then fall on his side. At this time your left knee touches the ground, and from this position you deliver a kick with your right foot to the adversary's solar plexus.

When the adversary attacks intending to slash your arm
The adversary attacks your wrist immediately after drawing his sword *(nuki uchi)*.

The situation is the same as the preceding one, except that the sword is aimed at your wrist from above. The sequence of the technique is pretty much the same.

When the adversary attacks you on an angle from above your left shoulder
The adversary attacks you on an angle *(kesa giri),* starting from above his right shoulder. You parry with the *jitte,* pushing upward and to the right. Then, by turning the *jitte,* you twist his hands holding the sword, grab his right hand with your left hand, putting your thumb on the inside, and yank it away from the sword handle. Then you move your right hand sharply to the side, pulling the sword out of his left hand. At the same time, you twist his right hand toward the outside with your left hand; then you change your hold on his right hand in order to apply a further twist that will throw him to the ground. Now immediately grab the upper collar of the adversary's garment with your left hand. In this way you can immobilize him.

When the adversary attacks you from above your head
This situation is about the same as the previous one. Here you add the following technique: Once you have immobilized the adversary with the previous technique, if he tries to get up, you execute a broad movement

to the right in order to put him flat on his stomach. Then press your knee into his back in order to immobilize him.

When the adversary attacks you on an angle from above your right shoulder

The adversary attacks you on an angle *(kesa giri)*, starting above his left shoulder.

You parry from below upward and toward the outside and you grab his right wrist with your left hand. Then you throw him in the *ippon zeoi* fashion (throwing over your shoulder and back an adversary you are holding by just one arm). Then you grab the upper part of his collar in your left hand as you place your left knee on the ground. When the adversary, who is now lying facedown on the ground, turns to get up, you put your right knee on the ground and move your left knee on top of his elbow to immobilize him.

The *Jitte* As a Complement to the Sword

The *jitte* is also used in fighting when you are on the attack. Then the idea is to parry the opponent's attack with the *jitte* and cut him down with the sword held in your other hand. In this case the *jitte* is generally held in the left hand and the sword in the right.

We may surmise that this manner of using the *jitte* contributed substantially to Musashi's development of his art of two swords. Indeed, it is possible to consider that in the School of Two Swords, the short sword substitutes for the *jitte,* and also that the *jitte*'s principal function (parrying and immobilizing the adversary's sword) is accomplished by crossing the two swords. In this school the short sword is held in the left hand; however, while you can parry with the short sword, it is not possible to immobilize the adversary's sword in the same way as with the *jitte*. But by crossing the short sword with another sword, you can form a sort of scissors with which it is possible to immobilize the adversary's sword momentarily or to hook it as a *jitte* would. In this way the two swords can function as a large *jitte*. In the School of Two Swords, Musashi not only substituted a short sword for the *jitte* but also realized one of the functions of the *jitte* through the use of both swords. We can see this by observing the techniques practiced today in Musashi's school, the Hyoho niten ichi ryu.

Thus, through the simultaneous use of two swords, Musashi succeeded in elevating the quality of the art he inherited from his family by adapting it to new circumstances. The *jitte* was a weapon intended for use on the battlefield. It was effective but cumbersome. In a more peaceful period, Musashi perpetuated the essence of its effectiveness by using the two swords that every warrior carried every day. This is an important point for understanding the formation of the School of Two Swords.

In the course of his apprenticeship in the *jitte,* Musashi doubtless developed the habit of wielding a *jitte* in one hand and a sword in the other—an essential experience for understanding that it is easier to handle a sword with one hand than with two if you manage to overcome the problem of weight. For example, holding the sword in two hands, it is easy to strike from above downward, but it is difficult to strike again immediately changing the direction to upward from below. By contrast, holding the sword in just one hand, all movements of the sword come easier. Musashi, who was quite strong from childhood onward, would easily have overcome the problem of the weight of the sword. He would have discovered the ease of handling the sword with just one hand, and this, in connection with the family practice of the *jitte,* would have led him to the idea of using two swords.

The *Shuriken,* a Secret Art

The art of the *shuriken* (literally, "a sword in the palm of your hand") is the art of throwing a knife or a short sword. This technique may well have played a role in the formation of the School of Two Swords. In the inscription on the Kokura monument, already cited above, we read: "Musashi also acquired the ability to throw either a sword or a wooden sword. Even if his adversaries ran or fled, none succeeded in escaping him. This throw had the power of a strong bow, and it never missed its mark. A superior adept would be unimaginable."

The *shuriken* had major significance for an adept of the sword, but this is not well known. A description of this art may help to provide a more complete picture of Musashi.

In a document of the eighteenth century, the *Nippon bujutsu meika den,* we read:

> This art teaches the use of a weapon that makes it possible to defeat enemies by gaining the initiative of attack. It is particularly useful when one is attacked by bandits while traveling. But it should not be thought that one can without fail kill an adversary with a *shuriken.* A man does not necessarily die from a single sword blow. It is a mistake to think one can kill with just the *shuriken.* It is a weapon that is effective in seizing the initiative of attack and in creating an opportunity to achieve victory. (9)

Generally, one is situated at a distance of more than 1.8 meters from the body of one's opponent, but when fighting against a *naginata* or a lance, the length of the blade of your own sword must be added. There is then a distance of about 2.7 meters between your body and your adversary's. The *shuriken* technique of the school of Musashi is to throw the short sword a distance of less than three meters.

At a distance of three meters, the sword is thrown by grasping it a little below the hilt. At four meters it is held closer to the hilt. You throw it with a ninety-degree movement of your arm, either from above downward or from below upward, either vertically or horizontally. If the sword is long, you throw it in the same way as a lance, holding the back of the blade near the center of gravity of the sword. These two techniques are called *jikida ho,* "throwing the sword without turning it." The maximum distance for these two techniques is around four meters.

A sword's center of gravity is near the handle, and that creates a problem in throwing it. To overcome this problem, different forms of the sword or knife were devised to make throwing easier. For example, a throwing knife is produced by removing the handle from a short sword. A tassel can also be added to improve its balance. There also exist throwing knives in the shape of spikes, with either round or square stems, which vary in length between eighteen and thirty centimeters. Most often the *jikida ho* technique was used for up to three meters, but when the distance was greater, the knife was turned between 180 and 360 degrees by changing the position of the hand holding it.

In the Negishi ryu, different types of *shuriken* were made for different distances, but in all schools the maximum distance for a *shuriken* throw was about fourteen meters. However, the throw was not expected to be highly effective beyond nine or ten meters.

The technique of throwing a sword was conceived of as a decisive measure, or at least one that could be used only once, since only two swords were carried and the long sword had to be kept in order to go on fighting. By contrast, it was possible to carry several throwing knives in addition to one's main swords. When the *shuriken* takes the form of either knives or spikes, speed of repetition becomes a key element for effectiveness. Hence the instruction "Throw five knives in one breath."[3]

Until recent times, the *shuriken* remained a secret art. Those who learned it had to swear an oath in writing to divulge to no one this knowledge that was directly transmitted as an extension of the ultimate teaching on the sword. The following formula was the usual one: "I will reveal what I learn to no one, not to my fellow disciples, nor my parents, nor my children. If I should reveal anything, may all the punishments of the gods fall upon me." Someone who did not have knowledge of this art was supposed to learn it at the same time as the defense techniques.

Why this secrecy?

First, because this was an art that was to be used by surprise for a decisive result. A *shuriken* practitioner was supposed to hide the possibility that he might throw a weapon until the last moment, so that in fighting against an adversary who was causing particular difficulties, he might throw the small sword by surprise. It was therefore essential for the adversary to have no notion whatsoever that a sword might be thrown at him. Keeping secret the existence of a particularly effective technique was a customary approach in all the ancient schools of the martial arts. The secret technique was usually concealed behind the cover of another technique that was close to it.

For example, in the bare-handed combat arts, a technique known as a nail kick is often hidden behind the appearance of a heel kick. When kicking is being drilled and the practitioner holds his foot vertically raised and then pushes forward with his heel, it is generally thought that he is practicing a heel kick. The more subtle and dangerous technique is to strike with the point of the foot with a vertical upward motion. But since an onlooker's attention will tend to be captivated by the heel, it is more or less impossible for him to catch on to the use of the point of the foot. Thus, to conceal an important technique, the usual thing was to provide another plausible explanation to distract the attention of prying eyes. If one were to hide the whole technique, practitioners from another school might continue to look until they found the secret. It was thought better to have another plausible technique to cough up at the right moment. In that way the intruders would be satisfied and give up their attempt to track down the secret. That was the approach habitually taken in transmitting secret arts.

This mode of transmission in the teaching of techniques became established in Japan during the Edo period, taking the form of the opposition between *omote* (surface) and *ura* (behind, or hidden). Apprenticeship in a particular school always began with the overt techniques *(omote waza),* and then selected students would learn the hidden techniques *(ura waza)*. Moving from the *omote waza* to the *ura waza* required a seniority that implied trust in the school and attachment to it. This was the prerequisite to opening the door to participation in the school's secrets. Sometimes the techniques were known as *ura gei* and *omote gei*. We must understand here that these were combat techniques that could mean life or death. Divulgence of secrets met with fatal sanctions.

Hidden arts of particular effectiveness, such as the *shuriken* for the art of the sword, have sometimes been characterized as perverse arts. The purpose of the art of the sword during the period of wars was to defeat the adversary by any means, but during the Edo period this objective slowly changed. From that point on, the rule was to win while observing the correct form of a discipline.

In this sense the technique of throwing a sword was part of the teaching of *ura waza* or *ura gei*. The possibility of throwing the short sword by surprise was hidden behind the appearance of holding it with one hand and using it for parrying and attacking. The more the function attributed to this way of using the short sword was visibly effective, the better it could be used to conceal the possible use of the short sword as a thrown weapon.

The *Shuriken* during "Travels for Improvement"

Schools of swordsmanship appeared beginning in the fifteenth century, and the practice of *musha shugyo* (traveling for improvement) became customary among warriors. Some men traveled with the idea of finding a liege lord, others to improve their art, and still others for both purposes. This last was the case for Musashi during a certain period of his life. For the feudal lords, receiving men doing their *musha shugyo* made it possible to obtain information from other regions. And for future vassals, the knowledge accumulated in the course of these travels became a useful stock in trade.

During these journeys a warrior traveled on foot, and if he encountered an adept worthy of facing, he asked him to fight. If this adept was the master of a dojo, it was often necessary first to fight against his disciples. In any case, the result of this type of bout, if one lost, could be serious wounds or even death. Even if one tended to win these combats, one could not remain forever unscathed. Many adepts perished in the course of these travels. Toward the end of the Edo period, training armor became widespread and the number of accidents diminished considerably, but in Musashi's time a bout between adepts often caused the death of one of the protagonists.

Thus the *musha shugyo* was a journey in the course of which one put one's life on the line in order to make progress in the way of the sword. The art of the *shuriken* was indispensable for this kind of journey, not only for fighting, but so that one could survive.

One of the greatest obstacles for the traveling practitioner of swordsmanship was hunger, because he did not always have money in his sleeve. Someone making a *musha shugyo* sometimes had to earn money in town and sometimes had to find his food in nature. He also had to sleep outside in the rain or snow. For the adepts of this period, the challenge of living rough in nature seemed like a suitable element for the strengthening of mind and spirit. Food gathering and small-game hunting were obligatory. In those days there were many wild animals in the forests and mountains. The art of the *shuriken* was not only useful but indispensable for those on *musha shugyo,* who had not only the explicit objective of facing adepts to improve their art but the implicit objective of getting through the trials of living under the hardest conditions.

Whether or not Musashi learned the art of the *shuriken* from his father, he must have practiced and developed it further himself in the course of the long years of traveling during which he shaped himself as an accomplished practitioner of strategy.

Musashi and the Art of the *Shuriken*

Throwing an object to defend yourself is a spontaneous reaction for anyone who has an object or a weapon in hand's reach. Especially in time of war, when responding to an unexpected lance or *naginata* attack, it was natural to throw a stick, a knife, a sword, or whatever one had. This is how the art of the *shuriken* must have developed—out of necessity.

Let us recall once more the text on the Kokura monument, which stresses Musashi's extraordinary skill in throwing a weapon, and also the passage previously quoted from the *Hyoho senshi denki:* "When he was a child, the master often criticized his father's art. One day, when he was nine years old, leaning against a post, he watched his father cutting some toothpicks. As usual, he criticized his father's art. His father lost his temper and threw a knife at him. The master dodged it with a slight movement of his head, and the knife stuck in the post." (9)

From this we may surmise that Munisai was skilled in throwing a knife and that he learned this art at an early age and developed it further later on.

Musashi is supposed to have taught the art of throwing the short sword to Lord Ogasawara as well as teaching his art of the sword to the lord's vassals.

According to Ozawa Masao, Lord Ogasawara Tadasane's interest in the *shuriken* went back to the battle of Osaka in the summer of 1615, in which Musashi participated. He cites the "Text on the Battle of Osaka of 1615" *(Osaka gunki):* "When Ogasawara Tadasane suffered a lance attack that pierced his armor and his skin, he drew his short sword and threw it at his enemy. In this way he succeeded in saving himself from a fatal attack." (9)

After this battle, in 1617 Ogasawara Tadasane became the lord of Akashi (Hyogo), an estate valued at a hundred thousand bushels *(koku)* of rice per year. Musashi stayed at Akashi for several years. He taught the *shuriken* to Lord Ogasawara, who found difficulties in throwing the sword because a sword's center of gravity is located well back because of the weight of the handle. Musashi developed a special form of knife for the lord, devised for ease of throwing. He had a famous sword smith named Sukesada forge a knife about twenty-seven centimeters long. At the end of the handle a red tassel was attached. This made it possible to draw the knife more easily from one's belt and also helped to keep it in balance while it was in the air. This *shuriken* is called the Ogasawara *shuriken*. Ogasawara always wore this knife in his belt. He was never without it, even when he went to the shogun's castle.

Musashi's third adoptive son, Takemura Yoemon, who propagated Musashi's school in the Hyogo region beginning in the 1640s, became famous for his *shuriken* art. Here is the account of Watanabe Koan, who knew Takemura:

> I was the student of Yagyu Tajimanokami Munenori, from whom I received the general transmission. I knew a great adept of the sword named Takemura Musashi, who was much stronger than Yagyu. He was invited by Lord Hosokawa Tadatoshi with a salary of rice for forty people. The son of Musashi was called Takemura Yoemon. He was also a great adept, not less great than his father, and he especially excelled in the art of the *shuriken*. He was capable of throwing his sword, which was forty centimeters long, and piercing a peach floating in the river. (9)

Watanabe Koan calls him Takemura Musashi, after his adoptive father. He doubtless knew Takemura Yoemon, as he is more specifically called, when the latter resided in the fief of Owari. This account confirms this adoption and gives us an idea of Takemura's abilities. This *shuriken* lineage is confirmed by the *Nippon bujutsu meika den* (eighteenth century): "On the *shuriken:* Chishin ryu. Niwa Orie Ujihari transmitted the art of the *shuriken* in the fief of Owari. This school originated with Takemura Yoemon, who was a disciple of Miyamoto Musashi. Takemura transmitted his art successively to Iijima Gentazaemon, Hioki Juemon, and then Asana Denemon. Niwa Orie learned the art of the *shuriken* from the last of these."

According to Ozawa Masao, the masters of the Yagyu school developed their art of the *shuriken* on the basis of meetings with Musashi.

Did Yagyu Sekishai Muneyoshi (1529–1606) invite Musashi and fight with him in order to study his art of the *shuriken*? According to Ozawa Masao, this is not a strong likelihood, given the difference in their ages. It would seem more likely that his son Yagyu Munenori (1571–1646) met Musashi or one of his disciples. Nonetheless, according to Ozawa Masao, Musashi fought Yagyu three times and defeated him three times. Ozawa thinks that, convinced of the effectiveness of this weapon, Yagyu persevered until he was able to defeat the attack of the *shuriken*.

However, it is difficult to imagine how Musashi could have defeated his adversary three times with the *shuriken* without seriously wounding him. It is also difficult to imagine that the young Musashi would have so easily revealed one of his secret techniques to the master of another school, who was in a certain sense his rival. (Later, Yagyu Munenori was to be the principal master of the shogun while Musashi was seeking this same position.) So what their relations were remains enigmatic. In any case, in my opinion, if Munenori did not study with Musashi, he nevertheless developed his techniques against the *shuriken* with the help of a meeting with an expert in this art who came from Musashi's school or a branch of it.

Yagyu Jubei, Munenori's eldest son, wrote concerning the *shuriken:* "Against the *shuriken,* you must make every effort to get a look at the inside of your adversary's hand. You must parry by crossing the *shuriken* with your sword. . . . Against a *shuriken* expert, you are too late if you react after having seen the thrower's movement. You must strike him before his movement takes shape." (9)

Jubei's technique consisted in parrying a *shuriken* attack by striking horizontally with the vertical part of your sword hilt, doing so immediately when the adversary raises his hand to throw. He called this movement a "strike in the form of a cross." At the same time, based on the idea of a parry in the form of a cross, the Yagyu school devised a *shuriken* in the form of a cross, with four points *(juji shuriken)*. This gave another school the idea of creating one with eight points *(happo ken)*, by putting one *juji shuriken* on top of another. Certain schools developed a similar one by putting two squares of steel on top of each other. This was called a *kuruma ken* (*shuriken* in the shape of a wheel). Using these *shuriken* increased the precision of the throw, but they had the disadvantage of possibly being blown off course by the wind once their speed reached a certain point. The target for a *shuriken* throw was an eye, between the eyes, or the throat.

Thus during the Edo period, the art of the shuriken was developed by several schools of swordsmanship. A passage in the text called *Oshu banashi,* transmitted in the fief of Sendai, elucidates this process:

> Ueno Izu was a vassal [of the fief of Sendai] around 1770. He was an accomplished practitioner of the martial arts and he developed a unique form of the art of the *shuriken*. He held a needle between his fingers and never missed his mark. He said he had developed this technique with the thought that he would be able to defeat any opponent if he could hit him in the eyes with needles. He always carried needles in his hair, four on each temple. . . . He said: "The art of the *shuriken* is not one that can be transmitted. I acquired this art by training assiduously in throwing needles." (9)

The needle he used measured twelve centimeters. It was called *izu bari* (Izu's needle) in reference to the inventor of the technique.

Thus the art of the *shuriken* was elaborated by samurais during different periods and in different schools, because the adepts who had had the experience of real combat realized the effectiveness of this weapon.

Musashi was doubtless an accomplished practitioner of this art. He influenced other schools in this domain and provoked the creation of new schools of swordsmanship that developed the use of two swords in different ways.

THE SCHOOLS OF TWO SWORDS

In general, when using the short sword as a throwing weapon, you take it in your right hand and hold your large sword in your left hand. This way of holding the two swords is called the *gyaku nito* guard position. *Nito* means "two swords," and *gyaku* means "reversed," the idea being the position of the two swords is reversed. This guard position is a preparation for throwing and not for continuing to fight using the two swords for parrying and slashing. The *gyaku nito* would be used mainly in fighting against a long weapon such as a lance or *naginata* in order either to facilitate and strengthen one's ability to parry or to throw the short sword at the propitious moment, thus creating an opportunity to seize the initiative against a weapon with a long reach. It goes without saying that in this latter strategy, the intention of throwing a sword must be concealed until the last possible moment.

By contrast with the schools that use the *gyaku nito* guard position, in Musashi's School of Two Swords the large sword is always held in the right hand. This is the reason it is generally thought that Musashi's art of two swords was derived from the use of the *jitte* rather than from the art of sword throwing. This is an essential point in comparing the schools that use both swords at once. In all the schools that use the *gyaku nito,* the practitioner has the intention from the beginning of finding an opening to throw the short sword; after that his principal attack will be executed with the large sword held in both hands. In such cases, the function of the short sword is more limited than in Musashi's school, where it is practically equivalent to that of the large sword.

Another hypothesis for explaining this difference in approach was that Musashi was left-handed. Certain scholars have advanced this idea based on analysis of both his calligraphies and the techniques of the School of Two Swords. However, we know that form was important in Japanese society and tended toward standardization. Left-handed people therefore became accustomed to performing movements of technique with their right hand, in accordance with the traditional manner of executing them. This was also true for calligraphy—the brush was held in the right hand. In Musashi's school, the large sword, the heavier of the two, the one most often used for slashing, is held in the right hand. If Musashi was a left-hander, he was a corrected left-hander whose assimilation to the dominant model enabled him to conceal the deftness of his left hand. In this case he would have been able to throw the short sword with his left hand with ease and conceal his ability to throw a sword at all behind an ordinary two-sword guard position. By contrast, against the *gyaku nito* guard position, an adversary would immediately suspect the possibility of the short sword's being thrown.

In the *Nitenki* we find the following passage:

> Musashi fought in the province of Iga against Shishido, an adept of the *kusari gama* [a sickle with a chain attached to it that had a steel weight on the end]. This combat took place in a natural setting. Before Shishido could strike with his sickle, Musashi threw his short sword, which pierced Shishido's chest. Immediately closing in, Musashi cut him down with his long sword. Shishido's disciples seized weapons and attacked Musashi. Under the brunt of Musashi's counterattack, they dispersed in all directions, and during this time Musashi calmly departed. (2)

To win the combat described above, it would have been necessary for Musashi to conceal his intention of throwing his sword until the last moment. And if he was really left-handed, he would indeed have been able to do so. In a confrontation, it is extremely difficult for a right-hander to hit his mark throwing a sword with his left hand, and especially since a sword is not made to be thrown, it is particularly difficult to make it penetrate point first. If we were to carry this hypothesis of left-handedness all the way, could we not say that it would be impossible to master the whole of Musashi's art if one were not left-handed? I think this position is defensible up to a certain point, because Musashi did not found his school to train disciples but to train himself. Each of his disciples had to find his own way of realizing Musashi's art, based on Musashi's teaching but without merely trying to copy him. We know of one of the branches of Musashi's school called Onko chishin ryu (School Where Innovation Is Known through Ancient Knowledge) in which the way the two swords are held is the reverse of Musashi's school: The long sword is held in the left hand and the short sword is held in the right.

In the *Gekiken sodan,* written by Minamoto Tokushu in 1843, we read the following passage concerning the School of Two Swords:

> The Onko chishin ryu is a school of two swords that is a branch of Musashi's school. In this school there is a secret technique called *hiryu ken* that is also called *gyaku nito.* It consists in holding the long sword in the left hand and the short sword in the right hand and throwing the short sword as a preparation to attacking rapidly with the long sword. This tradition has almost been interrupted—the only one who still holds it is the priest of the Shinto temple in the region of Bizen named Sugimura Hyoma. (1-f)

In any case the effectiveness of throwing the sword increases if it is done when the adversary is not expecting it, and that is why techniques for throwing a sword or a knife that were developed in different schools were transmitted secretly.

In contemporary kendo we sometimes see practitioners who use two *shinai,* but today, throwing a short sword is out of the question. When a practitioner assumes the *gyaku nito* guard position, he frequently does so because it is easier to score a point by striking an opponent's wrist from this guard position than from any other. However, it is not possible to use the criteria of modern kendo to assess the details of the swordsmanship of the warriors, given that in modern kendo usually only four techniques of attack are used: strikes to the head *(men)*, the side *(do)*, and the wrist *(kote)*, and the stab to the throat *(tsuki)*.

The techniques of the swordsmanship of the warriors greatly exceeds the range of techniques to which contemporary practitioners are accustomed. For example, Kanawa Goro, a sword adept of the end of the Edo period, was renowned for his favorite technique of *yoko men,* a diagonal strike to the temple. During training he won most of his bouts using this technique. He would pick up a handful of dirt, which he threw in his opponent's face, then strike him with his favorite technique. During the same period, the Ryugo ryu became popular. Its specialty was diving under an opponent and cutting his shin. The Kageyama ryu from the north of Japan transmitted the following secret technique: The practitioner first assumed a guard position holding the long sword in two hands; then, at the propitious moment, keeping hold of the long sword with his left hand, with his right he drew the short sword and threw it at once. In this technique one does not assume the guard position with two swords at the same time. (1-f, p. 225)

The particular quality of these examples is the use of a technique that is difficult for an opponent to elude; the difficulty of evading such an attack is increased by its being used at an unexpected moment. That is why these techniques were taught directly and revealing them was generally forbidden.

In Musashi's time the art of swordsmanship included varied techniques, because the long period of feudal wars, during which the martial arts were created and developed, had just ended. In the course of the two and a half centuries of feudal peace of the Edo period, the disciplines that corresponded to the practices of the warriors with different weapons (sword, *naginata,* lance, bow, jujutsu, and so on) became separated, and at the same time each of them became more refined and formal. By the end of the Edo period, confrontations with swords again became an actuality for warriors, and the techniques that had been undergoing improvement for more than two centuries once more found application. As a result of its renewed use for actual fighting, the refined art was now challenged by the reintroduction of elements from the period of feudal wars that had until then been viewed as perverse. The example I have cited above of Kanawa Goro is characteristic.

When the feudal social stratification was abolished in the Meiji period, the former warriors no longer had a reason or need to practice all the martial arts and especially not the less important ones. If a warrior then tried to assert his identity as a perpetuator of the tradition of the previous period, he certainly did not do so by practicing a secondary art. He practiced one of the principal arts, swordsmanship or another principal art in which he excelled. A discipline from the art of the warriors can survive in modern society only if it answers to an implicit expectation on the part of society, either a practical one or one that promotes a certain cultural identity. This situation led to the idea of *budo,* in which traditional elements were developed into modern practices. Within this framework, it was difficult for an art like that of the *shuriken* to survive as an independent discipline, hence its rarity today.

When we look at the martial arts of Musashi's time from the point of view of the martial arts of today, we run the risk of not taking the intervening evolution into account and thus falling prey to the illusion that the various disciplines continue to exist as they were several centuries ago. This illusion is all the stronger because these martial arts are practiced in traditional costumes that create the impression of living in the past.

‖ 2 ‖

Musashi's Duels

WHEN HE FOUNDED THE School of Two Swords, Musashi had in mind an art of the sword that was applicable to war as well as single combat. The pragmatic aspect of his approach is clearly stated in the *Gorin no sho*. Whereas Musashi's approach, developed at a turning point in Japanese history, relates to both forms of combat, the schools that followed him developed techniques only for individual combat.

Musashi wrote that before the age of thirty he had fought more than sixty duels, in most of which his opponents met death. He also took part in two wars. For Musashi the duel represented a confrontation in which he could make use of all his abilities, both technical and strategic, but it was also a privileged learning opportunity. He accumulated his skill and knowledge through encountering the techniques of his adversaries, each of them different, and also through relating to the different overall situations imposed on him by these duels. Thus the art of his youth developed through his contact with other adepts.

Consequently, in trying to understand Musashi's personality, it is useful to study his main duels, following their chronological order, looking into the technical lineage of his opponents, and discussing the different possible interpretations that arise when these duels are presented differently in several documents.

DUELS AND WARS FROM AGE FIFTEEN TO TWENTY

In 1599 Musashi left the village of Miyamoto. According to the *Tosakushi*, the registry of the Sakushu region, Musashi was then fifteen years old. Did he hope to become a great feudal lord? This period was a continuation of the warring period in which, with talent and luck, even a peasant could become a great lord. An example of this upward social mobility was Toyotomi Hideyoshi, who became Japan's greatest lord yet was said to have been the son of a poor peasant. Hideyoshi had just died a year earlier. This example of ascent through the social ranks must have made a strong impression on Musashi and his contemporaries. It is hard to imagine that at fifteen Musashi's main ambition was no more than to seek the way of the martial arts. The martial arts more likely represented for him the road to success.

The Duel against Akiyama

Shortly after leaving the village of his birth, full of youthful expectation, Musashi fought an adept named Akiyama in the neighboring fief of Tajima (Hyogo prefecture). In the *Gorin no sho* he wrote, "At the age of sixteen, I defeated a powerful adept by the name of Akiyama, who came from the prefecture of Tajima."

We have no further details on the way this confrontation unfolded.

In the *Tanji Hokin hikki* we find the following passage: "In 1599, when the master was sixteen years old, he defeated a powerful adept of the province of Tajima named Akiyama. He wrote of this in the Scroll of Earth, but we do not know any more details concerning this combat. I hope this passage will be completed through the research of our successors." (12, p. 42)

Moreover, on the Kokura monument, no more than the following appears: "The one named Akiyama was an adept of great power. Musashi killed him as fast as one can turn over one's own hand. His praises filled the town."

The Battle of Sekigahara

A year later, in 1600, war broke out between two clans, the Toyotomi and the Tokugawa. The feudal lords joined the opposing camps, and a decisive war took place that ended an era. It is thought that the young Musashi, then sixteen, fought with the army of the West on the side of the Toyotomi clan, with which Lord Shinmen, whose vassals Musashi's family had been for a long time, was allied. There is no document that states which army Musashi fought for, but if he did indeed participate in this war, it is difficult to imagine that it would have been with the army of the East.

In a letter Musashi presented to one of the principal vassals of the Hosokawa fief in 1640, he wrote: "Until now, from the time of my youth, I have participated in battles six times. Four times out of six, I was in the van, leading the army into battle. Everyone acknowledges this, and I have proof of it. In saying that, it goes without saying that I am not trying to advance myself in your estimation." (12, p. 109)

During this period, the act of leading the army into battle—which was called *sakigake*—was considered a highly meritorious deed for a warrior. It was customary for other warriors to bear witness to this feat in writing. Certain contemporary writers, reading passages of this sort in which Musashi speaks of himself and his exploits in wars and duels, criticize him for his lack of modesty. This criticism appears out of place in view of the customs of the time.

Musashi took part in three battles in the course of the year 1600. The first was the attack on Fushimi castle in the month of July. The second, in August, was the defense of Gifu castle, which had been encircled. The third battle was decisive for Musashi. It took place in the Sekigahara plain. It began about eight o'clock in the morning on the fifteenth of the ninth month, and by four o'clock in the afternoon it was all over. There is debate as to whether Musashi really participated in this battle. According to the *Hyoho senshi denki:*

Muninosuke, the master's father, fought valiantly in this battle. Whereas the master did not take part in it. He said: "I am no lord's

vassal, and my aim is to attain the essence of the way of strategy."
Thus he continued with perseverance in the study of strategy until
1614, traveling in the various regions once they had become more
calm. (9, p. 224)

This passage seems inaccurate to me, because it contradicts Musashi's statement "In my youth I was six times on the field of battle." This
figure can be reached only by including the battle of Sekigahara, and
other proofs exist that Musashi did indeed take part in that battle. However, the hypothesis could be advanced that Musashi fought in a different group from his father's while still fighting with the same clan.

The army of the West suffered a definitive defeat and many important lords were executed or died on the battlefield. Some succeeded in
escaping and returning to the countryside. The hunt for escaped warriors then began. Shinmen Sokan, liege lord of the Musashi family, took
refuge in the distant province of Kyushu. Nakanishi Seizo advances the
hypothesis that Musashi went down to Kyushu with his lord and his warriors, among whom was also his father. Fukuhara Josen, on the other
hand, thinks that Jirotayu, Musashi's elder brother, went to Kyushu with
Lord Shinmen, because he was related to the lord through his mother,
while Musashi, whose mother was Yoshiko, the daughter of Bessho, remained in the Banshu region, staying from time to time with his
mother's family. (16, p. 11) According to Nakanishi, Munisai had martial arts students in the Buzen region, in the north of Kyushu. According to him, Musashi lived for a while with his father; then for a few years
he lived on Hikosan, the sacred mountain of the region, working on
reaching a more profound level in his art.

However, there is no document that allows us to say with certainty
what took place in Musashi's life during this period. What is clear is that
he had already had the experience of two duels and three battles.

Some authors suggest that Musashi divided his time between training
in his art and Zen, but it does not seem to me terribly likely that between the ages of seventeen and twenty, at a time when he was seething
with a wild energy, Musashi spent much time doing *zazen*. This idea
seems to me to be a projection of those of our contemporaries who have

no experience of the practice of the martial arts. Even though he might be inclined toward introspection, a person of great physical strength who was exceptionally violent would feel a great need at this age to expend his energy in physical activity before reaching the point where he could immerse himself in spirituality. The young Musashi must have avidly pursued the practice of the sword, being still too young to conceive in concrete terms, as he did later, of the need to progress spiritually in order to advance in the way of the sword.

Musashi perhaps hoped to rise quickly in the military hierarchy by killing a great enemy general in the battle of Sekigahara, but we may suppose that his youthful dream collapsed in the face of reality. We do not know how Musashi occupied his time in the aftermath of this battle until the time when he arrived in Kyoto.

The Duels against the Yoshiokas

After the eclipse in our data for the period following the battle of Sekigahara, Musashi reappears in documents at the age of twenty. Between twenty and thirty years of age, he continued to shape his swordsmanship through encounters with various adepts. He fought sixty times in ten years. That is an average of a duel every two months. In the logic of those days, nearly every combat was to the death, which means that Musashi placed himself each time in a situation where he would be killed or would kill his opponent. He put an end to this period of duels, it seems, after participating in the battles of Osaka in 1614 and 1615.

Looking back on this period later on, Musashi wrote that he had fought in more than sixty duels during his youth but that on reflecting on this after he had reached the age of thirty, he realized that his victories had not been due to the perfection of his art but, rather, to the weakness of his adversaries and also to chance. Therefore he had ended up with relative results rather than a perfect art. If he had encountered superior adepts, he would not have survived. After this moment of realization, he went on developing his fighting art, which for him was inseparable from the art of life altogether. Thus we have reason to believe that Musashi entered a period of introspection at around the age of thirty.

In the *Gorin no sho* Musashi wrote, "At the age of twenty-one, I went up to Kyoto and fought duels with several accomplished practitioners of the sword from famous schools, but I never lost."

His most significant combats during his stay in Kyoto were those against the Yoshioka family. They took place in the spring of 1604.

The Yoshioka Family

For several generations the Yoshioka family performed the function of sword master to the Ashikaga shoguns. The Ashikaga shogunate came to an end in 1573.

Musashi's father fought in his youth against Yoshioka Kenpo Naokata in the presence of the shogun. Munisai won two out of three bouts against Yoshioka and received the title of "best adept in Japan" from the shogun. However, we cannot accept this fact without some reservation, since the various documents give different accounts of it. This was still during the period of feudal wars, the power of the shogun was weakened, and even if we accept this legend as valid, we should also consider that the shogun gave out titles of this kind quite readily.

In Kyoto at that time there were eight schools of swordsmanship that were called Kyo ryu, "schools of Kyoto." It is thought that these eight schools were founded by eight monks who had received teaching from a legendary master from the sacred mountain of Kurama. The Yoshioka school descended from one of these branches, which at the time was called the Kyo hachi ryu. Another possible derivation of this school is from the Shinto ryu mentioned earlier. Around 1540 Yoshioka Kenpo Naomoto was serving as a vassal to the shogun Ashikaga Yoshiharu (1511–1550), and he had distinguished himself in battle in the course of various wars. His younger brother Naomitsu succeeded him, taking the name of Kenpo, and became the shogun's sword master. His son, Matasaburo Naokata, succeeded him in the service of the last Ashikaga shogun, Yoshiaki (1537–1597), taking the name Yoshioka Kenpo Naokata. It is this Yoshioka who fought against Miyamoto Munisai. And Musashi fought successively against two of Yoshioka's sons and a grandson.

The head of the Yoshioka family took the name of Kenpo, which means "the law." According to a text on the Yoshioka family, this name derived from one of the heads of the Yoshioka family, an extremely upright and honest man who had received the epithet Kenpo, which had the sense of "a man as just as the law." This name stuck, and the head of the family bore it for four generations. However, there is another explanation for this name. Kenpo, written with a different combination of ideograms, means "the principle of the art of the sword."

The Yoshioka family was in the textile business and was particularly known for a dye unique to the family. There was in fact a dye called *kenpo zome,* so it was a play on words to superimpose the name Kenpo, which was simply that of a person, on *kenpo* in the sense of "the art of the sword," because a merchant excelling in the art of the sword was not a commonplace thing. It is not known exactly when the Yoshioka family took up the textile business. In 1614 the Yoshioka brothers took part in the battle of Osaka with the Army of the West, opposing Tokugawa Ieyasu, who won the victory. After their defeat, the Yoshiokas returned to Kyoto, but they publicly renounced the practice of arms. According to another version of their history, it was then that they learned dying techniques from one of their disciples, named Ri Sangan, and became artisans and merchants. Their dye became famous under the name *yoshioka zome* or *kenpo zome.* The practice of swordsmanship was no longer transmitted by them except within the family. (32, p. 142)

The Yoshioka family played an important role in the service of the Ashikaga shoguns, and the family still had a high reputation when Musashi arrived in Kyoto in 1604.

There are different versions of Musashi's fight against the Yoshiokas; here I will pass on only the best known. However, it should be noted that certain Yoshioka family documents give a different account of the combat. According to those, Musashi fought only Yoshioka Kenpo and Yoshioka won the victory. But the reliability of these documents seems to be highly questionable.

The Principal Documents concerning the Duels with the Yoshiokas
    The following passage is found in the *Hyoho senshi denki:*

There existed in the West an adept named Yoshioka Kenpo. Originally a cloth dyer, he transformed himself into a master of the martial arts, which was what he was inclined toward. One day the master challenged Kenpo, who accepted. But the day of the duel, the master had a cold and found it difficult to fight. Kenpo insisted on fighting on that day and sent him messages to this effect. The master refused twice. Kenpo insisted that the master appear, even if he had to be carried in a litter. Thus the master arrived in a litter in which he was warmly wrapped in a comforter. When he arrived, Kenpo opened the door of the litter to see what state he was in. The master, getting out immediately, smashed Kenpo's head with a small wooden sword with which he gave him several blows. Kenpo died, and Kenpo's students, who had accompanied him in large numbers, surrounded the master, intending to kill him. The master fought, drawing both his swords, and succeeded in getting away. It was on the basis of this experience that he devised his technique of fighting against numerous adversaries. (9, p. 225)

This text contains various inaccurate points that are in contradiction with other documents, notably as concerns Yoshioka's profession. Another version of the facts is found in the *Nitenki:*

Musashi's father, whose name was Shinmen Muninosuke Nobutsuna, was a sword adept of the Tori ryu. He was also an accomplished practitioner of the *jitte* and the two swords. One day, in the presence of the shogun Yoshiaki, and at his command, he fought against an adept named Yoshioka Shozaemon Kenpo, the best of the adepts then in Kyoto. Shozaemon won once and Muninosuke took the victory twice. Thus he received from the shogun the title "the best adept in Japan." According to some people, Muninosuke himself adopted the name of Shinmen when he deemed that he had sufficiently mastered the art of swordsmanship; according to others, he took this name the day he received the title from the shogun.

In the spring of 1604, Musashi fought at Rendaino, a place

located outside Kyoto, against Yoshioka Seijuro, the son of the famous adept Yoshioka Shozaemon. Seijuro fought with a real
sword, and Musashi struck him with a sword of wood. Seijuro fell
and ceased breathing. His students carried him home on a board.
Thanks to their care he revived, but he renounced the art of
swordsmanship from that day forward. He shaved his head and became a monk.

After that Musashi fought his younger brother Denshichiro on
the outskirts of Kyoto. Denshichiro, who was strong, used a
sword more than a meter and a half in length. Musashi took away
his sword and struck him a blow. Denshichiro died instantly. Intending to avenge themselves on Musashi, several dozen students
of Yoshioka's came together with Seijuro's son, whose name was
Matashichiro, but Musashi drove his enemies away and succeeded
in getting back to Kyoto. The Yoshioka family collapsed as a result
of this event. (2, p. 170)

This text also contains various inaccurate points that contradict other
documents. The Yoshioka family did not collapse at this point; at least
one branch of it continued to thrive after this event.

Finally, we find this passage in the Kokura monument inscription:

When Musashi returned to Kyoto where Yoshioka was, who was
considered number one in Japan, Musashi wanted to measure
himself against him. They fought on the field of Rendaino, located
outside Kyoto. Yoshioka was felled by a blow from Musashi and
ceased to breathe.

The combatants had agreed beforehand to deliver only one
blow, and this saved his life. For his students carried him away on
a board, and thanks to the medical attention he received, he ended
up reviving, but he abandoned martial arts and shaved his head.

After this event, Yoshioka Denshichiro came to fight with his
long wooden sword, measuring a meter and a half. Musashi, finding a good opening, tore the sword away from his adversary and
struck him with this weapon. Denshichiro died instantly. Yosh-

ioka's students decided to take revenge by employing means outside the usual rules of the art of strategy.

They came together at an appointed place near the Pine with
Low Branches—Sagari matsu—on the outskirts of Kyoto. They
worked out a strategy. The number of students was in the hun-
dreds, and they were determined to kill Musashi with various
weapons, notably with bows. Musashi was a person of high intelligence. He had figured out the strategy of the enemy and said to this
own students: "Be spectators and leave immediately. Even if the
many enemies form into herds, I see them as floating clouds. I am
not afraid of them. They are no more than scattered enemies."

He ended up hunting them down as a predator hunts down his
prey. The inhabitants of Kyoto admired this deed. It was a true
strategy that made it possible for one man to defeat ten thousand.
(17, pp. 215–216)

With the help of various documents (1-b, 9, 12, 15, 23, 29, 32) it is
possible to reconstruct Musashi's duels with the Yoshiokas, make some
corrections to the texts already cited, and offer some personal interpretations of them.

The Yoshiokas had the reputation of being at the top of the heap
among the eight schools of Kyoto, whereas Musashi at the time was an
unknown with a plainly provincial look to him. It was difficult for the
principal master of the Yoshioka dojo to accept a duel with him.

Musashi presented himself by letter as Miyamoto Musashi of the
Enmei ryu, and he added that he was the son of Miyamoto Munisai, who
in the past had fought the father of the present principal master of the
dojo and won two bouts out of three. *Enmei ryu* literally means "circle of
light school" (*en* means "circle," and *mei* means "brilliance" or "light").
The idea of a circle evokes perfection, that of the sun or moon, toward
which Musashi strove in his work on the way. The form and the light of
the sun and the moon were the essential inspiration for his swordsmanship. It is impossible to know whether Musashi had already conceived of
the image for his own school, the School of Two Swords, in connection
with the image of two swords being wielded so as to form a circle. The

basis for his own art was the Tori ryu, of which his father was an adept. The Enmei ryu is Musashi's elaboration of the basic material of that school.

Yoshioka Seijuro, the principal master of the school, replied immediately to Musashi's letter, informing of his acceptance and leaving to his opponent the choice of the place and time for the confrontation. Musashi thought it was best for him to fight somewhere outside the dojo, because he did not want anyone else to intervene. He also requested that if he won, his victory should be publicly recognized. The duel was set for the morning of March 8, in the field by the Rendaiji temple, just outside Kyoto.

The Kyoto school of which the Yoshioka school was a part was renowned for its subtlety, for the variety and speed of its techniques. Let us recall that this was the period during which the art of swordsmanship was being transformed; a new period had been inaugurated. Previously, because combatants had been protected by armor on the field of battle, light attack techniques were inefficacious, even if they were quick and varied. To cut down an adversary in armor, a powerful attack was needed; thus simple but powerful techniques were developed. The art of swordsmanship with armor is traditionally called *kaisha kenjutsu*. (121, p. 291) Now no longer on the battlefield, when warriors wore garments of ordinary cloth, a light blow of the sword could inflict a wound, and speed and subtlety became more and more important factors in the techniques. The Kyoto school excelled in this new form of swordsmanship, whereas Musashi's art lay somewhere between the two approaches. Under these circumstances, Yoshioka's technique was formidable.

The Duel with Yoshioka Seijuro

Yoshioka Seijuro was a formidable adversary; to fight him Musashi used a strategy that he described later in the *Gorin no sho* as "irritating one's opponent," "putting oneself in your opponent's place," and "frightening."

Here is how I see the situation:

Yoshioka Seijuro arrived early, ready to fight. When it was nearly ten o'clock, Musashi still had not arrived. A bell struck ten, but he still was not there.

Musashi had decided to arrive late. He had probably learned this strategy from his own experience. He was thus able to imagine what was taking place in Seijuro's mind. Putting himself in Seijuro's place, he saw anxiety about the confrontation arising in his opponent's mind; the longer he had to wait, the more images of death would arise. His imagination would generate fear, and he would begin to experience his body as heavier than usual. He would make every effort not to fall in with his opponent's strategy, but the more he labored against it, the more firmly the negative images would implant themselves in his mind. In the absence of the other, the combatant on the field would pass through repeated moments of dread.

But it would be a mistake to be too late, for Yoshioka could then leave and declare victory, saying Musashi had not appeared for the fight, even though he had set the place for the duel himself. For Musashi this would have been an ineffaceable blot on his honor, and Seijuro would have had a reason to reject his next challenge. That is why he had to irritate his opponent within the limits of his patience.

When Musashi arrived, Seijuro was indeed irritated. At the time of presenting themselves formally, Seijuro is said to have uttered a number of insults. Musashi is said to have responded calmly with a smile, which would have annoyed Seijuro further. Both combatants took up wooden swords and faced off at a distance of about six meters. They approached each other little by little, each one searching for the moment to attack. Musashi was naturally better at using the terrain to his advantage. He always trained outdoors, so this was an ingrained habit for him, whereas for Seijuro, this consideration was doubtless not a spontaneous one, since he trained for the most part on the smooth floor of his dojo. At a certain point the two combatants closed in on each other as though drawn by an invisible thread, and both struck at approximately the same time. Musashi's sword struck Seijuro's left shoulder. Musashi did not make a second attack, respecting the agreement for this duel that each combatant would make only one decisive attack.

Seijuro lost consciousness, but thanks to the care he was given, he revived. However, as a result of the blow to his left shoulder, he became incapable of using his left arm. He had been crippled and suffered a definitive blow to his honor; thus he gave over his responsibilities as head of the school and became a monk.

The Duel with Yoshioka Denshichiro

With Seijuro's retirement, his younger brother Yoshioka Denshichiro, whose level of attainment was considered as good as his brother's, succeeded him as the head of the Yoshioka dojo. He was a very strong and accomplished practitioner. This time it was Yoshioka who put out the challenge to Musashi, a matter of revenge. Musashi accepted immediately. The duel took place either on the outskirts of Kyoto or at the Sanjusangen-do temple in Kyoto.

Denshichiro decided to use his favorite weapon, which was either a simple staff reinforced with steel rings (1-b) or another quite unusual weapon—a long, thick staff of about a meter and a half, whose end was hollowed out and concealed a steel ball attached to the end of a chain. (8) This was a weapon that required exceptional strength to wield, which Denshichiro possessed.

Musashi used the same strategy again: irritating one's opponent by arriving late. He might have had thoughts to the effect that this time his opponent was impatient to take his revenge and restore the reputation of the Yoshioka family.

By the time Musashi arrived, Denshichiro was already quite nervous and irritated. According to the documents (1-b, 12, 23, 32), Musashi tore Denshichiro's weapon from his grasp and used it to deliver a fatal blow. From this the conclusion is usually drawn that Musashi initially faced his adversary empty-handed. To me this is inconceivable, because it is necessary to have attained a very high level to be able to fight empty-handed against an armed adept. In my opinion, therefore, Musashi carried, as before, a wooden sword, and in the course of the combat, when the combatants were already engaged at very close quarters, he dropped his own weapon so as to pull Denshichiro's away from him.

Yoshioka Matashichiro

The news of Musashi's successive victories against the Yoshioka brothers spread rapidly in Kyoto. To restore its family reputation, the Yoshioka clan challenged Musashi once again. They took as their nominal head Seijuro's eldest son, Yoshioka Matashichiro, who was twelve years old. An individual combat was no longer in question. For the Yoshiokas this confrontation was a battle for the family reputation. They prepared themselves with archers and riflemen. The number of combatants was several dozen. In the documents (1-b, 12, 17, 23, 32), this number actually varies between a hundred plus a few dozen and several hundred, but these numbers are not at all plausible, because a force of several hundred men was the size of the force that could be fielded by a major feudal lord. Moreover, if more than a hundred men had come together to fight in the immediate vicinity of Kyoto, it would have been impossible for the feudal police of the capital not to have intervened. The Yoshioka group was doubtless no more than a few dozen men, which was already quite out of the ordinary for a fight against a single adversary.

Musashi accepted this challenge. He no doubt thought that he had come to a decisive moment in his life. The place of combat was set for near the large pine tree of the Ichijoji temple, located east of Kyoto. Musashi adopted a different strategy from that of the two previous duels. This time, thinking that his adversaries would expect him to arrive late, he decided to arrive early. Musashi seems to have applied here several strategies that he formulated later in the *Gorin no sho*. For example, he wrote in the Scroll of Fire: "It is harmful to do the same thing several times in the course of combat. You can do the same thing twice, but not three times."

As he approached the place appointed for the combat, he passed a Shinto shrine and found himself before the altar to the god. He was just about to start praying to ask for divine help in his fight—which he could expect to come out of alive only with great difficulty—when he suddenly realized the significance of his gesture. "I was about to ask for the help of the gods just because I was about to face very powerful enemies, whereas ordinarily I never pray to the gods." Musashi then withdrew his hand from the string of the shrine bell and kept himself from ringing it, as is done to awaken the mind of the god of the shrine.

That is the interpretation of the novelist Yoshikawa Eiji (61, 62), who associates this moment with one of the precepts that Musashi formulated later in the *Dokkodo:* "Respect the Buddha and the gods without relying on their help."

At dawn Musashi was already at the combat site. He had been informed that the nominal head of the Yoshioka party was Matashichiro, a child of twelve or thirteen years of age. Musashi was the same age when he killed his adversary in his first duel. Hidden behind a bush, Musashi observed the arrival of the Yoshioka forces in the dawn light. He had to determine the number of guns and bows, but the most important thing was to locate Matashichiro. When they arrived, the Yoshioka forces thought Musashi would be late as usual. The two previous combats had given birth to this prejudice: Musashi always comes late.

Here we would do well to read what Musashi wrote in the Scroll of Fire ("Ripping Out the Bottom," page 182). To rip out the bottom in this situation, the head of the force had to be killed, because even if Musashi had killed a great many of the Yoshioka men, as long as their chief was still alive, he could not be considered to have won the battle. Thus he had to kill the chief before he was exhausted. That is why he attacked Matashichiro at the beginning of the combat, killing him with a single blow of his sword. Once the chief was dead, Musashi had to fight a multitude of enemies in order to get away.

It would also be good to read what Musashi later wrote in the Scroll of Fire ("Concealing Yourself," page 180) and the Scroll of Water ("Conduct against Many Adversaries," page 165). Do we not have the impression here of reading what he learned from his combat against the Yoshioka forces?

Although Musashi later defined his school as the School of Two Swords, he fought a great many duels with only one sword. He wrote that he formed the School of Two Swords in order to use both swords well. During his fight with the Yoshioka men, he doubtless drew both swords spontaneously in order to face his many adversaries while moving rapidly over the irregular terrain, as he describes in the *Gorin no sho.*

This third confrontation marked the end of one branch of the Yoshioka family.

Studying the Arts of Other Schools through Duels

Duel with a Representative of the Art of the Lance of the Hozoin School

Around 1604 Musashi visited the Hozoin temple. He was then twenty years old. It is not known with certainty whether this visit took place before or after his confrontations with the Yoshiokas. The documents diverge on this point.

The Hozoin temple in Nara was known for its art of the lance, developed by the monk Inei at the end of the sixteenth century. Inei (1521–1607) devoted himself to various martial arts from the time of his youth at the same time as he pursued his vocation as a Buddhist monk. He maintained close relations with Yagyu Muneyoshi (1529–1606), a famous adept of the sword who resided in the fief of Yagyu in the near vicinity of Nara.

We read in the *Honcho bugei shoden*, written in 1715: "Although he was a monk, Inei of Hozoin temple, which is located south of the capital, devoted himself to the arts of the sword and the lance. He also studied the art of the sword with Yagyu Muneyoshi under the direction of Kamiizumi Isenokami." (1-b, p. 189)

We have already noted that the martial arts were passing through a process of evolution during this period. Combat techniques had been accumulated over the course of centuries, and now certain adepts were no longer content to practice them purely as a means of war. They began to search for the profound significance of the martial arts, making this the goal of their life and seeking to attain the highest possible level. Around 1563, Kamiizumi Isenokami Nobutsuna (c. 1508–c. 1577) abandoned his position of feudal lord to dedicate himself to study of the way of the sword and to the transmission of his art. He was a feudal lord of middle rank who had distinguished himself many times on the battlefield. He was seeking a meaning more profound in the way of the sword than arose from its mere use in warfare. Kamiizumi was probably one of the first to have separated the way of the sword from its application in fighting.

Kamiizumi Nobutsuna lived in the fief of Yagyu. Inei and Yagyu

Muneyoshi became his disciples. Later Yagyu Muneyoshi became Kamiizumi's successor and founded the Yagyu shin kage ryu, which played an
important role in the history of the art of swordsmanship in Japan.

In the course of the 1570s, Inei perfected his art of the lance and
named his school Hozoin ryu, after the temple. Several years before
this, when a lance expert named Daizendayu Moritada was visiting
Nara, the monk Inei had asked for his instruction and invited him to stay
for several months at Hozoin temple. He continued to develop his art of
the lance further through studying with him, while also receiving the
advice of Yagyu Muneyoshi. Inei modified the shape of the lance blade,
adding a second crescent-shaped horizontal blade to it. He also short-
ened the length of the lance handle, setting its length at one and a half
times the height of its user. This type of lance was called *jumonji yari,*
"cross-shaped lance," or *kama yari,* "sickle lance."

The monk Inei died in 1607 at the age of eighty-seven. He had given
up practicing and teaching the art of the lance several years before, saying at last that he found it contradictory for a monk to study the art of
the lance, the purpose of which was killing. He had given all his weapons
to his disciple Nakamura Ichiroemon. The continuity of the Hozoin
school was now in the hands of the monk Inshun, who had received
Inei's teaching for several years only and then had to abstain from practicing the art of the lance until his master's death. Since he had become
a monk at Hozoin in order to practice the art of the lance, Inshun was
unable, after Inei's death, to remain faithful to his master's wishes not to
practice an art that involved killing, and he moved on to the Okuzoin
temple, which was attached to Hozoin, and sought instruction from a
monk of this temple who had been a disciple of Inei's.

The school had instructions that took the form of poems; for example:

Hands are waiting, feet are ready to attack,
Like a waterbird about to take flight.

This poem is understood as instruction for a particular piece of
footwork associated with this school, called "the foot of the waterbird"
(mizudori no ashi). One had to move like a waterbird sliding on the sur-

face of the water. For that it was important to learn a particular position in which one's center of gravity is placed on the forward foot and this foot is moved forward with a sliding step just by relaxing the muscle tension in this leg, using the weight of the body, which is tending forward.

When Musashi came to the temple, Inei was eighty years old. He had given up the lance, and the monk Inshun, who had succeeded him, was only sixteen. Musashi fought the monk from Okuzoin and defeated him. Here is the pertinent passage from the *Nitenki:*

> This took place in the ninth year of the Keicho era [1604]. The Buddhist monk Nichiren-shu, who was called Okuzoin and was a disciple of the monk Inei from Hozoin temple in Nara, was an adept of the lance. Musashi met him and measured himself against him. The monk was armed with his lance. Musashi chose a short wooden sword and fought him twice, but the monk was unable to gain an advantage. He expressed admiration for Musashi's art and asked him to stay at the temple, where he received him. They talked until dawn. With the first light, Musashi departed. (2, p. 72)

The Duel with Shishido

Earlier on I cited a document giving an account of the duel with Shishido. His first name is not given in any document. In his novel on Musashi, Yoshikawa gives him the personal name Baiken.

Here is the interpretation Yoshida Seiken gives of this confrontation:

> Shishido used a special kind of weapon called a *kusari gama*. It was a sickle that had a chain with a steel weight attached to the end of it. . . . As he was traveling in the province of Iga, Musashi learned of Shishido's reputation. Intrigued by this unique weapon, the *kusari gama,* Musashi asked him to fight. The name of Musashi was not unknown to Shishido, who accepted this challenge from an adept of the martial arts. He had confidence in his own art, since until then he had never lost.

The size of the *kusari gama* was variable, depending on the person using it. Generally the blade and the handle were each about forty centimeters in length, and the chain with a steel weight on the end of it measured about two meters. In the guard position, the sickle was usually held in the left hand, and the weight was spun holding the chain in the middle [with the right hand]. There were three guard positions—high, middle, and low—as to how the sickle was held, but the way of spinning the weight remained the same.

It is often thought that the attack was carried out with the sickle and the weight on the chain alternately, but the reality is different. The moving weight can always be thrown, whereas the sickle can be used only close up. Therefore it is enough just to pay attention to the weight as long as the distance is sufficient. The particular way in which the chain was used should also be noted. If it is stretched taut between the two hands, it can act like a steel rod in parrying a sword blow. For the opponent, it is difficult to approach an adept who wields this weapon well. Especially if he throws the weight and the chain wraps itself around your arm; you are caught in trap. The *kusari gama* adept will then yank the chain downward and to his right, and will then come at you with the sickle held in his left hand. These movements are very fast. There is no question of pulling little by little on the chain as in the popular story. You have to think that as soon as the chain has wrapped itself around your arm, the adversary will come at you immediately. Through this analysis, we can see that it is very difficult to fight against an adept of the *kusari gama*. How, then, did Musashi fight?

The duel took place outside. As soon as they had faced off, Shishido began to spin his chain. Musashi regarded this technique with admiration. He immediately began looking for a tactic to defeat it, and in order to gauge the attack range of the weight, he switched his long sword to his left hand and drew his short sword with his right hand, assuming the *gyaku nito* guard position. He came forward twirling the short sword above his head. He adjusted the cadence of his short sword to the spin of the weight at the end of the chain. Shishido was stunned by this strange guard position. The small sword twirling above the head of his adversary made him uneasy. If he tried to catch it with his chain, the long sword would become dangerous. Both swords became disconcerting for him. Musashi moved forward, whereas Shishido began to back away. Musashi then sensed that he had to get things over with quickly, and his plan took shape. The moment Shishido began backing up, Musashi threw his short sword, which stuck in his opponent's chest, and at this moment he leaped forward and cut him down.

The technique Musashi used in the duel with Shishido was transmitted in the School of Two Swords under the name of *sanshin to,* "the sword with three minds." One mind spins the short sword to draw the adversary's attention, another mind prepares to parry his attack with the short sword, and the third mind runs the adversary through with the large sword held in the left hand. (35, pp. 198–200)

Such is Yoshida's interpretation, made on the basis of techniques handed down in Musashi's school. Some authors maintain that Musashi held the large sword in his right hand and threw the small sword with his left. If Musashi was left-handed, as some researchers think, throwing the sword with his left hand would have been natural. Other scholars have a different interpretation. Their idea is that Musashi drew his short sword only at the last moment. Shishido then threw his weight and wrapped the chain around Musashi's sword, and it was as he was pulling Musashi toward him that Musashi drew his short sword and threw it.

The Fight against Oseto Hayato and Tsujikaze

According to the *Nitenki,* after fighting Shishido, Musashi went to Edo, where he fought two adepts of the Yagyu ryu. These duels probably took place during his first stay in Edo around 1605 or 1606, when he was twenty-two or twenty-three years old. The following anecdote was told by Ujii Yashiro, who was sword master to Lord Hosokawa when Musashi arrived in Kumamoto in 1640 and who was defeated by Musashi in a bout arranged at the request of Lord Hosokawa:

> During his trip to Edo, Musashi met two powerful adepts named Oseto Hayato and Tsujikaze, who were part of the Yagyu school. They asked Musashi to fight, and he accepted immediately.
>
> When Oseto was about to attack, Musashi took the initiative and struck his adversary before he made a move. His adversary was defeated. It was then Tsujikaze's turn to attack, but he was thrown backward, and his back crashed into a stone bowl in the garden, and he fainted. He quickly came to, but when he sat up, he suddenly died. (2, pp. 178–179)

The fight with Tsujikaze reminds us of the passage "Banging into Your Opponent" in the Scroll of Water (page 163).

The Meeting with Hatano Jirozaemon

In the *Nitenki* we read:

> When Musashi was in Edo, he met an adept named Hatano Jirosaemon from Marume Mondo's Ichiden ryu. Hatano asked Musashi to give him some advice on improving his art. Musashi communicated to him the principle of his art. On the basis of Musashi's instruction, Hatano founded his own school and named it Itten ryu. He became a monk with the name of Soken. His art was remarkable and his school became famous. It had a great number of students. (2, p. 180)

The Ichiden ryu was founded in the Joshu region (Gunma prefecture) by Marume Mondo, who excelled in the art of drawing the sword *(batto jutsu)*. Hatano was his student.

The Duel with Muso Gonnosuke

We may surmise that Musashi's duel with Muso Gonnosuke took place between 1608 and 1611, when Musashi was between twenty-five and twenty-eight years old. According to the *Nitenki,* Musashi fought Muso Gonnosuke in Edo.

> When Musashi was in Edo, he met an adept named Muso Gonnosuke, who asked to fight him. Gonnosuke used a wooden sword. Musashi was in the process of making a small bow; he picked up a piece of firewood. Gonnosuke attacked him without even bowing, but he received a blow from Musashi that made him fall down. He was impressed and left. (2, p. 172)

According to the *Kaijo monogatari,* a document written in 1666, this combat took place during Musashi's stay at Akashi. Here are the main points from this text:

> Muso Gonnosuke was a big man who traveled with eight disciples. He dressed in an outer garment of a loud color, and attached to his shoulder was a strip of cloth on which was written in gold ink: "The greatest adept in the whole history of Japan: Muso Gonnosuke."
>
> One summer day, Gonnosuke visited Musashi to ask him to fight a duel. He said, "In the past, I had the opportunity of seeing the art of your father Munisai. Today I would like to see the art that you have developed."
>
> At first Musashi tried to refuse the duel, saying, "My art is not very different from my father's." But Gonnosuke insisted. Musashi finally accepted his request and went down into the garden with a piece of a small bow he was in the process of making.
>
> Gonnosuke was armed with his usual weapon, which was a staff reinforced with steel of about four *shaku* [1.2 meters] in length, and he attacked him without even bowing. For a while

Musashi treated his opponent lightly, then seizing an opening, he struck him in the middle of the forehead. His adversary fell immediately.

After this experience, Gonnosuke persevered. He took up residence on Mount Homan-zan in the Chikuzen region [Fukuoka]. He developed his art further and ended up founding a school using a staff of four *shaku* and two *sun* [1.28 meters] in length. He named his school Shinto Muso ryu, because he had previously studied the swordsmanship of the Shinto ryu under the guidance of Sakurai Osuminokami Yoshikatsu. (27, p. 174)

Later Muso Gonnosuke became a vassal of Kuroda and his school was transmitted in the fief of Kuroda. According to an account of the Shinto ryu, during his long career as an adept, Gonnosuke lost just once— against Musashi—and he finally defeated Musashi after he perfected his new method. However, there is no other record of any second encounter with Musashi.

Auxiliary Combat Arts in Musashi's School

Certain documents tell us that after his defeat, Muso received instruction and advice from Musashi and that as a result he was able to improve his art of the staff and develop a new form of it. His art is practiced today in the Shinto Muso ryu. By giving advice to Muso Gonnosuke, perhaps Musashi gained a better understanding of the specific qualities of the staff as a weapon. Later Musashi accepted a student named Shioda Hamanosuke who was also an adept of the art of the staff. According to a document handed down in the Niten ichi ryu, Shioda showed Musashi all his staff techniques, saying to him that they were deplorable. Instead of rejecting them, Musashi made certain modifications to improve them. Thus it may be that his encounter with Muso Gonnosuke had aroused his interest in these techniques. In any case, Musashi later introduced staff techniques as part of the instruction of his school.

We have noted that in Musashi's time, duels were often a matter of life or death. The experience of duels was cumulative—a victorious adept received precious instruction from his opponent. In some sense, killing an adversary did not mean destroying his art but, rather, incorporating it. During his period of dueling, Musashi's adversaries constituted for him a kind of master from whom he learned the essence of the art of swordsmanship.

Musashi's school is characterized by the use of two swords, but as he explained in the *Gorin no sho,* his art extended beyond mere swordsmanship. It seems that Musashi attempted to apply the principle of his art to all the weapons that he encountered. Among the great many weapons he studied, the following disciplines are still practiced in his school today:

- Techniques for the large sword *(tachi seiho).* There are twelve basic techniques and four techniques for high-level practitioners.
- Techniques for the short sword *(kodachi seiho)* against the large sword. There are seven techniques.
- Techniques for both swords *(nito seiho).* There are five techniques based on Musashi's five forms.
- Knife techniques *(aikuchi roppo).* The *aikuchi* is a hiltless knife of about thirty centimeters. There are six techniques.
- Techniques for the *jitte* against the sword. There are five techniques *(jitte to jutsu).*
- Techniques for the staff. There are seven techniques for the staff against the sword and thirteen techniques for the staff against the staff *(bo jutsu).* (3, p. 79)

The staff is without a doubt one of the most rudimentary weapons. Handling a staff is considered one of the foundational techniques for certain martial arts disciplines and it is like an extension of the body for the others. For example, a staff can be used as an extension of the upper limbs in a bare-handed combat art such as karate, jujutsu, aikido, and so on. A staff can be a weapon in itself, but it can also be looked at as a lance or *naginata* that has lost its metal part. In the first case, techniques are developed for the staff as a weapon per se. In the second case, the techniques are developed in parallel with those for the lance or the *naginata.*

For warriors it was important to be able to continue to wield their weapons even if they were partly broken.

THE DUEL AGAINST SASAKI KOJIRO

The first period of Musashi's duels came to an end with a famous duel. In 1612, at the age of twenty-eight (twenty-nine according to the old way of counting), Musashi fought an adept by the name of Sasaki Kojiro on the island of Funajima, later called Ganryujima. Of the combats of his youth, this is probably the one that marked him most deeply.

Let us examine this passage from the *Gorin no sho:*

> At the age of thirty, I reflected and saw that although I had won, I had done so without having reached the ultimate level of strategy. Perhaps it was because my natural disposition prevented me from straying from universal principles; perhaps it was because my opponents lacked ability in strategy.
>
> I continued to train and to seek from morning till night to attain a deeper principle. When I reached the age of fifty, I naturally found myself on the way of strategy.

From this time on, Musashi sought to reach a deeper understanding of his art. The duel against Kojiro seems to have marked the end of his first stage as an adept. We might well ask ourselves what brought about this change in Musashi's attitude.

Who Was Sasaki Kojiro?

Some points concerning the life of Sasaki Kojiro remain obscure, notably his age at the time of the duel.

According to the *Nitenki:* "From the time of his childhood Sasaki Kojiro received the instruction of Toda Seigen, a master of the school of the short sword *(kodachi),* and having been the partner of his master, he excelled him in the wielding of the long sword. After having defeated his master's younger brother, he left him to travel in various provinces. Then he founded his own school, which was called Ganryu." (2, pp. 172–173)

According to this text, Sasaki Kojiro was eighteen when he fought Musashi, but that seems improbable. According to the most credible document available to us, in 1610 Sasaki Kojiro became the principal sword master of the fief of Hosokawa, located in the north of Kyushu. Supposing that he was eighteen when he fought Musashi, he would have been sixteen when he became the principal master of the fief, which is unthinkable. Moreover, he could not have been the student of Toda Seigen, who died in the 1590s, unless he was at least ten years old at the time of this master's death. That is why some authors think Sasaki Kojiro was more than fifty when he fought Musashi. Others think he was the student of Kanemaki Jisai, Toda Seigen's disciple. In any case, while the age of Sasaki Kojiro remains uncertain, it is generally said that he came from the Echizen region (Fukui prefecture).

All the documents agree that he received the training of the Chujo ryu from Toda Seigen, the famous sword master of Echizen. This school excelled in the art of the short sword *(kodachi)*. One trains with a short sword against one or several adversaries who are using the long sword. It is possible that it was while serving as a combat partner for his master, who used the short sword, that Sasaki Kojiro became an expert with the long sword.

In the Chujo ryu, one of Toda Seigen's disciples, Kanemaki Jisai, used a sword of medium length *(naka dachi)*. He had a student named Ito Ittosai, who founded the Itto ryu, which later exercised a direct and very important influence on the practice of contemporary kendo.

Sasaki Kojiro's favorite technique is known by the name of *tsubame gaeshi,* which means "to turn the sword with the speed of a swallow," or according to another interpretation, "the sword that cuts a swallow."

There is no text that directly explains this technique, but in connection with it the old texts make reference to the Itto ryu technique known as *kinshi cho ohken* or to the Ganryu technique called *kosetsu to.* The analysis that follows compares the two techniques with the idea of showing their common characteristics.

Here is the paragraph concerning the *kinshi cho ohken* (royal sword of a golden bird) technique from *The Supreme Teaching of the Itto Ryu* by Sasamori Junzo:

> The *kinshi cho* is a large bird whose wing measures ninety thousand leagues. It can soar in the sky but it is too large to descend and dive into the sea. The glance of this bird flapping its immense wings in the sky threatens the dragon that is in the sea. The surprised dragon dives to the bottom of the sea, full of fear and also anger. When he can no longer tolerate the situation, the dragon emerges on the surface of the sea thrashing his scales among the waves, and the *kinshi cho* swoops down and devours him.
>
> The point here is to assume a high guard position with which you threaten your opponent. And when he becomes agitated and his mind wavers, you strike to defeat him. (50, p. 526)

In this technique you take a high guard and, with a strong will, you threaten your opponent. At the moment he reacts, either to flee or to attack, you strike downward from above with a decisive stroke. From this we may retain, as an element in the *tsubame gaeshi,* the attack downward from above at the moment when the mind of the opponent becomes disconcerted.

The *kosetsu to* technique transmitted in the Ganryu provides us with another key. *Ko* means "tiger," *setsu* means "cutting through," and *to* means "sword." But in the name of this technique, the word *ko* has a series of meanings. Although *ko* means "tiger," in the tradition of this school, through its proximity in pronunciation to the ideogram *go,* which means "behind," it has this meaning as well. Understood in this sense, the word has the connotation of "yin" or "negative," that is, the back in relation to the front, the low in relation to the high, a shadow in relation to the light. Including these implicit meanings is necessary to grasp that *ko setsu to* means "the sword that cuts starting from below" or "starting from behind."

Remember that the expression *tsubame gaeshi* means "to turn" *(gaeshi)* and "swallow" *(tsubame),* which expresses a movement in the midst of a strike—a rapid change of direction like that of a swallow.

We are thus able to piece together what Sasaki Kojiro's favorite technique was. It involved striking downward from above and then, instantly, striking again from below upward or from below toward the rear, then upward on an angle, like an eagle climbs again immediately after having stooped.

This reconstruction is confirmed by the following passage in a document of the Edo period, the *Gekiken sodan,* written in 1843:

> In the east of Japan, many schools bear the name Ganryu. In these schools there exists a technique called "one mind for one sword" *(isshin itto).* . . . This involves moving forward, adopting a guard position in which one is immediately ready to strike downward from above, and then, approaching the adversary more closely, delivering a stroke that carries all the way down to the ground. Next one must immediately lower oneself and take the victory by striking from below upward as the adversary is attacking downward from above. (1-f, p. 197)

In my view Sasaki Kojiro did learn the art of the Chujo ryu under the guidance of Toda Seigen or his disciple. In any case, it can be stated that his training was in the tradition of Toda Seigen, a tradition also called Toda ryu, which places great emphasis on speed in the execution of all techniques. Instead of confining themselves to rapid execution using the short sword or a sword of medium length, its adepts worked on rapid execution with an especially long sword. Having confidence in his longsword technique and having perfected his *tsubame gaeshi* technique, Sasaki Kojiro founded his own school, called Ganryu, "School of Rock." Yoshida Seiken writes:

> Kojiro proved his great speed in the art of the sword by cutting in half swallows flying under the bridge over a river. To cut a flying swallow in two, one has to reach the point of being able to wield

a sword with speed and precision. Just wielding the sword with speed is not enough, because a swallow's sharp sight enables it to avoid danger. To cut through a swallow with certainty, one must have the ability to judge the change in the trajectory of its flight as it is moving to avoid the sword stroke. One must strike accurately while instantly changing the direction of the sword blade. Sasaki Kojiro had mastered this technique to a high degree. (35, p. 206)

I do not know what Yoshida Seiken's interpretation is based on, and I also do not know if it is possible to cut a flying swallow in half "with certainty." All the same, with his art of the *tsubame gaeshi,* Sasaki Kojiro had traveled in various regions without ever losing once, and with each combat, his reputation had increased. When he arrived in Kokura in the north of Kyushu, he was received by Lord Hosokawa Tadaoki, who made him the principal master of arms of his fief. His reputation was widespread not only in Kyushu but also in the country of the West, as far as Kyoto.

According to the most common version of the event, Musashi heard of this adept in Kyoto and desired to measure himself against him. He addressed a request for a duel to Lord Hosokawa Tadaoki, using as an intermediary Nagaoka Sado, one of the lord's principal vassals, who had at one time been a student of Musashi's father. Lord Hosokawa gave his permission and the duel was set for April 13, 1612, at eight o'clock in the morning, on the island of Funajima, located in the strait separating the southern tip of Honshu from the north of Kyushu.

The Duel between Musashi and Kojiro according to the *Nitenki*

The choice of the place for the duel between Musashi and Kojiro was up to Lord Hosokawa Tadaoki. When he heard of Musashi from one of his principal vassals, Nagaoka Sado Okinaga, he told him to arrange the duel on the island then known in Kyushu as Mukojima (yonder island) and in Nagato, on the other shore, as Funajima (boat-shaped island). Today, as a memorial, it is known as Ganryujima.

Why did Lord Hosokawa choose this island that is not very easy to reach? Doubtless he wanted to avoid any trouble in his fief that might have resulted from this simple duel between two adepts of *hyoho*. For Sasaki Kojiro had a large number of students among Hosokawa's vassals. The name of Musashi was not as yet well known. If Kojiro lost to an adept who was not well known, his disciples—following a custom of the period—would not let the victor go in peace, and a disturbance would be inevitable. This was doubtless a major reason for his decision.

The basic document most often cited with regard to this duel is the *Nitenki,* from which the entirety of the pertinent passage is given below.

There was an adept named Ganryu Kojiro. He came from the village of Jokyoji-mura in Usaka in the Echizen region. He was an adept of very great talent and his strength was incomparable. From his childhood he had been the disciple of a famous adept from the same country, Toda Seigen. He learned his master's art living under his roof.

As he was growing up, he became Seigen's practice partner. Seigen practiced with a short sword of forty-five centimeters against Kojiro, who attacked with a sword of more than ninety centimeters [length of the blade]. Kojiro could not defeat his master with his long sword. He trained further and reached a level where he could defeat all of Seigen's other disciples. In a duel, he defeated Jibuzaemon, Seigen's younger brother.

Without his master's permission, Kojiro himself founded a school whose techniques were unique and called it the Ganryu. He traveled in different regions, having bouts with famous adepts and not losing even once. Finally he arrived at Kokura, where he entered the service of Lord Hosokawa Tadaoki as sword master of the fief.

In the month of April 1612, Musashi, age twenty-nine, arrived at Kokura, having come from Kyoto. He was received by Nagaoka Sado Okinaga, a former student of Munisai, Musashi's father.

Musashi said to Okinaga: "I hear Ganryu Kojiro is staying here. It seems that his art is fabulous. I would like to measure myself against him if that is possible. Would you kindly grant me the favor of taking the necessary steps so that I can realize my desire?"

Okinaga agreed to present a request to his lord, and he provided Musashi with lodging in the meantime. Later he received Lord Tadaoki's consent for them to fight on the island of Funajima, or Mukojima, which is located off the coast near Kokura. Today this island is sometimes called Ganryujima. It is located on the border between Buzen and Nagato. It is one league away from both Kokura and Shimonoseki in the Nagato region.

The people were informed in advance that it was forbidden to watch the duel and also prohibited to take sides with one party or the other.

Okinaga said to Musashi: "You will fight Kojiro at eight o'clock tomorrow morning on the island of Mukojima. Kojiro will go there in Lord Tadaoki's boat, and you will go in my boat."

Musashi, visibly satisfied, thanked him for having made his wish come true. But that night Musashi disappeared. People looked for him all over the town, but no one found a trace of Musashi. Finally people said, "He doubtless fled, having learned during his stay that Kojiro is much stronger than he supposed."

Okinaga was upset by this talk, but he could do nothing. He finally said: "If Musashi fled out of fear, why did he wait for this day? He could have left long before. I think he has something in mind. I remember that before arriving here, he stopped at Shimonoseki. It is possible that he is at Shimonoseki at this moment and that he is intending to reach the island from Shimonoseki. So send a messenger right away."

When the messenger arrived, he found that Musashi was indeed staying with a wholesaler named Tarozaemon. The messenger conveyed Okinaga's words to Musashi, who replied with the following letter: "For tomorrow's duel, you offered to take me in your own boat. I am very grateful for your thought. However, Kojiro and I are for the moment in the position of two adversaries. If Kojiro were to go in Lord Tadaoki's boat and I in yours, it seems to me this would be awkward for your relationship with your lord. I therefore request you to take no account of my lot. If I had told you that directly, I know you would not have accepted. That is why I decided to disappear on the spur of the moment. I ask you to excuse me for this. Tomorrow morning, I will go to Mukojima by my own means. Please do not worry.

"The twelfth of the fourth month, Miyamoto Musashi

"To Lord Sado"

That is how Musashi replied to Okinaga [Sado]. (2, pp. 172–175)

Musashi's reasoning was that since for the moment he was the enemy of Sasaki Kojiro, principal sword master of the fief of Hosokawa, the situation in fact made him an enemy of the fief of which Nagaoka was a principal vassal. Since Sasaki Kojiro was going in Lord Tadaoki's boat, if Nagaoka took Musashi in his personal boat, he risked compromising his position. Musashi's thinking might seem a bit rigid, but he considered his duel as a battle, not a mere individual combat. For Musashi, the duel already began the moment it was officially declared.

When he got Musashi's letter, Nagaoka Sado calmed down.

But the following morning, dawn had already broken, and it was getting late, and Musashi was still in bed. The head of the Tarozaemon house was getting worried, and he let Musashi know that it would soon be eight o'clock. At the same time, a messenger arrived from Kokura to find out if Musashi had left yet.

Musashi replied he would be leaving soon. Then he washed and got dressed and had his breakfast. He asked the head of the house to give him a rowboat oar, from which he fashioned a wooden sword. During this time, another messenger arrived to tell him to leave immediately.

Musashi put on a lined silk kimono, put a towel in his belt, and took with him a quilted cotton jacket. Then he got into the boat, which was rowed by one of Tarozaemon's servants. In the boat he twisted some odds and ends of paper to make a string, which he put beneath his kimono sleeves and crossed behind his back. In this way his sleeves would not get in the way. Having finished this work, he put on his jacket and lay down in the boat.

The island was guarded by the supervisors of the duel, and approaching it was strictly forbidden to the public. When Musashi arrived it was already past ten o'clock.

He had the boat stop in a sandy shallow, left his jacket and his long sword in the boat, and turned up the bottoms of his pants *(hakama)*. Barefoot, he got out of the boat with his wooden sword in his hand. As he walked a few dozen steps in the water, he made the towel into a headband and put it on.

Kojiro had put on a red vest reinforced with dyed leather and was wearing straw shoes. He was carrying a long sword, the blade of which, more than ninety centimeters long, had been made by Nigen Nagamitsu.

Kojiro was tired of waiting for Musashi to arrive. As soon as he saw him, he ran in anger to the water's edge and said: "I got here early. Why are you arriving so late? Did you get scared?"

Musashi acted as though he had heard nothing and gave no reply. Kojiro drew his sword and threw the scabbard into the water. He waited for Musashi at the water's edge, but Musashi stayed in the water. Then he smiled and said: "Kojiro, you are lost. For if you expected to be the winner, why would you throw your scabbard in the water?"

With this Kojiro's anger came to a head, and when Musashi approached him, he attacked with the intention of cutting his head down the middle. Kojiro's sword cut the knot of Musashi's headband, and it fell to the ground. Musashi also launched his attack at the same moment, and his blow hit the head of his adversary, who fell instantly.

According to Yoshida Seiken's version, Musashi first held his sword in both hands, and then to extend the range of his weapon, he struck holding it with only his left hand.

Musashi approached with the wooden sword in his hand and prepared to strike again by raising the sword above his head. Kojiro,
lying on the ground, struck horizontally and cut the cloth of his
kimono above the knees over a length of about nine centimeters,
while Musashi's wooden sword was breaking Kojiro's ribs. Kojiro
fainted and bled from the nose and mouth.

After a moment, Musashi put down his weapon and approached Kojiro and put his hand in front of his adversary's nose
and mouth to see if he was really dead. Then he bowed to the ref-
erees of the duel, picked up his sword, and got back in his boat.
Helping the oarsman with a long bamboo stick, he got away
quickly.

Back in Shimonoseki, he wrote a letter of thanks to Okinaga.
He returned several days later to Kokura and requested another
duel with one of Lord Tadaoki's vassals. The principal vassals met
to discuss this and did not respond to this request. Musashi returned to Shimonoseki.

Ganryu called himself Sasaki Kojiro, and it is said that he was
eighteen years old at the time of the duel. He was a man of great
quality, and Musashi himself regretted his death. Toda Seigen [his
teacher], formerly called Gorozaemon, was a famous adept of the
Chujo ryu. Having had an eye ailment, he shaved his skull and
took the name of Seigen. His younger brother's name was Jibuzaemon, and he became heir to the family lineage. (35, p. 205)

The Strategy

The wooden sword Musashi used was particularly heavy and measured
1.26 meters in length. On the reasons for his using this wooden sword,
Hirayama Shiryu-gyozo (1759–1828), a sword master, wrote in his
work "Discourse on Swordsmanship" *(Kensetsu):*

Ganryu Sasaki Kojiro used a sword whose blade measured ninety
centimeters in length. It was nicknamed "the clothes-drying

pole." Judging that it would be to his disadvantage to use two swords, both of which were shorter than that of his opponent, Musashi asked the boatman to give him an oar, from which he made a large wooden sword. With that he could kill his adversary by smashing his skull. Musashi's talent was this ability to change his means as appropriate for a given adversary. (1-g, p. 370)

This commentary is not entirely correct, since Musashi's long sword also measured more than ninety centimeters. Thus the sword length of both combatants was about the same. In my view Musashi wanted to fight with a weapon whose length was greater than Sasaki Kojiro's and he carried out his strategy in such a way as to conceal it until the last moment. Initially he kept the end of his weapon immersed in the water, putting his back to the sun. Then, during the combat, he held it at an angle over his shoulder. Did he not make all the strategic moves necessary to begin the fight without giving his opponent an instant to get a look at the nature of his weapon? There is not enough objective data to permit an analysis of how Musashi fought. An interpretation like Yoshida Seiken's is based on his own practice. Nevertheless, we can form an idea of Musashi's approach on the basis of the *Gorin no sho*.

Looking at the duel between Sasaki Kojiro and Musashi, we can conclude that during this period a confrontation between adepts was seen as like a battle. From the moment the duel was scheduled, Musashi considered himself an enemy of the fief as a whole. He applied his strategy accordingly. Thus he had to get away immediately after defeating his opponent in order to avoid the vengeance attacks of Sasaki Kojiro's disciples. It would not be appropriate to judge Musashi's actions on the basis of our current notions of sports matches. Feudal society had just emerged from a long period of war—more than a century— and individual confrontations then had a strong connotation of battle. Thus the two adepts entered into a state of combat the moment they agreed to fight.

To reach the island, Musashi had to get across the particularly strong current that runs between the islands of Honshu and Kyushu. The speed of this current can be as high as eight knots. The current changes four times a day. Musashi arrived more than three hours late, which greatly upset his adversary. Some authors suggest that Musashi was delayed by this current but that this accidental delay had produced a positive strategic effect. And indeed, still today, it is impossible for a small motorboat to make headway against this current. Being from this area myself, I have several times witnessed the following spectacle: The boat seems to be standing still, but if you look closely, you see that it is very slowly advancing against the current, with the motor full out. If you are taken by this strong current, it is impossible to get anywhere directly against it while rowing. Was Musashi's lateness due to the current?

This hypothesis seems unlikely to me when we recall the passage in the *Gorin no sho* entitled "Getting Past a Critical Passage." Does Musashi not describe in this passage how it is necessary to prepare in advance for any navigation on the sea and with what determination it is necessary to do this? If this idea was already in Musashi's mind, it is difficult to imagine that he failed to look into the nature of the currents when he arrived at this place—but we might also conclude that this wisdom came to him as a result of bitter experience. In that case, the hypothesis might be correct.

Going back to the description of the duel in the *Nitenki*, we find there that Kojiro's strike did not reach Musashi:

The third of the first month, Musashi was invited to the ceremony of chanting celebrating the new year at the Hatanaka house in the Hosokawa fief at Higo Kumamoto. Before the beginning of the ceremony, Shimizu Hoki, a highly placed functionary, addressed these words to Musashi from the upper box: "Some people say that when you fought Sasaki, his sword touched you first. Is that true?"

Musashi, without replying, approached Hoki with a candle-holder in his hand and sat down next to him. He said: "When I was a child, I had a pimple at the root of my hair. It was to hide the trace of it that I grew my hair out. In the combat with Kojiro, he fought with a real sword and I fought with a wooden one. If I received a blow from his sword, I should have a scar. Would you be so kind as to take a look?"

Saying this, Musashi took the candleholder in his left hand and put his head close to Hoki and lifted his hair with his right hand. Hoki, backing away, said: "No, I see no trace of any." But Musashi insisted: "Please be so kind as to look carefully." Hoki then declared: "Yes, I have looked at it with certainty." With that, Musashi contented himself with going back to his seat. During this exchange, all the warriors around them had held their breath, their palms wet with perspiration. This story, which was popular for a time, was interpreted as a mistake on Hoki's part. (2, p. 182)

The vagueness of the figure of Sasaki Kojiro is due to the fact that he was killed in the duel. Only a victor has a chance to leave behind the signs of his passage. Some critics hold the view that Sasaki Kojiro's ability with the sword was superior to Musashi's, who was able to defeat him only by having recourse to a trick or a tactic. This hypothesis is no better founded than its opposite, but if we adopt it, we should bear in mind the fundamental difference between the contemporary practice of the martial arts and the practices of Musashi's period. A single mistake could sentence an adept to eternal silence, to death. Even if he had enormous talent, there was no way he could get a return match. This is the incisive premise on which Musashi's whole practice and consciousness of the martial arts was built. Without this consciousness, it is difficult for us to gain a true idea of Musashi's image or his thought.

Some Problems Posed by the *Nitenki* Account

The text of the *Nitenki* (2) has functioned many times as the basis for novels on Musashi's life, and it is often considered to be a historical text. Despite all this, however, an attentive reading immediately reveals problems and contradictions in the account, some examples of which follow.

"He asked the head of the house to give him a rowboat oar, from which he fashioned a wooden sword." (2, p. 173) It is difficult to imagine that someone who was about to fight a duel to the death should get his weapon ready only a few hours before the combat; all the more so, since the wood from which oars are made is very hard. Working on it with a knife

or other tools would tire out one's arms, which any combatant would avoid before a fight.

"*Barefoot, he got out of the boat with his wooden sword in his hand. As he walked a few dozen steps in the water, he made the towel into a headband and put it on.*" (2, p. 174) This scene is pretty much impossible. How could Musashi have made a knot with one hand while holding a heavy wooden sword in the other hand and approaching a formidable adversary at the same time?

There are several other problems, especially regarding Sasaki Kojiro, of whom we know little.

In a text of Minamoto Tokushu dating from 1843, we find the following description of the fight between Musashi and Sasaki Kojiro:

> When he fought Ganryu, Musashi asked a boatman for a piece of an oar to make two swords, whereas Ganryu fought with a real sword. Musashi won and Ganryu died. The details of the combat are already known. I will describe them no further.
>
> I will provide other information.
>
> When the duel between Miyamoto Musashi and Sasaki Ganryu was decided upon, the disciples of both adepts were very concerned. One of Musashi's disciples, named Yamada, encountered a man named Ichikawa, a disciple of Ganryu's. Both spoke of the exceptional qualities of their teachers.
>
> Yamada said: "Master Musashi made a wooden sword to gain the victory by smashing his opponent, because he knows Ganryu likes to use an especially long sword."
>
> Ichikawa said: "My master's technique places no importance upon the strength of the adversary, whoever he may be. Until now, all his strong opponents have been vanquished by his art."
>
> Returning home, Yamada informed Musashi of this conversation.
>
> Musashi then said: "Ganryu's technique is called *kosetsu* (sword that cuts down a tiger) and I already know the particularities of this technique."
>
> The day of the duel arrived. Musashi allowed his adversary to

use his *kosetsu* technique, but since Musashi was a man of exceptional agility, he eluded the *kosetsu* strike by jumping in the air. Ganryu's sword cut into the bottom of Musashi's leather pants, while Musashi crushed Ganryu's skull. (27, p. 178)

Other Versions of the Duel

The documents cited below provide an entirely different picture of the duel between Musashi and Kojiro.

The text on the Kokura monument reads as follows:

Musashi wanted to fight an adept of the martial arts named Ganryu. The latter said, "Let's fight with real swords." Musashi replied, "You fight with a real sword; as for me, I will use a wooden sword to express my art." Thus they came to an agreement concerning their duel.

The two adepts found themselves at the same time on the island of Funajima, which is situated between the two regions of Nagato and Buzen. Ganryu manifested his art by risking his life with his sword, whose blade measured ninety centimeters in length. Musashi killed him by delivering a blow with his wooden sword with a speed that seemed faster than lightning.

So, according to this text, Musashi and Ganryu arrived at the same time.

According to the text of the Numata family:

One year, when Lord Nobumoto was at Moji, Miyamoto Musashi Genshin arrived in the region of Buzen and taught the art of the School of Two Swords. During this time, a man named Kojiro was also teaching his art of the Ganryu.

The disciples of the two schools had a dispute regarding the superiority of their respective schools, which led to the duel between Musashi and Kojiro. The place set for the combat was the island of Hikoshima, located between Buzen and Nagato. It was agreed that none of the disciples of either party would be present at the duel. Kojiro lost the duel and died.

The disciples of Kojiro did not come, as per the agreement, but Musashi's disciples came covertly.

After the duel, Kojiro revived, but Musashi's disciples arrived and killed him.

Kojiro's disciples, learning this, arrived in a group on the island. Musashi fled amid the dangers as far as Moji, where he came to ask protection from Lord Nobumoto, who took him to his castle to provide him with a secure situation. Later, he sent Musashi to Bungo.

By the lord's order, Ishii Mitsunojo succeeded in taking Musashi to the house of a man named Munisai in the neighboring region of Bungo. On horseback, he led a group of riflemen who provided security for Musashi's journey. (17, pp. 124–127)

According to Harada Mukashi (17, p. 125), this text was written during the Genroku period (1688–1704) by a secretary of the Numata family who had been given the responsibility of putting the family documents in order. The basis of this text is the journal of Numata Nobumoto, one of the witnesses to the duel, who wrote an account of it.

At this time the legislation limiting the number of castles to one per fief was not yet in force. Thus each lord had several castles. The Hosokawa fief had seven castles. The castles other than the principal one were each administered by a principal vassal (jodai). At that time Numata Nobumoto exercised the function of jodai of Moji castle, the closest one to the island of Funajima. He was one of the witnesses of the duel, and this text was written on the basis of his having been there. Numata Nobumoto later took the name of Nagaoka Kageyuzaemon. Nagaoka is one of the family names that only families owing fealty to Lord Hosokawa were authorized to use.

The "Little Tales of the Martial Arts of Japan" (Honcho bugei shoden) was written in 1715 by Hinatsu Shigetaka. In it, Nakamura Morikazu gave an account of the duel of Miyamoto Musashi based on what he heard from his elder.

The day of the duel, a great number of people of all classes crossed the sea to go to the island of Funajima as spectators. Ganryu arrived at the port, got on a boat there, and asked the boatman, "Tell me why there are so many people in the port today?"

The boatman replied: "Don't you know that today on the island of Funajima there is a duel between two adepts of strategy named Ganryu and Miyamoto Musashi? It is to watch this show that the people have been going to the island without a break since dawn."

Ganryu said, "I am Ganryu."

The boatman, surprised, whispered: "If you are Ganryu, I am going to steer this boat in the opposite direction and you can make a quick escape to another region. Because they say that your art is divine, but Musashi is surrounded by his people, and you will never be able to get out of this alive."

Ganryu said: "I've heard the news and I do not think that I can survive. But I made a firm promise with regard to today's duel. Even if I die, a worthy warrior must never go against his word. After my death, please pour some water on my grave to assuage my soul." And then saying, "Even though you are not a warrior, I am very grateful for your sympathy," he got out a small bag and gave it to the boatman.

The boatman was deeply moved and cried to hear these words of a brave man. When the boat arrived at the island, Ganryu leaped out and awaited Musashi, who soon arrived. The two fought. Ganryu fought courageously, now like lightning, now like thunder, but unfortunately, he left his life on the island of Funajima. . . .

Some people say that in the boat on his way to the island, Musashi asked his boatman for a piece of an oar and that, using his short sword *(wakizashi)*, he trimmed one end of it to make gripping it easier. When he got out of the boat, he fought with this weapon, while Ganryu used a sword whose blade was more than ninety centimeters long. This sword had the name *monoboshi zao* (clothes-drying pole). Today Ganryu's grave is on the island of Funajima. (1-b, p. 180)

Such are the different accounts of the duel between Musashi and Sasaki Kojiro that are to be read in the classical documents and that present a certain number of contradictions. The version that has inspired the greatest number of novels on Musashi is the one in the *Nitenki*. The majority of scholars consider it to be a historical document, whereas for Harada Mukashi, it is no more than a work of fiction.

The Interpretation of Harada Mukashi

Harada relies on the *Text of the Numata Family,* which in his opinion is the most faithful to reality, and on the *Bugei shoden,* which is close to it. Working from those, he develops an original interpretation. (17, pp. 114–141)

According to Harada, Musashi won the duel, but contrary to general opinion, it was not an honorable victory. As we read in the text of the Numata family, Musashi had to flee in the midst of dangers and ask for the protection of Lord Nobumoto. He ended having to be escorted by men with guns to Bungo, where his father lived. This picture is very distant from the one to which we have become accustomed.

According to Harada, Ganryu was a native of the Buzen region, where the Sasaki clan had lived for a long time and exercised considerable power. (To this day the Sasaki family is still very numerous in this region.) When Lord Hosokawa established himself in the north of Kyushu after the battle of Sekigahara (1600), one of his major preoccupations was finding a way to govern in these regions where traditional local forces were prominent. The Sasaki clan was a considerable obstacle for him. Harada puts forward the hypothesis that Musashi was hired by Hosokawa in his effort to weaken the Sasaki forces. According to him, Ganryu is the name of the school of the Yamabushi, monks with a syncretistic religion that tends toward mysticism who lived on the sacred mountain Hikosan. The adept named Sasaki Kojiro represented both the Ganryu of the Yamabushi and the Sasaki clan.

In the duel, Kojiro did not die from the blow Musashi gave him but was killed by students of Musashi or retainers of Hosokawa who were hidden on the island. Learning of the assassination of Kojiro, his students tried to kill Musashi, who was forced to flee and request protection from Hosokawa's principal vassal. That is why this duel was a bitter experience for Musashi, who must have reflected upon the precariousness of the life of an adept at the mercy of political forces. It was in this way that this duel marked the end of one of the periods of his life. After this duel, he gave up seeking situations of individual combat.

Let us note in addition that the island of Funajima ended up being called Ganryujima and not Musashijima. Is this not the expression of great sympathy in the region for Ganryu? If Ganryu was an adept from a distant place, why was not the name of Musashi, the victor in the duel, given to the name of the island where he fought so valiantly?

Harada's interpretation seems convincing to me, given the political situation of the moment. If this interpretation is an accurate reflection of history, then we must conclude that the account given in the *Nitenki* is largely fictitious. Taking into account the existing documents, this is not a hypothesis that should be entirely ruled out. Concerning Sasaki Kojiro, the mystery lives on.

Literary Divagations

The images of Musashi and Kojiro have passed into the collective imagination through a variety of literary works, which have made them popular while simultaneously helping to distort them.

In 1746 Yamojiya Jisho wrote a theater piece *(Hana ikada Ganryu jima)* that made the duel between the two warriors into a popular theme. It is a story of vengeance, of which the following are the main outlines:

Sasaki Ganryu is a man of mature years. He falls in love with the daughter of a warrior named Yoshioka, who does not consent to Ganryu's courting his daughter. Ganryu flies into a temper and finally kills Yoshioka.

Yoshioka had a boy named Musashi, who decides to avenge his father and travels through different regions trying to find Ganryu. He finally arrives in Kyushu, where he is adopted by a warrior named Miyamoto Muemon. At that point he takes the name of Miyamoto Musashi.

MIYAMOTO MUSASHI, *Cormorant.*
Hanging scroll, ink on paper.
Eisei Bunko Foundation.

||||

IT MAY SEEM SURPRISING that
a great swordsman should also be
a fine painter, but in Japan it is
believed that all forms of art can
enrich each other. In addition, the
frequent connections between Zen
monks and samurai may have led
Musashi to follow the tradition of
ink painting. Appropriately, he
followed the style of Kaiho Yusho
(1533–1615), a major artist from a
samurai family who was famous for
the strength of his brushwork and
boldness of his composition.
Musashi's own paintings have a
visual tension and suppressed
energy in both their composition
and brushwork that attest to his
fierce spirit.

This painting is rare among the
works of Musashi because it bears
his signature as well as his seal. The
diagonal sweep of the cliff leads to
the opposing diagonal of the bird's
body, from which the neck sits so
the beak can jut out to the left. The
evocative sense of visual ambiguity,
here created by the rough black ink
of the cormorant's feet and nearby
rocky forms, is characteristic of
Musashi, as are the quivering
brushlines on the cormorant's neck
and belly; these have been called
"fighting brush" for their tensile
strength of expression.

MIYAMOTO MUSASHI, *Screens of Waterfowl. A pair of six-fold screens, ink and gold dust on paper. Eisei Bunko Foundation.*

||||

MUSASHI PAINTED THESE screens of waterfowl for the *daimyo* (feudal lord) Hosokawa Tadatoshi, who died in 1641 and they are still in the Hosokawa Collection. Since Musashi had arrived in the Hosokawa fief in 1640, the

screens can be securely dated to four or
five years before the artist's death in
1645. Most of Musashi's paintings were
presumably produced during these later
years, but there is little evidence of
specific dates for his other works.

The composition of these screens
follows models by earlier ink painters,
especially the panels in Shinju-an sub-
temple of Daitoku-ji attributed to Soga
Jasoku (fifteenth century). The curving
tree trunks at the end panels of the

screen act as visual parentheses,
containing the total composition and
focusing attention on the activities of
the waterfowl. These enfolding shapes
are echoed in one screen by a bending
branch and in the other by the graceful
arc of a goose's neck as it flies down for
a landing. Contrasts of light and dark
are especially effective in these screens,
not only between the birds and the grey
and gold washes behind them, but also
in the trees, reeds, and subtle land

forms. Although the subject of
waterfowl is not uncommon in the
ink-painting tradition, the emphatic
placement of the birds in the
foreground and the rough strength of
the brushwork mark these screens as
masterworks of Musashi's art.

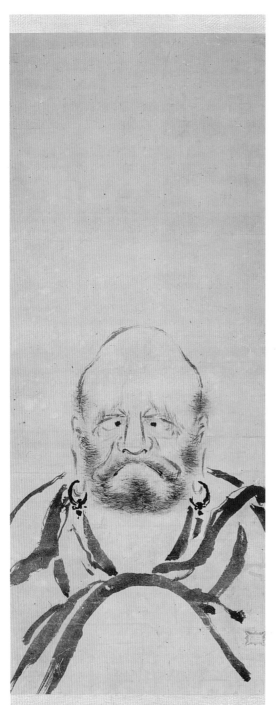

MIYAMOTO MUSASHI, *Daruma Meditating*. Detail, hanging scroll, ink on paper. Eisei Bunko Foundation.

||||

THIS PAINTING DEPICTS the first patriarch of Chan (Zen), and is also a portrait of meditation itself. We can see the great intensity of both the subject and the artist in the direct composition and immediacy of brushwork. Compared to works by professional artists of the time, Musashi's composition is bolder and there is less restraint in his brushwork.

There is a legend that Musashi once painted a Daruma in front of his *daimyo*, but was not satisfied with the result. Awakening at midnight, he took up his brush and painted a masterwork—at ease without the *daimyo* watching him. Here the crossed eyes of the patriarch signify intense meditation. The robes are depicted with strong, rough lines of black ink, while the hair and beard are rendered in dry, gray, overlapping strokes. The bold curve of the mouth, resembling the shape of Mount Fuji, gives added impact to the painting.

MIYAMOTO MUSASHI, *Dove on a Red Plum Tree. Hanging scroll, ink on paper. Eisei Bunko Foundation.*

||||

THE PLUM TREE is a symbol of physical endurance, since it blossoms early in the spring when there may still be snow on its branches. In addition, its old and gnarled limbs often seem to be dead, yet they will once again bear flowers to herald the arrival of spring. The dove, in contrast, is softly rounded, and offers painters the opportunity to experiment with merging ink tones. Here Musashi has emphasized the long "spirit-branches" of the tree, which shoot upwards in bold contrast to the "broken ink" treatment of the tree trunk. The artist achieves compositional balance between the heavy twisting trunk of the plum and its long branches by the gentleness of the dove, perched delicately like a giant blossom.

ARTIST UNKNOWN, *Edo Period,*
Portrait of Miyamoto Musashi.
Hanging scroll, ink and colors on paper.
Kumamoto Prefectural Museum of Art.

||||

SEVERAL PORTRAITS of Musashi
exist, although not all were done
during his lifetime. Here we see the
famous warrior seated, one sword
at his waist and the other placed by
his side. While the portrait
generally follows a tradition of
samurai depictions, we can sense
some of the controlled power of
Musashi through the intensity of his
face and the strong blunt lines that
define his robe.

Portraits frequently are
inscribed, usually by the sitter, but
here we can supply our own
imagined commentary through
everything that we know about this
remarkable man.

At last he meets Sasaki Ganryu in the town of Kokura and fights him, fulfilling his vow of vengeance.

Because of the popular success of this play, another play of the same type *(Nito eryuki)* appeared shortly afterward. The plot is as follows:

At the end of the sixteenth century, Sasaki Ganryu was the head of a dojo for swordsmanship in the town of Himeji. Ganryu had a dog that one day attacked a warrior named Yoshioka Tarozaemon, who killed it, cutting it down with his sword. Ganryu, becoming angry, killed Yoshioka and fled from the town.

Yoshioka had a disciple named Miyamoto Muemon who tried to avenge his master, but before he was able to accomplish this, he died of an illness. Muemon had a son named Musashi, who took the vow of vengeance upon himself.

Musashi traveled through various regions looking for Ganryu. He finally found an adept named Ganryu teaching his art in the town of Kokura under the name of Sasaki Kantaro. He succeeded in provoking a duel with him and killed him with a wooden sword that he had made from a piece of oar.

During the Edo period, several more plays were written that were inspired by these two. They were all stories of vengeance in which Sasaki Ganryu played the role of the "villain."

Musashi at the Battle of Osaka

We have no documentary evidence on Musashi for the two years following his duel with Kojiro. We only know that he participated in the battle of Osaka.

Tokugawa Ieyasu, who saw the Toyotomi family as a threat to his regime, gathered an army to attack Toyotomi Hideyori. The latter concentrated his forces at Osaka castle. The first confrontation, in 1614, was indecisive. A truce was negotiated with the condition that Toyotomi would fill in the moats surrounding his castle, which would make the castle vulnerable. A battle took place in May of 1615 in which Toyotomi's army suffered a total defeat. With this, Tokugawa made firm his power over all other feudal powers in Japan He was then seventy-four years old and died the following year. He had exhausted his vitality in solidly establishing the Tokugawa regime.

Most scholars think that Musashi fought on the Toyotomi side, as he had the previous time.

On the Kokura monument, this piece of evidence appears: "When [ ] Lord Hideyori raised his armies, everyone had heard the name of Musashi and was talking about his valor." (17, p. 213)

In this sentence, there is a blank space [ ], a space big enough for one letter that appears right before the name of Lord Hideyori. This is a traditional method called *ketsu ji ho* that was used to indicate respect toward a person whose name was cited in a text. It was customary to use this method for the emperor or for a great feudal lord.

Harada Mukashi is of the opinion that the sign of respect is an indication that Musashi fought in the battles on the side of Toyotomi Hideyori, but I don't think this expression of respect is sufficient to prove he was on that side. In classical Japanese literature, such expressions of respect are linked to rank and not to considerations of affinity. Going into this theory a little deeper, it could be pointed out that the expression "raised his armies" *(hei ran)* could be interpreted as an expression of revolt against a more legitimate power. Thus Harada's reasoning is not convincing on this point, since the text could also indicate that Musashi fought against Hideyori.

For anybody who had even a modicum of insight, it would not have been difficult to predict the outcome of this battle. We could almost say that everybody knew in advance that the army of the East would prevail. Could we be sure that Musashi, a man of strategy who had developed relations beyond his own clan, would stake his life on the losing side?

Most of those who think Musashi took the side of the army of the West, the Toyotomi side, reason as though Musashi's position had remained unchanged since the previous battle, fourteen years earlier. But at this time the criteria for fealty to a feudal lord were still flexible. Moreover, the alliances among the feudal lords had considerably changed since the battle of Sekigahara. Therefore it seems unlikely to me that Musashi remained rigidly fixed in his choice of which army to support.

In 1612, on the occasion of his duel with Sasaki Kojiro, Musashi had established a significant relationship, which was later confirmed, with a number of the principal vassals of Lord Hosokawa. A little before the battle of Sekigahara, this lord had sided with the East, the side of the Tokugawas. Moreover, we know that three or four years after the battle of Osaka, Musashi made an important relationship with Lord Ogasawara, who belonged to a family that was close to the Tokugawas. If he had been persecuted for having fought with the army of the West, it would be difficult to imagine this relationship developing. We may surmise that this relationship dates from the period of Musashi's duels.

These factors militate in favor of the hypothesis that Musashi fought with the army of the East. This is contrary to the usual theory; nevertheless, it seems more plausible to me. Moreover, during the ten last years of Musashi's life, he benefited from extraordinary manifestations of esteem on the part of the two lords, Ogasawara and Hosokawa.

On the whole, in the absence of proof positive indicating which side Musashi took in these battles, we must confine ourselves to stating hypotheses.

‖ 3 ‖

Deepening the Way

IF MUSASHI DID FIGHT in the army of the West, he would have had to spend several years in hiding to escape the pursuit of the Tokugawa warriors. If he was part of the army of the East, he would not have had this concern.

Even though there is very little documentary evidence for Musashi's life between the ages of thirty-one and fifty, we may surmise that this was a period of withdrawal into himself, of digesting the bloody experiences of the previous years. From this point on, he conducted any duels he had in such a way as not to kill his opponent. The last years of his life, during which he consolidated his teaching and composed his major works, are better known.

MATURITY

Musashi probably lived in Himeji for a few years between 1615 and 1624. After the Osaka war (1614–1615) the region of Banshu to the west of Osaka was divided into two fiefs, Himeji and Akashi. In 1617 Honda Tadamasa and his son Tadatoki received Himeji castle from the shogun, and Ogasawara Tadasane received Akashi castle. The families of Honda and Ogasawara were both very close to the Tokugawas. The strategy of the Tokugawa government was to stabilize its power by dividing territory among the feudal lords. It divided the fiefs in such a way that lords whose lineage was close to the Tokugawa family or those who had been allied with it for a long time were in a position to control the other lords in whom they had less confidence. Thus at the beginning of the Edo period, there was much moving about of feudal lords.

Honda and Ogasawara, whose lineages were linked with the Tokugawa family, had an important role to play vis-à-vis the other lords, especially those who had formerly been Tokugawa enemies. Nevertheless, the main priority for them was to strengthen and stabilize their power in their own fiefs. They had need of talented vassals. These were the circumstances when Musashi arrived in Himeji. According to Tominaga Kengo: "Himeji was located in the region of Banshu, of which Musashi's mother was a native. Banshu was adjacent to the region of Musashi's birth. Musashi doubtless spent a part of his childhood in the Banshu region. . . . I suppose that when he returned to Himeji, Musashi lived there for a rather long period of time." (12, p. 89)

During this period, Musashi adopted two children, who took the names of Miyamoto Mikinosuke and Miyamoto Iori.

The Adoption of Miyamoto Mikinosuke

Musashi's adoption of Mikinosuke is described as follows in the *Hyoho senshi denki:*

One day Musashi was traveling on horseback on the Settsu road. At the inn at Nishinomiya, a boy of fourteen or fifteen took his horse for him. Musashi perceived that the boy had extraordinary qualities. Talking with him, Musashi recognized his worth.

Musashi said: "Wouldn't you like to become my son? I would find a good lord for you."

"You are very kind to make such an offer, but I have old parents. The reason I am working as a hostler is to take care of them. If I became your adoptive son, my parents would immediately fall on hard times. I must therefore tell you no, with my thanks."

After listening to him, Musashi asked the boy to take him home with him, and he met his parents. He explained his plans for their son to them and received their consent to adopt him. He gave them a small sum of money so that they could live without difficulty and asked their neighbors to take good care of them. Thus he took the boy away with him.

Musashi educated him for a certain period of time; then he presented him to Taiyu [Honda Tadatoki], the lord of Himeji castle in Banshu, who thought highly of him and gave him the name Mikinosuke. In this way he rose to a considerable rank.

Later, for an unknown reason, Mikinosuke took leave of his lord and went up to Edo, during which time unfortunately Lord Taiyu died. When Musashi learned this news at Osaka, he concluded that Mikinosuke would surely come in the next days and decided he would receive him with a farewell feast. And in fact, Mikinosuke did arrive, and learning that Musashi knew in advance that he would come, he was very happy and took pleasure in the feast.

While he was with Musashi, picking up a glass of sake, Mikinosuke said, "I drink this glass to bid you farewell."

Even though he had taken leave of his lord, in learning of his death, he returned to Edo to follow him in death. He went to say his good-byes to his adoptive father. Such an attitude can only arouse sympathy. (9, p. 230)

When Honda Tadaoki died in 1626, Mikinosuke killed himself by seppuku in order to follow his lord. In this way he expressed his thanks to this lord, through whom he had attained the respectable rank of warrior.

The act of a vassal who follows his lord into death to serve him in the beyond is called *junshi*. In Japan this custom remained current until the middle of the seventeenth century. The Tokugawa regime prohibited it in 1663 by military decree. During the period when Mikinosuke died, this act was highly esteemed.

We may suppose that the adoption of Mikinosuke took place not long after the battle of Osaka, because according to the text cited above, Musashi educated him "for a certain period of time" before presenting him to Honda Tadatoki, whom Mikinosuke served for a number of years. Honda Tadatoki died in 1626. Thus all these events took place in a period of eleven years.

If Musashi raised Mikinosuke for three or four years before the boy entered into Honda's service, to attain a considerable rank Mikinosuke must have worked at least a few years with the lord—four or five years, presuming that he left his service a year before Honda's death.

Calculating in this way, I conclude that Musashi adopted Mikinosuke between 1615 and 1617. Now, after the battle of Osaka (1615), the Tokugawa government persecuted the warriors from the army of the West. If Musashi had to flee, it is difficult to imagine that he would have traveled openly on horseback on the road from Nishinomiya, in the immediate vicinity of Osaka. If Musashi was able to accommodate the ambition of this child and was able to convince his parents to allow him to adopt him, it is probable that he was not forced to conceal himself. All that would have been impossible if Musashi had been a man pursued by the Tokugawa government. That would not only have meant the loss of any hope of employment but also have imperiled his very existence.

Quite to the contrary, in adopting a child Musashi doubtless was hopeful he could find an interesting situation for him. This supports my hypothesis that Musashi fought in the battle of Osaka on the side of the East.

The genealogy of the Shinmen family attributes a completely different origin to Mikinosuke. According to this genealogy, Mikinosuke was the grandson of Shinmen Sokan and the cousin of Musashi, but no other evidence is provided to confirm this line of descent. A possible theory is that this line of descent was concealed because of Shinmen Sokan's having sided with the army of the West.

Here is the pertinent excerpt from the Shinmen family genealogy as reproduced by Harada Mukashi:

Miyamoto Mikinosuke, a lad of exceptional beauty, was skilled in the art of the sword. Being related to Musashi, he served as a page to Nakatsukasa Taiyu Tadatoki, a descendant of Honda Mino no kami Tadamasa, lord of Himeji castle in Banshu. Later on he became the head page and received seven hundred *koku*.

Died following Lord Tadatoki, the third year of the Kanei period [1626]. (17, p. 156)

Harada thinks that Musashi participated in the planning of the town of Himeji during the years that he lived there with Mikinosuke.

In addition, several authors, without clearly specifying their source, cite a document according to which "Mikinosuke was the grandson of Shimanosuke, the military prefect of Lord Mizuno Katsunari, lord of Fukuyama castle in the region of Bigo [Okayama]." (2, p. 136)

The Duel with Miyake Gunbei

Two versions exist of Musashi's combat with Miyake, a vassal of Honda Tadamasa, lord of Himeji castle. One is related in the chronicles preserved in the fiefs of the region (*Bisan hokan* and *Nokokujin monogatari*). The other is told in the *Nippon kendo shi,* a collection of chronicles from the Edo period. I have translated them here as they were given by Tominaga Kengo in his *Shijitsu Miyamoto Musashi*.

The first version is as follows:

Lord Honda was famous among the Tokugawa lords for his bravery, and a number of his vassals were important adepts of the martial arts. Some years after Lord Honda was established at Himeji as governor of the region, Musashi opened a dojo in the town and put up a sign saying: "Miyamoto Musashi, the number one adept of the sword in Japan."

Seeing this sign, Honda's vassals became indignant and wanted to run him out of town or kill him. Lord Honda then said: "If Musashi is really the number one adept of the sword in Japan, I would like to take him on as my vassal. If he is not, you only need defeat him in combat and send him away." He sent Miyake Gundayu, the best adept among his vassals, to test Musashi's abilities.

Miyake visited Musashi, who kept him waiting for more than an hour, during which time Miyake said: "What an ill-mannered man! Keeping me waiting, me, one of the principal vassals of the fief, whereas he is a warrior without a lord!"

Miyake had to wait still longer before Musashi came out to see him. Miyake immediately asked to fight with him. Musashi, laughing, replied: "If I had been informed that the purpose of your visit was for us to measure ourselves against each other in combat, I would have come sooner. Only I was in the midst of playing *go* with a guest. Would you care to come out in the garden? I will leave the choice of weapons up to you, either a real sword or a wooden sword, as you prefer."

Miyake was irritated, but his purpose, on his lord's orders, was to test Musashi's ability and not to kill him. He cut a piece of bamboo in the garden and took it for his weapon. Musashi took his own wooden sword.

The combat was over in an instant, and Miyake was beaten. He acknowledged that the title Musashi had arrogated to himself was accurate. He gave this information to his lord.

Lord Honda wished to take on Musashi as his vassal. Musashi refused this offer. He accepted only to teach his art to Honda's vassals and to receive two hundred *koku*. This is the way that Musashi's Enmei ryu spread in this region. (1 2, pp. 87–89)

The second version is as follows:

During his stay at Himeji, Musashi made the acquaintance of the various vassals of Lord Honda, and he helped design the plans for the construction of the town of Himeji as well as the various temples and gardens.

It was during this period that he received a challenge from an adept named Miyake Gunbei. Gunbei was a warrior who had fought in various battles. He was a sword adept of the Togun ryu and also of the bare-handed combat art of the Araki ryu. Everyone recognized him as the number one adept of the fief.

Being confident in his art, Gunbei visited Musashi with three of his friends when he learned of his arrival in the fief of Himeji. When they arrived, Musashi kept them waiting for a moment; then he came out with two wooden swords in his hands. After a brief exchange of introductions, Musashi said, "All four of you can attack me at once, if you like."

Gunbei got angry and took his place facing Musashi alone, holding his wooden sword. Intending to win with a single blow, Gunbei raised his weapon over his head, whereas Musashi backed up all the way to the entrance and adopted the crossed-sword guard position.

After a moment of tension, Musashi advanced toward Gunbei with this crossed-sword guard. Gunbei struck, aiming at the top of Musashi's head. Musashi parried, separating his two swords; then he crossed them again, pressing down on Gunbei's sword. Freeing his sword, Gunbei attacked again, and Musashi parried as he had before, then he backed one step away and recrossed his swords. Musashi now had his back to the wall. Gunbei, thinking that he had found a good opportunity, lowered his sword to the level of his chest and leaped forward to run his opponent through.

Musashi shouted: "That's not what you should do!" and parrying Gunbei's attack with the small sword in his left hand, touched the point of his other sword to his adversary's cheek. Gunbei was wounded because of his own momentum and was bleeding at the cheek.

Musashi gave him some medicine and a towel, calmly told him to wipe away the blood, and waited.

Gunbei realized that he was far from Musashi's level and decided, along with his friends, to become his student. Later he said: "When Musashi came out with his two swords in his hands, I was seized by a sense of dread stronger than that which I felt at the time of the battle of Sekigahara, when just before the two sides clashed, the two armies were taken with a deep and horrifying calm."

It seems that Musashi stayed at Himeji for some years, not as Lord Honda's vassal, but as his guest.

The Adoption of Miyamoto Iori

Before presenting a translation of the account of Musashi's second adopted son as reported in the *Nitenki,* it might be good to explain the origin of this document, since many authors who have written about Musashi regard it as a faithful account of his life.

The *Nitenki* (Writings on the Two Heavens) is a text begun in 1712 by Toyoda Seigo, a vassal of Lord Matsui who was an adept of the sword from Musashi's school. He recorded comments he collected from Musashi's direct disciples. His son Seishu added remarks that he himself collected, and his grandson Toyoda Kagefusa reworked and completed the text in 1755. This work cannot be accepted without some critical reservations, because it contradicts other documentary sources that are more reliable. It is based on historical facts and also doubtless on the accounts of firsthand witnesses of the last period of Musashi's life, but the text, which has been revised a number of times, is in essence a literary effort that leaves room for considerable doubt about the veracity of the details it reports. We must also take into account that it relates the master's history as an exemplary story based on the accounts of his disciples, which were doubtless embellished.

The Adoption of Miyamoto Iori according to the *Nitenki*

In the course of a journey in the province of Dewa [Yamagata], while traveling through the region of Hitachi [Ibaraki], Musashi passed a place called the Shohoji Field. He saw a young boy of thirteen or fourteen who was carrying a pail full of loaches. Musashi asked if he could buy a few. The boy offered to give them all to him, including the pail. Musashi said, "That's too much for just me. A few will be enough; I'll take them wrapped in a cloth."

The boy, laughing, said: "I'll give you all of them, including the pail. There's no point in being stingy." And off he went, leaving everything behind. Musashi accepted with thanks.

The following day he crossed some wild country, lost his way, and was unable to find an inn. He went on walking for three leagues after the sun went down. He was wondering what to do, since to get to where there were houses, he would have had to go back four or five leagues. At this moment he saw a light at the foot of a mountain. Going toward it, he found a small house. When he called out, a strange young boy came out and asked what he wanted. Musashi said, "I am a traveler who has lost his way in the night and I can't find a place to stay. Could you put me up for the night?"

The boy said: "It's only a little hut made of grass. I don't even have anything to eat myself, so how could I provide hospitality for a guest?"

Musashi said: "For a traveler like myself, just a roof will be enough."

At this moment the boy recognized Musashi and said, "You're the gentleman to whom I sold the loaches yesterday!"

Musashi, surprised, recognized the boy: "So, it's you!"

"If it's you, then come in."

He had Musashi sit down and made tea.

Musashi asked: "Why are you living here by yourself? Where are your parents?

The boy replied: "I was born in the village of Shohoji. My father gave up farming and decided to live here. But my parents are dead. I have a sister married to a farmer who lives three leagues from here."

As he was talking, he offered Musashi a little rice mixed with millet. The night was getting on, and the autumn wind was glacial.

Musashi went to sleep but was awakened in the middle of the night by the loud sound of a blade being sharpened. He yawned and wondered if this lad was perhaps in cahoots with some bandits. Then the boy, hearing him moving around, said, "Why aren't you sleeping?"

Musashi replied, "I was awakened by the sound of you sharpening a blade."

The boy replied, laughing, "You look like a strapping fellow, but are you maybe a coward? I am so weak, how could I kill you, even with a knife?"

"So why are you sharpening a blade now?"

The boy replied: "I will tell you without hiding anything. My father died yesterday. I want to bury his body next to my mother's grave, which is farther up the mountain behind us. But since I am not able to carry him, I thought I would cut his body in two. I could carry it in two trips."

Musashi was surprised and moved by his story. He said: "Fortunately, I'm here this evening. I can help you carry him so he can be buried."

Musashi and the boy carried the dead man. Musashi took the shoulders, and the boy took the feet. They went up the mountain together and buried him next to the boy's mother. Then they put up a board with the dead man's name on it. By the time they got back to the house, it was already dawn.

The boy said, "I'm alone now, you can stay here for a while."

Musashi said, "Instead of staying here by yourself, if you came with me, you would have the chance to become a warrior.

"I could follow you anywhere, but if the idea is to be your servant the rest of my life, I won't come. I will come with you only if I have a chance to become a great warrior who can carry a lance and who travels on horseback. Otherwise, it's better for me to stay here."

Musashi said, "If you come with me, you'll have that chance."

Happy, the boy put his sword in his belt and walked toward Musashi.

"Are you ready to leave any time?"

"Yes, sir, I can leave immediately. Because I haven't had any news of my sister for a long time. It is not necessary to inform her. So it's useless to leave this house behind."

He set fire to the house and followed Musashi.

They traveled through various regions and arrived at Bizen-Kokura. The boy took up residence there. He took the name of Miyamoto Iori and became a vassal of Lord Ogasawara. Thus he became a warrior who could carry a lance, ride a horse, and pass down his status to future generations. Iori's father had earlier been a vassal of Lord Mogami in the province of Dewa. Having become a *ronin* (warrior without a lord), he went to live at Shohoji Field and worked as a farmer. Iori, having become the adoptive son of Musashi, took Miyamoto as his family name.

In the ninth year of the Kanei period [1632], Lord Ogasawara Ukyodayu Tadasane was appointed governor of the Bungo region, replacing Lord Hosokawa Echizen no kami Tadatoshi, who had been appointed governor of the Higo region. In the eleventh year of the same era, Musashi arrived in Kokura. Lord Tadasane welcomed him warmly, and Musashi remained there for some years. He was then fifty-one years old.

In the fourteenth year of the same era [1637], Christians in revolt attacked Shinabara castle in the Bizen region and occupied it. Lord Tadasane went off to fight them, and Musashi, now fifty-six, accompanied him. After the battles, when contributions to the military effort were being evaluated, Miyamoto Iori, who had gone with Musashi, was singled out for his exceptional conduct and was promoted to the rank of vassal. He later became one of the principal vassals and received two thousand *koku*. In addition, Lord Tadasane officially recognized his status as an adoptive son of Musashi, appointed to serve him. (2, p. 176)

According to this version, Iori's father was a vassal of Lord Mogami. In 1622 the fief of Mogami was shaken by an internal conflict in the course of which a group of vassals attempted to take power. The Tokugawa government punished the Mogamis by banishing them from their fief. The vassals were then without a lord. It was probably as a result of these events that Iori's father became a farmer.

Although this relationship is the one most often accepted, I and a number of other authors are of the opinion that the account of the meeting between Musashi and Iori given above is a literary fiction, because it is in contradiction with what Iori wrote on the signboard at the Tomari shrine and also with the genealogy of the Miyamoto family, according to which Iori was a nephew of Musashi's. (17, pp. 97–98) By contrast, the rest of the account is in agreement with other documentary sources.

The information available about Iori provides us with some reference points for Musashi's life during this period. The year of the death of Mikinosuke, Musashi's first adoptive son, was 1626. His voluntary act of following his lord into death was very highly thought of, and this surely redounded to Iori's benefit. That same year, thanks to his adoptive father, Miyamoto Iori, at the age of fifteen, entered into the service of Lord Ogasawara, initially as a page. We may therefore surmise that that year Musashi was already at Akashi, the fief adjacent to Himeji.

If Iori was fifteen in 1626, he was eleven when his father found himself without a lord, and if he was adopted by Musashi at the age of thirteen, this would have been in 1624. In that case, if we are to believe the account in the *Nitenki,* Musashi would have left Himeji at one point to travel in the north of Japan, then would have returned to Akashi around 1626. According to the other hypothesis, Musashi adopted Iori not far from Himeji.

About Iori

Iori entered Lord Ogasawara's service as a page at fifteen. A short time later he became an official vassal. He was twenty when Ogasawara established his seat in the north of Kyushu in 1632. At that point he received twenty-five hundred *koku*[1] (two thousand according to another source) and became one of the principal vassals. Ogasawara governed at Akashi for fifteen years, during which time he took on seventy-six new vassals. Iori was just one of those seventy-six vassals to begin with, but six years after having entered Ogasawara's service, at the age of only twenty, he was given a rank beyond other vassals who had been in service for many years. Iori's rise was exceptional. Moreover, in 1638, six years later, Iori received fifteen hundred *koku* more because of his efforts in the battles connected with the siege of Shimabara. Thus at the age of only twenty-six, he occupied the first place among the principal vassals, with an income of four thousand *koku*. Ogasawara's other principal vassals did not receive much more than two thousand *koku,* and during this period a warrior who received two hundred *koku* was regarded as already doing quite well. It is difficult to find another rise in the hierarchy during this period as rapid as Iori's.

It is difficult to imagine that Iori, even if he was very gifted, could have achieved such a level of promotion at such a young age in such a short time on his own. However, the name of Musashi does not appear in the official Ogasawara papers. What role did Musashi play in supporting Iori's rise?

Harada Mukashi's view, which I share, is that Musashi had a long-term strategy of acquiring a position for his family within the feudal system:

> Musashi shared the tragic destiny of certain other feudal figures— he did not have the good fortune to have a lord to serve. With his innate intelligence, Musashi planned to integrate the Miyamoto family into the feudal system. In this system, if a lord met a tragic destiny, his vassals were obliged to die with him. By having his talented adoptive children become part of different fiefs, he had a high probability of succeeding with at least one of them. In this way, Iori met his expectation. (17, p. 31)

Musashi's Diverse Activities

Harada cites the following passage from *Writings on Lord Ogasawara Tadasane:*

> Next to the third building of Akashi castle, there was a long piece of abandoned ground, the development of which was entrusted by the lord to the famous Miyamoto Musashi. This piece of land was transformed into a garden in which there was a fountain, some miniature mountains, trees, flowers, a tea house, and also a

field for playing ball. He had alpine plants brought in from the regions of Miki and Akashi and stones from Awa, Sanuki, and the island of Shodo. Work on this lasted for a year. (17, p. 163)

So it seems Musashi worked on various building and development projects at Himeji and also Akashi. His gifts in the various artistic domains are pointed out in the text on the Kokura monument: "He was well versed in all the artistic domains. Moreover, there was almost nothing he did not know regarding the arts of craftsmanship and construction." (17, p. 121) We may suppose that Musashi had practical experience in the art of carpentry, which he wrote about in the *Gorin no sho*.

Musashi took journeys to the various regions of Japan. Tominaga Kengo writes: "I think Edo is one of the towns in which Musashi stayed for the longest time. Edo was the political, economic, and cultural center. A number of important adepts of the martial arts lived there, among others, Yagyu Tajimanokami, Ono Tadaaki. . . . There was a significant number of public dojos. It would have been impossible for Musashi to overlook this town." (12, p. 85)

Ogi Kakubei wrote in his *Shinmen Musashi ron* in 1851: "Lord Hojo Akinokami and Musashi were each other's disciples. The former taught Musashi military strategy, while the latter taught Akinokami individual strategy. Musashi went to Edo several times and stayed there a fairly long time." (27, p. 240)

Hojo Akinokami was born in 1608 and was thus twenty-four years younger than Musashi. It is difficult to imagine that he could have taught Musashi, being that much younger. Consequently, we may surmise that they were in touch with each other during the last years of Musashi's stay in Edo. If Musashi was then nearly fifty, Hojo must have been twenty-six. It is also possible that attributing the position of teacher to Hojo was a matter of politeness in view of his high position. Musashi was then completing his thinking on strategy, and it is hardly conceivable that a young man of twenty-six could have been his teacher on the way of strategy, which he had been pursuing since his youth.

Musashi also stayed for some years in Nagoya. Tominaga Kengo gives a passage from a document on Lord Owari's genealogy that mentions him:

> In the article on Lord Koyo, we find the following passage:
> The lord was a large man, and he liked the martial arts. That is why adepts from all over Japan came to Nagoya. There were more than two hundred masters, each of whom represented a school. Thus Miyamoto Musashi, the greatest adept in Japan, came. The lord, seeing his art, admired him, saying that his was an exceptional art of sublime subtleties. The lord proposed that he become his vassal, but Musashi refused. He remained as a guest and stayed for three years. (12, p. 95)

There are various anecdotes about Musashi's time in Nagoya.

During this period, Musashi's center of gravity was at Himeji and Akashi, but he traveled in various regions of Japan, staying several years in Edo, Nagoya, and Osaka.

Duels of the Mature Period

When he reached maturity, Musashi stopped looking for opportunities for combat. The duels he engaged in were requested by his adversaries or more or less required by the lords of the towns in which he lived. We have already described the duel with Miyake Gunbei.

The Fight with Two Vassals of Tokugawa Yoshinao

After staying at Himeji, Musashi traveled in various regions and stayed for a time at Nagoya in the fief of Owari.

Hatta Kuroemon, a vassal of Lord Owari's, wrote a chronicle of the martial arts in 1684, in which he provides the account that I give below in a slightly abridged translation:

> While he was traveling, Musashi stopped at Nagoya, the capital of the fief of Owari. Lord Tokugawa Yoshinao invited him to be his

guest, and at the lord's request, he fought two adepts of the fief. For this combat, Musashi used two wooden swords. Taking the presence of the lord into account, he avoided striking a blow in defeating his adversaries.

Against his first adversary, Musashi adopted the crossed-sword guard position and advanced toward him. His opponent backed away, pushed back by the energy emanating from Musashi and his swords. Being unable to get away from the points of Musashi's swords, which were directed at his face, he was pushed all the way to the wall. Once he had his back against the wall, he was forced to back along the whole length of the dojo wall until he ended up having gone around the complete circumference of the hall.

Musashi said, "My lord, such is my way of fighting."

He prevailed over the second opponent in the same way.

After this confrontation, the name of Musashi was known throughout the Owari region, and many adepts came to become his students. Takemura Masatoshi and Hayashi Shiryu excelled, and they propagated Musashi's school.

Hayashi Shiryu was initially an adept of the Shinto ryu, and before becoming Musashi's student, he fought against him. Musashi defeated him rather badly, and he lost consciousness as he was leaving the dojo. Musashi felt that Hayashi had shown talent for the art in the way he had fought, so he had his students take care of him. When he had healed, Hayashi became Musashi's student. When Musashi left the region, Hayashi continued to study in the School of Musashi under the guidance of Takemura Yoemon, one of Musashi's most senior students, and he eventually received the final transmission of the Enmei ryu. (27, p. 183)

Thus Musashi's Enmei ryu spread successfully in the Owari region. In 1744, 99 years after Musashi's death, the adepts of the Enmei ryu came together with Souda Busuke, who was the head of the Hayashi branch, and they put up a monument to Musashi that still stands. In 1794, 149 years after Musashi's death, another branch of the same school erected another monument in Musashi's memory. These monuments bear witness to the major presence of the School of Musashi in this region.

We can be fairly sure that Musashi's stay in Nagoya occurred around 1630, when Musashi was forty-five. Here is a famous anecdote from that period:

> During his stay in Nagoya, Musashi saw a warrior in the street whose way of carrying himself he found striking. He approached, and the warrior looked at him also. At the moment they were passing each other, Musashi said, "Aren't you Lord Yagyu Hyogonosuke?"
>
> "I am. Aren't you Lord Miyamoto Musashi?"
>
> Though they had never met each other before, each adept had recognized the other, concluding that, because of his way of carrying himself and the martial energy that he emanated, it could not possibly be anyone else. Thus, instead of measuring themselves against each other in combat, they conversed like old friends at Yagyu's house. (9, p. 43)

This anecdote is often told as an example of the recognition of the high quality of one great adept by another adept of an equivalent quality, but its historical authenticity is dubious.

The Encounter with the Lance Adept Takada Matabei

In 1634 Musashi, who was then fifty years old, fought in Kyushu against Takada Matabei, a lance adept of the Hozoin ryu. Musashi showed his superiority but in such a way as to save the honor of his adversary. (See the account of this combat on page 115).

Lord Matsudaira Izumo no kami Noamasa and His Vassals

Lord Matsudaira Naomasa was himself a valiant warrior. He fought in the battles of Osaka of 1614 and 1615, and killed more than thirty enemies by beheading them, and he received particular praise from Tokugawa Ieyasu. For this reason he encouraged the practice of the martial arts in his fief, which boasted a large number of adepts.

The *Tanji Hokin hikki* reports the following anecdote:

During Musashi's stay at Izumo [Shimane], Lord Naomasa invited him to fight against his strongest vassal.

The library garden was chosen as the place for the combat. Musashi's opponent chose as his weapon an eight-sided staff 2.4 meters in length and took up a position next to a stairway that descended into the garden. Musashi slowly walked down the stairs holding his two wooden swords. When he had gone down two steps, he suddenly took up a middle-level guard position and aimed the points of his weapons at his opponent's face. The adversary, surprised, took up a guard position with his staff. Musashi launched an attack and struck both his arms and then his head. His opponent fell to the ground.

Lord Naomasa was angered by the ease with which his strongest vassal had been defeated and wanted to fight himself. Musashi replied: "In truth, to understand strategy, the best thing is to practice oneself."

Though his vassals attempted to dissuade him, Naomasa took up a wooden sword and assumed a position facing Musashi. But just by taking up a guard position against Musashi, Naomasa was pushed back all the way to the wall. This combat was repeated twice, and the third time, Naomasa had to back up all the way to the *tokonoma* in the library. Gathering his courage, Naomasa made a strike; Musashi broke through. Naomasa's wooden sword was broken in two, and the violence of the blow was such that the part that was broken off flew upward and crashed through the ceiling.

This combat convinced Naomasa of Musashi's capabilities, and he himself became his student. Musashi remained for some time at Izumo and taught his art in the fief. (27, p. 184)

Matsudaira Naomasa came to Izumo in 1638. If this combat took place in that year, Musashi would have been fifty-four years old.

Musashi wrote in the Scroll of Earth, "When I reached the age of fifty, I naturally found myself on the way of strategy. Since that day, I live without needing to search further for the way." This calls for two remarks.

First of all, with regard to what Musashi wrote, the way he fought with Matsudaira Naomasa seems to have been a bit harsh, close to his way of fighting in his youth.

Second, did Musashi really go off on another journey at the age of fifty-four, eight years before his death? If we go by the most reliable documentary evidence, it would appear that Musashi settled down after 1634 into a more sedentary lifestyle; it was for the first time in his life and lasted for the rest of it. So the question remains open.

The Encounter with Shioda Hamanosuke Shosai

From 1640 until his death, Musashi resided in the fief of Higo as the guest of Lord Hosokawa Tadatoshi. He transmitted the most mature form of his art in this fief.

Shioda Hamanosuke, formerly a student of Musashi Munisai, Musashi's father, was a vassal of Hosokawa's, an adept of the art of the staff and of jujutsu. Here is what is reported in the *Bokuden:*

A short time after Musashi's arrival in Higo, Shioda requested Musashi to fight him.

Shioda's weapon was a staff 2.6 meters long, whereas Musashi chose a small sword of wood. Each time Shioda tried to penetrate and attack, Musashi prevented him from starting his movement. Thus Shioda was defeated. Musashi said: "This time, we are going to fight attempting immobilization in the jujutsu style. I will sit down here without a sword. If you succeed in getting within a distance of one *ken* [1.8 meters] of me, I will consider myself beaten."

Angered, Shioda tried to immobilize Musashi, but he was unable to cross the line Musashi had indicated, as though there were an energy field around Musashi's body that protected him. Persuaded of Musashi's art, Shioda asked to be allowed to take his place among his students. Since he also appreciated Shioda's art of the staff, Musashi had his students study it. What is usually called "the staff of the School of Musashi" has its origin in Shioda's art. (27, pp. 185–186)

The Encounter with Ujii Yashiro

In 1640, at the request of Lord Hosokawa, Musashi fought Ujii Yashiro, an adept of the Yagyu school of swordsmanship. Musashi defeated him without delivering a blow (see the account of this encounter on page 125). Musashi was then fifty-six years old and would die in five years.

This combat and the one before it were probably the last ones in his life.

The Significance of Musashi's Last Duels

Musashi's combats during the years of his maturity recall what is known today in kendo as *kizeme,* literally "*ki* offensive," at its highest level. Toward the end of his life, Musashi fought his duels by dominating his adversaries without striking a blow. This way of defeating an adversary would in the future become the ultimate goal of the Japanese martial arts, in the form they acquired during the Edo period.

In the course of the preceding centuries, fighting had generally meant taking someone's life, whereas starting in the seventeenth century, succeeding in dominating one's opponent without killing him became the objective that little by little came to pervade the martial arts. This change of purpose went hand in hand with the transformation of the lifestyle of the Japanese warrior.

But what does "dominating the opponent without killing him" mean in a fight to the death? What is worthy of thinking about here is that this has nothing to do with the application of an ethical outlook; rather, it is the culmination of a development in combat technique. In the warrior culture, which was based from the beginning on pragmatism, ethics and philosophy are the products of technique. Technique here came to take in the total human being. The technical quest thus included the mental state without which it is impossible to reach technical perfection.

What is going on when Musashi is able to dominate his adversary merely by pointing his sword at him? Why is the adversary compelled to back away? Why was Shioda unable to move closer to Musashi's body than 1.8 meters?

These questions are being explored in other forms today by contemporary kendo.

MUSASHI'S LAST YEARS

Musashi's life up to this point was a series of journeys and adventures. It seems that from this point on, having reached the summit of his art, he was looking for the stability that would allow him to establish his school in a lasting fashion.

The Kokura Period

In 1634 Musashi was fifty years old. He went to Kyushu, to the town of Kokura, where his adoptive son Iori was in the service of Lord Ogasawara. It must be said that not all scholars agree on this point. Some think that Iori remained with Musashi until 1634, and it was only in that year that Musashi got him into Lord Ogasawara's service. According to this theory, Iori traveled with Musashi until 1634. As we saw above, I favor the hypothesis according to which Iori entered Ogasawara's service in 1626. In support of this view, here is the text written by Iori on a signboard at the Tomari shrine: "From the time I wore a child's hairstyle, at Akashi in the province of Banshu [Harima], I have served Lord Ogasawara Tadasane, who came from Shinshu. Today, I have come to Kokura, following my lord."

From this it appears evident that when Musashi arrived in Kokura in 1634, Iori was already one of the vassals of Lord Ogasawara, who had been appointed there only two years earlier.

According to the *Tanji Hokin hikki,* when Musashi arrived in Kyushu, before going to Kokura he visited Lord Kuroda Tadasuke at Chikuzen Fukuoka:

When he heard of Musashi's arrival, Lord Kuroda proposed to the committee of his principal vassals that he be taken on as the master of strategy with an income of three thousand *koku*. But no one agreed with him. And two or three days later, someone said to the lord: "Musashi's face is strange, and we do not think he is capable of being a good teacher for young people. On top of that, we understand that he has no intention of entering into official service." Lord Kuroda then said, "Fine, act as though I didn't say anything the other day." (12, p. 104)

If Musashi had not intended to offer himself as the master of arms of the fief, why did he go to Fukuoka without stopping at Kokura, which was on the way? Is it true, as some scholars think, that he had tried up to that point to find an important position as a teacher without ever being able to do so satisfactorily? As far as his own ambition was concerned, was his life a series of failures?

During the previous period, Musashi had gone to Edo several times and had stayed there altogether a relatively long time. Some authors think that Musashi tried in vain there to acquire the position of master of strategy to the shogun. Ozawa Masao gives the following interpretation, based on a variety of documents:

Musashi, who had been presented by Hayashi Razan [famous Confucianist scholar, teacher to the shogun] was summoned to the castle. Shogun Iemitsu questioned Yagyu Munenori on Musashi's personality. Yagyu replied: "His strategy is good, but his face is strange, with long uncoiffed hair. I do not think he is worthy of being the shogun's teacher."

Iemitsu was convinced by Yagyu and gave up the idea of testing Musashi, but since he had been summoned to the castle, he thought it would be a pity to send him away without having him do anything. The principal vassals were familiar with Musashi's reputation as a painter. So the shogun asked Musashi to paint a screen. Musashi painted wild ducks on it.

When Matsudaira Masayuki, Shogun Iemitsu's younger brother, was transferred to the fief of Aizu, he took this screen with him, and it was preserved as a family treasure. It was lost in the fires that followed the bombings of 1945. . . .

Later, in a letter addressed to Nagaoka Sado, Musashi expressed his regret at having lost the chance to convince the shogun of his art: "I regret that I did not have an opportunity to prove my talents." (9, p. 50)

Does this mean that Musashi was unable to realize his greatest ambition? Some authors think that he tried to achieve what he had not been able to accomplish by himself through his adoptive sons and the students he took on later in his life.

In fact, Musashi does seem to have taken steps to acquire a position with various great feudal lords. According to Nakanishi Seizo, Musashi's pride prevented him from working in the service of a lord with less than 500,000 *koku*. He presented himself to the shogun, and in Nagoya he presented himself to Lord Owari, who had 620,000 *koku*, and to Lord Kuroda, who had 523,000 *koku*. Lord Ogasawara of Kokura had only 150,000 *koku*.

After visiting Fukuoka, Musashi arrived at Kokura castle in the Buzen region. He was received by Lord Ogasawara Tadasane. In the regional historical chronicle of Buzen, entitled *Buzen kokushi,* we find the following passage:

Lord Tadasane of Kokura was well versed in strategy. He invited as his guest Miyamoto Musashi, the best adept of strategy in Japan. The lord took as masters in his fief Musashi Genshin for the sword and Takada Matabei for the lance. Respect was expressed for these masters by saying, "We have the two eyes, one of which is the best sword and the other the best lance. (12, p. 105)

Takada Matabei was a famous lance adept, a disciple of Nakamura Ichiroemon, who was trained by the monk Inei, the founder of the lance school of Hozoin.

The monk Inei, having studied the art of the sword in his youth under the guidance of Kamiizumi Nobutsuna and the art of the lance with Daizendayu Moritada, developed an art for lances with cruciform blades. Though his name became famous, it was not Inei's intention to propagate his art, since he found it contradictory, being a Buddhist monk of the Nichiren shu order, to study an art intended for killing. Deeming that his vocation was not the martial arts, he gave all his weapons to his disciple Nakamura Ichiroemon. He died in 1607 at the age of eighty-seven. The succession of the Hozoin school was taken over by the monk Inshun, but he was only nineteen years old at the time of Inei's death, and he had not received the founder's ultimate teaching. He received supplementary teaching from a monk of Okuzoin temple, a subsidiary of Hozoin temple. According to the *Nitenki*, Musashi fought in his youth against this monk from Okuzoin and defeated him.

An account of the bout between Musashi and Matabei is given in the *Hyoho senshi denki:*

> Takada Matabei, a vassal of Lord Ogasawara, was an adept in the art of the lance. During the master's [Musashi's] stay in Kokura, Matabei visited him frequently to receive his teaching. One day Lord Ogasawara requested them to fight. Matabei wished to refuse, but on the orders of the lord, he was compelled to fight. The master chose an ordinary wooden sword, and Matabei chose a bamboo lance.
>
> When Matabei attacked with the lance, the master calmly penetrated in close using the middle-level guard and won twice. The third time, when the master penetrated as before, the lance slid between his legs.
>
> The master said: "I was touched, therefore I lost this time." He told the onlookers that Matabei was a true adept of the lance.
>
> Later on, Matabei said: "Master Musashi is a true adept whom I was unable to touch. It was to save my face that he acted as though I had won once out of three times." (9, p. 234)

In *Miyamoto Musashi no subete,* Hiroshi Kato, basing his account on a variety of documentary evidence, writes:

Takada Matabei was an adept of the lance whose art was highly appreciated by Shogun Iemitsu. He was born in 1590 in the Iga region [Mie prefecture], and he entered Lord Ogasawara's service in 1623, when Ogasawara was at Akashi in the Banshu region. One document says that he fought Musashi in 1632, but Musashi came to Kokura with Iori in 1634. The combat must have taken place that year. Musashi was then fifty and Matabei forty-four.

The combat took place on the occasion of the January 1 holiday. Matabei chose a training lance that had a hook on the end, Musashi a wooden sword. Their weapons crossed three times and both made movements forward and backward. In the eyes of the onlookers, the match seemed equal, but Matabei suddenly let go of his weapon and declared himself beaten.

Since Lord Tadasane did not understand what had happened, Matabei explained to him: "The lance is long and the sword is short. The lance has an advantage. Although we crossed weapons three times, I was unable to win; therefore I can only consider myself to have been defeated."

Lord Tadasane, praising Musashi, proposed that he become his vassal. Musashi, instead of accepting, asked him to take Iori in his place. (27, p. 184)

Kato therefore espouses the view that Iori entered Ogasawara's service in 1634 on Musashi's recommendation, but we have seen that this hypothesis is hardly plausible.

In any case it seems clear that Musashi took up residence in Kokura and stayed there for six years. If Iori did indeed enter Ogasawara's service in 1626, it is probable that Musashi came in order to be near him. Some scholars think he was then already sick, following a difficult and ascetic life, and that he felt old age coming on.

But three years later, in 1637, a Christian revolt broke out at Shimabara in the Bizen region, also located on the island of Kyushu.

The Battles at Shimabara (1637–1638)

The Christian revolt that shook the shogunate in its process of consolidation had the effect of allowing the shogunate to strengthen the severity of its rule and to close the country to the outside world.

In 1543 Lord Tanegashima bought guns from the Portuguese. The value of guns was much appreciated by the Japanese, and they quickly began manufacturing them. In addition, Francis Xavier arrived in Kyushu in 1549 and began energetically preaching Christianity, which he continued to do over the course of two years. Christian culture penetrated into Japan in a spectacular fashion during the second half of the sixteenth century. The spread of Christianity went hand in hand with the development of commerce, which reached its peak toward the end of the sixteenth century. From the beginning of the Tokugawa regime, various measures were adopted to block or brake the introduction of Western culture.

In 1614, just before the battles of Osaka, the Tokugawa government promulgated a decree prohibiting Christianity on all Japanese territory. The application of this prohibition became more and more stringent and finally reached its culmination in the battles of Shimabara. These were later followed by definitive measures of *sakoku,* the closing off of Japan to the outside world, which remained in force for more than two centuries.

The Christians were numerous in the southern part of Kyushu, where resentment against the Tokugawa government was on the rise. Lord Matsukura of Shimabara castle carried out a severe policy against the peasants, who finally revolted and defeated his armies. The peasants of the island of Amakusa and the former vassals of the Christian lords joined forces. Thirty-eight thousand people, mostly Christian peasants, occupied Hara castle under the command of a boy of sixteen, Amakusa Shiro Tokisane, nicknamed the Child of Heaven. The rebels put up a cross on the top of the castle and fought under banners ornamented with crosses and images of the Virgin Mary. It took the government five months and 120,000 warriors to subdue the revolting peasants. The government even received military aid from the Dutch, who fired on the castle with their ships' cannons. It became a real war for the Toku-gawa government, which, following these events, strengthened its con-servative policies. After the battles of Shimabara, the government decided to exterminate the Christians, and in 1639 it closed Japan to the Western world, with the exception of limited contact with the Dutch.

Along with the prohibition of Christianity, the government estab-lished a system of attaching the population to regional Buddhist tem-ples. Each family was attached to a temple in its locale. This system was called *danka sei*. It continues in attenuated forms to the present day.

Musashi took part in the battles of Shimabara three years after his ar-rival in Kokura.

Harada reproduces a letter of Musashi's, which was found among the correspondence of the Arima family of the Maruoka fief of Echizen [Fukui]:

> Miyamoto Musashi
> To Lord Yuzaemon through the intermediary of pages
> I did indeed receive your papers and I would like to thank you. I am very glad that my son Iori was entrusted with the role of eval-uating military actions after the battle. I think I guided your vas-sals to appropriate positions. Everyone admired the way in which you and your father reached the main building of the castle. Hav-ing had some stones fall on my shin, I am having trouble walking. I therefore ask you to excuse me for not coming to greet you. Please allow me to express my great respect.
> I am highly honored to address to you these words of respect.
> At four in the morning,
> Genshin [hand-executed seal] (17, p. 240)

This letter was probably written the twenty-eighth of the second month of 1638 at the *tatsu-koku* hour, which is actually the equivalent of eight o'clock in the morning, right in the middle of the final attack on Hara castle by the governmental army.

At the siege of Shimabara, Musashi seems to have worked as part of the general staff of the Ogasawara forces. This was his sixth and last battle. Musashi probably advanced to the vicinity of the castle, close enough to have caught a stone thrown by the peasants on his shinbone. We do not know what Musashi did, but we know that Iori's work was greatly appreciated, because he received fifteen hundred *koku* more after the battle and rose to the rank of principal vassal.

Three years after the Shimabara insurrection was crushed, Musashi left Ogasawara to go to the fief of Hosokawa in Higo, where he passed the last five years of his life. Musashi had been closely connected to Lord Hosokawa from the time of his childhood. In 1612 it was under the protection of one of Hosokawa's principal vassals, Nagaoka Sado, that Musashi fought his duel against Sasaki Kojiro. During this period Hosokawa governed the north of Kyushu from Kokura. In 1632 Ogasawara established himself at Kokura to govern the region of Buzen, while Hosokawa went down to Higo region to govern a fief of 540,000 *koku*.

Nakanishi presents these circumstances in Musashi's life as follows:

At the time of the final attack of February 28, 1638, Musashi met Nagaoka Sado, principal vassal of Hosokawa, on the battlefield. Nagaoka knew that Musashi lived in Ogasawara's house, but he learned at this time that it was his son Iori who was in Ogasawara's service and that Musashi was there as a guest. He also learned that Musashi had no intention of entering the lord's service and that he was taking part in this battle on the general staff in order to be able to advise his son.

Returning to Higo, Sado began nursing an idea. He was thinking of undertaking the necessary steps to get Musashi taken into the service of his fief, since he knew that Lord Hosokawa was also interested in Musashi's personality. But Lord Hosokawa, who was well schooled in the wisdom of the feudal system, ordered him to act prudently, because even though Musashi's current situation was such as they knew it, he was residing with Lord Ogasawara, in relation to whom it would be a mistake to show any discourtesy.

Sado first wrote a letter to Musashi, because these steps had to be taken in the most discreet manner possible. Musashi replied politely, rejecting his proposition, saying that he had already given up the idea of having a lord. In 1639, when Nagaoka Sado passed through Kokura on official business, he took advantage of the occasion to visit Iori's house in order to see Musashi, to whom he communicated his lord's wish as well as his own. Musashi did not immediately give a positive reply, but after Sado's departure, he decided to accept the Hosokawa offer, not as a vassal but as a guest. Because according to the logic of the feudal relationship between members of a family, since Iori was already an Ogasawara vassal, it was not easy for Musashi to become attached to another lord.

After a certain number of administrative exchanges between the Ogasawara and Hosokawa fiefs, Musashi's decision was implemented. (8, pp. 174–175)

Musashi's Last Home

During the first month of 1640, Musashi left for Kumamoto with a Hosokawa vassal named Iwama Rokubei, who was sent to accompany him. Through Iwama Rokubei, Lord Hosokawa asked Musashi to formulate his desires. Musashi wrote an answer to Sakazaki Naizen, who served as an intermediary in his relations with Lord Hosokawa:

> You had Iwama Rokubei ask me what my situation and my intentions are. Since my answer was difficult to give orally, I am taking the liberty of writing this to you.
>
> Until now, I have never been officially in the service of a lord. And time has passed; moreover, in the last years I have often been sick. That is why there are not so many things that I desire. If you allow me to reside in your fief, if it were to occur that you went to battle, I would like to bear suitable arms and have two horses, one of them being a spare.
>
> I am an old man who has neither wife nor child. I am not concerned about a house or furniture.
>
> From the time of my youth, I have participated in battles six

times. Four times out of six, I was in the van, leading the army into battle. Everyone acknowledges this, and I have proof of it. In saying that, it goes without saying that I am not trying to advance myself in your estimation.

I can be useful teaching the way weapons are used and what is suitable conduct on the field of battle.

I can be useful in elaborating how to govern in relation to the situation.

What I have written in these last lines relates to the domain in which I have long persevered—since the time of my youth.

I have tried above to formulate the answer to your question.

In the second month, seventeenth year of Kanei [1640]

Miyamoto Musashi

To Lord Sakazaki Naizen (8, p. 185; 12, p. 109)

Musashi was accepted under the following conditions: He would have the status of guest of the lord; he would receive an allowance of seventeen warriors or three hundred *koku;* his rank would be equal to that of a general of a division. (12, p. 109; 17, p. 51)

Musashi's allowance was not a high one, but it was not a vassal's income, since Musashi was a guest of the lord. If this allowance had been given him in the capacity of vassal, this sum would have been humiliating for him.

In this connection, Naoki makes the following comment:

If Musashi was the number one adept in Japan, it is inconceivable that Hosokawa could have engaged him for 300 measly *koku.* Being nearly sixty years old, how could a man like Musashi have accepted such a small sum? Yagyu Munenori, who was also a politician, received 11,500 *koku* from the shogun. Toda Shigemasa received 10,000 *koku* in the fief of Echizen. Yagyu's disciples also received 500 *koku.* Kamiizumi Mondo, the younger brother of the great Kamiizumi, received 3,000 *koku.* If Musashi's salary was only 300 *koku,* I think that this was the reflection of a just assessment of his value. (21, p. 194)

Naoki's comparison is not entirely objective, since Yagyu's position was not that of a mere sword master. He played the role of political advisor to the shogun, and at the same time he was the director of the secret police, which had infiltrated throughout the whole of Japan. Toda, for his part, had been a vassal of the fief of Echizen since the time of the feudal wars and his high position had been acquired in the course of previous generations. Kamiizumi Mondo was the younger brother of Kamiizumi Nobutsuna, a legendary master who had trained, among others, Yagyu Muneyoshi, father of Yagyu Munenori, the master to the shogun. His good position was due to his older brother.

Contrary to what Naoki seems to be saying, the salary of an adept who became a vassal in the capacity of martial arts master was most often on the order of a few hundred *koku*. For example, Kamiizumi Yoshitane, grandson of the great Kamiizumi, a master of *iai* (the art of drawing the sword) in the fief of Owari, received 200 *koku* in this capacity. In the same fief, Yagyu Hyogonosuke, the grandson of Yagyu Sekishusai and the nephew of Munenori, who was sword master to the lord, received 500 *koku*. Let us remember that Owari was a branch of the Tokugawa family and ranked among the greatest fiefs. Shogun Tokugawa had two sword masters, Yagyu Munenori and Ono Tadaaki. The latter, who was only a master of the sword and not involved in politics, first received 200 *koku,* and his income rose as high as 600 *koku* by the end of his life. His son Ono Tadatsune succeeded to his father's position, and in 1633 he received 800 *koku* from Shogun Iemitsu. Tamiya Nagakatsu, an *iai* master, received 800 *koku* from Lord Tokugawa of Hamamatsu castle. His son Tamiya Heibei, the founder of the Tamiya ryu batto jutsu, first received 250 *koku* and then 800 *koku* when he succeeded his father. Oguri Jinemon, the founder of the Oguru school of swordsmanship and jujutsu, received 200 *koku* from Lord Yamanouchi of Tosa.

All of these examples are of contemporaries of Musashi's, each of them in his specialty a principal master of arms of a fief. If we are to study the status of masters of swordsmanship or of the martial arts objectively, these are good examples of the norms of the period. It is true that Musashi's income would not have been a high one if he had been a vassal who was the master of martial arts of a fief, but it would not have been as low as Naoki indicates.

In reality, Hosokawa's concern was to determine the suitable circumstances in which to receive Musashi, taking into account his pride, taking into account his own vassals, and considering also the fief of Ogasawara, where Musashi's son was in service. All the elements of this complex situation had to be considered.

To take Musashi on officially as a master of arms to the lord, three thousand to four thousand *koku* would perhaps have been necessary, and it would not have been certain that Musashi would accept. Moreover, this figure went well beyond what the other principal vassals of Hosokawa received. In a certain way, even an offer of five thousand *koku* would perhaps not have been enough to satisfy Musashi's pride. Indeed Iori received four thousand *koku* from Ogasawara, and if a neighboring lord made an offer to Musashi, it would have been difficult to make him one on a lower level than his son. True, an income of four thousand *koku* was an exceptionally high one.

If Hosokawa thought about all these aspects of the problem, Musashi thought about them too. Already old, he does seem to have given up the idea of officially serving a lord. Considering that his son was already in Lord Ogasawara's service, Musashi deemed it impossible for him to enter officially into the service of another lord. This was valid reasoning, even though Musashi always had the choice of separating himself from the feudal unit of his adoptive son's family by granting him familial independence. Musashi therefore doubtless adopted the position that he did in order to resolve certain problems. Hosokawa and he both avoided setting a price on Musashi's art, preferring to let it be understood that it was "priceless."

As a result, Hosokawa gave Musashi the exceptional status of guest of the lord and the rank of a general of a division. His income was paid directly by the lord and not by his administration, as was done for the vassals. Thus Musashi was not made an official subject. Musashi was a guest, having the capacity of a master of strategy and general advisor to Lord Hosokawa.

In Harada's opinion, "Since the Ogasawara and Hosokawa families had a very close relationship, it was rather Ogasawara who sent Musashi so that he could contribute to the consolidation of the Hosokawa fief." At the time when Hosokawa had just set himself up at Kumamoto, there were particularly strong tensions among the vassals who were natives of the Higo region and those who came there with Lord Hosokawa. Thus Harada thinks that Musashi was invited into this situation of instability at a time when Hosokawa was in need of people he could depend on.

The old castle of Chiba, which was right next to Kumamoto castle, where the lord lived, was chosen as Musashi's residence. Though his income was low, he received a maximum of privileges and comforts in exchange for his activities of private teacher and counselor.

Thus Lord Hosokawa Tadatoshi received Miyamoto Musashi as a guest. Officially, Musashi was his master of strategy, but they also communicated with each other on political and diplomatic matters as well as matters connected with the arts: tea ceremony, calligraphy, painting, and Noh theater.

In the *Tanji Hokin hikki* we find an account of Musashi's life during this period:

> Musashi had a taste for sculpture and the art of casting metals. He also made a great number of *bokuto* (wooden swords). He had a powerful frame and was 1.8 meters tall. His strength was well above the average. During his life he did not comb his hair or take a bath. During his prime his hair hung down to his belt, and when he was older it still reached his shoulders. He wore a long silk jacket without sleeves, lined in red, that came down all the way to his feet. His *katana* (long sword) and *wakizashi* (short sword) both had wooden grips reinforced with copper. When he was old, he separated himself from his sword and carried a cane a meter and a half in length. He never lacked money during his life, and many unemployed samurai *(ronin)* followed him. (9, p. 70)

Hosokawa Tadatoshi practiced the sword of the Yagyu shin kage ryu and had received its general transmission. The principal sword master of the fief was an adept of this school—Ujii (his personal name is given variously in different documents as Yashiro or Magoshiro). Lord Hosokawa wanted to arrange a match between Ujii Yashiro and Miyamoto Musashi. Musashi hesitated because, even though Ujii was younger than he, Ujii had precedence of rank over him in the fief and had the status of master. But Ujii accepted without problem, and Musashi finally agreed.

Let us cite the *Nitenki:*

An adept named Ujii Yashiro came to Higo on the recommendation of Yagyu. That happened before Musashi's arrival. In the Hosokawa fief, the Yagyu school was popular, since Lord Tadatoshi himself had attained the level of the general transmission of that school with Master Tajima [Yagyu Munenori]. The lord often trained with Yashiro. Musashi, invited by the lord, arrived from Kokura and took up residence in this country.

Musashi fought Yashiro in the presence of the lord, who sent away all his vassals with the exception of one, who bore his sword.

The two adepts fought three times. Yashiro could not defeat Musashi, who did not deliver a blow. Taking into account the presence of the lord, Musashi contented himself with dominating his adversary by rendering all his techniques ineffective.

After that, Lord Tadatoshi himself fought Musashi, but it was impossible for him to land a blow. He expressed his admiration, saying: "I never imagined there could be such a difference in levels of accomplishment!" From that moment on, he studied the School of Musashi. (2, p. 79; 9, p. 219)

Yagyu Munenori, master of the Yagyu school and sword master to the Edo shogunate, had officially delegated Ujii to Hosokawa as a sword master of his school but probably had also sent him as a secret agent. As a matter of fact, Yagyu, an advisor to the shogun, sent sword adepts from his school into most fiefs with a secret mission of gathering information. He was thus in possession of very large amounts of information on each fief. Yagyu taught the art of the sword of his school to a great number of feudal lords during their stays in Edo. And despite the mediocrity of their level, he often granted them the complete transmission of his school, which gives authorization to teach the art of a school officially.[2] We may suppose that the certificate of transmission that Lord Hosokawa received from Yagyu was of this nature.

Hosokawa Tadatoshi was able to receive instruction from Musashi for only a few months. He was doubtless already sick when Musashi arrived. We read in the *Nitenki:* "At the request of the lord, in the second month of the eighteenth year of Kanei [1641], Musashi presented his work *Hyoho sanju go kajo.* And on the seventeenth of the third month of the same year, Lord Tadatoshi died at the age of fifty-six."

So Lord Hosokawa died in 1641 at the age of fifty-six. His eighteen vassals followed him into death *(junshi).* The death of Tadatoshi seems to have had a strong effect on Musashi, who thought that he had finally found a lord with whom he could bring to fruition his science of strategy and that, in the service of Hosokawa, he could live the remainder of his life, identifying it fully with his art.

As cited by Tominaga Kengo, Ogi Kakubei wrote in 1851 in his *Shinmen Musashi ron:*

> With his art of the sword, Musashi placed himself under Lord Hosokawa, whose talent he esteemed; and he had intended to help him with the politics of his fief. The lord, who was clear-sighted, was very quick to spot Musashi's talent, and he often called Musashi to him for intimate discussions. It was therefore said that if the lord had remained alive longer, all political matters would have been entrusted to Musashi. . . .
>
> After the lord's death, Musashi never again had a lord who was capable of appreciating him. He got older and older and died as a simple adept of strategy. Only his art of swordsmanship was transmitted in our fief. This is highly regrettable. (12, p. 91)

The Enmei Ryu

Up to this point, Musashi had called his school Enmei ryu (School of the Shining Circle), but at this time he changed the name to Niten ichi ryu

(School of the Two Heavens United, or School of Two Swords Raised to the Heavens Becoming One).

Musashi had adopted a third son, Hirao Yoemon. According to Harada Mukashi (17), he was descended from the paternal side of Musashi's family and therefore kept his patronymic. Yoemon is without doubt, among Musashi's adoptive sons, the one who stayed with him the longest. We do not know the date or the circumstances of this adoption, but a letter from Musashi recommending Yoemon, addressed to Terao Sama, one of the principal vassals of the Owari fief, has been preserved. (13, 17) The Terao clan was native to the Sakushu region, where Musashi spent his childhood. A part of the clan moved to Kyushu, doubtless following the battle of Sekigahara, and became Hosokawa vassals. The two Terao brothers, Musashi's closest disciples, came from this part of the family. (2, 17)

Here is the text of this letter from Musashi:

> ... Concerning this Yoemon, who is about to move to your fief, I would appreciate your lending him some support. ... As for me, I have become older and no longer go out much; my condition does not permit me to practice strategy. I have the wish, accompanied by much longing, to see you again once more. However, this person named Yoemon is the one to whom I have transmitted strategy over many years, and he has attained a good level. ...
>
> The twenty-seventh of the eighth month
> Miyamoto Musashi Genshin [signature]
> To the Honorable Terao Sama and to those close to him (13, p. 162)

Owing to the support of Terao Sama, Hirao Yoemon was able to set up in the fief of Owari as a master of the sword. He then took the name Takemura Yoemon. He transmitted the Enmei ryu of Musashi in this region. He bestowed on several of his students copies of the *Hyoho sanju go kajo*. (13) As we saw, Musashi finished this work in 1641 and presented it to Lord Hosokawa Tadatoshi. Thus we may surmise that the letter above was written between 1641 and 1643, the year in which Musashi went into retreat in the cave at Reigando.

In the *Hyoho sanju go kajo,* Musashi already uses the phrase Hyoho nito ichi ryu as the name of his school. Yoemon, who received a copy of this work and probably at the same time the transmission of the School of Musashi, must have left after this time. Why did he keep the name Enmei ryu? It is possible that Musashi had not yet definitely changed the name of his school, or else that he wanted to transmit the name of Enmei ryu to Yoemon, and therefore changed the name of the school he himself would continue to direct.

COMPOSITION OF THE *Gorin no sho* AND MUSASHI'S DEATH

The death of Hosokawa Tadatoshi profoundly shook Musashi. After a year of mourning, Musashi began staying at Reigando cave, located on Mount Iwato, a dozen kilometers southwest of Kumamoto.

He wrote the following letter to Lord Hosokawa Mitsuhisa, Tadatoshi's son:

> I am going to go up to Mount Iwato in order to fulfill your command to explain the general ideas of the strategy that I have worked on throughout my life. I will therefore be absent for a period of time. On the questions concerning *hyoho,* you can ask the adepts of the disciplines in question or Buddhist scholars. It will be of no use to visit me to alleviate my solitude.
>
> The eighth of the tenth month
> Shinmen Musashi Genshin (9, p. 72)

From the cave one can see the Ariake Sea to the west. The cave was surrounded by several waterfalls, and on the inside there was a shrine dedicated to Kannon. On the outside were five hundred statues of stone and stones heaped in the form of towers, among others, towers of five stories, or *gorin to.* It was there that Musashi, who had been ill for some years and felt his death coming, began to compose the *Gorin no sho* on the tenth day of the tenth month, 1643. The title of the work and the atmosphere of Reigando with its *gorin to* seem to me to be connected in Musashi's inspiration. Sometimes he wrote in the cave, sometimes he practiced *zazen*.

In the "Anecdotes about the Deceased Master" *(Hyoho senshi denki)* we find the following account:

> The master fell sick after arriving in Higo [fief of Hosokawa]. Especially from the beginning of 1645, he was unable to swallow food, and several doctors tried to treat him. The master knew that he had developed an incurable ailment and refused to take medicine. But on the insistence of Lord Hosokawa, he yielded from time to time. One day one of the principal vassals, named Sawamura Daigaku, visited him and said, after examining the master's condition: "Take care of yourself; with rest, I am sure you will heal completely."
>
> Once the visitor had left, the master said, "Daigaku is an adept who has considerable experience of war; these words of his do not suit him." (9, p. 239)

In the second month of 1645, Musashi finished writing the *Gorin no sho* and became weaker. He moved back and forth between his residence in Chiba castle at Kumamoto and Reigando cave. Sensing the imminent approach of death, he chose to die at Reigando cave.

On the thirteenth of the fourth month, he wrote to three principal vassals who were his friends:

> I have been sick these last years, and especially since the beginning of this year my condition has grown worse, and it is difficult for me to stand up. It is because of my illness that I have been held back in my desire to fulfill my functions in the fief. The late lord liked strategy, and I was able to teach him and to communicate to him the overall mind of my school. That was my greatest happiness. His death caused me to lose hope.

The lord asked me to write on the principles of strategy, but with the wish that he could come to understand sooner, I wrote succinctly. I wrote down my new way of looking at strategy without recourse to ancient expressions such as those of Confucianism or Buddhism or to traditional examples of martial principles. This is my original thought on the essence and the principle. I consider it to correspond to the way of the arts and of human qualities. It is a way that would be applicable as a universal principle. I regret not having been able to apply it. Until now, most adepts have considered strategy as a way of making a living. This explains why true strategy has sickened.

Since I am an adept who has excelled in times past and up to the present day, I should transmit the essence of my school, but I can no longer move my limbs and I think that the end of my life is near. So I prefer to spend my last days in the mountains, hiding my dying body from the sight of others. Would you please be so kind as to convey all this to the others.

The thirteenth of the fourth month

Miyamoto Musashi

To Lord Shikibu

To Lord Kenmotsu

To Lord Uemon (12, p. 131)

Surprised by this letter, the three principal vassals went to the cave to try to convince Musashi to return and let himself be cared for at his home in town. This shows the importance that Musashi had acquired in this fief: The three principal vassals would not have undertaken such a journey for a mere master of strategy.

A week before his death, Musashi composed "The Way to Be Followed Alone" (Dokkodo), which seems to be the distillation of an existential attitude. He bequeathed his possessions as keepsakes to his close friends and disciples. For example, he bestowed his large sword on Nagaoka Sado and asked that his small sword be sent to the house where he was born. He dedicated his last work, the Gorin no sho, to his disciple Terao Magonojo and gave the latter's younger brother, Terao Motomenosuke, his own copy of the *Hyoho sanju go kajo*. Musashi certainly considered these two brothers to be his last disciples.

Musashi died the nineteenth of the fifth month of 1645, in the presence of his adoptive son Iori and his disciples. Some authors say that he died at home, others that he had himself carried to Reigando, where he waited for death meditating in *zazen*.

The death of Musashi is described this way in the *Hyoho senshi denki:*

At the moment of his death, he had himself raised up. He had his belt tightened and his *wakizashi* put in it. He seated himself with one knee vertically raised, holding the sword with his left hand and a cane in his right hand. He died in this posture, at the age of sixty-two. The principal vassals of Lord Hosokawa and the other officers gathered, and they painstakingly carried out the ceremony. Then they set up a tomb on Mount Iwato on the order of the lord. (9, p. 239)

Musashi's hair was buried on Mount Iwato. According to his desire, he was dressed in his battle armor and interred in the village of Yuge, on the outskirts of the town of Kumamoto, following the wish he had formulated:

I served and received great favors from the two lords Tadatoshi and his son Mitsumasa. After my death, I will protect the peace of the Hosokawa family as thanks for the favor these lords showed in my regard. I wish to be able to bow to my lord when he travels to Edo to render his duty to the shogun. Would you be so kind as to choose the location of my interment in a place that will permit me to fulfill these wishes. (8, p. 242)

The correspondence of Iori with Lords Nagaoka Shikibu and Nagaoka Kenmotsu has been preserved. Here is the content of it in summary:

Allow me to write you respectfully here.

My father Musashi has fallen ill and you are caring for him

warmly. My infinite thanks to you for this. I should visit you to thank you in person, but I am held here by my functions. Would you kindly have the indulgence to excuse me for this.

Thanking you again, I commend my father into your care.
Miyamoto Iori
The fifteenth of the eleventh month [signature]
To Lord Nagaoka Shikibu Shoho
and to his family

I am in receipt of your letter.
Mr. Musashi fell ill in the mountains outside Kumamoto. We have sent a doctor and attempted to treat him with medicine, but his condition has not improved. We are unable to provide him with adequate care in this place. We asked him to return to Kumamoto with us, but he did not accept. It was only the day before yesterday that he finally acceded to our request and returned to Kumamoto.

We would like to see you too, but we understand your situation very well. Mr. Musashi is a friend of long standing of my father Okinaga, and I am myself a friend of his. I ask you not to worry yourself over his care.
Nagaoka Shikibu Shoho
The eighteenth of the eleventh month
To the Honorable Miyamoto Iori (17, pp. 194, 198, 202)

This letter shows clearly that Musashi did not want to leave Reigando cave, where he intended to die. Musashi's condition improved for a short time, but in the month of May it again grew worse. Receiving this news, Iori arrived in haste from Kokura and was present at Musashi's death on the nineteenth of the fifth month, 1645.

The funeral ceremony having taken place, Iori returned to Kokura on the twenty-third of the fifth month and wrote to Nagaoka Kenmotsu:

During the last period of Musashi's illness, Lord Hosokawa Mitsumasa had the kindness to have him assisted by Terao Motomenosuke, who bled him. I thank you for the ceremony and also for erecting the tomb.

I thanked by letter Mr. Iwama Rokubei of Edo. I ask you to convey my thanks to him once again.

I am sending you a package of peaches and a package of dried fish, which are no more than a humble token of my thanks.

Miyamoto Iori

The twenty-ninth of the fifth month [signature]

To Lord Nagaoka Kenmotsu

and to his family

In 1654, nine years after Musashi's death, Miyamoto Iori had a monument raised to his memory in the town of Kokura. The text on this monument is a funeral eulogy to Musashi. It is known by the name of the Kokura *hibun*.

TWO

MUSASHI'S WRITINGS

||| 4 |||

"Writings on the Five Elements" (*Gorin no sho*)

On problems of translation of the Gorin no sho *and on the meaning of some important terms, see appendix 1.*[1]

THE SCROLL OF EARTH

School of the Two Heavens United, Niten ichi ryu,[2] is the name that I give to the way of strategy.[3] In this text I am going to explain for the first time what I have been studying in depth for many years. At the beginning of the tenth month of the twentieth year of Kanei [1643], I came to Mount Iwato in the Higo[4] prefecture of Kyushu to write. I pay homage to heaven, I prostrate to the goddess Kannon, and I turn toward the Buddha. My name is Shinmen Musashi no kami, Fujiwara no Genshin,[5] and I am a warrior, born in the prefecture of Harima.[6] My life now adds up to sixty years.[7]

I have trained in the way of strategy since my youth, and at the age of thirteen I fought a duel for the first time. My opponent was called Arima Kihei, a sword adept of the Shinto ryu, and I defeated him. At the age of sixteen I defeated a powerful adept by the name of Akiyama, who came from the prefecture of Tajima.[8] At the age of twenty-one I went up to Kyoto and fought duels with several adepts of the sword from famous schools, but I never lost.

Then I traveled in several fiefs and regions in order to meet the adepts of different schools. I fought more than sixty times,[9] but not once was I beaten. All that happened between my thirteenth and my twenty-eighth or twenty-ninth year.

At the age of thirty I reflected, and I saw that although I had won, I had done so without having reached the ultimate level of strategy. Perhaps it was because my natural disposition prevented me from straying from universal principles; perhaps it was because my opponents lacked ability in strategy.

I continued to train and to seek from morning till night to attain to a deeper principle. When I reached the age of fifty, I naturally found myself on the way of strategy.

Since that day I have lived without having a need to search further for the way.[10] When I apply the principle of strategy to the ways of different arts and crafts, I no longer have need for a teacher in any domain. Thus, in composing this book, I do not borrow from the ancient Buddhist or Confucianist writings; I do not use ancient examples from the chronicles or the tradition of the military art.

I began writing on the tenth of the tenth month, at night, at the hour of the tiger,[11] with the aim of expressing the true idea of my school, letting my mind reflect in the mirror of the way of heaven and the way of Kannon.

Strategy is the practice that is necessary in warrior families.[12] A person who directs warfare must learn it, and soldiers must also be familiar with it. Nowadays those who know the way of strategy well are rare.

As far as the way is concerned, several of them exist. The law of Buddha is the way that saves people. The way of Confucianism is the way that leads to correctness in literature. Medicine is the way that cures illnesses. The poet teaches the way of poetry. There exist a number of ways in the arts—that of the man of taste,[13] that of the practitioner of archery, and those of other arts and crafts. Adepts train in these in their fashion, according to their manner of thinking, and are fond of them in accordance with their dispositions. But very few like the way of strategy.

First of all, warriors must familiarize themselves with what is known as "the two ways," literature and the martial arts. That is their way. Even if you are clumsy, you must persevere in strategy because of your position.

That which a warrior must always have in his mind is the way of death. But the way of death is not reserved only for warriors. A monk, a woman, a peasant—any person—can resolve to die for the sake of a social obligation or honor. In the way of strategy that warriors practice, the aim of action must be to surpass others in all domains. A warrior has to win in combat against one or several opponents, bring fame to his lord's name and his own, and establish his position owing to the virtue of strategy. Some people perhaps think that even if they learn the way of strategy, it will not be useful in real practice. On this point, it is sufficient to train in it for it to be useful at all times and to teach it for it to be useful in all things. This is how the true way of strategy must be.

Concerning the Way of Strategy

From China to Japan, over a long time, a person who practices this way has been known as an adept of strategy. For a warrior, it is not possible not to study it.[14] Nowadays there are certain people to be found everywhere who declare themselves accomplished practitioners of strategy, but in general they practice only the sword. Recently the Shinto priests of Kantori and Kashima in the prefecture of Hitachi[15] have founded schools, saying that their art was transmitted to them by the gods, and they have propagated their art in various fiefs.

Among the ten talents and the seven arts that have long been known,[16] strategy is considered to be a pragmatic domain.[17] Since it is a pragmatic domain, it is not appropriate to limit it just to the technique of the sword. On the basis of the principles of the sword alone,[18] you will not be able to understand the sword well, and you will be far from being in accord with the principles of strategy.

There are people who make a profession out of selling the arts.

They treat themselves as articles of merchandise and produce objects with a view to selling them. This attitude is tantamount to the act of separating the flower from the fruit. And it must be said that the fruit in this case does not amount to much. They adorn the way of strategy with flowery colors, lay out a display of techniques, and teach their way by creating first one dojo, then another. Someone who might want to learn such a way with the goal of making money should keep in mind the saying "Strategy, inadequately learned, is the cause of serious wounds."[19]

In general, four ways exist for traversing human life: those of the warrior, the peasant, the artisan, and the merchant.[20] The first is the way of the peasant. Peasants prepare various tools and are vigilant with regard to the changing of the seasons, year after year. That is the way of the peasant.

The second is the way of the merchant. A manufacturer of sake, for example, buys the necessary materials and makes profits that correspond to the quality of his product—this is the way he goes through life. All merchants pass through human life making more or less profit from their businesses. That is the way of business.

The third is the way of the warrior. Warriors must make various weapons and know the richness[21] of each weapon. That is the way of the warrior. Without learning how to handle weapons, without knowing the advantages of each of them, a warrior is lacking somewhat in education.

The fourth is the way of the artisan. A carpenter follows his way by skillfully making various tools and knowing well how to use them. He correctly lays out construction plans using black cords and a square.[22] He goes through life with his art without wasting a moment.

This is the way the four ways should be, those of the warrior, the peasant, the artisan, and the merchant.

I am going to speak of strategy by comparing it to the way of the carpenter. This comparison has to do with a house constructed by carpenters. We speak, for example, of a noble house, a warrior house,[23] or the Four Houses.[24] We also speak of the decline or continuation of a house;

in the realm of art, we also speak of a house in the sense of a school or a style.[25] It is because the term *house* is used in these ways that I make the comparison with the way of the carpenter.

The word *daiku*, carpenter, is written *dai*, "fully," *ku*, "to be very clever at." In the same way, the way of strategy is built upon ingenuity of great fullness and scope. That is why I compare it to the way of the carpenter. If you want to learn strategy, you must contemplate these writings and train ceaselessly, the master and disciple together, so that the master is like the needle and the disciple is like the thread.

Comparison of the Way of Strategy with the Way of the Carpenter

A general, like a master carpenter, should know the overall rules of the country and adjust the rules of his own province to fit with them, just as the way of the master carpenter consists in regulating the measurements of the house he is going to construct.

The master carpenter learns the structural pattern for building a tower or a temple and knows the construction plans for palaces and fortresses. He builds houses by making use of people. In this way the chief carpenter and the chief warrior resemble each other.[26]

In constructing a house, one must first choose wood that is suitable. For the front pillars, wood is chosen that is straight, without knots, and of good appearance. For the rear pillars, one chooses wood that is straight and sturdy, even if it has a few knots. It is appropriate to use woods that are less strong but of handsome appearance for the sills, the lintels, the sliding doors, and the shoji.[27]

The house will last for a long time even if knotted or twisted wood is used, on the condition that the strength needed for the different parts of the house is accurately assessed and the qualities of the wood used are carefully examined. It is appropriate to use somewhat weak, knotty, or twisted wood for scaffolding and then afterward for heating.

In using men, the master carpenter must know the qualities of the carpenters. In accordance with their high, medium, or low ability, he must assign them different tasks, such as construction of the *toko-noma*;[28] of the sliding doors and the shoji; or of the sills, lintels, and ceilings. It is appropriate to have support framing done by those with not much skill, and wedges made by the most unskillful. If one is able to discern the qualities of men in this manner, work progresses quickly and efficiently.

Being fast and efficient; being vigilant with regard to the surroundings;[29] knowing substance and its function;[30] knowing the high, medium, or low level of ambient energy;[31] knowing how to energize the situation; and knowing the limits of things: Above all, a master carpenter must possess all those. It is the same for the principle of strategy.

The Way of Strategy

Both a vassal and a soldier are similar to a carpenter.[32] The latter sharpens his tools, makes other tools, and carries them in his carpenter's box. Following the orders of the master, he accomplishes his work efficiently; his measurements will be exact for the smallest detail work as well as for the long external corridors.[33] Sometimes he roughs out the pillars and beams with his adze or planes the posts of the *tokonoma* and the shelves; sometimes he carves openwork in planks or sculpts wood. Such is the law of the carpenter. If he learns to practice the techniques of woodworking and also learns how to draw up plans, he can later become a master.

A carpenter must keep his tools well sharpened and always maintain them. Only a specialist in woodworking knows how to make a precious box for a statue of the Buddha, a bookshelf, a table, a stand for a lamp, all the way down to a chopping block or a lid. Either a vassal or a soldier is similar to a carpenter. They should ponder this well.

A carpenter must always keep his mind attentive to the following things: The wood must not lose its shape, the joints must hold, he must plane well but avoid oversmoothing, the wood must not warp later on.

If you study the way of strategy, it is necessary to examine attentively what I write here, down to the least detail.

I Write on Strategy in Five Scrolls

I write my work in five scrolls, the scrolls of Earth, Water, Fire, Wind, and Heaven, in order to show clearly the qualities of each of the five ways.[34]

In the Scroll of Earth, I present an overall vision of the way of strategy and the point of view of my school. It is difficult to arrive at the true way relying on the way of the sword alone. It is appropriate to understand details on the basis of a broad vision and to attain depth by beginning on the surface. It is necessary to plot a straight path through terrain that has been leveled. That is why I have given the name Earth to the first scroll.

The second is the Scroll of Water. You should learn what is essential regarding the state of the mind from the nature of water. Water follows the form of a square or round vessel. It is a drop and also an ocean. The color of its depths is pure green, and taking this purity as my inspiration, I present my school in the Scroll of Water.

If you succeed in clearly discerning the general principle[35] of the art of the sword and in this manner easily defeat one person, you can defeat any opponent. The mind is the same whether it is a matter of defeating one person or a thousand or ten thousand enemies.

The strategy of a general consists in applying on a large scale what he has studied on a small scale. This is the same thing as designing a large statue of the Buddha on the basis of a model[36] of thirty centimeters. It is difficult to explain it in detail, but the principle of strategy is to know ten thousand things from a single thing. It is in this way that I write about the content of my school in the Scroll of Water.

The third scroll is that of fire. In this scroll I write about war, for fire symbolizes a blazing mind, whether small or large. The way of war is the same if the situation is one against one or ten thousand against ten thousand. This should be examined well, making the mind now large, now small.

Seeing what is large is easy, seeing what is small is difficult. It is difficult to change strategy quickly when you are many, whereas a single person quickly changes his tactics in accordance with his state of mind;

that is why for such a case it is difficult to foresee the minute details. This should be examined well.

That which I write about in the Scroll of Fire happens in a short time.[37] Therefore it is necessary to train in it and habituate oneself to it every day so that an immutable mind can become the ordinary thing. This is an essential point of strategy; it is in relation to this mind that I write about war and individual combat in the Scroll of Fire.

The fourth is the Scroll of Wind. What I write in this scroll is not about my own school but deals with the strategies of other present-day schools. We use the expressions the ancient wind and the modern wind, and also the wind of such and such a family.[38] I explain the strategies of the other schools and their techniques in the Scroll of Wind.

Without knowing others, one cannot really know oneself. In the practice of all the ways and in all manners of working with things, the danger exists of deviating from the true way.[39] Even if you practice the way daily and think you are on the right track, it is possible to deviate from the true way if your mind has turned away from it. You can recognize this if you know how to observe on the basis of the true way. If you are not progressing along the true way, a slight twist in the mind can become a major twist. This must be pondered well.

In other schools it is thought that just the way of the sword constitutes strategy, and not without reason. But what I understand by the principle and the techniques of strategy is quite different. I write about the other schools in the Scroll of Wind so as to acquaint you with their strategy.

The fifth is the Scroll of Heaven [or Emptiness].[40] With regard to that which I mean by heaven, how could one distinguish between the depth of it and its entrance,[41] since what we are talking about is emptiness? After having realized the principle of the way,[42] it becomes possible to move away from it—you will find yourself naturally free in the way of strategy and you will naturally reach a high level of ability.[43] You will naturally find the cadence that is appropriate to the moment, and the stroke will appear all by itself and strike home by itself. All of that is in the way of emptiness. I write in the Scroll of Heaven of the manner of entering naturally into the true way.

I Give My School the Name School of Two Swords

I describe my school in terms of two swords, since all warriors, from the vassal to the ordinary soldier, must wear two swords firmly at their sides.[44] Formerly, these two swords used to be called *tachi* and *katana;* today they are called *katana* and *wakizashi*. It goes without saying that all warriors wear these two swords[45] in their belts. Whether they know how to use them or not, in our country, carrying the two swords is the way of the warrior. It is in order to make the advantage of carrying the two swords understood that I describe my school in terms of the two swords. The lance and the *naginata*[46] are weapons to be used outside, on the field of battle.[47]

In my school a beginner learns the way by taking the large sword and the small sword in his hands at the same time.[48] This is essential. If you are going to die in battle, it is desirable to utilize all the weapons you are carrying. It is deplorable to die with weapons left in their scabbards without having been capable of using them.[49]

But if you have a sword in each hand, it is difficult to handle each of the two swords as you wish. That is why you have to learn to wield the large sword with just one hand. It is normal to wield a large weapon like the lance or the *naginata* with two hands, but the large sword and the small one are weapons to be utilized with just one hand.

Holding a large sword with two hands is a disadvantage when fighting on horseback, when fighting on the run, when fighting in marshy terrain, in a deep rice paddy, on stony ground, on a steep road, or when you are in the midst of a melee. When you are holding a bow,[50] a lance, or any other weapon in your left hand, you must hold the sword with the right hand.[51] That is why holding a sword with two hands is not appropriate in the true way. If you do not succeed in killing your enemy with just one hand, it is enough to use two hands at that point. It is not a very complicated matter.

It is in order to learn to handle the large sword easily with one hand that we learn to wield the two swords.[52] At the beginning everyone has difficulty handling the large sword with just one hand because of its weight. It is the same thing in any form of new beginning. For a beginner it is hard to draw a bow, and handling a *naginata* is also hard. Whatever the weapon, the important thing is to get used to it. In this way you may succeed in drawing a strong bow, and by exercising every day, you will achieve the ability to wield the sword easily by acquiring the strength that is fitting for the way.

The way of the sword is not a mere matter of the swiftness of the strike. I will explain this precisely in the second scroll, the Scroll of Water. The large sword is used in an open space and the small sword in a confined space—that is the starting point[53] of the way.

In my school one must win with a long weapon as well as a short one. That is why I do not fix the length of the sword. To be ready to win with all the weapons—that is the essence of my school. The advantage of using two swords instead of one becomes manifest when one is fighting alone against many adversaries and when one is fighting in a closed-in place. It is not necessary to write more about this now. It is necessary to know ten thousand things by knowing one well. If you are to practice the way of strategy, nothing must escape your eyes.[54] Reflect well on this.

Knowing the Meaning of the Two Ideograms *Hyo Ho*[55]

Customarily in this way, someone who knows how to handle a sword is called a man of strategy. In the way of the martial arts,[56] someone who knows how to shoot a bow is called an archer, someone who knows how to shoot a gun is called a gunner, someone who is skillful with the lance is called an expert with the lance, and someone who handles the *naginata* well is called an expert with the *naginata*. Thus someone who excels in the techniques of the sword should be called an expert with the long sword or an expert with the short sword. The bow, the gun, the lance, and the *naginata* are all weapons of the warrior; each one of them is part of the way of strategy. Nevertheless, strategy is usually used to designate the art of the sword. There is a reason for this.

It is through the virtue of the sword[57] that one rules a country and that one behaves in a fitting manner oneself. The sword is at the origin of strategy. By mastering the virtue of the sword, one person can defeat ten. If one can defeat ten, a hundred can defeat a thousand, and a thousand will defeat ten thousand. It is in this sense that in my school the principles are the same for one as for ten thousand, and what I mean by strategy includes the practices of all warriors.

We may speak of the way of the Confucians, of the Buddhists, of tea masters, of masters of etiquette, or of dancers, but these ways are distinct from the way of the warrior. Nonetheless, anyone who understands the way in great depth will find the same principle in all things. It is important for each person to persevere[58] in his own way.

Knowing the Advantage of Each Weapon in Strategy

If you know well the advantages of the different weapons, you can use any weapon appropriately[59] in accordance with the situation of the moment.

The small sword is advantageous in a confined place and when you get close to your opponent. The large sword is suited to nearly all situations and presents advantages in all of them. On the battlefield the usefulness of the *naginata* is slightly less than that of the lance, for if you compare the two, the lance allows one to take the initiative better.[60] If there are two practitioners of the same level and one has a lance and the other a *naginata,* the one with the lance will have a slight advantage. The effectiveness of the lance and the *naginata* depends on the situation of combat; they will not be very effective in a confined space nor when you are surrounded by enemies in a house.[61] They are weapons especially for the battlefield, indispensable in situations of war.

You can learn and develop the subtleties of technique indoors,[62] but they will not be appropriate if you forget the true way. The bow is appropriate[63] when you are moving troops forward or back in the strategy of battles. It makes possible rapid fire in parallel with the use of lances and other arms. It is therefore particularly useful on battlefields in open terrain. But its effectiveness is insufficient for attacking fortresses or for combating enemies who are farther than thirty-six meters away.[64]

At the present time, there are many flowers and little fruit in archery—this goes without saying, and goes for the other arts as well.

If an art is nothing but that, it cannot be useful in a really important situation. The interest is great.[65]

From within a fortress, there is no weapon more effective than a gun. On the field of battle also, the interest of the gun is great before an encounter. Once, however, the encounter has begun, its effectiveness diminishes. One of the advantages of the bow is that the trajectory of the arrow is visible, and the deficiency of the gun is that the ball cannot be seen. It is appropriate to examine well this aspect of things.

As far as the horse is concerned, it must be strong, resilient, and without bad habits. Generally, as for all the weapons of war, you should choose horses that are large and good for marching. The swords, both the short and the long, should be large and sharp,[66] the lance and *naginata* large and well honed. You must have bows and guns that are powerful and are not easily ruined. You should not have a predilection for certain weapons. Putting too much emphasis on one weapon results in not having enough of the others. Weapons should be adapted to your personal qualities and be ones you can handle. It is useless to imitate others. For a general as for a soldier, it is negative to have marked preferences. You should examine this point well.

Cadences in Strategy

Cadence is inherent in all things, especially as far as strategy is concerned.[67] It is not possible to master cadence without thorough training.

In this world we can see that different cadences exist. The cadences of the way of the dance and of musicians with their stringed or wind instruments are all concordant and without distortion.[68] Going through the various ways of the martial arts, there are different cadences depending on whether you are shooting a bow, firing a gun, or riding a horse.

You must not go against cadence in any of the arts, nor in any handcraft. Cadence also exists for that which does not have a visible form.[69] Regarding the situation of a warrior in the service of a lord, according to the cadences he follows, he will rise or fall in the hierarchy, for there are cadences that are concordant and others that are discordant.

In the way of business, there are cadences for making a fortune and cadences for losing it. In each way, there exist different cadences. You must discern well the cadences in conformity with which things prosper and those in conformity with which things decline.

In strategy, different cadences exist. First it is necessary to know the concordant cadences and then to learn the discordant ones.[70] Among the large or small and slow or fast cadences, it is indispensable for strategy to discern striking cadences, interval cadences, and opposing cadences.[71] Your strategy cannot be sure if you do not succeed in mastering the opposing cadence.

At the time of strategic combat, you must know the cadences of each enemy and utilize cadences that they will not think of. You will win by unleashing the cadences of emptiness that are born from those of wisdom. In each scroll, I will write about cadence. Examine these writings and train well.

IF YOU PRACTICE DILIGENTLY, from morning till night, the way of strategy I teach, your mind will spontaneously broaden. I am transmitting to the world my strategy in its collective and individual dimensions. I am expounding it for the first time in writing in these five scrolls of Earth, Water, Fire, Wind, and Heaven.

Those who would like to learn my strategy should apply the following rules in order to practice the way:

1. Think of that which is not evil.[72]
2. Train in the way.
3. Take an interest in all the arts.
4. Know the way of all professions.
5. Know how to appreciate the advantages and disadvantages of each thing.
6. Learn to judge the quality of each thing.
7. Perceive and understand that which is not visible from the outside.
8. Be attentive even to minimal things.
9. Do not perform useless acts.

You must train in the way of strategy keeping these general principles in mind. Particularly in this way, if you do not know how to see the right things in broad perspective, you will not be able to become an accomplished practitioner of strategy. If you master this method,[73] you will not lose, even alone against twenty or thirty opponents. First of all, because you maintain your vital energy constantly in your strategy[74] and you practice the direct way, you will win through your techniques and also through your way of seeing. Since you have free mastery of your body[75] as a result of your training, you will win through your body; since your mind is accustomed to this way, you will also win through your mind. Once you reach this stage, how can you be defeated?

Regarding grand strategy, you must be victorious through the quality of the people you employ, victorious through the way in which you utilize a great number of people, victorious by behaving correctly yourself in accordance with the way, victorious by ruling your country, victorious in order to feed the people, victorious by applying the law of the world in the best way. Thus it is necessary to know how not to lose to anyone—in any of the ways—and to firmly establish your position and your honor. That is the way of strategy.

The twelfth of the fifth month of Year 2 of Shoho [1645]
Shinmen Musashi
For the Honorable Lord Terao Magonojo
The fifth of the second month of Year 7 of Kanbun [1667][76]
Terao Yumeyo Katsunobu for the Honorable Lord Yamamoto Gensuke[77]

THE SCROLL OF WATER

The mind of strategy of my School of Two Swords takes water as its fundamental model.[78] Therefore I title this text the Scroll of Water, because the idea here is to practice a method of pragmatic effectiveness.[79] For this reason I elucidate the sword techniques of my school in this part of my writing. It is difficult, in writing, to explain this way in detail as I would like to do. Even where words are inadequate, you should understand the principle intuitively.[80] It is necessary for you to pause and reflect on each of the words and ideograms I have written in this text. If you read superficially, you run a great risk of deviating from the way.

Regarding the principle of strategy, even though I may describe [the situation] as though talking about individual combat, it is essential to understand this with broad vision—as the principle of a battle among tens of thousands of people. You are in danger of falling into a bad way if you wander and choose the wrong path, for the slightest error in judgment can have grave consequences, especially in this way. If you content yourself with reading what I write here, it will be impossible for you to reach a high level in the way of strategy. Read this text thinking that it is written for you;[81] do not think that you are just reading or learning written things. Instead of imitating what I write, make this text yours, like a principle that you have brought forth from your own thought. It is necessary to ponder well by putting yourself into the situation.

State of Mind in Strategy

In the way of strategy, one's state of mind[82] need not be distinct from the ordinary one. In daily life as well as in strategy, it is necessary to have an ample and broad mind and to carefully keep it very straight, not too tight and not at all loose. In order not to have your mind too much off to one side, it is necessary to place it in the center and move it calmly so that it does not cease to move even in moments of change.[83] All that has to be examined well.

Even at a calm time, the mind is not calm; even at a moment of great speed, the mind is not at all fast. The mind must not be carried along by the body, nor the body by the mind. The mind must be wary when the body remains unguarded. The mind must not be insufficient or even a little bit too much. When the surface of the mind is weak, its depth must be strong so that the opponent cannot perceive one's state of mind. Those who are small [either in size or in number] must know well those who are large [in size or number], and those who are large must know those who are small. The large as well as the small must keep their mind straight and not overestimate themselves.

It is necessary to keep the mind pure and broad, and wisdom will find its place within this breadth. The important thing is to polish wisdom and the mind in great detail. If you sharpen wisdom, you will understand what is just and unjust in society and also the good and the evil of this world; then you will come to know all kinds of arts and you will tread different ways. In this manner, no one in this world will succeed in deceiving you. It is after this stage that you will arrive at the wisdom of strategy. The wisdom of strategy is entirely distinct. Even right in the middle of a battle where everything is in rapid movement, it is necessary to attain the most profound principle of strategy, which assures you an immoveable mind. You must examine this well.

Posture in Strategy

Regarding posture,[84] it is appropriate to keep the face neither lowered nor raised, nor leaning nor frowning; to keep the eyes unperturbed, the forehead without wrinkles but with creases between the brows; not to move the eyeballs and not to blink, though keeping the eyelids slightly lowered. In this way you shape a beautiful, luminous face, keeping the nose straight and the lower jaw slightly protruding.

Keep your neck straight, putting some force in the hollow of the nape; lower your shoulders, with the sensation that the torso from the shoulders down forms a unity; keep the back straight, do not stick out your buttocks, push your force downward from your knees to the tips of your toes. Advance the belly slightly forward so that the pelvis does not lose its stability; remember the adage "squeeze from one corner," which recommends pressing the scabbard of the small sword (wakizashi) firmly against the belly so that your belt does not loosen up.

In sum, it is necessary for you to have as your posture for strategy just the ordinary one, and it is essential that the posture of strategy be the ordinary one for you. This must be examined well.

The Way of Looking in Strategy

Your look must be broad and ample. Looking and seeing are two different things.[85] Look powerfully, see gently. It is necessary to look at what is distant as something that is close and what is close as something that is distant—this is essential for strategy. It is fundamental in strategy to know the sword of the adversary without ever looking at it. You must exercise well in this. Whether it is a matter of strategy on the individual scale or strategy on the large scale, the way of looking is the same. It is essential to look to both sides without moving your eyes.[86] But without preparation, you will not be able to achieve this way of looking at the time of combat. That is why you had better study well what I write here; you must accustom yourself to looking all the time in this way in order to be able to keep this way of looking in any situation. Examine this well.

The Way of Gripping the Sword

You should grip the sword holding the thumb and index finger as though they were floating, the middle finger neither tight nor slack, the ring and little fingers very tight. It is bad to have an empty space inside your hand. Hold the sword with the thought of slashing your opponent. When you slash your opponent, the posture of the hand remains the same, and your hands must not tense up. It is with the sense of just slightly moving your thumb and index finger that you beat back your opponent's sword, that you receive it, strike it, or exert pressure on it. In all these cases, you should grip the sword with the thought of slashing. Whether you are training at slashing an object or in the thick of combat, the way of holding the sword remains the same—it is held with the intent of slashing your opponent. In sum, it is not good to let the hand or the sword become fixed or frozen.[87] A fixed hand is a dead hand; a hand that does not become fixed is alive. It is necessary to master this well.

The Way of Moving the Feet

To move from one place to another, you slightly raise your toes and push off your foot from the heel, forcefully. According to the situation, you move your feet with a large or a small step, slowly or rapidly, but always in the manner of walking. There are three ways of moving it is necessary to avoid: jumping, moving with a floating step, stomping heavily.[88] The essential instruction related to moving from place to place is alternate movement of the two feet,[89] positive foot and negative foot. Which means you should not move just one foot. When you slash, when you back away, when you parry, you must always move the right and left feet alternately. You must never move only one foot. This should be examined with care.

The Five Guard Positions

The five guard positions are the high, middle, low, and those of the two sides, left and right. Five guards can be distinguished, but all of them have as their goal to slash the opponent. There is no guard position other than those five. Whatever guard position you assume, do not think of taking a position, instead think of being ready to strike.

The choice of a wide or narrow guard depends on your assessment of the situation. The high, middle, or low guard positions are the substantial positions, and the side positions, right and left, are circumstantial ones.[90] Thus, when you are fighting in a place of limited height where one of the two sides is obstructed, take the side guard position, either right or left. You choose between the right and left in accordance with the situation.

Do not forget this instruction: The middle-level guard position is fundamental. In fact, the middle-level position is the original guard.[91] Observe that as you broaden your strategy, you will understand that the middle-level guard position corresponds to the place of the general. Four other positions come after that of the general. You must examine this well.

The Pathway of the Sword *(Tachi no Michi)*

Here is what I call knowing the pathway *(michi)* [92] of the sword: When you handle the sword that you carry all the time, you can handle it freely even with only two fingers if you know well the pathway *(michi)* of the sword. If you are preoccupied about moving the sword fast, the pathway of the sword will be troubled and that will cause you difficulties. It is enough to move the sword appropriately and calmly. If you attempt to move the sword fast like a fan or a small knife, you will have difficulties, because you are straying then from the nature *(michi)* of the sword. You cannot slash a man by thrashing about with your sword as though you were chopping something with a knife. If you strike downward from above, you raise the sword up again, following a pathway that naturally reflects the reaction of the force. Likewise, if you strike horizontally, afterward you bring the sword back along the horizontal following a suitable pathway. In all cases, you must move the sword broadly and powerfully, amply extending your arms. [93] That is the way *(michi)* of the sword.

If you master the five formulas of technique of my school, you will strike well, because the path *(michi)* of your sword will be well stabilized. [94] It is necessary to train well.

The Series of Five Technical Forms [95]

First Technical Form

Take the middle guard position and point your two swords at your opponent's face—confront your opponent in this manner. When he launches an attack, deflect his sword to your right and, pressing on it, make your attack with the point of your sword. [96] If your opponent attacks you again, strike him from above downward, turning the point of your sword one quarter of a circle, and leave your sword in the position it has reached. If your opponent attacks once again, cut his arm starting with your sword in this low position. [97] All of this constitutes the first form. [98]

It is not possible to understand the five forms just by reading; it is necessary to assimilate them by practicing them with your swords in hand. By making a thorough study of these five forms of the sword, you will understand the way of your own sword, and consequently you will be able to face all kinds of attacks on the part of your opponents. Know that there are no other forms apart from these five in the School of the Two Swords. It is necessary to train in this.

Second Technical Form

In the second form, you hold the two swords high and strike with a single blow at the moment your adversary launches his attack. If your blow is deflected, leave your sword in the position it has reached and strike from below upward at the moment your opponent launches another attack. Do the same if this situation repeats.[99]

This form includes different ways of directing your mind and various cadences. If you exercise in the techniques of my school, striking according to this form, you will be able to attain precise mastery of the five principles (michi) of the sword and you will obtain the ability to win, no matter what your way of doing it is. It is necessary to train in this well.

Third Technical Form

In the guard position of the third form, you hold the sword with the point down, as though it were hanging, and you strike the wrist of the adversary from below at the moment he attacks. If the adversary parries and tries to force your sword down by striking it, you turn your sword aside with a passing cadence[100] and cut his upper arm horizontally. The essence of this formula is to win with a single blow starting from the low guard position the instant your opponent launches his attack. In training in the way, you will encounter this low guard position, which is used when combat is fast as well as when it is slow. You must exercise in it with your swords in hand.[101]

Fourth Technical Form

In the guard position of the fourth form, you hold the two swords horizontally on your left side and strike the wrist of your opponent with an upward motion[102] at the moment he launches his attack. If he attempts to knock down your upward-moving sword, you follow your intention of striking his wrist in accordance with the way of the sword,[103] and you extend the stroke obliquely up to the height of your own shoulder.[104] This technique conforms to the way of the sword. If your adversary launches another attack, you will defeat him in the same manner in accordance with the way of the sword. You must examine this well.[105]

Fifth Technical Form
The fifth form has to do with a guard position where you hold the swords in the right-side guard position, horizontally. Relating to the opponent's attack, starting from this position low and to the side, you strike diagonally upward and then slash directly downward from above. This form is also important for knowing the way of the sword well. If you train in handling the swords in accordance with this form, you will reach the point of being able to move the heavy swords easily.[106]

Giving more details regarding these five forms is not necessary. Above all, it is through continuously applying the techniques of these five forms in their full depth[107] that you will learn the whole of the way of the sword of my school, master the general cadences, and perceive the qualities of the sword of your opponents. At the time of combat against opponents, you will thoroughly and fully apply these sword techniques, and you will win, in whatever way, by employing various cadences in response to the intentions of your opponent. You must learn well how to see with discernment.[108]

The Teaching of the Guard without a Guard[109]

Here is what is called the guard without a guard—this is not having in your mind the idea of adopting a guard position. Nevertheless, the five positions that I have mentioned can become guard positions. You will find yourself placing your sword in a variety of positions depending on the openings furnished by your opponent[110] and depending on the place and the situation of combat—but no matter what the situation, you must always hold the sword in such a way you that can slash well at your opponent.

You hold your sword in the high position, and if in accordance with the moment you lower it a little, your guard will become that of the middle level, and then if it becomes advantageous to raise it a little, your guard will again become the high one. In the same way, if in responding to the occasion you slightly raise your sword from the low position, that will become the middle-level guard. If you hold the sword to the right or the left, and in response to situations you move it inward, you will pass into the middle or low guard. It is in this sense that I recommend the guard without a guard. Whatever the situation is, you hold the sword so that you can slash your opponent.

You parry your opponent's sword, which is coming to strike you; you touch, press against, or graze it—all that becomes the occasion for you to strike him.[111] You should keep that clearly in mind. If you think of parrying, if you think of striking, if you think of touching, of pressing, of grazing, you run the risk of your slashing action being inadequate. The essential is to think that anything you are doing has to become the occasion for slashing. You must examine this well.

As for group strategy, the placement of troops corresponds to the guard position, and what is necessary is to aim at creating an opportunity to win. Letting a situation fixate[112] is bad. You should work this out well.

A Single Cadence for Striking Your Adversary[113]

Here is what I call the single-cadence strike: You are near your opponent, at a distance apart at which you can just reach each other, and you strike very rapidly and directly without moving your body,[114] not letting your will to attack become attached anywhere, seizing the instant when he does not expect it. You strike him with a single blow just at the instant when he is not even thinking of pulling back his sword or moving it out of the guard position or attacking. After having learned this cadence well, you must train in striking rapidly with the interval cadence.[115]

The Passing Cadence in Two Phases

Here is the passing cadence in two phases:[116] You are just about to attack and your opponent backs away or parries quickly. You feint striking him and then actually strike him at the moment when he relaxes after having started a parrying movement or after having backed up. That is the passing cadence in two phases. It is difficult to master this strike just from reading this text, but you will understand it immediately when it is taught to you directly.

The Strike of Nonthought[117]

In a situation where both you and your adversary are just about to launch an attack, make your body into a body that is striking, make your mind into a mind that is striking. Then your hand will strike spontaneously out of emptiness, with speed and power, without taking note of the starting point of the movement. This is the strike of nonthought. It is of prime importance. You will often encounter this kind of strike. You must study it and train in it well.

The Flowing-Water Strike

Here is what I call the flowing-water strike:[118] You are fighting an equal battle with your opponent and each of you is searching for an opening. In this situation, when your opponent tries in haste to back off or to disengage his sword or to push yours back, you expand your body and your mind. You strike broadly and powerfully by moving your body forward first and then your sword, with a movement that is apparently quite slow, like flowing water that seems to be stagnating.[119] By mastering this technique, you will gain ease and confidence. It is indispensable here to discern the level of your opponent.[120]

The Chance-Opening Blow[121]

When you strike, your opponent tries to parry by blocking or hitting your sword. You put yourself fully and completely into the action of striking with your sword and you strike whatever you encounter in your path, whether it is the head, the arms, or the legs [of your opponent]. Strike in this way, following the single way of the sword—this is the chance-opening strike.[122] If you learn this approach well, you will find an application for it at all times. You must minutely discern the details in the course of training bouts.

The Blow Like a Spark from a Stone[123]

In a situation in which your sword and your opponent's are about to cross, strike extremely hard without raising your sword at all. That is the blow like a spark from a stone. To execute this technique, you must strike quickly with the three combined forces of your legs, your body, and your hands.[124] This blow is difficult to execute if you do not exercise in it frequently. With diligent training you will be able to increase the force of its impact.

The Crimson-Leaves Strike[125]

You cause your adversary's sword to drop by striking it, then you immediately bring yourself back to a readiness to strike. That's what I call the crimson-leaves strike. When the opponent assumes a guard position facing you, at the moment he is thinking of striking, hitting, or parrying, you strike his sword either with the strike of nonthought or with the strike like a spark from a stone. You strike with force, and if you extend the force of your strike[126] by executing it so that the point of your sword is directed toward the ground, your opponent's sword will definitely drop. By training assiduously, you will arrive at being able to make your opponent's sword fall with ease. You must train well.

The Body Replacing the Sword

Instead of "the body replacing the sword,"[127] I could as well say "the sword replacing the body." In general, when you strike, the movements of body and sword are not simultaneous. Taking advantage of the opportunities created by your opponent's strikes, first you put your body in striking position, and your sword will strike without taking your body into account. It can also happen that you strike solely with the movement of the sword without moving your body, but generally first you put your body in a striking position, and the sword will strike afterward. As you learn the strikes, you must examine this well.

The Strike and the Hit

A strike and a hit[128] are two different things. Striking is striking consciously, deliberately, whatever the manner of the strike. The hit is like a chance encounter, and even if it is strong enough so that your opponent dies from it at once, it is a hit. Whereas a strike is carried out with awareness. This must be examined. A hit might get to the adversary's arm or leg, but this hit must be followed by a potent strike. A hit means having the sensation of touching [by chance]. As you learn this, the difference becomes obvious. Work this out well.

The Autumn Monkey's Body

The autumn monkey's body[129] expresses a combat posture in which you do not use your hands. In getting in close to your opponent, do not think of using your hands. Think of quickly getting your body in close[130] before striking your opponent. If you think of reaching out with your hands, your body will inevitably remain distant.[131] That is why you must think of getting your whole body in close quickly. When you are at a distance[132] at which you exchange sword blows, it is easy to get in close to your opponent.[133] You must examine this well.

The Body of Lacquer and Paste[134]

By speaking of lacquer and paste, I teach getting very close to your opponent and staying stuck to him. When you get in very close to your adversary, behave as though you were strongly glued to him with your head, your body, and your feet. In general, fighters have a tendency to put their heads and feet forward, but the body often hangs back. You must try to paste your body against your opponent's without leaving any place where your bodies are not touching. You must examine this well.

Comparing Heights

Here is what I call comparing heights:[135] When you get in close to your opponent, whatever the circumstances, penetrate forcefully and avoid shrinking; as though you were comparing heights, stretch the limbs, the pelvis, and also the neck. Set your face over against that of your adversary and enlarge yourself, as though to defeat him in a comparison of heights. It is important to move forward forcefully with this attitude. Work this out well.

Making Your Movements Stick[136]

In a situation where you and your opponent are both striking with your swords, when your opponent parries your attack, you stick your sword to his and get in close to him while maintaining this sticky quality. This stickiness should produce the sensation that your swords are difficult to separate, and you must get in close without having too much of a feeling of forcing. When you stick your sword to your opponent's and maintain this adhesion, it is possible for you to get in close to him with complete confidence.

There is a difference between sticking and getting tangled up. Sticking is powerful, getting tangled up is weak. These should be distinguished.

Banging into Your Opponent[137]

At the moment of coming in close to your opponent, you bang into him. You tilt your face slightly to the side, stick out your left shoulder,[138] and bang into his chest. In banging into him, you fill your entire body with force, and you strike with a cadence of concordance with the breath[139] and with a sensation of rebounding. By mastering this technique, you can strike so violently that your opponent will be knocked back a distance of two or three ken.[140] Your impact can be such that your opponent dies of it. You should train well.

The Three Parries

Here are what I call the three parries:[141] When you come in close to your opponent, if he strikes at you, you parry his sword with a movement as of stabbing[142] his eye with your large sword, thus deflecting his sword over your right shoulder.

Here is what I call the stabbing parry: You parry the sword of your adversary, who is attacking you, as though you were going to stab his right eye, with the sensation that you are going to slit his throat with the continuation of this movement.

Finally, at the moment when your opponent attacks, you parry with your short sword as you come in close to him, doing this as though you were going to punch him in the face with your left fist and without giving any thought to the length of the blade of the sword you are holding. For this third parry,[143] you should think that you are delivering a punch with your left hand.[144]

You should train in these well.

Piercing the Face

Here is what I call piercing the face:[145] In the course of combat, the two combatants are face-to-face, separated by a certain distance, each holding his sword pointing toward his opponent. At this time it is essential to think constantly of piercing the face of your opponent with the point of your sword. By applying your mind to piercing the face of your opponent in this way, his face and body will be pushed back.[146] After having repulsed the adversary in this manner, different opportunities to defeat him will present themselves. You must work this out well. During the combat, if you succeed in pushing back the body of your opponent, you will already have won. That is why you must never forget what I call piercing the face. You must acquire this approach in the course of your training in strategy.

Piercing the Heart

Here is what I call piercing the heart:[147] When the place of combat is tight with regard to height and breadth and you have difficulty in executing slashing movements, stab your opponent. Elude his strike with the sensation of directly showing him the back of your sword,[148] then bring the point of your sword back into a straight line and from this position stab him in the chest.[149] You should apply this technique when you are tired or when your sword is not cutting well anymore. You must understand this well.

Katsu-totsu

Here is what I call *katsu-totsu*:[150] When you attack, driving your opponent back, or when he tries to riposte in response to your attack, you lift your sword from below upward as though to stab him, then you reverse this movement—lowering your sword—in order to strike him. In all cases, you strike with a rapid cadence, *katsu-totsu*—that is, you raise your sword upward in order to stab, *katsu,* and then you strike, *totsu.* In the course of combat, you will very often encounter this cadence. You execute *katsu-totsu* by first raising the point of your sword as though to stab your opponent and then lowering it immediately in order to strike him. You must train well in this cadence and examine it.

The Parry with the Flat of the Sword

Here is what I call the parry with the flat of the sword:[151] In the course of combat, when the exchanges of attacks and defenses between adversaries become stagnant and repetitive in a cadence of *totan-totan*,[152] you parry an attack with a slap of your sword, which you apply to the sword of your opponent side against side, and afterward you strike. Do not slap too hard and do not think about parrying. The proper way to react to your opponent's attack is to slap his sword and strike him immediately as an extension of the same effort. You must take the initiative through the movement of slapping your opponent's sword and take the initiative through the strike. If you slap his sword with the right cadence, with the sensation of stretching your arm slightly,[153] even if your opponent's strike is very strong, the point of your sword will not be knocked down. You must study this well and examine it.

Conduct against Many Adversaries

What I call "conduct against many adversaries"[154] applies when you are fighting alone against many adversaries. Draw both your large and small swords and take up a guard position with them held wide apart, as though you were tossing them horizontally to both sides of you. Even if your opponents come at you from four sides, you will fight them by driving them back in a single direction. Distinguish clearly in the conduct of your opponents the order in which they are launching their attacks; you face first those who come at you first. Look all around, strike at the same time in opposite directions with the right sword and the left sword in response to the tactics of your adversaries. It is bad to wait after having struck. Immediately resume your guard position on the two sides, and as soon as someone advances, strike him forcibly and in this way shake your opponents. Extending this momentum, assault those who advance each time with the intention of making them crumble. Continually make every effort to push your opponents back so they will be forced into one rank, one behind the other, like fish strung on a line.

As soon as your opponents pile up one behind the other, sweep them away by slashing with force, without letting this moment escape. It is not very effective to continue to beat back opponents who form into a compact group. It is also ineffective to face off with adversaries each time they approach you, because you then place yourself in a situation of waiting. Perceive the cadences of your adversaries, recognize the moment in which they will crumble, and you will be victorious.

Train from time to time with many partners and exercise in the way of driving them back. If you grasp this nuance, you will be as at ease fighting against ten or twenty opponents as against a single one. You must train well, then examine.

The Principle of Combat

In strategy it is by the principle of combat[155] that you will know victory with the sword. I do not have to write about the details. The important thing is to train well and learn how to win. This has to do with sword techniques that express the true way of strategy. The rest must be transmitted orally.[156]

The Single Strike

Gain the capacity to win with certainty by keeping in your mind the single strike.[157] It is impossible to acquire this strike without studying strategy thoroughly. It is by training in this strike that you will achieve a free mastery of strategy. This is the way of victory at will in any combat. You must exercise well.

Direct Communication

The mind of transmission of direct communication[158]—that is what I will transmit to he who has received the true way of my School of Two Swords. It is essential to train well so that your body becomes strategy. The rest will be communicated orally.

I have written above in this scroll the general teaching of my school of the sword.

In strategy, to know how to win with the sword, it is necessary first to learn the five forms of striking in conjunction with the five guard positions. Mastering by this means the pathway *(michi)* of the sword, the body will be free and the mind will come alive to grasp the cadences of the way *(michi)*. Your sword and your technique will be naturally remarkable, since your body will be available from head to toe to move with free mastery. It is in this way that you will be victorious first over one, then over two, and that you will finally be able to understand what is good and what is bad in strategy. Train by following one by one the instructions I have written down in this text, and you will progressively obtain the principle of the way *(michi)* by practicing combat with different opponents. Never fail to have this attitude of mind, go forward without hurry, learn the essence of things through frequent experiences, taking advantage of every occasion. Fight against all kinds of people and be aware of their mind. Follow a road that is a thousand leagues long one step at a time. Be without haste and be convinced that all these practices are the duty of a *bushi*. Be victorious today over what you were yesterday; tomorrow be victorious over your clumsiness and then also over your skill. Practice in accordance with what I have written without letting your mind deviate from the way.

Even if you gain victory over the most formidable of adversaries, unless it is in conformity with the principle, this victory cannot be considered part of the true way *(michi)*.[159] By assimilating this principle, you will become able to conquer several tens of adversaries. Then, through the wisdom of the art of the sword, you will be able to master individual strategy and group strategy.

A thousand days of training to develop, ten thousand days of training to polish. You must examine all this well.

The twelfth of the fifth month of the second year Shoho [1645]
Shinmen Musashi
For the Honorable Lord Terao Magonojo

The fifth of the second month of the seventh year of Kanbun [1667]
Terao Yumeyo Katsunobu
For the Honorable Lord Yamamoto Gensuke

THE SCROLL OF FIRE

I write about battle and combat in this scroll of fire,[160] for it is through the image of fire that I think of battle in the strategy of the School of Two Swords.

In this world, people are alike in having too limited a conception of strategy. Often strategy is thought of in a small way. Some seek trivial advantages by using the ends of their fingers and an area of the wrist of five or three *sun* in length.[161] They know how to be victorious in combat through movements of the forearm that they teach with a fan. Others teach the advantages of slight increases in speed with a *shinai*[162] through developing techniques of the arms and legs, and they attribute the greatest significance to any increase in speed, as slight as it might be.

I have engaged in combat many times in accordance with my strategy, at the risk of my life. I have discerned the principle that makes it possible to situate oneself between life and death, and I have learned the way of the sword. I have also learned to recognize the strength and weakness of the adversary's sword, and I have understood the meaning of the edge and the back of the sword.[163] In training to strike your adversary a mortal blow, you cannot even think of small and feeble techniques. Especially if you are seeking to gain advantage in combat where armor is worn,[164] you cannot even think about small techniques.

The way of my strategy, again, is to know with certainty the principle *(michi)*[165] that makes it possible to be victorious alone against five or against ten opponents when your life is at risk. Where, then, is the difference in the principle of the way[166] between "winning one against ten" and "winning a thousand against ten thousand"? That must be examined well.

However, in ordinary training it is impossible to exercise in the way with a thousand or ten thousand people. That is why, in single combat, you probe the tactics of each of your opponents, you try to be aware of the strength and weakness of their techniques; in this way you will understand how to win against any person,[167] thanks to the wisdom of strategy. In this fashion you will become an accomplished practitioner of this way.

Thinking, "Who besides me in the world is going to attain direct communication[168] in strategy?" and also "I will surely achieve this one day," train from morning till night. When in this manner you have finished polishing, you will spontaneously acquire freedom and excellent ability, and in this way you will be able to gain access to supernatural power.[169] This is the vital essence[170] of the practice of the method of the art of war.

Regarding the Place of Combat[171]

Regarding the evaluation of the place, a first teaching is to situate yourself with your back to the sun; assume a guard position with the sun behind your back. Depending on the situation, if it is impossible to place yourself with your back to the sun, you should place yourself with the sun on your right.

The same goes for light when you are fighting in a house. Place yourself with the light behind you, and if not, on your right. It is preferable to place yourself without having your back right up against the wall, leaving some space on the left side and not leaving any space on the right side.[172]

At night, if your opponents are visible, you should also situate yourself with your back to the light or with the light on your right, keeping present in your mind your guard position as in the previous situations.

You should try to situate yourself on higher ground, however slightly; this is what is called "looking at your opponents from above." If you are in a house, consider the rear of it as the high place.[173]

In the course of combat, you should try to direct your opponents toward your left side and drive them back in such a way that they have their backs to the difficult place. In any case, it is important to drive your opponents toward a difficult place. Drive them back without relenting, so that they will not have a chance to turn their heads to recognize the difficulty of the place. When fighting in a house, drive them back in the same way without allowing them to turn their heads so that they cannot recognize that they are getting close to the threshold, the lintel, the sliding door, the porch, or a pillar.

In all cases, you should force them in the direction where the terrain is bad, where there are obstacles. Taking the advantages and disadvantages of the location clearly into account, you must try to win first through your grasp of the site. You should examine this all well and train.

The Three Ways of Taking the Initiative *(Sen)*

In combat there are three ways of taking the initiative *(sen)*.[174]

The first consists in attacking before your opponent. I call this "attacking before your opponent" *(ken no sen)*.[175]

The second consists in taking the initiative when your opponent attacks first. I call it "taking initiative at the time of an attack" *(tai no sen)*.

The third consists in taking the initiative when the two adversaries are getting ready to attack each other. I call it "the initiative at the time of a reciprocal attack" *(tai-tai no sen)*.

These are the three ways of taking the initiative.

Whatever the form of combat, there does not exist any other way of taking the initiative once the fighting has started apart from these three. Taking the initiative is essential for strategy, since it is through this that a quick win in combat will be determined. There are details to be mastered in relation to taking the initiative, but it is pointless to describe them, because it is a matter of winning through the wisdom of your own strategy by discerning the intentions of your opponent and choosing the way of taking the initiative that is appropriate to each moment.

First, attack before your opponent does *(ken no sen)*. When you want to attack, you remain calm at the beginning, then you take the initiative of attacking all of a sudden. Take the initiative with a state of mind that remains calm in its depth while being strong and fast on the surface.

Maintain a mental disposition that is very strong, move your feet somewhat more quickly than usual, and as soon as you near your opponent, take the initiative by acting very fast.[176] All through the combat, preserve an untroubled mind[177] with the sole idea of crushing your opponent; in this way you will gain a victory with a mind that is strong to its depth. All these examples are ways of taking the initiative by attacking before your opponent does.

Second, taking the initiative at the time of an attack *(tai no sen)*.[178] When your opponent attacks you, pretend to be weak and remain without a reaction. At the moment when he approaches, make a broad and vigorous move back, then, with a leap, feint an attack, and the instant he relaxes, strike him, straight on and with force. Take the initiative to win in this way. When the adversary attacks you, oppose him with the greatest vigor—he will modify the *hyoshi* of his attack; take control of him in this moment of change and defeat him. Such is the principle of taking the initiative at the time of an attack.

Third, taking the initiative at the time of a reciprocal attack *(tai-tai no sen)*.[179] When your opponent attacks fast, face him calmly and powerfully. Then at the moment he gets near you, pretend suddenly to abandon your riposte. From this, the instant your opponent relaxes in anticipation of an illusory victory, you gain the victory by striking directly. Against an opponent who attacks you calmly, attack in a lively manner, rather quickly—approach him and exchange a series of sword blows. Following his reactions, you will defeat him with strength. These are two ways of taking the initiative at the time of a reciprocal attack *(tai-tai no sen)*.

It is not possible to give the details in writing. You must find out for yourself along with reading this text. You will be able to execute these three ways of taking the initiative by adapting to the evolution of the situation and applying the principles. Although you may not necessarily be able to attack first, it is preferable to try to force your opponent to move through your initiative. In any case, in order to be able to take the initiative, train your mind well to strive toward a flawless victory by employing the wisdom of strategy.[180]

Holding Down on the Headrest

What I want to express by "holding down on the headrest"[181] is a way of conducting yourself in combat in which you do not allow your opponent to raise his head. In the combat of strategy, it is harmful to allow yourself to be led by your opponent and to place yourself on the defensive. It is necessary at all costs to work to lead your opponent in accordance with your will. However, if you are thinking that, your opponent is thinking that also. It is therefore impossible to lead him in a way that is favorable for you unless you are able to foresee his actions. You block a strike, you parry the sword that is coming to stab you, or you get loose when your opponent is holding you—you are then behind your opponent in strategy.

What I mean to say by "holding down on the headrest" is different. If you are fighting as one having arrived at the true way *(michi),* you can perceive the will of your opponent before he makes a move.[182] If he intends to strike, you grasp the first letters of strike—*stri*—and you do not allow him to complete his striking movement. That is the sense of "holding down on the headrest." For example, when your opponent means to attack, you grasp the letters *att* in *attack,* when he means to jump, you take hold of the *ju* in *jump,* when he means to slash, you seize the *sla* in *slash.* All these have the same sense. In the course of combat, you allow him to do useless things while preventing him from doing anything effective. This is essential in strategy.

However, working to prevent each movement your opponent tries to make is following his initiative. The essential is for you to exercise in all the techniques following the way correctly, and in this manner you will come to the point where you can foresee the will of your opponent and prevent him from actualizing it by rendering all of his movements ineffective. Dominating your opponent in this manner proves that you are a true adept who has spent long years in training. You should examine well what I mean by holding down on the headrest.

Getting Over a Critical Passage

Here is what I call "getting over a critical passage."[183] I will take the example of navigation at sea. In certain straits the currents are fast, and a distance of forty or fifty leagues constitutes a critical passage. Also in traversing life,[184] a person encounters numerous critical passages.

In navigating at sea, it is necessary to know the dangerous places, the position of the ship, and the weather. Without having a pilot ship, it is necessary to know how to adapt to each situation. The wind might blow from the side or from behind or even change. You must have the determination to row for a distance of two or three leagues in order to reach port. That is the way you can get over a critical passage in a ship at sea. This way of being also applies to traversing life. You must get over a critical passage with the idea that this event is unique.[185]

It is important during a combat of strategy, also, to get over critical passages. You get over them by precisely evaluating the strength of your opponent and your own capacity. The principle of this is the same as for a good captain who is navigating a passage at sea. Once the critical place has been passed, the mind becomes calm. If you get past the critical point, your opponent will come out of it weakened, and you will begin to take the initiative. You have then practically already won. In group strategy and in individual strategy, it is essential to be determined to get over the critical passage. You should examine this well.

Realizing the Situation

Here is what I call "realizing the situation."[186] In group strategy it is necessary to recognize the moments when your opponents are at a high point and when they are at a low point, to know their numbers and their intentions, to take into account the conditions of the place, and to discern their situation clearly. You must be able to deduce from these things a way to direct your forces applying the principle of strategy, which will lead with certainty to victory, and to fight knowing how to take the initiative.

In individual strategy, you must have knowledge concerning your opponent's school,[187] discern his personality, and find his strength and his weakness. Use tactics that thwart his intentions,[188] and it is important to seize the initiative of attack by perceiving the rises and falls of your opponent's combativeness and by knowing well the cadences of his intervals. If the strength of your wisdom is sufficient, you can always perceive what the situation is. If your body moves freely in the realm of strategy, if you accurately probe the mind of your adversary, you will find many ways of winning. You must work this out.

Crushing the Sword with Your Foot

"Crushing the sword with your foot"[189] is an expression that is unique to strategy.

In group strategy the adversaries first shoot with bows and guns or attack in some other way. If you make your assault after their bow and gun volleys, it is difficult to succeed in penetrating by force, because they have time to draw their bows again and to refill their guns with powder. That is why it is necessary to make a rapid assault while your adversaries are shooting their bows or firing their guns. As soon as the enemy acts, break their actions by reacting in accordance with principle. Thus you will obtain victory.

In individual strategy, if you strike by responding after each of your opponent's attacks, the combat will stagnate and become a repetition of the same cadences.[190] If you think of crushing your opponent's sword under your foot, you will vanquish him the instant of his first attack so as to take away his chance of acting a second time.

You do not crush only with your foot; you must also know how to crush with your body, with your mind, and also, of course, with your sword[191] in order to interdict any second move by your adversary. It is in this way that you can take the initiative *(sen)* in each situation. You act at the same time as your opponent not in such a way as to collide with him but so as to pursue him after the encounter.[192] You must examine this well.

Recognizing the Instant of Collapse[193]

For each thing there exists an instant in which it collapses. A house, a person, an adversary, collapses over the course of time following discordances in cadence.[194]

In group strategy, once you have grasped the cadence of collapse of your adversaries, it is essential to place them under attack without leaving them a single instant's interval. If you let them have a breather when they are about to collapse, you will give them a chance to recoup their forces.

In individual strategy, it may happen that during the combat your opponent begins to collapse as a result of a discordance in cadence. But if you slack off at this moment, you will give him an opportunity to reestablish himself, and you will lose a chance to defeat him. At the moment your opponent fails to collapse, persist in pushing him back by means of firm attacks so that he has no further chance of raising his head. Drive him back with a direct and powerful mind and strike him in a way that makes the blow carry a long way, so that he will not be able to recover. You must understand well this strike that causes the blow to carry a long way.[195] If you do not put some distance between you and your opponent, this strike is difficult to execute.[196] This must be worked out.

Becoming your Opponent

Here is what I call "becoming your opponent."[197] This is the thinking you do when you put yourself in his place. In life there exists a tendency to overestimate the power of the adversary. Take for example a robber who, not having succeeded in fleeing, locks himself up in a house. If you put yourself in his place, surrounded, with all society as his enemy, you are desperately upset. Someone who locks himself up this way is a pheasant, and the person coming in to kill him is a falcon. You should think all that over well.

In group strategy, there also exists a tendency to overestimate the strength of your adversaries and to assume too prudent an attitude. You do not have to be afraid if you have a sufficient number of soldiers, if you know the principle of strategy, and if you know how to create an opportunity to win.

In individual strategy also, you must think on the basis of putting yourself in your opponent's place. Having to face an adept of *hyoho* who has perfectly mastered the principle and the techniques, he will consider himself to have lost in advance. You should examine this well.

Undoing Four Hands

Here is what I call "undoing four hands."[198] If you and your opponent are both doing the same thing, pushing one another back, the combat will not unfold to your advantage. As soon as you feel that you are being drawn into restraining your opponent by making an effort similar to his, drop what you are doing and seek to win by another means.

In group strategy, if you fight with the approach of the fight of four hands, you will not be able to come to a favorable result, and you will lose troops. It is important to drop this approach quickly and to win through means that your adversaries have not thought of.

In individual strategy, as soon as you feel that you are fighting in the manner of four hands, change your attitude. You must win by employing a radically different means, recognizing clearly the state of your opponent. You must understand this well.

Moving Your Shadow

Here is what I call "moving your shadow."[199] This is to be applied when you are unable to discern what is in the mind of your opponent.

In group strategy, when the state of your adversaries is unfathomable, pretend to attack forcefully and you will discover their tactic. Once you have discovered their tactic, it will be easy to defeat them through the use of an effective means[200] adapted to it.

In individual strategy, when your opponent takes up a guard position with his sword held back or to one side,[201] feint an attack and his mind will then be reflected in the movement of his sword. Having unveiled his state of mind, you will employ an effective means against him, and you will surely win. But if, in doing this, you let yourself relax, you will lose the appropriate cadence. Examine this well.

Constricting the Shadow

Here is what I call "constricting the shadow"[202] when you see that your adversary intends to act.

In group strategy, you constrict the instant your adversaries are about to launch their action. If you show forcefully that you are constricting the effective means used by your adversaries, they will change their tactic, because they will be constricted by your strength. At this moment you change your own tactic and gain the victory by taking the initiative of attack with an empty (ku) mind.[203]

In individual strategy, at the moment your opponent is about to attack you with a strong will, you get him to give up his action by using an effective cadence. During the cadence of his retreat, you find an effective means to defeat him, and you take the initiative of attacking. You must work this out well.

Infecting

Here is what I call "infecting."[204] This exists in everything: Sleep is infectious, yawns are infectious, and this goes for time too.[205]

In group strategy, when you perceive in your adversaries a quality of indecision and haste, pretend not to notice it and act extremely slowly; that will influence your adversaries and they will relax their attitude. When you judge that you have infected them sufficiently, seize this opportunity to win by attacking fast and strong with an empty (ku) mind.

In individual strategy, it is important to win by attacking powerfully and fast in order to grasp the initiative by seizing the moment in which your opponent has relaxed because he has been infected by the relaxed quality of your body and your mind.

You can also intoxicate your opponent by a similar process. Here you introduce dreariness, indecision, and weakness into his mind. You should work this out well.

Irritating Your Adversary[206]

One can become irritated in different ways, for example, as a result of the feeling of brushing the limits of danger, of facing the impossible, or of surprise. You should examine this well.

In group strategy, it is important to know how to irritate your adversaries. Launching a violent assault at a place your adversaries have not thought of, before their minds have a chance to stabilize,[207] take the initiative of attack, making the best of this advantage. To win in this way is essential.

In individual strategy also, show yourself as slow to begin with, then attack abruptly with force, and following the ups and downs of your opponent's concentration and movements, take advantage of this opportunity to defeat him without slacking off even to the slightest extent.[208] This is essential. You should examine it well.

Frightening[209]

Anything can frighten. One allows oneself to be frightened by what one does not expect.

In group strategy, you can frighten your adversaries not only by a direct action but also sometimes by making noises, sometimes by making a small thing look large, sometimes by making sudden attacking movements off to the sides. You should gain victory by relying on the advantage offered to you by the cadence of your adversaries' fright.

In individual strategy, you can frighten with your body, with your sword, and also with your voice. It is essential to win directly by taking advantage of the opportunity that arises at the moment when your opponent is frightened by acts that he will not have imagined. You should examine this well.

Coating

Here is what I call "coating."[210] When your adversary approaches you and you clash with him forcefully and then the development of the combat stagnates, coat your adversary as though you constituted but one single body. Try to find a chance to win in this melee.

In group strategy and also individual, when the combat stagnates because the two opponents are clashing equally, coat your opponent in such a way that it is impossible to distinguish yourself from the other. In this situation seize the opportunity to win and gain the victory with power. Examine this well.

Hitting a Corner

Here is what I call "hitting a corner."[211] You cannot always cut something down directly, especially if it is powerful.

In group strategy, first you must look at the number of enemies and create an opening by beginning attacking at the point where the enemy force forms a protrusion. If a corner is weakened, the whole will be influenced by this and weaken. While one corner is deteriorating, it is important again to find other corners where you can apply the same tactic in order to win the victory.

In individual strategy, if you wound a corner of your opponent's body, this will weaken him, however slightly, and he will begin to crumble. It is then easy to win. You should examine this well in order to master the principle of winning.

Troubling

Here is what I call "troubling."[212] It is preventing the adversary from having a confident mind.

In group strategy, probe the mind of your adversaries on the field of battle; trouble them with the skillfulness of your strategy. Draw them here and there, make them think this and that, make them sometimes think slowly and sometimes think fast. Make the most of the cadence of their troubled state to defeat them with certainty.

In individual strategy, vary your techniques according to the moment. Feint striking, stabbing, getting in close. Grasp the manner in which your opponent's mind is becoming troubled and win with ease. This is essential for combat; you must examine it well.

The Three Types of Cries

The three types of cries,[213] those for the beginning, middle, and end of a combat, are distinct. Depending on the situation, it may be important to sound a cry. Cries come from a surge of energy—people cry out at the time of a fire, in the course of a storm when there is wind and waves. You can tell someone's force from their cry.

In group strategy, at the beginning of a battle it is necessary to cry out as loudly as possible,[214] beyond what could be imagined; during the confrontations, it is appropriate to cry out in a low tone that comes from the bottom of the belly; and after having won you should make great, powerful cries.

In individual strategy, cry out *ei*[215] while pretending to attack in order to cause your opponent to make a move, and strike with your sword after this cry. Sound a cry also after having won in order to declare your victory. These two cries are called "cries of before and after."[216] Do not sound a great cry at the same time as you strike with your sword. If you cry out during combat, the cries should fit in with your cadence and be low ones. You should examine this well.

Concealing Yourself

Here is what I call "concealing yourself."[217] When two large groups oppose each other in battle, if your adversaries are powerful, conceal yourself by attacking first in one direction, then, as soon as you find your adversaries beginning to crumble, leave them as they are and redirect your attack toward other powerful groups. Move more or less as though you were zigzagging down a slope.[218]

This strategy is important when you are fighting alone against many opponents. Do not try very hard to win on each side, but as soon as you have made one side fall back, attack on another side where your opponent is strong. Perceiving the cadence of your adversaries, move with the cadence that suits you, from left to right as though you were zigzagging down a slope, while following the reaction of your opponents. When, after having discerned the force of your opponents, you go in among them to strike them, you must not in any way have the slightest notion of backing off, and you will obtain the opportunity of winning with strength. This strategy can also be applied when you are facing a single powerful adversary in order to get close to him.[219] To conceal yourself, you must not have in your mind the least thought of backing away. You must understand clearly what is meant by, "going forward while concealing yourself."

Smashing

Here is what I call "smashing."[220] For example, it is important to have in mind to smash the adversary, determinedly considering him to be weak while viewing yourself as strong.[221] In group strategy, if the adversaries are few in number or even if they are many, they are in a state of weakness when they are moving about indecisively in a disoriented condition. Smash them, starting with the head, adding to this an oppressive burst of energy[222] that has the sensation of pushing them and smashing them. If you do not smash them enough, it is possible they may regain their strength. So smash them as though you held them in your hands. You must understand this well.

In individual strategy, when you are fighting against an inferior opponent or when your opponent backs away as the result of a discord in his cadence, it is important not to give him a moment to breathe and, without meeting his glance, to continue straight on and smash him completely. It is of vital importance not to give him the least opportunity to recover, however slightly. You should examine this well.

Change from the Mountain to the Sea[223]

Here is what I call "the mind of the mountain and the sea." It is harmful to do the same thing several times in the course of combat. You can do the same thing twice but not three times. If you fail with a technique, you can begin it over again once more, but if you do not succeed this time, abruptly apply another, completely different technique. In this way, if your opponent is thinking of the mountain, you apply the sea; if he is thinking of the sea, you apply the mountain. Such is the way of strategy. You must examine this well.

Ripping Out the Bottom

Here is what I call "ripping out the bottom."[224] When you fight against an opponent, it might happen that you get the impression of having won on account of the advantage of the way, but it could be that the mind of your adversary has not been broken and that his defeat has been superficial, while in its depth his mind has not been defeated. In this case, abruptly renew your mind and batter him until his mind has been broken and he feels completely defeated.[225] It is essential to ascertain this.

You rip out the bottom [of his resistance] with your sword, with your body, and also with your mind. It is not appropriate to think of this in just one way. It is when he has collapsed from the very bottom that you no longer need to maintain your vigilance—otherwise, you must maintain it. But as long as in its depth he maintains his mind, it is difficult to bring him to collapse. In group and individual strategy, you should train well in order to learn how to rip out the bottom.

Renewing Yourself

Here is what I call "renewing yourself."[226] If at the time of a combat, you feel yourself entangled with your opponent and the fight is stagnating, you throw off your preceding sensations and renew your thoughts as though you were doing everything for the first time. In this way you employ a new cadence to achieve victory.[227]

As soon as you feel a grating indecisiveness in your contact with your opponent, immediately renew your mind so you can make use of a completely different opening in order to win. In group strategy as well, it is important to know how to renew yourself. This is something you will find immediately through the wisdom of strategy. You should examine it well.

A Mouse's Head and a Bull's Neck

Here is what I call "a mouse's head and a bull's neck."[228] In the course of a combat, it sometimes happens that the two combatants become entangled because both of them have gotten hung up on details. In this situation you should always keep in mind that the way of strategy is like a mouse's head and a bull's neck, and while you are fighting with small techniques, all of a sudden enlarge your mind and transform those small techniques into big ones. This is an integral part of strategic thought. It is important for a warrior to think every day that a person's mind is like a mouse's head and a bull's neck. For group and individual strategies, it is necessary always to have this way of thinking present. You should examine all this well.

The General Knows His Soldiers

Here is what I call "the general knows his soldiers."[229] This is applicable in all battles. If you practice this method unremittingly and if you succeed in realizing the way as you understand it, you will obtain the power of the knowledge of strategy. You will then be able to consider all your opponents as your own soldiers, with whom you can have done whatever you like. You will have the sense of directing your opponents according to your will. You are then the general and your adversaries are your soldiers. You must work this out well.[230]

Letting Go of the Sword Handle

What I call "letting go of the sword handle"[231] has several senses. It is the state of mind of winning without having a sword and also the state of mind of not winning with the sword. I shall not write down all the ways of conducting oneself that flow from this mind. You should train well.

The Body of a Rock

Here is what I call "the body of a rock." He who has mastered the way of strategy can immediately become like a rock. At that point he will never receive a sword blow and nothing will be able to move him.[232] The details will be given orally.

I HAVE WRITTEN in the foregoing what I think uninterruptedly in the practice of the sword of my school. This is the first time I have written on this principle. There are therefore confusions in the organization of the sentences, and I have not been able to express myself down to small details. Nonetheless, this text will serve to guide the mind of those who study this way.

I have devoted myself to the way of strategy since my youth. I have exhausted the knowledge of the hand and body in all the techniques of the sword, and my thought has passed through several stages. I have visited a variety of schools and I have seen in some of them skillful explanations being given and in others subtle techniques of the hand being shown. They have a nice appearance, but none of them manifests a correct mind. I think it is possible to develop a certain skill of body and a certain finesse of mind by learning these techniques, but all this training becomes, for the way, a source of faults. These persist without ever disappearing, and because of them, the correct way of strategy fades away and the way is lost.

For mastering the true way of the sword and for defeating your adversary in combat, the principle is in no way different. If you obtain the power of the knowledge of my strategy and if you act correctly, there will be no doubt of your victory.

The twelfth of the fifth month of the second year of Shoho [1645]
Shinmen Musashi
To the Honorable Lord Terao Magonojo

The fifth of the second month of the seventh year of Kanbun [1667]
Terao Musei Katsunobu
To the Honorable Lord Yamamoto Gennosuke

THE SCROLL OF WIND

Knowing the Way of Strategy of Other Schools

I write the Scroll of Wind[233] on the subject of the other schools of strategy in order, in this scroll, to explain what they are. You cannot know with certainty the way of your own school without knowing the way of others.

I have visited and observed other schools of strategy. In one school they use a large sword of great length and merely seek for power in their technique. In another school the way is practiced with a small sword called a *kodachi*. Another school has elaborated many varied techniques; there the way is transmitted with different guard positions for the sword, and they distinguish between surface training and depth training.[234] In this scroll I write the reasons why all these trends are not the true way and I explain their advantages and disadvantages.

The principle of my school is quite different. In the other schools, techniques are displayed like merchandise adorned with colors and flowers, so they can be turned into a way of making a living, which is not the true way. The strategies propagated in this world are limited to the single small domain of the art of the sword,[235] and it is thought that to win it is enough solely to acquire techniques by training in handling the sword and in movements of the body. Neither of these two ways is a sure one.

I explain here what is lacking in the other schools. It is necessary to thoroughly examine all of this together as a whole in order to understand the advantage of my School of Two Swords.[236]

Schools That Use a Particularly Long Large Sword

There are schools that prefer a particularly long large sword.[237] From the point of view of my strategy, these are weak schools. For their preference for the long large sword comes from the idea of trying to win by placing oneself far from the sword of your opponent; they think that this is the advantage of a long sword. This attitude comes from a misunderstanding of the principle that consists in defeating the adversary no matter what the situation is.

People say that the longer one's limbs are, the better it is,[238] but this idea comes from those who are ignorant concerning strategy. Instead of relying on the principle of strategy, they try to win by means of length and situating themselves far away from their opponent. This approach comes from mental weakness; it is in this sense that I consider their strategies to be weak.

If you fight from a short distance away, at a distance from which you might well be able to close in to a hand-to-hand range, the longer your sword is, the less well you are able to strike, the less well you are able to swing it around—and a long sword becomes a weight on you. Someone who has a small sword,[239] or even someone who has nothing in his hands, can have the advantage in this sort of situation. Those who prefer a long sword may be able to justify their choice, but their reasoning is valid only for themselves. If you look from the point of view of the true way of this world, there is no reason for that. How can you say that with a small sword you will inevitably lose against someone with a big sword? When you fight in a space that is tight in width or height, or when you are in a house where it is permitted to carry only a small sword, preference for a large sword has bad consequences, because this preference comes from uncertainty about your own strategy. In addition, some people do not have the main force to handle a large sword.

As a proverb has it—"something large can replace something small"—so I do not unconditionally reject length, but, rather, it is the prejudice in favor of length that I repudiate. In group strategy, the large sword corresponds to a large number of troops and the small sword to a small number. Is it impossible for a small number to fight a large number? We know of several examples where a smaller force has carried off the victory. In my school I reject this sort of narrow preconceived outlook. You should examine this well.

Schools That Use the Sword with Brute Force[240]

It is not appropriate to set up a distinction between a strong sword and a weak sword. If you strike with the intention of producing force, your sword technique will be crude, and it is difficult to achieve victory with crude technique. If you try hard to cut through a human body using force, you will not succeed. If you try to cut through various objects,[241] you will see that it is bad to strike with force.

In fighting a mortal enemy,[242] no one would think of cutting him down weakly or strongly; when you want to kill someone, you do not do it strongly, and of course not weakly, but simply in such a way that he dies.

In practicing the sword with brute force, if you slap the other's sword forcefully in making a parry,[243] the force will spill over, and that is always bad. If you hit the other's sword with a great deal of force, your sword might break in two.[244] Thus it makes no sense to advocate using the sword with brute force.

In group strategy, if you try to win in a battle through sheer power—with strength in troops—then your opponents will also try to have strength in troops and they will want to fight with brute force. The two sides will thus be thinking the same way. It is impossible to win in any domain without the principle of the way.[245] In the way of my school,[246] you must never consider the impossible and you must learn to win in all ways thanks to the power of the knowledge of strategy. You must work this out well.

Schools That Use the Short Sword

Trying to win with only the short sword[247] is not the true way. From ancient times the large and the small sword have been talked about; this clearly expresses the usefulness of having a long and a short one. In this world a strong person can easily handle a large sword; there is no point in limiting him to a short sword. When you need a long weapon, you can even take a lance or a *naginata*.[248] With a small sword, trying to look for a fault in your opponent's attack in order to cut him down, trying to penetrate in close by leaping, or making an attempt to catch hold of the body of your opponent—all these approaches are partial and no good. Looking for a fault as the opening for your attack amounts to submitting to the initiative of the other[249] and should be avoided, because you run the risk of becoming entangled with him.

When facing many opponents,[250] if you have a short weapon in your hand, the idea of getting close enough[251] to them to fight hand to hand or to catch hold of them is ineffective. If you are particularly trained in the use of the short sword, even when you want to drive back many adversaries by slashing at them, or when you want to leap about freely or spin energetically, all of your sword technique becomes defensive, and you have a tendency to fall into confusion. Therefore this is not a sure way.

To the extent to which it is possible, you must repulse your opponents by getting them to jump about and become disconcerted, while you yourself keep straight, with power, in order to obtain the victory with certainty. This is the way. The principal is the same for group strategy. To the extent to which it is possible, the essence of strategy is to crush your enemies immediately through the power of great numbers by driving them back all of a sudden.[252]

In this world, if you continually accustom yourself in the course of your apprenticeship to certain techniques of parrying, dodging, disengaging, and warding off an attack, your mind will be steered by these ways of doing things *(michi)*,[253] and you will run the risk of letting yourself be controlled by others. Since the way of strategy is straight and true, it is important to dominate your adversary by harrying him with the true principle. You should examine this well.

Schools That Have a Large Number of Techniques

Teaching people a large number of sword techniques[254] is turning the way into a business of selling goods, making beginners believe that there is something profound in their training by impressing them with a variety of techniques. This attitude toward strategy must be avoided, because thinking that there is a variety of ways of cutting a man down is evidence of a disturbed mind. In the world, different ways of cutting a man down do not exist. Whether you are an accomplished adept or a noninitiate, a woman or a child, the ways *(michi)* of striking, slapping, and cutting are not all that numerous. Apart from these movements, there are only those of stabbing and slashing broadly on the horizontal. Because what is primarily at issue is the way *(michi)* of cutting someone down, there cannot be many differences.

All the same, whatever the place and situation of combat might be, for example, a place that is closed in with regard to height or width, one must hold the sword without being discomfited by the place. It is from this necessity that the five ways of holding the sword come. All five are necessary.

Apart from that, it is not fitting to the true way to cut someone down by pivoting one's wrists, twisting one's body, jumping, or pulling back.[255] Because you cannot perform the act of cutting a man down by pivoting, twisting, jumping, or pulling back. These are entirely futile movements.

In the strategy of my school, keep your body and mind straight and make your opponent go through contortions and twist about. The essence is to defeat him in the moment when, in his mind, he is pivoting and twisting. You should examine this well.

Schools That Insist on the Importance of the Guard Position in the Art of the Sword[256]

It is erroneous to think that the guard position is essential in the art of the sword. In this world it is when there is no adversary that one can establish a guard position.[257] The reason is that, in the way of combat, there is no place for the setting up of laws, whether they relate to current custom or present-day rules. In strategy the point is to do whatever creates a disadvantage for the adversary. What is called the guard or guard position involves having recourse to immobility. For example, to construct a fortress or establish the order of a battle, one must have a powerful and immovable mind, even if the enemy attacks; this is a fundamental attitude. Whereas in the way of strategic combat, it is necessary to take initiative after initiative in any situation. Now to assume a guard position is to wait upon the initiative of the other. You must work this out well.

In the way of strategic combat, you shake the other's guard; you employ techniques he is not thinking of; you get him to panic, to become irritated, frightened; and you defeat him by becoming aware of the cadence in accordance with which he is getting lost in the situation of combat. In this practice it is bad to take up a guard position, which is waiting upon the other's initiative. It is in this sense that I insist in my school on the guard without a guard,[258] that is to say, even if there is a guard, it is not a rigid guard.

In group strategy, you must be informed of the number of your adversaries and the conditions of the place and know your own numbers and the abilities of your camp. The essential is to have an idea of the potential import of these elements when you begin combat maneuvers with your troops. Between the two situations, that in which your adversary has seized the initiative of attack and that in which you have taken the initiative, the disadvantage and the advantage vary from single to double.

Firmly setting up a guard position as a preparation to blocking the sword of your opponent and thoroughly beating it back amounts to moving a lance or a *naginata*[259] about in such a way as to set up a barrier.[260] If you strike your opponent, it is best for you to take the approach of pulling up a stake from the fence to use it as a lance or *naginata*. You should examine this well.

Schools That Teach Particular Ways of Gazing[261]

Certain schools teach particular ways of directing the gaze. This teaching varies from one school to another—you are to focus your gaze on the sword, the hand, the face, or the feet of the adversary. But to fasten the eyes in this way on a particular spot is liable to interfere with the mind and is a fault in strategy.

I will explain myself by giving some examples: Someone playing ball[262] kicks without fixing his gaze on the ball. Sometimes he kicks as he is stroking his temples,[263] sometimes while catching up to the ball on the run, sometimes as he spins. Once accustomed to it, he has no need to maintain a fixed gaze. The same is true of an acrobat.[264] An expert in this art is capable of juggling several swords while balancing a door over his nose.[265] Things are seen naturally as a result of unremitting training and not on account of looking at them fixedly.

In the way of strategy, by accumulating experiences with different opponents, you will learn the lightness or weight of the mind of each one. By practicing the way in this manner, you can see everything that is far away or close and also assess the speed or slowness of the adversary's sword. Generally, in strategy you place your gaze on the mind of your opponent.[266] In group strategy your gaze is directed onto the situation and the state of the enemy troops. There are two things you can do: looking and seeing.[267] It is necessary to look hard, to the point of perceiving the mind of your adversary and the condition of the site. It is also necessary to look broadly in order to perceive the dynamic state of the battle and the strength and weakness of the moment. You must win like this, in the right way. In group strategy and also in individual strategy, it is out of the question to fix one's gaze narrowly. As I have already said, as a result of narrow and minutely detailed vision, you will let something big escape you, and your mind will become uncertain, which will lead you to let a sure chance of winning get away from you. You should examine these reasons well and train well.

Schools That Teach Various Kinds of Footwork[268]

There are schools that teach different ways of moving the feet so as to vary movements from place to place and make them faster. These are, for example, floating foot, leaping foot, hopping foot, stamping foot, and crow's foot.[269] From the point of view of my strategy, all these movements have deficiencies.

Floating foot is to be avoided because in situations of combat, there is always the tendency to have the sensation of floating in the feet; therefore one should move with firm steps.

Leaping foot is not good because at the moment of leaping, there is a pushing-off movement, and you make a movement to dampen the impact at the moment of landing on the ground that holds the body back.[270] There is no reason to leap several times in a row during a battle. Therefore leaping foot is to be avoided.

With hopping foot, the mind will be hopping too, and you will not be able to fight effectively.

Stamping foot is particularly bad, since it involves a wait.[271]

There is also crow's foot and several other ways of moving rapidly.

But sword combat can take place in a variety of conditions, for example, in a marsh, in a deep rice paddy, or in the mountains; on the banks of a river, in a stony field, or on a narrow path. In some places you cannot leap or hop, and you will not be able to move rapidly either.

In my strategy the way of moving is no different from normal walking on a road.[272] You move rapidly or calmly in accordance with your opponent's cadence. In all cases, move without the movement of your feet being disturbed, without missing a step, without any excess in your step, with a suitable body posture.

Movement from place to place is equally important in group strategy, for if you launch an attack without knowing the intention of your adversary, with imprudent speed, your cadence will be thrown off, and it will be difficult to gain victory in these conditions. If your steps are too slow,[273] you will not be able to find the moments when your adversaries become troubled and are on the verge of collapse—one of the elements of victory will elude you and you will not be able to win quickly. Discern the moment when your adversaries become troubled and are foundering, and do not give them the least chance to catch their breath. Winning in this way is essential. You must train well in this.

Schools That Stress Speed[274]

Speed is not part of the true way of strategy. When you say "fast," this means a lag has occurred in relation to the cadence[275] of things; that is what is meant by "fast" or "slow."

In whatever the domain, the movements of a good, accomplished practitioner do not appear fast. For example, there are messengers who cover forty or fifty leagues at the run in a single day, but they do not run fast from morning till night. Whereas, a beginner cannot cover such a long distance, even if he has the wind to run the whole day.

In Noh theater, when a beginner sings following a good, accomplished practitioner,[276] he has the impression of lagging behind and sings with the feeling of haste. In the same way, in the drumbeat for "Old Pine" ("Oimatsu"),[277] which is a slow melody, a beginner has the feeling of lagging behind and having to catch up. "Takasago"[278] is a rather fast song, but it is not appropriate to play the drum too fast. Speed is the beginning of a fall, because it produces a deviation in the cadence. Of course, excessive slowness is also bad. The movements of a good, accomplished practitioner look slow, but there is no dead space between his movements. Whatever the domain, the movements of an expert never appear hurried. Through these examples, you should understand a principle of the way.

In the way of strategy, it is bad to try for speed. I will explain. In places such as a marsh or deep rice paddy, you cannot move either your body or your legs fast. This is all the more true for the sword—you must not try to cut with speed. If you try to cut with a fast movement, the sword—which is neither a fan nor a knife—will not cut because of the speed. You must understand that well.

In group strategy also, it is bad to think of hurrying up in order to attain speed. If you possess the attitude of mind of "holding down on the headrest," you will never be late. If your adversaries act too fast, you apply the opposite approach, you calm yourself and avoid imitating them. You must train yourself well in developing this state of mind.

Schools That Distinguish Depth and Surface

In questions of strategy, what is meant by surface and what is meant by depth?[279] In the different arts, there is a manner of distinguishing the depth from the entry[280] that refers to the ultimate teaching or the secret transmission.[281] But as to the principle that comes into play at the time of combat with an adversary, you cannot say that you fight him with techniques of the surface and cut him down with those of the depth.

In my school's teaching of strategy, you teach techniques that are easy to assimilate for those who are beginning in the study of the way, giving them an explanation that they can understand right away. Observing the degree of their advancement,[282] you progressively give them explanations that direct them toward more and more profound principles. However, in general you teach them things that correspond to situations they are really in; there is no need to distinguish between depth and entry in the teaching. This can be connected with the adage according to which if you continue to go deeper and deeper into the mountains, you will come out by a different entry.[283]

In all the ways, it might turn out that the depth technique is effective or that the entry technique is.[284]

With this principal of combat, why should you hide one thing in order to show another? That is why, in the transmission of my school, I do not have written oaths, accompanied by penalties.[285]

Observing the student's level of intelligence, you teach him the correct way and help him to free himself of the five or six bad ways of strategy.[286] You cause him to enter naturally into the true way that conforms to the principles of the warriors, so that his mind will be free from doubt. Such is the way (michi) of teaching strategy in my school.

You should train well in this.

IN THE SCROLL OF WIND I have written succinctly about the strategy of other schools in nine sections. I should have written about each of these things in greater detail, going from the entry to the depth, but I intentionally avoided mentioning the names of the schools and the names of the techniques. For in every school, the ideas and the explanations concerning such and such a way can vary from person to person in accordance with the way he understands, and every person has his way of reasoning. Thus there are small differences in thought within a single school. That is why I mentioned neither the name nor the techniques of the schools, thinking about their development in the future.

I have outlined the general characteristics of the other schools in these nine sections. If we observe things from the point of view of the way of the world and also from that of correct human reasoning, these schools follow partial ways, because one of them is attached solely to length, another touts the advantage of the short sword, and the others are partial because of one single preoccupation, whether it is strength and weakness or coarseness and fineness. I do not need to be specific about whether I am talking about the entry or the depth of such and such a school, because everybody knows.

In my school there is neither depth nor entry for the art of the sword, and there are no fixed guard positions. The essence of strategy is solely that the mind learns virtue from it.

The twelfth of the fifth month of the second year of Shoho [1645]
Shinmen Musashi
For the Honorable Lord Terao Magonojo

The fifth of the second month of the seventh year of Kanbun [1667]
Terao Musei Katsunobu
For the Honorable Lord Yamamoto Gensuke

THE SCROLL OF HEAVEN

In this scroll of heaven,[287] I elucidate the way of strategy of the School of Two Swords. The meaning of emptiness is space where there is nothing, and I also envisage emptiness as that which cannot be known. Emptiness, of course, is where there is nothing. Knowing that which does not exist while knowing that which exists—that is emptiness.

In this world, some people think of emptiness in an erroneous fashion, interpreting it as not distinguishing anything. This is the product of a mind gone astray. It is not true emptiness.

In addition, for the way of strategy, emptiness does not mean disregarding the law in order to practice the way of the warrior. Some also speak of emptiness as existing where they find nothing to do because of many doubts, but that is not true emptiness.

The warrior must learn the way of strategy with certainty by practicing the different disciplines of the martial arts, and he should not disregard anything connected with the practice of the way of the warrior. He should put it into practice from morning till night without tiring and without letting his mind wander. He should polish his mind and his will and sharpen the two visions—the one that consists in looking and the one that consists in seeing. He should know that true empty space is where the clouds of uncertainty have completely dissipated.

As long as you remain ignorant of the true way, even if you think you are on a sure way and that you are doing well in accordance with Buddhist laws or in accordance with the laws of this world, you will deviate from the true way, because you overestimate yourself and your way of seeing is distorted. You understand it if you see things with the direct way of the mind and take into account the great code of this world.

Know this state of mind and take as fundamental that which is straight, conceive of the way with a sincere mind, practice strategy broadly, think on a large scale with accuracy and clarity, think of *void* as the way and see the way as *void*.

In emptiness the good exists and evil does not exist.

Knowing exists, the principle exists, the way exists, and the mind—is void.

The twelfth of the fifth month of the second year of Shoho [1645]²⁸⁸[288]
Shinmen Musashi
For the Honorable Lord Terao Magonojo

The fifth of the second month of the seventh year of Kanbun [1667]
Terao Musei Katsunobu
For the Honorable Lord Yamamoto Gensuke

||| 5 |||

The Texts Preceding the
Gorin no sho

"THE MIRROR OF THE WAY OF STRATEGY" (*Hyodokyo*)

1. The state of mind of strategy
2. The way of looking
3. The way of holding the sword
4. About sword combat
5. The way of moving from place to place
6. The way of holding the body
7. The way of cutting
8. How to change the situation in the midst of combat
9. Getting the other to drop his sword
10. Yin in combat
11. Yang in combat
12. How to discern the other's state
13. Delivering a blow
14. How to take the initiative
15. Striking while turning the point of the sword

16. Attacking the legs
17. Attacking the hand
18. How to avoid the point of the adversary's sword
19. How to pass above the adversary's sword
20. Moving with sliding steps
21. Discerning the real intention
22. The two swords
23. How to throw a *shuriken*
24. Fighting against many opponents
25. Using the *jitte*
26. How to draw the various swords
27. The ultimate strike
28. The state of direct communication *(jiki tsu)*

Miyamoto Musashi no kami, Fujiwara Yoshitsune,
the Enmei Ryu,
the Best Adept in Japan
To Mr. Ochiai Chuemon,
the auspicious day of the tenth year of the Keicho period [1605]

|||| *"The Mirror of the Way of Strategy"* (Hyodokyo) *is Musashi's first work. It is a work of his youth, written between the ages of twenty-one and twenty-four. Two copies of it are extant today. Each is addressed to a different person and carries a different date. One of them is composed of twenty-one articles and the other of twenty-eight articles. I have given a partial translation of the latter.*

I have translated only the article titles of this work because its content is less developed than that of the Gorin no sho, *and it would seem repetitive here. The work is confined to the practice of the sword in individual combat, but the subject matter that would be developed in the* Gorin no sho *is present in embryonic form.*

I consider this text a proof that Musashi was not self-taught. It seems impossible to me that a young man of twenty-two, living in the conditions of his time, could have acquired the whole of the art of sword combat through his own experience and formulated it in such a systematic form.

This text appears to me to be a proof that Musashi had received the general transmission of a school, which could only have been that of his own family. This hypothesis is reinforced by the fact that in the twenty-fifth article, Musashi mentions the jitte, a weapon of which his father was a master. Thus Musashi had already received a systematic teaching, which he tried to reproduce when he granted a certificate of transmission to his first student.

"Thirty-five Instructions on Strategy" *(Hyoho sanju go kajo)*

|||| *In 1641, two years before beginning to write the* Gorin no sho, *Musashi wrote a work called "Thirty-five Instructions on Strategy." It was written for Lord Hosokawa, whose guest Musashi was. The* Gorin no sho *can be considered an elaboration of this work.*

If we wish to get a closer idea of Musashi's thought, it seems essential to bring together these two works, which were written some years apart. We find several articles whose subject matter is identical, but with variations in expression and also some different ideas. Comparison of the two works is useful for an in-depth reading of the Gorin no sho, *because Musashi sometimes uses different words to express the same idea, which makes it possible to get a clearer impression of his meaning. However, in some cases it is not clear whether Musashi was using a different word or whether a copyist's error has occurred (for example, jiki tsu for jikido).*

We should not forget that Musashi's works were not intended for the public and that each of them was addressed to a specific person. This is something that should be borne in mind when comparing the two texts. For this reason, even if certain passages are repeated in both, it is not accurate to consider the Hyoho sanju go kajo *purely as a work preparatory to the* Gorin no sho. *It has an original character of its own.*

The Gorin no sho *was written by Musashi for Lord Hosokawa Tadatoshi. At the end of his life, Musashi accepted the invitation of Hosokawa Tadatoshi, a lord of the south of Japan (Kyushu), to live at his court. But he was received there as his guest, not as his vassal. Lord Hosokawa practiced swordsmanship himself. In his youth he had lived for several years in Edo, where he practiced the art of the sword of the Shogun Tokugawa school. From the principal master of this school, Yagyu Munenori, he received the transmission of the school's highest level of accomplishment. When he returned to his fief in Kyushu, he practiced the sword with a certain pride and self-confidence. When he received Musashi in his fief, he faced him himself in order to gauge his level. He was mastered in just a few seconds and immediately became aware of Musashi's exceptional ability. Hosokawa also greatly appreciated Musashi's great talent in a very broad range of activities. They were both about the same age and entered into a friendship of sorts in spite of their separation in the hierarchy. That is why Hosokawa received Musashi as a guest rather than a vassal. To take Musashi in and offer him a fixed income (as he would have done for a vassal) would have been in some sense to buy him at a certain price. Whereas a guest is priceless. For this reason Hosokawa refrained from offering Musashi a position as his retainer.*

Quickly persuaded of Musashi's qualities as an adept of strategy and as a man, Hosokawa became his student. After a year of practicing with Musashi, Lord Hosokawa had not succeeded in grasping the essence of his school, so he asked Musashi to compose a text to guide his practice. Musashi then began to compose the Hyoho sanju go kajo, *which he presented to the lord a year later.*

In the translation that follows below, I confine myself to giving only the titles of those articles that more or less replicate ones in the Gorin no sho. *I have translated the others and, in my commentary, situated them in relation to the* Gorin no sho.

To help understand the nature of this text, it should be pointed out that in his introduction Musashi uses a special verbal form to express his respect for Lord Hosokawa. This is a nuance that is difficult to render in an English translation.

I write for the first time here, in your honor, on my School of Two Swords, which is the result of many years of training. Considering that it is you I am addressing, this text is insufficient to communicate that which is difficult to say. It deals with how one must handle oneself with a sword in the strategy that you usually practice. I write below about the principal aspects of this in the way that they come to my mind.

1. Why I Named My School "School of Two Swords"

|||| *The ideas in this article are presented again and further developed in the Scroll of Earth of the* Gorin no sho. *However, after explaining why he uses two swords and indicating that it is through training that one becomes capable of handling a heavy sword with ease, Musashi adds:*

Among the people also, a sailor with a rudder or oars or a farmer with a spade and a hoe each in his way succeeds in accustoming himself to his action. You too can acquire strength through regular exercise. Nonetheless, it is appropriate for each person to choose a sword that corresponds to his strength.

2. The Manner of Understanding the Way of Strategy

The way is identical for group strategy and for individual strategy. I am writing here about individual strategy, but it is appropriate to look at this keeping in mind, to take an example, the image of a general—the limbs correspond to vassals and the torso corresponds to soldiers and to the people. It is thus that one must govern the country and one's own body. In this sense I say that the way is the same for group strategy and for that of the individual.

To practice strategy it is necessary to integrate the whole of one's body, without having any imbalances. Nobody is strong and nobody is weak if he conceives of the body, from the head to the sole of the foot, as a unity in which a living mind circulates everywhere equally.

3. The Way of Holding the Sword

|||| *After a brief description of the way of holding the sword, similar to that in the* Gorin no sho *(the Scroll of Water), Musashi continues:*

Life and death exist for the sword as well as for the hand. When you adopt a guard position or parry an attack, if you forget to slash your opponent, your hand is going to forget an essential dynamic and will become fixed. That is what is called a "dead hand." A living hand is one that does not become fixed in a gesture. You will then be at ease with the possibility of slashing properly, since both the sword and the hand will be adapting flexibly to successive actions. I call that "living wrists." The wrist must not be slack, the elbow must not be too tense nor too bent. A sword should be held with tension in the lower part of the arm muscles and relaxation in the upper part of these muscles. You should examine this well.

4. Posture

It is appropriate to hold the head neither lowered nor raised. The shoulders are neither raised nor contracted. The belly is forward but not the chest. The buttocks are not drawn in. The knees are not fixed. The body is placed in a facing position, so that the shoulders appear broad. The posture of strategy should be well examined so that it also becomes one's ordinary posture.

5. Movement of the Feet

|||| *This section is nearly identical to the* Gorin no sho *(the Scroll of Water, "The Way of Moving the Feet").*

6. The Way of Looking

|||| *This is almost identical to the* Gorin no sho *(the Scroll of Water, "The Way of Looking in Strategy").*

7. Sizing up the *Ma*

Different schools give different instructions on the way to assess the *ma,* but I find that they tend to fix or rigidify your strategy; that is why I advise you not to take into consideration what you have learned before.

Whatever the discipline may be, it is by repeating exercises that you arrive at the point of being able to assess the *ma.* In general you should think that when your sword reaches your opponent, he can also reach you. When you want to kill an opponent, you have a tendency to forget your own body. You must reflect well on this.

|||| *Let us recall that* ma *is not exactly distance but is a description of the space-time of a relationship.* Ma *also refers to the action of the mind by which this spatial and temporal phenomenon is grasped.*

In this text Musashi is doubtless alluding to the habits acquired by Lord Hosokawa in the Yagyu ryu.

8. Regarding State of Mind

The mind should be neither solemn nor agitated, neither pensive nor fearful; it should be straight and ample. This is the state of mind that should be sought after. The will should not be heavy, but the depth of one's awareness should be; in this way you make your mind like water that reacts appropriately to shifting situations. Whether it is a drop or an ocean with blue depths, it is water. You should examine this well.

9. Knowing the Three Levels of Strategy

Someone who adopts guard positions in strategy and displays different guard positions while handling the sword sometimes slowly, sometimes fast, practices strategy of a low level.

Someone who has refinement in strategy and who appears magnificent due to the subtlety of his techniques, who is a master of the cadences and has an elegant bearing, practices at an intermediate level.

The supreme strategy appears neither strong nor weak, neither slow nor fast, neither magnificent nor bad, but broad, straight, and calm. You should examine this well.

|||| *In Musashi's text the three levels—low, intermediate, and high (or supreme)—are expressed by the terms* ge, *"low,"* chu, *"intermediate," and* jo, *"high." When these words are associated, the usual order is* jo-chu-ge; *this expression refers to level or quality.*

10. A Graduated Cord Measure

You must always have a graduated cord measure in your mind. If you measure your opponent by adjusting the cord to him, you will be able to ascertain clearly his strength and weakness, his straightness and crookedness, where he is relaxed and where he is tense. With this measure you must size up all aspects of your opponent—round, square, long, short, crooked, or straight. You should examine this well.

|||| *"A graduated cord measure,"* ito gane: Gane *is the connecting form of the word* kane, *which means "metal ruler"; the expression refers to a cord that is used as a measure.*

11. The Pathway of the Sword

Without knowing the pathway of the sword, you cannot handle it freely. You cannot properly slash your opponent if you put too much force into it, if you do not have a sense of the back and side of the blade, if you shake the sword around like a knife or a spoon for serving rice. You must train in hitting your opponent well, always knowing the pathway of the sword and moving it calmly, following its weight.

12. The Strike and the Hit

|||| *This is almost identical to the* Gorin no sho *(the Scroll of Water).*

13. The Three Kinds of *Sen*

|||| *This is almost identical to the* Gorin no sho *(the Scroll of Fire).*

14. Getting Past a Critical Passage

You often find yourself in a situation where you and your opponent can reach out and touch each other. In this situation, you strike. And if you see before finishing the strike that your opponent is in the process of avoiding your sword, get up as close as possible to him, moving your body and your feet.

If you get past this critical moment, you are in no danger. For this you must understand well what I have written concerning how to take the initiative.

15. The Body Replacing the Sword

|||| *This idea is developed more completely in the* Gorin no sho *(the Scroll of Water).*

16. The Two Steps

You should move your feet in two movements (one foot, then the other) in making a single strike. This is what I call "the two steps." When you parry, pressing on your opponent's sword, or when you move forward or backward, you must move your feet in two steps, as though one foot were taking over from the other. If you move with a single step when making a strike, your body will be held by this movement and it will be difficult for you to react immediately for the next movement. Ordinary walking is the basis for the two steps. You should examine that well.

17. Breaking the Sword with Your Feet

|||| *This is almost identical to the* Gorin no sho *(the Scroll of Fire).*

18. Leaning on the Shadow

Here is what I call "leaning on the shadow." If you observe clearly what is happening in the body of your opponent, you can discern where his mind is excessively full and where it is absent. If you place your sword on the shadow of the place where his mind is absent, while at the same time vigilantly watching the place where it is overly full, your opponent's cadence will be disturbed, and your victory will be facilitated by this. Nonetheless, it is important never to miss a strike as a result of attaching your mind to your opponent's shadow. This must be worked out.

19. Moving Your Shadow

|||| *This idea is more completely developed in the* Gorin no sho *(the Scroll of Fire).*

20. Disconnecting the Cord

There are situations in which it seems you are attached to your opponent by a cord that is pulling you together. At this point you disconnect the cord. You must disconnect it without delay, as much with your body as with your sword, as much with your feet as with your mind. It will be easy for you to disconnect it if you make use of that which your opponent does not have in mind. This must be worked out.

21. The Teaching of the Small Comb

The idea of the small comb is to disentangle. You have a small comb in your mind and you should disentangle yourself each time your opponent snags you with a thread. Snagging with a thread and pulling with a cord are similar, but pulling is strong and snagging is weaker. You should examine that well.

22. Recognizing a Gap in a Cadence

A void in a cadence should be discerned in relation to your opponent, who could be either fast or slow.

When you are fighting a slow opponent, without moving your body at all and without letting him see the beginning of your sword movement, you strike him fast on the basis of the void. This is the cadence "in one" *(ichi hyoshi* or *hiotsu hyoshi).*

Against a fast opponent, you feint a strike with your body and with your mind, your opponent will move, and you will strike after his movement. This is the double *hyoshi* for passing over the top, *koshi.*

Your body is ready to strike, your mind and your sword are kept back, you strike with force starting from the void—at the instant when a gap *(ma)* arises in the will of your opponent. This is the "strike of non-thought" *(munen muso).*

When your opponent is ready to strike or parry, you make a striking movement that is deliberately slow, braking the movement during its trajectory, and you strike at the point where a void *(ma)* appears in his attention. That is the delayed cadence *(okure hyoshi).*

You should examine that well.

|||| *The term* ma *is used here in the sense of a gap or a void in perception.*

23. Holding Down on the Headrest

24. Recognizing the State of Things

25. Becoming Your Opponent

|||| *The ideas in the previous three articles are developed more completely in the* Gorin no sho *(the Scroll of Fire).*

26. Holding and Letting Go of One's Mind

Depending on the situation and the moment, you must either hold your mind or let go of it. In general, when wielding a sword, you must launch your will but hold on to the depth of your mind. When you strike your opponent with certainty, you must let go of your mind deep down and hold your will. These two states of mind, holding and letting go, can take on different forms, depending on the situation. This must be worked out well.

‖‖ *"Holding the mind," and "letting go of the mind" in Musashi's text trans-late* zan shin *and* ho shin, *respectively. These terms are used in contemporary martial arts.*

27. The Chance-Opening Blow

28. Paste and Lacquer

29. Body of the Autumn Monkey

30. Competition in Size

‖‖ *The ideas in the previous four articles are developed more completely in the* Gorin no sho *(the Scroll of Water).*

31. The Door Teaching *(Toboso)*

When you are glued to your opponent, take a position in which you straighten up your body and accentuate its breadth, as if you were covering the sword and the body of your opponent with your body, without leaving any gap between him and you. Then pivot, keeping your profile quite straight and making it as narrow as possible. Then deliver a powerful blow to your opponent's chest with your shoulder so as to knock him over. You must train well in this.

‖‖ *Regarding "the door teaching,"* toboso no oshie, toboso *refers to the mechanism for holding in place and closing a door that pivots on a central axis. It is composed of two pivot points situated in the middle of the door on the floor and above the door.*

32. The General and His Troops

|||| *This is almost identical to the* Gorin no sho *(the Scroll of Water, "The General Knows His Soldiers").*

33. The Guard without a Guard

|||| *This idea is developed more completely in the* Gorin no sho *(the Scroll of Water, "The Teaching of the Guard without a Guard").*

34. The Body of a Rock

The body of a rock is the state of an unmoving mind, powerful and large. Something inexhaustible that comes from the universal principle exists in the body. It is through this that the power of the mind resides in every living being. The grass and trees, which do not have a consciousness, are powerfully rooted in the earth. This mind is also found in the rain and the wind. You must examine well what is meant by "the body of a rock."

35. Spotting Opportunities

You must know how to spot opportunities: those that come sooner or later, the opportunity to escape or not escape. In my school the ultimate teaching consists in spontaneous emanation of the universal energy, *jiki tsu*. The details of this teaching are given through oral transmission.

All reasons and principles come from emptiness. The meaning of this sentence is impossible to explain—be so good as to reflect on it yourself.

I have described above the principal aspects of my conception of strategy and state of mind in thirty-five articles. A number of sentences are inadequate, but it all has to do with what I have already explained to you. I have not written down the technical details of my school, which I teach you directly and orally. If you run across an obscure passage, be so kind as to permit me to explain it to you directly.

The auspicious day of the second month of the eighteenth year of
  Kanei [1641]
Shinmen Musashi Genshin

"Forty-two Instructions on Strategy"
(Hyoho shiju ni kajo)

|||| *Nowadays, few people know of the* Hyoho shiju ni kajo, *and even fewer read it attentively. It is true that Musashi's thought is presented in the most comprehensive manner in the* Gorin no sho, *and people generally are content with reading that alone.*

The "Forty-two Instructions on Strategy" (Hyoho shiju ni kajo) is a copy of the "Thirty-five Instructions on Strategy" supplemented by additional articles. It was handed down by Terao Motomenosuke, one of Musashi's disciples.

As I already explained, the "Thirty-five Instructions on Strategy" (Hyoho sanju go kajo) was written at the request of Lord Hosokawa Tadatoshi. Musashi presented this work to him in 1641; Hosokawa died that same year.

We might surmise that Musashi, as was the custom at the time, made a copy of his manuscript and gave it to one of his disciples before he died, in this case, Terao Motomenosuke. Terao Motomenosuke was the younger brother of Terao Magonojo, to whom Musashi bequeathed the Gorin no sho.

Musashi seems to have had great confidence in these two brothers. A few years before his death, he wrote:

> *Up to this point I have traveled in more than sixty provinces, and I have transmitted my art to those who desired it. But I never met a person to whom I could pass on the transmission of my whole school. I was thinking, with regret, that my way was going to pass away with my own death until the day I met a disciple like Motomenosuke. Thanks be to heaven I had a student like him.*

We can imagine from this expression the confidence Musashi must have had in Terao Motomenosuke.

The two texts, the "Thirty-five Instructions on Strategy" and the "Forty-two Instructions on Strategy," are composed, to a great extent, of identical articles. The second contains everything from the first with the exception of the fourteenth instruction ("Getting Past a Critical Passage") and contains eight additional articles as well. Here is the translation of those eight.

Making Your Movements Stick

You and your opponent attack each other. At the moment when he blocks your sword, you close in on him and make your sword stick to his. You must glue your sword to his as though it were impossible to make it come unstuck, but without putting too much force into it. In making your movements stick, you can never be too calm. You must distinguish between sticking and becoming entangled. Sticking is strong, becoming entangled is weak.

|||| *"Making Your Movements Stick,"nebari o kakuru: The description here is simpler than in the article of the same name in the Gorin no sho (the Scroll of Water), written four years later.*

Regarding the Place of Combat
Combat against Many Adversaries

|||| *The previous two articles are more or less identical to those in the Gorin no sho (the Scroll of Fire and the Scroll of Water, respectively).*

Regarding the Five Directions of the Guard

|||| *The five articles below are grouped under the title "Regarding the Five Directions of the Guard"(Goho no kamae no shidai). The five guard positions described here are not the same as in the Gorin no sho.*

1. The middle guard position (kanjitsu no kamae) *with your blades held slightly at an angle*
When your opponent is far away, you approach him just to the limit of his range of attack, holding your swords slanting downward and keeping your body straight. You situate yourself facing him and adopt a guard position as follows:
You raise your arms, with your elbows neither raised nor lowered,

and cross your large and small swords in a forward position and at a middle level, broadly but without putting them too far forward. The point of the large sword is tilted slightly upward and placed above the line that runs between the middle of your body and your opponent's. The blades of your swords are neither raised nor held flat on the horizontal. They should be held on an angle.

In this position, keep your will mobile and the depth of your mind stable. Avoid your opponent's attack by detecting the movement of his will. Jab the point of your sword toward his face; this will disconcert him, and on account of that he will be drawn into launching his attack. At that point strike his arm from top to bottom by bringing the point of your sword back into position. After striking, leave this sword at the point it has reached, as though you had abandoned it, without moving your feet. And when your opponent attacks again, strike his arm from bottom to top in such a way as to hit him when he is a third of the way into his movement of attack.

Generally speaking, it is appropriate to keep your attention on the unleashing of your opponent's will to attack. You can then detect what he is about to start doing. This is a situation that is encountered all the time. You must understand it well.

2. The high guard position of gidan (gidan no kamae)

Place your right hand at the level of your ear, slanting your large sword slightly toward the inside—this is what I call the guard position of *gidan*. You hold the sword neither too tight nor too loose, with the point of the sword aimed toward the center line of your opponent's body. You strike, depending on your opponent's attack, either low, at the middle level, or high. The speed, depth, and force of your strike depend on his.

To dominate your opponent from the outset, strike his wrist by moving your large sword forward. But you must not strike downward. Strike with the feeling of piercing your opponent's hand, being quite sure of the direction of the blade of your sword. Then, whether your opponent parries or not, you immediately raise your sword, striking from below upward. To carry out this technique, you must hold the sword correctly and strike swiftly. It contains a sequence in the course of which it is possible to have a chance to cut your opponent down. But at a short distance, this technique is difficult to execute; in this case you must try to achieve dominance after having parried. You must use your judgment.

3. The right-side guard position (uchyoku no kamae)

Hold your large sword down on the right side and your small sword up, as though you were going to make a broad horizontal slashing movement.

When your opponent attacks, you strike him in such a way as to hit him when he is a third of the way through his move. If he tries to strike your small sword so as to make you drop it, you lower it slightly to make him cut in the void, then you slash your opponent by straightening the direction of the blade of your own sword. Speed is necessary for this strike. You must watch to make sure you keep the direction of the blade of your sword correct at the moment when you turn the point.

4. The left-side guard position (juki no kamae)

There are two kinds of left-side guard positions. For the first you move your right hand, which is holding the large sword, to the left, with the point of the sword forward and rather low, directed to the right. When your opponent attacks, you strike a third of the way through his movement. Your striking movement is as follows: You raise the sword, reaching with your arm in such a way that your hand goes beyond the point of your opponent's sword. After this strike, you must immediately turn the blade of your sword over.

For the second, you hold your sword rather low with the point directed to the left. Your hand then touches your right leg, and the blade of your sword is turned toward your opponent. You strike him as soon as he shows his intention to attack. Adjust the depth and force of your strike depending on your opponent. You must examine this strike well.

5. The low guard position (suikei no kamae)

You hold the two swords with the points coming near one another, downward and toward the inside, with the elbows broadly separated, without extending the arms. In this position, the small sword is placed forward. That is the low guard position.

When your opponent attacks, as you cross his sword you strike him on the central line, raising your sword up to the level of his forehead. You must strike broadly and fully, straight ahead. It is bad to cross the adversary's sword by moving your sword from the left side. After this strike, you must immediately turn the blade of your sword over. Depending on the situation, you could then adopt the right-side guard position. You must use your judgment.

WITH THESE FIVE GUARDS you can deal with all situations. Without conforming to the principle of the nature of the sword, you will not be able to cut down your opponent.

|||| *The following final sentences are no longer present in the* Hyoho sanju go kajo.

I have written here the general principles of my school. To learn the principle of victory with the sword through strategy, you must master the five guards by means of five technical forms. Through this you will be enabled to recognize the nature of the sword and you will obtain flexibility of body. You will be able to find cadences that conform to the way on any occasion.

|||| *These five articles are not found in any of Musashi's other writings.*

According to Ozawa Masao (9, p. 251), six articles were added by Terao Motomenosuke to the "Thirty-five Instructions on Strategy" (Hyoho sanju go kajo), and together these constitute the "Forty-two Instructions on Strategy" (Hyoho shiju ni kajo), which he passed down to his disciples. Ozawa does not explain his reasons for this assertion, which is not very precise, because the difference between the two documents involves eight articles and not six. [Ozawa counts the title as one article.] By contrast, Mitsuhashi Kanichiro, a kendo master of the end of the nineteenth century, claims that this text was written by Musashi himself for his favorite disciple.

Several hypotheses are possible:

1. Musashi wrote the Hyoho shiju ni kajo *in tandem with the* Hyoho sanju go kajo. *He gave the latter to Lord Hosokawa, and by adding a number of articles to this, he generated the copy intended for his disciple.*

2. Musashi wrote out two or more copies of the Hyoho sanju go kajo *and he bestowed one of these on his disciple.*

3. Before presenting the Hyoho sanju go kajo *to Lord Hosokawa, Musashi allowed his disciple to copy down its contents.*

We have no historical basis for concluding in favor of any one of these three hypotheses. Nevertheless, I have to say that the five last articles added in "Regarding the Five Directions of the Guard," which I have translated above, are particularly difficult to understand. In addition, if these are compared with all the other texts by Musashi, their style is found to be quite different. Why is Musashi's writing so unclear in these five articles? Translating the entirety of his works makes the difference in style between these five articles and the rest of his works stand out quite clearly. But does the English, which forces one to give a certain logical construction to the text, show this difference clearly?

In view of this difference in style, I adopt the hypothesis that these articles were written by Terao Motomenosuke.

The text is followed by a postface in which Terao, as was the custom, affirms the authenticity of the transmission, mentioning the founding master of the school.

Postface

What I have written above comes from my master Genshin [Musashi]. The master persevered from his youth in the way of strategy and was able to attain the ultimate level in all the domains of the art, thanks to the principle of strategy. He engaged in more than sixty combats, either with the sword or with the *bokuto* (wooden sword), without ever losing. In this way he defeated the most famous adepts of all Japan. He continued to look for a more profound way, training from morning till night. Only after the age of fifty did he attain the ultimate state from which an extraordinary energy spontaneously emanates, and from that day on, he no longer had the need to go deeper.

The master did not write anything about his art until he met Lord Hosokawa Tadatoshi of Hishi [Kumamoto], who pursued this way. This lord had studied the strategy of several schools and had received the highest transmission from Yagyu Tajimanokami [Munenori], the most celebrated master of strategy in Japan. The lord secretly believed he had attained the highest level. At the time of his meeting with the master, they fought and the lord was completely dominated. He was astonished at the master's ability, and he asked him a number of questions.

The master then replied: "As far as the principle of strategy is concerned, this is true for all the schools: if the way of ultimate sincerity does not become one with what one is trying to do, it is not a true way."

The lord said, "Although I am not very skillful, I will persevere until I arrive at this way."

That is how the Master came to begin teaching him the way in private, and he presented to him his first writing. The lord swiftly attained mastery, thanks to his previous achievements in strategy.

The lord said, "I have persevered in the art of the sword *(kenjutsu)* from the time of my youth and I have studied several schools in a conscientious manner, but I have understood that none of this was part of the true way. Everything that I had learned over a long period of time turned out to be useless and disappeared." In this, his joy was great.

As for me, thanks be to heaven, I was able to meet my master, who granted me his special attention, and I was able to benefit from the depth of this relationship. I was able to attain the way by drinking at the spring of my master's mind by means of training.

The master complimented me, saying, "Until now, I have taught a great number of people, but none of them was able to enter into the real way. Without attaining a true way, it is impossible to give a real transmission. Nobuyuki [Terao's name], you have great intelligence in strategy, and you can understand ten things on the basis of one. And thanks to your exceptional ability, you have reached the state where an extraordinary energy spontaneously emanates from your person."

But this way is not a mere method of the sword *(kenjutsu),* and very few people pursue it. Even if there are people who search for it, if they do not do so with a sincere mind and with great perseverance, it is better not to speak to them of anything, because they will never arrive at it. I passed a number of years without ever showing my art to anybody, saying to myself that teaching my art amounted to touching my nose to indicate my mouth.

In this situation I have a trustworthy friend, Yasumasa, with whom I have been training for a long time, and I wish to be able to continue to do so for the rest of my life. I know the real sincerity of his mind, through which he inevitably reaches success, and how could he fail? Therefore I have transmitted everything to him, and he has attained the ultimate state of the way. It is for this reason that I bestow on him this text that comes from my master. This is an extraordinary occasion.

The school that will be perpetuated for all eternity is called Niten ichi ryu (the School of Two Swords toward the Sky). This is the strategy of the reality that has the fullness of a circle. The master gave it this name because "all principles arise from emptiness. If there is no communication, there is no response."

The fifteenth of the eighth month of the sixth year of Kanbun [1666]
Terao Motomenosuke Nobuyuki

"The Way to Be Followed Alone" (Dokkodo)

1. Do not go against the way of the human world that is perpetuated from generation to generation.

2. Do not seek pleasure for its own sake.

3. Do not, in any circumstance, depend upon a partial feeling.

4. Think lightly of yourself and think deeply of the world.

5. Be detached from desire your whole life long.

6. Do not regret what you have done.

7. Never be jealous of others, either in good or in evil.

8. Never let yourself be saddened by a separation.

9. Resentment and complaint are appropriate neither for yourself nor for others.

10. Do not let yourself be guided by the feeling of love.

11. In all things, do not have any preferences.

1 2. Do not have any particular desire regarding your private domicile.

1 3. Do not pursue the taste of good food.

1 4. Do not possess ancient objects intended to be preserved for the future.

1 5. Do not act following customary beliefs.

1 6. Do not seek especially either to collect or to practice arms beyond what is useful.

1 7. Do not shun death in the way.

1 8. Do not seek to possess either goods or fiefs for your old age.

1 9. Respect Buddha and the gods without counting on their help.

2 0. You can abandon your own body, but you must hold on to your honor.

2 1. Never stray from the way of strategy.

|||| *"The Way to Be Followed Alone" was written by Musashi in the few days preceding his death. We presently have two versions of the Dokkodo. One has nineteen articles and the other twenty-one. Articles 4 and 20 are absent from the shorter version.*

We know of certain moments in Musashi's life from a later text entitled Nitenki (Writings on the Two Heavens), according to which, one week before his death, Musashi gave away his personal objects to people close to him. On that occasion he composed the twenty-one points entitled Dokkodo (the way where one walks alone), which are a reflection on his life at the moment of death. He dedicated these thoughts to his disciple Terao Magonojo, to whom he had also addressed the Gorin no sho. Terao Magonojo took them as precepts.

The sentences in the Dokkodo are short, concentrated expressions. That is why their meaning is difficult to understand in the original text. Unless some commentary is added, the translation might be somewhat incomprehensible or lead to misunderstandings.

These twenty-one thoughts of Musashi's require us to unpack the meaning of each word in order to get a sense of their overall signification, since each sentence distills Musashi's thought in a very few words and contains a great number of implicit notions meant to be understood by someone who has received his teaching at firsthand. For this reason a literal translation of this text, even if very well done, does not permit us to get at its meaning. Strictly speaking, Musashi himself and the disciple to whom these words were addressed doubtless remain the only ones able to decipher their meaning fully. We can get more or less close to the meaning of the text by elucidating the implicit notions the text contains.

For each precept I give the Japanese pronunciation, because the sonority of the words contributes to their message. I then explain the meaning of the main words, situating them in relation to their context.

1. Do not go against the way of the human world that is perpetuated from generation to generation *(yo yo no michi o somuku koto nashi).*

|||| Yo: *"society" or "the world of human beings," and in a broader sense, "the world." The repetition of the term denotes the idea of succession and movement over time.*

Michi: *"the way" or "principle."*

Somuku: *"to go against."*

Koto nashi: *a negation applied to a verb. Nashi corresponds to the negation ("not"), and koto to the nominative form taken by the verb in this sentence.*

Yo yo no michi: *"the way of the human world that is perpetuated from generation to generation." According to Imai Masayuki, the present-day and tenth successor of Musashi, this expression designates the way of wisdom, the true way that traverses time from the past to the future. This idea belongs to the tradition of Buddhism. According to Imai Masayuki, this sentence indicates the state of a man who is independent yet, acting freely, conforms to a truth of human nature.*

2. Do not seek pleasure for its own sake *(mi-ni tanoshimi o takumazu).*

|||| Mi: *"the body," "oneself."*

Tanoshimi: *"pleasure," "enjoyment."*

Takumazu: *negative form of the verb takumu, which means "to elaborate, look for a good means."*

In this precept it is not only physical pleasure that is meant but, in a more general sense, that which is pleasant and which Musashi has given up seeking intentionally. Would it be accurate to describe this ascetic at-

titude as masochism, as certain contemporary critics do? In my view labels of this type result in hiding the true image of Musashi behind a smoke screen of current-day thinking. This may produce a clear image, but it is an illusory one.

Renouncing pleasure, for Musashi, is a basic condition for arriving at what is essential. In this he is following the path that has been followed by other great accomplished practitioners of the martial arts. Asceticism of this sort is connected with a view of life that sees the agreeable aspects of existence as obscuring its depth, which is hard and heavy. Musashi seeks to avoid being detained at the level of pleasure, which would only distract him from the essential. His idea is to confront the deeper and weightier aspect of life directly in order to attain the essence of his art, which is inseparable from life itself. Such a conception of life is derived from a synthesis of Buddhist thought with more ancient Japanese notions of nature and the world. One of the contributions of Buddhism to this synthesis is the notion that life contains apparently contradictory aspects that are nevertheless inseparable from one another: There is old age in youth, death in life, hatred in love, separation in meeting, bitterness in pleasure, and so on. In his effort to see the true face of existence, Musashi goes directly toward this most pithy and substantial aspect of it. Becoming detached from the power of his own desire enables his mind to discover true emptiness (ku)—on that basis a new dimension opens before him. Although Musashi does not mention Buddhist doctrine (in which the notion of emptiness is another key element), his orientation is deeply permeated by Japanese Buddhism.

3. Do not, in any circumstance, depend upon a partial feeling (*yorozu ni eko no kokoro nashi*).

|||| Yorozu: literally, "ten thousand; a very large number of things or phenomena; everything."

Eko: "dependency; that on which one is dependent; partial point of view; personal interest."

Kokoro: "heart, mind, thought."

The point here is to have an attitude toward all things and all persons that is neither dependent nor partial nor egotistic. This clear-sighted attitude, applied even to those close to one, might give an impression *of coldness, and this is indicated by some documents on the subject of Musashi.*

4. Think lightly of yourself and think deeply of the world *(mi o asaku omoi, yo o fukaku omou).*

|||| Mi: *"the body, oneself."*

   Asaku, asai: *"not deep, shallow."*

   Fukaku, fukai: *"deep."*

   Omoi: *"to think, to consider."*

   First we should point out the opposition here between self and the world. The word-for-word translation of the beginning of this sentence would be "think not deeply with regard to oneself."

   Musashi is telling us here that the proper way to look at things is not putting oneself at the center of them and not overestimating the weight of one's own existence. Such a self-centered view is often dominated by egocentric ideas and desires. He is inviting us to meditate on our own smallness in relation to a world that is moving in time, in eternity.

5. Be detached from desire your whole life long *(issho no aida yokushin omowazu).*

|||| Issho: *"all one's life."*

   Aida: *"during."*

   Yokushin: *"cupidity, lust."*

   Omowazu: *"not thinking of, not having in mind, being detached from."*

   According to Imai Masayuki, man is tormented by lusts of the following three kinds: the desire to be viewed favorably by others; the egotistic desire for material riches; the desire to surpass others, to defeat them. According to Imai, the point here is to live in a state of detachment from these kinds of desire.

6. Do not regret what you have done *(waga koto ni oite kokai o sezu).*

|||| Waga koto: *"one's own affair, what one has done." These ideograms can also be read* ware koto. *In this case,* ware *is the subject, and the meaning is approximately the same.*

Oite: *"in, concerning."*
Kokai: *"regret."*
Kokai o sezu: *"do not regret."*

7. Never be jealous of others, either in good or in evil *(zen aku ni ta o netamu kokoro nashi).*

|||| Zen-aku: *"good and evil, in any case."*
Ta o: *"toward others."*
Netamu: *"to be jealous."*
Kokoro: *"heart, mind, thought."*
Nashi: *"do not have."*

8. Never let yourself be saddened by a separation *(izure no michi nimo wakare o kanashimazu).*

|||| Izure no michi nimo: *"in all ways, whatever the situation in which one finds oneself."*
Wakare: *"separation."*
Kanashimazu: *"do not be saddened"; this is the negative form of kanashimu.*

The sadness of momentary separation or the separation of death is considered in Buddhism to be one of the causes of being drawn away from the essential. It arises from the illusion of seeing as immutable that which is transient. Let us not forget Musashi's own experience—he spent the greater part of his life traveling.

9. Resentment and complaint are appropriate neither for yourself nor for others *(ji ta tomoni urami kakotsu kokoro nashi).*

|||| Ji: *"oneself."*
Ta: *"others."*
Tomoni: *"both together, as well as."*
Urami: *"resentment."*
Kakotsu: *"complaining."*
Kokoro: *"heart, mind, thought."*
Nashi: *"negation."*

10. Do not let yourself by guided by the feeling of love *(renbo no michi omoi yoru kokoro nashi)*.

|||| Renbo: *"love (being in love)."*
    Michi: *"road, way, direction, orientation."*
    Omoi yoru: literally, *"to think of and come near, to incline one's feeling toward a person."*
    Kokoro: *"heart, mind, thought."*
    Nashi: *"negation."*
    Musashi never had a child. The documents we have do not tell of his having relations with a woman. Some interpret this as a will to control his desire so as to dedicate himself to the way; others see it as a sign of homosexuality. This dictum militates in favor of the first hypothesis.

11. In all things, do not have any preferences *(mono goto ni sukikonomu koto nashi)*.

|||| Mono goto: *"each thing."*
    Ni: *"in, concerning."*
    Sukikonomu koto: *"preference, predilection."*
    Nashi: *"negation."*

12. Do not have any particular desire regarding your private domicile *(shitaku ni oite nozomu kokoro nashi)*.

|||| Shitaku: *"domicile"* or *"private house."*
    Ni oite: *"in."*
    Nozomu: *"to desire."*
    Kokoro: *"heart, mind, thought."*
    Nashi: *"negation."*
    For Musashi it was necessary to be able to live wherever he was, whatever the conditions were. It was not a question of seeking out discomfort but of not being attached to the quest for comfort in a dwelling place. There is no hindrance here to appreciating good things, but one must not be attached to them. All through his life, Musashi had to be able to be at home wherever he was, whether it was in a house or in a natural setting with the sky as his roof. Realizing this may help us to understand why he

chose to spend the last two years of his life in a cave, although he had a comfortable house at his disposal.

13. Do not pursue the taste of good food *(mi hitotsu ni bishoku o konomazu).*

|||| Mi: *"one's body, oneself."*
    Hitotsu: *"alone."*
    Bishoku: *"delicacy, good meal."*
    Konomazu: *"do not prefer, do not love."*
    This means not allowing oneself to be drawn by the taste of a good dish and being able to nourish oneself, whatever the nature of the food available. In the life of a bushi, it was necessary to face situations of war in which material conditions could reach levels of extreme privation. One had to be able to avoid being weakened by unfavorable material conditions. In addition, daily life was regarded as a preparation for war. In Musashi's time, wars began to occur more rarely, and keeping oneself in condition to deal with war became an ethical matter.
    Another interpretation is possible. For a follower of the way like Musashi, the taste of sophisticated cuisine would be a negative element, because it would run counter to his effort to relate to the profound nature of things, which is better reflected by the taste of simple food not requiring fussy preparation.

14. Do not possess ancient objects intended to be preserved for the future *(suezue shiromono naru furuki dogu shoji sezu).*

|||| Suezue: *"in the future, posterity."*
    Shiromono: *"merchandise, object."*
    Furuki: *"ancient, old."*
    Dogu: *"object, utensil."*
    Shoji sezu: *"do not possess."*
    One becomes attached to an old object and tries to preserve it. One can possess an object but can also be possessed by an object.
    A man might possess an object that came into his hands in a certain particular way and attach a special value to it for that reason, especially if that object came down to him from his ancestors.

One must be wary of this sort of attachment, particularly if it comes into play in choosing a weapon. An antique object may be precious, but what is important here is usefulness. Therefore it is necessary to free oneself from conditioning that is based on a value that is perverted from the point of view of one's primary goal.

15. Do not act following customary beliefs *(wagami ni itari monoimi suru koto nashi).*

|||| Wagami: *"my body, myself."*
    Ni itari: *"concerning."*
    Monoimi: *"to avoid something because of a belief."*
    Suru koto: *"doing"(nominative form)*
    Nashi: *"negation."*

    There are many customs of monoimi *in traditional Japanese usage. For example, one must not choose a course of action or a date without taking into account mandatory divinatory indications. For another example, it is believed that a person must preserve the purity of the body in order to please the gods, and numerous purificatory procedures exist. For this reason also, a person must avoid certain places and certain acts. As an expression of mourning, close relatives are required to remain shut up indoors for a longer or shorter period, from a week up to a hundred days. A number of these ancient beliefs are still observed in present-day Japan.*

    The important point here is that in a period in which most Japanese were subject to a great number of superstitious beliefs, Musashi dared to reject them in order to try to see the world as it is.

16. Do not seek especially either to collect or to practice arms beyond what is useful *(hyogu wa kakubetsu yo no dogu tashinamazu).*

|||| Hyogu: *"arms, weaponry."*
    Kakubetsu: *"particularly, especially."*
    Yo no: *"supplementarily, in surplus, outside of."*
    Dogu: *"utensil, object."*
    Tashinamazu: *negative form of* tashinamu, *"dc not like to practice or collect."*

For Musashi, under no circumstances were weapons collectible objects, even if they had great aesthetic qualities. One had to know how to use them correctly and have the ones that were necessary. If they were not available, one had to know how to make them oneself. Musashi himself hand made a considerable number of weapons.

17. Do not shun death in the way *(michi ni oitewa shi o itowazu omou).*

|||| Michi: *"the way."*

Ni oitewa: *"in."*

Shi o: *"toward death."*

Itowazu: *negative form of itou, "do not detest, do not avoid or shun."*

Omou: *"to think, to consider."*

Musashi also presents this idea in the Scroll of Earth in the Gorin no sho.

18. Do not seek to possess either goods or fiefs for your old age *(rogo ni zaiho mochiyuru shoryo ni kokoro nashi).*

|||| Rogo ni: *"having grown old, being old."*

Zaiho: *"treasure."*

Mochiyuru: *"to possess."*

Shoryo: *"fief."*

Kokoro: *"heart, mind, thought."*

Nashi: *"negation."*

19. Respect Buddha and the gods without counting on their help *(busshin wa totoshi, busshin o tanomazu).*

|||| Busshin: *"Buddha and the gods."*

Totoshi: *"respectable."*

Tanomazu: *"not depending on, not counting on someone," negative form of tanomu.*

20. You can abandon your own body, but you must hold on to your honor *(mi o sutetemo myori wa sutezu).*

|||| Mi: *"the body, oneself."*

Sutetemo: *"even if one abandons"* (steru: *"to abandon").*

Myori: *"reputation, honor."*

Sutezu: *"to not abandon"(negative form of* suteru*).*

21. Never stray from the way of strategy *(tsune ni hyoho no michi o hanarezu).*

|||| Tsune ni: *"always, at any moment."*

Michi: *"the way."*

Hanarezu: *"to not stray from, not deviate from" (negative form of* hanareru*).*

The Dokkodo *brings out the asceticism that Musashi advocates in connection with the way of strategy. The life and works of Musashi have been the object of systematic eulogies and passionate critiques. Thus some of our contemporaries have described him as obsessive, paranoid, and the like. But these judgments do not take into account the lifestyle of his period. Nonetheless, we can also adopt a critical attitude.*

Musashi represents a form of fruition of the practice of the arts of his time, and the works he left behind are a reflection of this. In order to understand Musashi's personality, we must see what he did in relation to what he was seeking to do and also take into account the innovative qualities of his quest when seen within the context of this period in history. His writings show that his mental and spiritual stance does not arise from the context of the ordinary preoccupations of ordinary people; rather, his entire life was structured around the extended dynamics of the way of strategy. However, we shall see from other examples that this total concentration of his on the way, as rare and exceptional as it was, had an exemplary value for the society in which he was living. Is strategy not a positive way of shaping the human energy of society as a whole, a way that does not hide either from life's harshness or from death?

Thus, both in connection with the martial arts and in terms of daily life, it would be unjust to judge Musashi's thought on the basis of the forms of security and comfort that we are familiar with, on our values and our conception of death.

⫴ 6 ⫴

Notes of Musashi's Disciples on the Practice of His School

⫴ *The following four sections, which are notes written by disciples of Musashi's, are presented in a collection of texts on Musashi's school made by Mitsuhashi Kanichiro, one of his successors as head of the school. Mitsuhashi was a kendo master of the early twentieth century who in contemporary kendo circles had the reputation of being "the Musashi of today." He does not give the source of these documents. I must suppose that he copied them from among the secret transmission texts of a few schools that transmitted the art of Musashi. He has the following to say of them:*

> *These notes were not necessarily written by Master Musashi. They were without doubt written by his disciples, who noted down what they had heard from their master. That is why the words and the ideas are the same as those of the master. Nonetheless, it is possible that in certain passages the disciples introduced details based on their own experience and thought. If we take these points into account when reading them, it will surely be helpful for our practice of kendo. (6, p. 18)*

NOTES ON MIND, ENERGY, AND THE BODY IN STRATEGY *(Hyoho shin ki tai oboe gaki)*

1. Stretching, stagnating, hardening by curling up, contracting, closing oneself off, "squeezing" the body, and slacking off—all these are ailments in strategy, because every one of these states hinders freedom of action.

For example, if the tendons or the muscles have been overly stretched—to the point of causing a cramp—this would be like a stretched cord. Stagnating amounts to being in a sitting position without being able to get up. If you harden up, this is like water freezing. If you close yourself off, you cannot move well from place to place. You must make a distinction between "squeezing" the belly by putting it under pressure from a belt and tensing the body, which is a negative state. If you slack off through laziness, that will lead you to a state of weakness.

Every time you stand up with your swords in hand to train, you must be aware of the state of your vital energy and your body so that you can be quite relaxed and put yourself in a waterlike state by melting the ice. In this way the body will become completely free.

You should know that the eyes do not always precede actions.

2. There should be no faults in your mind or your vital energy.

A fault is a void caused by a break (in your perception). A true adept does not have such faults. Those who are not true adepts have more or fewer faults or lapses, depending on their level. You must carefully examine your own state in order to do away with major faults. It is a sign of training and reflection to be aware of the problem of faults. A true adept detects the least sign of a fault in the mind or in the energy of his opponent, and he defeats him by not letting the moment when he is vulnerable escape. This phenomenon will appear strange only to those who are not familiar with the way of strategy.

Someone who does not train enough will not find the fault in others. Even if he succeeds in perceiving a fault, he will not be able to achieve victory by penetrating into this fault. Someone who has persevered over a long period of time knows what a defeat due to a break (in perception) is and knows how to recover from his own fault.

3. If when you train you move around very vigorously at the beginning of the session, it is because you do not know how to expend your energy calmly. But that depends on a person's state. You should know that you can hardly examine the principle of the mind when you are speeding around physically.

4. It is important to place yourself in a state of calm and to work out your way of mastering your own mind and work on the manner in which your vital energy emanates from you. However, if you are lacking in resolve when you place yourself in a state of calm, your mind, your energy, and your body will fall asleep and weaken. You will have the mind and energy of a corpse.

Even if you perceive the moment in which the mind and energy of your opponent are about to go out or go in and the moment in which he is thinking about or working out a strategy, it is not sure that you will be able to react to this effectively.

You are in danger of suffering an enormous defeat if you strike or if you close in without having first reestablished your own wholeness, whereas your opponent is ready to take the initiative the moment he has reestablished the calmness of his mind.

At the moment of a strike, cadences that are appropriate as to speed and force are only realized in a state of calm and harmony. It is the force of the belly and the movement of the feet that make it possible to realize the cadence of speed. You must examine this well and work on it.

5. Entanglement of the mind, of the energy, and of the body cannot be seen with the eyes. In this state you will be unable to distinguish between emptiness and fullness in your opponent. You must at all costs avoid falling into this error.

6. If you are capable of mastering your own mind by placing yourself in a state of calm, you will be able to see clearly what is happening in your opponent.

7. If you move from place to place with too great a spread between your two feet, your freedom of movement will be reduced, because your body and your energy will not be evenly distributed. Too small a spread is not good either. When you perceive a collapse in the mind and

the energy of your opponent, you should move forward with a large step, even pounce with a leap. That is the reason there is no rigid rule and everything depends on your opponent. Moving your feet uselessly should be avoided, but you should do it if it is to take the initiative. When there is a disturbance in the movement of the feet, neither your mind nor your energy is sure. A large amount of useless footwork will lead you into a major defeat.

8. You should master separately the three domains of the mind *(shin),* the will and vital energy *(ki),* and the body *(tai).* If you are not able to distinguish these three domains, it is impossible to realize instructions by the master such as

- Not letting the mind be influenced by the state of the body
- Keeping the mind calm, even when you are moving rapidly
- Holding back the mind while launching the body into movement
- Keeping hold of the depth or core of the mind while letting the mind go
- Taking the initiative of a movement of attack in order to bring about a collapse in the will of your opponent
- Keeping the mind calm in the midst of violent movements

You should work on these, being aware of the distinctions.

9. Distinguish a reach *(nobi)* from a passing movement *(koshi)* in the energy of the will.

10. Distinguish between projecting your energy *(ki)* toward your opponent and preceding it.

11. You should know that fear hinders courage and stimulates the will of your opponent.

12. You must know how to guide yourself by discerning the degree of the vitality of your mind, your will, and your body. Carrying on without having an accurate awareness of these leads to death.

13. A mind that is strong, unmoving, and calm, whose vigilance is a wakefulness devoid of useless tension, becomes clear when it is necessary. This is the fundamental state.

14. Will and vital energy must be emanating from you with power in order for you to create true impetus and momentum.

15. You must hold your body accentuating its central axis. In this posture the belly is forward and the whole body is dynamic.

It is not fitting to be partial in any area. Neither excess nor insufficiency is good. You should reflect in order to find several things in reading a single instruction or a single teaching. You should not look at the infinity of the sky from the point of view of the small aperture of a box. You must have an ample vision in order to encompass the universal principal. It is also necessary to perceive the details, without which strategy would be a crude thing.

Mere apprenticeship amounts to a loan. To adapt what you learn to yourself, you must create your own strategy on the basis of a profound understanding. If your mind and wisdom are correct, there is no risk of error.

ATTITUDE TOWARD TRAINING

1. Reflect and work on it every time you run across a doubt in your training. It is after having found a solution to it that a profound understanding will come. Even if you are lacking in knowledge and you are awkward, the future is wide open.

2. If you learn without examining things for yourself, who will really continue to instruct you?

3. He who is too skeptical will live in doubt and will never get beyond the frame of reference of his stupidity. Doubt is the disease of the way. You should meditate on this ancient teaching: "A small understanding is born from a minor doubt and great understanding is born from great doubt."

4. One who is awkward and one who is nimble will both find their way through sincerity and through accumulation of work.

THE SCHOOL OF THE FIGHTERS OF THE TWO HEAVENS (*Senki niten ryu*)

The current of a river in winter reflects the moon
Like a mirror, and it is transparent.
(Kan ryu tsuki o obi, sumerukoto kagami no gotoshi.)

|||| *This is a famous poem by Musashi. The notion of water in winter evokes the coldness of a blade as well as lucidity of mind. This water does not stagnate but flows uninterruptedly as one's mind and will should do during combat. The water is highly transparent, yet its surface distinctly reflects the bluish color of the moon.*

This poem is frequently cited to express the state of mind of the art of the sword.

(The contents of items 8 to 16 below are identical to instructions found in the Gorin no sho, *the Scroll of Water.)*

Here is what the master said:

1. Your opponent moves forward or you move forward. Know how to win from the inception of the first step.

The master also said that every defeat comes about through an error. You must be concerned mainly with seeking out how to avoid committing an error.

2. The instruction on the three colors refers to ways of reacting in response to the adversary. Three colors are found in the adversary: He comes on, he backs away, or he stagnates. These distinctions are essential.

3. One masters oneself and one also governs a country by the virtue of the sword. It is in this sense that strategy is the root of principle.

4. Through knowing what is advantageous in combat, you should attain victory with the sword and in strategy. The sword expresses the essence of strategy.

The essential is to acquire and master strategy. Only by training diligently can you obtain the means of being victorious whenever you wish. The most important thing is training in conjunction with reflection.

5. You must smash the depth or core of your opponent with your body and your mind as well as with your sword. If your opponent crum-

bles in his depth, you do not need to put your mind to it. Otherwise you must remain vigilant. If the mind of your opponent remains alive, he has not yet collapsed. You must train well in this.

6. If your strategy is in the true way, defeating an opponent will be part of your daily training and you should acquire an unchanging mind. It is necessary to be sure that a victory is nothing other than the expression of the correctness of the way.

7. As soon as you have moved past the boundary of attack range, even before your opponent can become aware of it, strike him very swiftly and directly with the feeling of not moving your body or your mind. This is the strike of a single *hyoshi*. This means striking even before the thought occurs to your opponent of pulling back his sword or parrying or striking.

8. The strike of nonthought.

9. The flowing-water strike.

10. The strike like a spark from a stone.

11. The body replacing the sword.

12. Banging into your opponent.

13. The three parries.

14. Piercing your opponent's face.

15. The parry by a slap of the sword.

16. Regarding cadence.

The State of Mind of Those Devoted to the School of Musashi (*Musashi ryu shugyo kokoroe no koto*)

1. There is no hierarchical order of importance in the techniques that you train in every day.

You must conduct yourself with courtesy and sincerity. The most important thing is to train calmly, without hesitation, without disturbance, and with a very confident depth or core energy.

2. Ordinary training should be carried out without stagnation and without distortion.

3. When you adopt the middle guard position, be calm in appearance while the depth of your mind remains strong. In daily training, you should always think of taking the initiative in combat.

4. When you fight with a short sword that has no guard on it,[1] it is not good to try to win with trivial techniques. You must keep your mind broad and especially not fail to take the initiative. However, if your emotional tension is too high, you are in danger of not succeeding. You must conduct yourself with determination to win by a single blow. This is not achievable unless your will is completely filled with energy.

If you let your opponent draw his sword and you parry his attack, even if you carry off the victory, you might be stiff afterward. In general, in a combat where you use a short sword without a guard, from the beginning to the end you must get the jump on your opponent by taking the initiative. That is what will determine the result of the combat. You must remember the three ways of taking the initiative [given by Master Musashi]. In order to achieve this attitude, you must work on it thoroughly.

5. Those who study the school of Master Musashi must seek to master their vital energy every day. The essential is to behave in conformity with the principle of the universe. The reason and the principle of strategy arise from the subtlety of nature.

Even if you work on the way without any other thought, about halfway along the road comes the danger of your intention's going astray. You must keep this in mind in order to devote yourself to the way.

The nineteenth of the eleventh month of the ninth year of Tenpo [1838]

I HAVE COMPOSED this at the order of my master Asai.

That which I have written above was transmitted to me as the ultimate teaching by my master on the twenty-seventh of the ninth month of the tenth year of Tenpo [1839] at the time of a journey outside the country.

The master fell ill the eighth of the tenth month and died the eighteenth of the same month of the tenth year of Tenpo [1839] around seven in the evening. He was seventy-four years old. He was buried at the Myokyoji temple.

The name of my master was Asai Shinemon.

The nineteenth of the fifth month of the fourth year of Koka (1847), I am transmitting this ultimate teaching to my successor.

THREE

MIYAMOTO MUSASHI AND THE MARTIAL ARTS

‖ 7 ‖

The School of Musashi
(Hyoho niten ichi ryu)

MUSASHI CHOSE THREE of his disciples—the two Terao brothers and
Furuhashi Sozaemon—to be responsible for the transmission of his
school, which spread and went on to be divided into several branches.
The Terao brothers bestowed the final transmission on several adepts,
each of whom returned to the fief he came from and there in his turn
opened the School of Musashi. Furuhashi opened his school in Edo at
the same time as the School of Musashi was continuing in Higo.

BRANCHES OF THE SCHOOL

Before naming his school Niten ichi ryu, Musashi called it Enmei ryu.
Each of Musashi's disciples received the transmission of his school at a
particular moment of the master's life and at a particular stage in the development of his art. They continued to elaborate their own art on the
basis of what they received from Musashi, adding to it their own
achievements. Thus they founded schools teaching their art, always
claiming that it was the School of Musashi. Such was the case of Aoki
Jozaemon (1586–1661). He met Musashi during his stay in Edo, when

Musashi was not yet twenty-eight years old, and became his student in the Enmei ryu. After Musashi left, Aoki Jozaemon established himself in Edo, opened a dojo, and called his school Tetsujin ryu, "School of the Man of Steel." He chose this name to go along with his idea of making his mind and body as strong as steel, but the general content of the techniques was that of the Enmei ryu. In a short time this school divided in two, with one branch in Edo and the other in Osaka.

For a time Musashi had called his school Musashi ryu (School of Musashi), and today there are several schools with this name in the Kyushu region. We find information on these schools in the *Gekiken sodan,* a collection of documents dated 1843:

The Musashi ryu (called Enmei ryu)
Musashi ryu is the school of Miyamoto Musashi. . . . His father was named Shinmen Munisai and was an adept of the art of the *jitte*. Musashi also trained in this art. But later he reflected on the fact that the *jitte* was not a weapon to be carried at all times. The essence is to win at any moment with the swords one is carrying. Thus he developed his School of Two Swords. . . .

Musashi ryu is a general name and I think this branch was part of the Enmei ryu. . . . The authorizations to teach that Musashi conferred in 1607 all bear the name Enmei ryu. . . .

For the final stage of this school, the following poem is taught:

The spring wind blows the day the peach flowers bloom,
This is also the time when dew falls on the paulownia
leaves.

The teaching of the final phase is expressed in this poem.
Kyushu is where Musashi's School of Two Swords is most numerous. . . .

At Hasa no ike in Saga, there is a master called Seki Heidayu. He teaches the art of two swords. I suppose that he too is from the lineage of the School of Musashi.

The Onko chishin ryu

The Onko chishin ryu is also a school of two swords. It is a school that is derived from Musashi's school. (1-f, pp. 225–226)

There were still other names for the School of Musashi. For example, there is Nito Masana ryu, which means "the Masana School of Two Swords." Masana was Musashi's warrior name. The Niten ichi ryu has also sometimes been called just Niten ryu.

The Shin gyoto ryu (Shin keito ryu)

Iba Hideaki (1648–1713) was an adept of the Shin kage ryu, but he concluded that this school was not sufficiently realistic, and he traveled around looking for a school that suited him better. He had a match with an adept of the Enmei ryu in Nagasaki (Kyushu region), lost, and afterward became the disciple of the man who had defeated him. Later he changed his name to Iba Zesuiken and founded a school, the Shin gyoto ryu, by merging the Shin kage ryu with the Enmei ryu. The name of this school means "School of the Sword That Shapes the Mind." What he means by this name is, at the time of combat one is in the grip of two attitudes of the mind—that of attacking and that of fleeing because of fear. To give another shape to this mind that is driving one to flee, first one has to deepen one's level of technical accomplishment in order to create an unshakable form.

Matsuura Seizan (1760–1841) was an adept of this school. When he received the final transmission, he took the name of Joseishi in connection with his practice of swordsmanship. Under this name he wrote a great number of essays, many of which are on the art of the sword, notably "Kendan," "Kenko," "Koshi yawa." (1, 77) His work is considered to be one of the foundations for the study of Japanese swordsmanship. Musashi's thought, viewed from another angle, is somewhat visible in it.

The School of Musashi developed, forming branches, some of which have lasted down to the present day.

THE SCHOOL OF MUSASHI TODAY

Today there exist several schools named Hyoho niten ichi ryu, the name used by Musashi to designate his school toward the end of his life. Each of these schools claims to have an authentic lineage going back to the School of Musashi.

Here are the lineages of three of them:

1. Miyamoto Musashi, Terao Motomenosuke, Terao Goemon, Yoshida Josetsu, Santo Hikozaemon, Santo Hanbei, Santo Shinjuro, Aoki Kikuo, Kiyonaga Tadanao, Imai Masayuki.

This school is located on the island of Kyushu, and its principal master is presently Imai Masayuki. Its headquarters is in Oaza-Joi, Usa, Oita, Japan.

2. Miyamoto Musashi, Terao Motomenosuke, Terao Goemon, Yoshida Josetsu, Santo Hikozaemon, Santo Hanbei, Santo Shinjuro, Aoki Kikuo, Miyakawa Takashi, Komatso Nobuo.

The principal master is presently Komatso Nobuo. The seat of the school is at Shiomidai, Suma-Kobe, Hyogo, Japan.

3. Miyamoto Musashi, Terao Motomenosuke, Terao Goemon, Yoshida Josetsu, Santo Hikozaemon, Santo Hanbei, Santo Shinjuro, Aoki Kikuo, Miyakawa Yasutaka.

The principal master is presently Miyakawa Yasutaka. The seat of the school is at Tenjin-cho, Hida, Oita, Japan.

We see that all three schools have the same lineage up to the eighth generation. The eighth successor, Aoki Kikuo, was part of the first generation following the Meiji period. The feudal tradition then underwent a reform that shattered it. From that time on, there was a great increase in social mobility as well as in changes of residence. The development of diverging branches of Musashi's school is in part explained by these overall social changes.

Transmission in the School of Musashi at the Present Time

Succession in the School of Musashi does not follow a hereditary pattern. It is attested by the conferral of two objects: a scroll on which is written the name of all the techniques and the approach to them that must be transmitted in order to perpetuate the school, and a wooden sword that Musashi made himself, with which he trained, and which he used as a cane during the last years of his life.

In the School of Musashi, today called the Hyoho niten ichi ryu, the following techniques are transmitted:

- *tachi seiho,* techniques with the long sword: twelve forms
- *kodachi seiho,* techniques with the short sword: seven forms
- *nito seiho,* techniques with both swords: five forms (these correspond to the five forms in the Scroll of Water)
- *aikuchi roppo,* knife techniques, six forms
- *jitte to jutsu, jitte* techniques against a sword: five forms
- *bo jutsu,* staff techniques: twenty forms (3, p. 79)

One of the branches of the Hyoho niten ichi ryu today is directed by Master Imai Masayuki Nobukatsu, the tenth-generation successor of this school. Until the eighth generation, the school remained in the prefecture of Kumamoto, where Musashi spent the last years of his life, but in the ninth generation the school was transferred to the town of Usa in the prefecture of Oita, adjacent to Kumamoto. Imai Masayuki continues the training inherited from his predecessors in his dojo, located next to the Shinto shrine of Usa.

In Musashi's time it was customary to take the name of a master when succeeding him. The history of Japanese swordsmanship furnishes numerous examples of this. In warrior circles this custom facilitated the perpetuation of the school, but more than that, it corresponded to the belief that the spiritual and physical presence of the person whose name one has taken lives on in the person who has taken it.

From the point of view of the transmission of the art, this identification with the master had a certain effectiveness. We are presently less sensitive to this aspect of lineage succession, and it is no longer common for us to take on the exact name of someone else, but does not someone who bears the first name of an ancestor experience a particular attachment to him?

Inheritance of physical objects also in some sense has a similar effect. If we hold on to the intimate possessions of a dead person whom we knew well and live with them, when we touch these objects, how can we not evoke the presence of this person by incorporating them in some way into our own lives? In this way a phantom can have an existence.

Someone who takes the name of a master and at the same time receives physical possessions of his, as well as assuming his functions, can never escape from the image of the master. It will live with him, and the moment he lets himself go, this image will persecute him, evoking the model associated with the master.[1]

‖ 8 ‖

The Transmission of Musashi's Art

THE ROLE OF MUSASHI'S WRITINGS IN THE TRANSMISSION OF HIS ART

Around 1640, in the fief of Hosokawa, the number of Musashi's students reached one thousand. Three of them, Terao Magonojo, his younger brother Terao Motomenosuke, and Furuhashi Sozaemon, had attained a remarkable level, which led to their being viewed as Musashi's future successors. Musashi dedicated the *Gorin no sho* to Terao Magonojo and gave him the actual text. To Terao Motomenosuke he gave the *Hyoho sanju go kajo*. It seems that Musashi was counting on these two brothers to succeed him as the head of his school.

Nakazato Kaizan cites a text written in the Edo period that describes a scene in which Musashi was training Terao Magonojo:

Among Musashi's numerous students, Terao Magonojo, from the town of Kumamoto, persevered in his training for years, and he received the transmission for the whole of Musashi's teaching. Musashi often trained Terao with the *kodachi* (short sword). Once when training him, Musashi attacked with a large wooden sword and Terao parried with a short wooden sword and counterattacked. After several repetitions, Terao's sword broke in the middle at the moment Musashi was striking downward from above. Musashi's sword stopped short just shy of the skin of Terao's forehead. Thus he was not injured. This degree of control was usual for Musashi. (23, p. 86)

Precision and ability to control were without a doubt essential elements in the effectiveness of the swordsmanship of Musashi. The transmission of the School of Musashi includes techniques for the short sword *(kodachi)*, and this document confirms that the practice of the school was not limited to the art of two swords, which was nonetheless one of the principal foundations of its training.

We know the circumstances of the key meeting in which Musashi passed on the *Gorin no sho* from the commentary that accompanies the second copy of the *Gorin no sho,* which is less known and was transmitted under the name *Ihon gorin no sho*. This copy was transmitted by Furuhashi Sozaemon to his disciples, who added some passages recounting what they had heard from Furuhashi: "Master [Musashi] died the nineteenth of the fifth month [1645]. A little before his death, on the twelfth of May, he called Terao Magonojo, Motomenosuke, and me and told us: 'You must attain in practice everything that I communicated to you day by day without having any need to note anything down. There is no written text for my school. Once you have read what I have written, you must make an end to it with fire.'"

What did they actually do?

Terao Magonojo assumed the role of successor first, then yielded this responsibility to his younger brother Motomenosuke. Perhaps he did burn the original of the *Gorin no sho* as his master had ordered him to do, because this original has never been found. A few years later, Motomenosuke transmitted to his disciples, under the title *Hyoho shiju ni kajo,* a document in which he added seven instructions to the *Hyoho sanju go kajo.* (9, p. 66)

Furuhashi borrowed for a few days the *Gorin no sho* that Magonojo had kept, and on the order of Lord Hosokawa Mitsuhisa, he made a copy of it, which he gave him. Furuhashi made for himself a second copy that he transmitted to his successor under the name of *Ihon gorin no sho*. This copy ends with the following notice:

> The twelfth of the fifth month of the second year of Shoho [1645]
> Shinmen Musashi no kami Genshin
> For the Honorable Terao Magonojo
> For the Honorable Furuhashi Sozaemon

The copy that is best known today is the one that was preserved by the Hosokawa family, which ends with the following notice:

> The twelfth of the fifth month of the second year of Shoho [1645]
> Shinmen Musashi
> For the Honorable Terao Magonojo

Then, in another handwriting:

> The fifth of the second month of the seventh year of Kanbun [1667]
> Terao Yumeyo Katsunobu
> For the Honorable Yamamoto Gensuke (10, pp. 23, 46, 68, 83, 87)

We do not know whether this was the copy made by Furuhashi or a copy transmitted by one of the Terao brothers within his school that was then appropriated by the seignorial Hosokawa family, as the notice at the end of this copy seems to indicate. Some present-day scholars advance the hypothesis that both the known copies are the work of Furuhashi. Doubtless we would never have known the *Gorin no sho* if Furuhashi had not copied it on the order of his lord, thus contravening the last wishes of his master, Musashi. It is also through him that we know of these last wishes.

It seems that the work had such power for Musashi's three disciples that they were unable to resolve to destroy it. In transmitting it, they manifested their respect for their master, but at the same time they were aware of betraying him. Why did Terao Magonojo yield the successorship to his brother? We might consider the idea that the dilemma posed by the transmission of the *Gorin no sho* played a role in this decision.

Let us continue our reading of the recollections of Furuhashi's disciples:

> For us this text is the memorial of our master [Furuhashi]. We would like to add to it our recollection of his words, although our writing brushes are mediocre. Those who read this text must exercise their judgment and work things out for themselves. We have all read it with a feeling of special gratitude. Thanks to this text, we have been able to clarify the problems of the way. It is a clear matter of life and death. This text should never be communicated outside the school.
>
> Master [Musashi] was already old at the time of his stay in the fief of Kumamoto, and his art had fully ripened. These were the circumstances when he chose only three disciples. He said that when he was young, his character was too bad to train disciples.
>
> These three disciples were Terao Magonojo, his younger brother Motomenosuke, and Furuhashi Sozaemon. The master considered all three as his only successors. He had not adopted the system of a written oath at the time of initiation into his school, nor had he made a point of secret techniques, since he said that a true adept would never neglect the essence. Among his three disciples, Furuhashi was inferior to the two others, and we are disciples of the Furuhashi branch.
>
> What the master communicated to his three disciples:
>
> Before dying, the master communicated his last will to his three disciples. According to that, anyone who declares himself to be an adept of his school should write the following oath: "If I lose in combat against another school, I will end my life."
>
> They took it. And they had to require the same oath when they themselves conferred to someone their permission to call

himself an adept of their school. This was a serious system. That is why, at the moment of combat, one must commit oneself fully, without holding anything back, with the mind of dying. (9, pp. 67–68)

After Musashi's death, Furuhashi left Lord Hosokawa's service and left the island of Kyushu to live in Edo. He set himself up there as a master of *hyoho*. He taught swordsmanship to the vassals of the Owari fief. Chikamatsu Shigetomo, the master of strategic theory for the Owari fief, refers to the teaching of Furuhashi in a text entitled *Mukashi banashi*. This is a later document and is therefore less reliable than the one cited above. I will summarize it nevertheless, because it is interesting for an understanding of the attitude of adepts of that period toward written texts:

Some days before his death, Musashi called two of his disciples, Hayashi Magokuro [this refers to Terao Magonojo] and Furuhashi. Musashi said that Magokuro excelled in technique but that he was lacking in reflection, and that Furuhashi excelled in reflection but his technique was inadequate. Neither one nor the other of them was perfect, but he had to transmit to them the secret of his school, because he had found no one else. Musashi showed them a text and said: "Read it now."

When the two disciples had read it through quickly, Musashi burned this text. But Furuhashi was a person with an exceptional memory. After reading it, he could recite all its sentences. Fearing he would forget, he secretly wrote down what he had read in the presence of his master. Later he was a master of strategy in Edo. He got old, and then one day he fell sick. He could not resolve to let this precious text be lost that contained the teaching of his late master, who was exceptional. He finally decided to transmit it to one of his disciples, Matsui Ichimasa, a vassal of the Owari fief. Matsui was the most brilliant of Furuhashi's disciples. He was also a great adept of the bow, and Furuhashi held him in high esteem.

One evening Furuhashi visited Matsui in the house of the Owari vassals and said to him: "I think my life will not last much longer. I would like to transmit to you the text of my late master. But I must respect his wish. Read it once and try to remember its contents."

Matsui said: "I am very honored, Master. But I do not have an excellent memory. It is impossible for me to memorize it in a single reading. I would like to ask you the favor of lending it to me until tomorrow morning. I will try to memorize it by reading it as many times as possible by tomorrow morning."

Furuhashi finally agreed to lend him the text if he swore not to copy it. Matsui wrote out the oath required of him. He read the text over and over until the following morning and at last learned it by heart.

He awaited the visit of Furuhashi, who had said he would return the following morning. Noon passed. Matsui, worried, went to visit his master in order to return the text to him. When he arrived at Furuhashi's house, he was informed that the latter had died suddenly the previous night. It was in this manner that Musashi's text, written in Furuhashi's hand, was transmitted to Matsui.

Matsui preserved this text under the name "Wisdom of the Warrior" *(Shichi)*. (9, pp. 85–88)

A Text Parallel to the *Gorin no sho*

The text of the *Ihon gorin no sho,* the copy written and preserved by Furuhashi, is, with the exception of a few details, identical to that of the *Gorin no sho*. I made my translation using both texts.

The *Shichi* contains a certain number of passages from the *Gorin no sho,* completed by a few passages that are not in the latter, of which I give the essentials below. I have tried my best to convey the difference in tone, which is quite clear in Japanese, between this text and that of the *Gorin no sho*.

Recognizing the changes in heaven and earth

In the course of each of the four seasons, inevitably, if the good weather continues for a period of time, rain, wind, or snow follow. One must always think of the changes in heaven and earth. In the same way, one must be prepared for changes in the mind of a person and win without risk through foresight. This is the essence of the way of strategy.

Reshaping things

It is easy to transform things. For example, we ferment grain, we cook rice, then we make sweet sake, and by cooking it more, we make caramel. Someone lacking in wisdom does not know how to transform from one to the other. It might happen that he will cast blame on someone who has had the intelligence to do so, saying that he has changed his attitude. One of the foundations of strategy is to correct geography so as to locate yourself on the high ground and to transform your own mind.

Water in the dark of night

To see the reflection of the moon in water, the ordinary mind thinks it is enough to wait for the moon to appear. Someone who is wise fills a bucket with water before night so that the moon will be reflected there when it appears. This analogy is simple: If you study without fault and if you prepare correctly in advance, the advantage of strategy will be reflected in your upright mind.

Knowing what you do not see

There are precursory signs in all things; this is a principal of the universal order. Reacting to what has appeared is ordinary. In traversing human life and in governing society, it is important to perceive even before the precursory signs appear. That is what I call "knowing what you do not see." By polishing your mind from morning till night in the way of my school, you can obtain the wisdom of strategy that makes it possible to apprehend the universal order in this manner.

Discriminating the true from the false
One of the techniques of the way of commerce is to show as your own something that is borrowed. In the different arts, there exist techniques intended to give the illusion of superiority through an abundance of decoration. It is essential in *hyoho* to discriminate through wisdom the true from the false.

The Role of the Text in the Transmission of the Art

In Musashi's time, in the realm of the arts, the transmission of written texts was rare, and taking notes during teaching and practice—and even afterward—was forbidden. It is probable that those who did write down their master's words wrote what they understood, reformulating the expressions involuntarily in one way or another. Sometimes it was just a modification of style, but sometimes the meaning was changed. In the martial arts the most important thing is an intuitive understanding that comes from the body. In my experience, taking in the meaning of an instruction in itself on a profound level is all but incompatible with being able to reproduce literally the words that served as a vehicle for it. In other words, depending on whether the effort you make is to faithfully memorize some words or to capture the fullness of their meaning and what they are trying to convey, your intellectual activity will be of a different order, and what you retain will not be the same. All one has to do is remember the experience in school of learning material by rote to grasp the difference that exists between these two attitudes. Rejection of transmission by means of writing reflected a recognition of the importance of real intuitive comprehension on a personal level. After that the point is to be able to communicate in the same fashion to others what one has most deeply understood oneself. In this case, faithfulness or accuracy is not on the level of words. Hence the rejection of indirect transmission by means of a text, which is considered unfaithful or inaccurate.

At the same time, the weight given to words was different from what it is today. The oath required by Furuhashi is an example of this. The sense of a word that binds was understood here, and the relationship between the two interlocutors was included as a part of this. In certain situations the words of a master were taken as a riddle or a subject of meditation, and the weight given to exact wording took on maximal importance in this connection. Furuhashi, with his exceptional memory, developed by his function of official scribe for Lord Hosokawa, doubtless had a special ability to provide a faithful transcription.

In the martial arts, experience has proven that it is not always effective to take notes while instruction is being given, at which time one must maximize one's entire intuitive and physical availability so as to be able to understand what is being taught and be able to do it oneself. When we write things down right after receiving instruction, we can somewhat easily capture what we have heard even if we have not understood everything. It often happens that we understand these words only later on. From this point of view, it is useful to take notes, but when everything has yet to be understood, the effort made to faithfully reproduce in writing what we have heard during the lesson tends to stifle the seed of intuitive and physical understanding. The fabric of written words provides a reference point for later reflection. But such reference points sometimes form a barrier that puts an end to the process of intuitive fermentation by which one might succeed in capturing the practical meaning. However, thanks to notes, if the associated images are recalled with precision a long time afterward, words can give birth to a new understanding.

Thus in *budo,* whether or not to take notes immediately after instruction poses a veritable dilemma. Tradition resolved this by prohibiting the taking of notes.

Comparison of the texts of the *Shichi* and the two copies of the *Gorin no sho* illustrates the diversity of processes of transmission. From this point of view, the *Hyoho shiju ni kajo* of Terao Motomenosuke is closely related to the *Shichi*.

THE TRANSMISSION OF MUSASHI'S ART THROUGH PRACTICE

Terao Motomenosuke Nobuyuki received the complete transmission of the School of Musashi. Musashi had the greatest confidence in him. At the time of his death, Musashi gave him both his swords and a certificate of complete transmission.

Motomenosuke at first refused to teach, and he sent what he had received from his master to Miyamoto Iori, Musashi's adoptive son. Iori immediately gave everything back, saying: "I can be heir to the name and warrior's honor of Musashi, but I cannot take on the succession of his school. It is my wish that you, to whom Musashi passed on his art, succeed him. Please be kind enough to accept."

Thus Motomenosuke took over the position of head of the School of Musashi. Motomenosuke's and Iori's actions were manifestations of mutual respect. For Motomenosuke's part, his action was an expression of a great respect and sense of consideration toward his dead master that extended on to his son. For Iori's part, it was natural to return these gifts; this confirmed his recognition of Motomenosuke and showed his implicit agreement with his succeeding to Musashi's position as the head of his school.

Motomenosuke's fourth son had great talent in the martial arts. His father had him take the name of Shinmen Bensuke and gave him the complete transmission of the School of Musashi. Musashi had said to his favorite disciple, "If you have a capable lad, in having him succeed me, give him the name Shinmen." Shinmen was the name of the familial clan to which Musashi belonged.

In this way the continuity of the first two successions was assured, but Bensuke died at the age of forty-five, and the school began to divide up. As in the history of transmission of all schools of the arts, more branches appeared from generation to generation.

The schools that issued directly from that of Musashi and were formed under its influence were Enmei ryu, Tetsujin ryu, Onko chishin ryu, Mirai chishin ryu, Hozan ryu, Ippo ryu, Imaeda ryu, and Shin gyoto ryu.

Transmission of the Art of the School of Musashi through Katas

In every school the effective techniques are formalized in order to facilitate training and transmission. Exercising in these techniques constitutes a framework that each practitioner must use to develop his personal art. Depending on the school, the number of these essential techniques varies from around ten to twenty, but sometimes a school will have only two of these formalized techniques. In that case they are both essential, and all the technical variations will be built around these two techniques, repeated thousands of times every day.

The technical forms that distill the essence of each school are called katas. Each kata has a particular name that evokes its technical content. Generally each sword kata expresses a single essential technique and is composed of a few precise and concentrated sequences of movements. In contrast to a martial art such as karate, whose katas are composed of a number of interlocked sequences of defense and attack movements that contain many techniques, each sword kata is simple in appearance and short.

The system for naming the technique that constitutes a kata must be clarified. Let us recall that Musashi described techniques such as the strike of nonthought, the flowing-water strike, the strike like a spark from a stone, the crimson-leaves strike, the autumn monkey's body, the body of lacquer and paste, and so on. These names are all evocative and attach an image to each technique. Such a system is common within a school, but from one school to another, the same technique is called by different names. Why is this?

The function of the name of a technique is to communicate the essence of that technique within the limited group of the members of a single school. The same name, within one school, can convey different things depending on a person's level. The name of a technique should communicate something but at the same time hide it from the outside. That is why the name must evoke an image, but its interpretation can be manifold. The communication is based on a precise meaning, but at the same time intentions are concealed behind the ambiguity produced by the multiple meanings of a single word. This opacity also shows that there is something of considerable value involved, and this is necessary for the assertion of the school's dignity.

The Same Technique Transmitted under Different Names

In schools that are considered to be branches of the School of Musashi, the same technique is transmitted under different names. I rely here on descriptions of the techniques given by Yoshida Seiken (35) and Sasamori Junzo (50).

For example, in the Enmei ryu there is a kata technique called *sagosetsu*, and in the Shin gyoto ryu this technique is called *togosetsu*. These names are derived from the ancient Chinese pronunciation of certain ideograms. The same technique in the Tetsujin ryu is called *awase giri*, pronounced according to the Japanese system. The two last ideograms of all the names are the same. If we read the names of the first two techniques with the Japanese system that is used for the third, the first one would be read *sashi awase giri* and the second, *katana no awase giri*. Thus the final part, *awase giri*, is common to all three. In the first, *sashi* refers to the movement of stretching the arm, and in the second, *katana no* refers to the sword. The function of these initial parts is primarily as modifiers. What is essential here is *awase giri*.

So what does this term mean?

The three names correspond to the following technique: You approach the adversary holding the two swords with the points directed downward *(gedan)*. When he attacks downward from above toward the top of your head, you raise your hands to the level of your chest, and from this position you put forward the crossed blades of your two swords and cut into the hand of your adversary with a scissors motion. And indeed, *awase* means "to cross" or "to superimpose two objects," and *giri* (or *kiri*) means "to cut." Thus the name of the technique expresses its content.

The Understanding of Techniques and Images

In the Enmei ryu there is a technique called *tenpen hassu kurai*. *Tenpen* means "to turn and change," that is, it refers to a rapid and diversified development. *Hassu* means "to emanate," "to depart," or "to attack." *Kurai* means "state, guard position." Thus this name expresses the idea of a guard position that allows one to change one's position freely in order to attack the adversary.

More concretely, in this technique you place both your swords on your right side, which corresponds to the side guard *(waki gamae)* of the school of Musashi. The points of the swords are directed toward the rear. Your body is at an angle, with the left shoulder forward. Your body is open on the front and on the left side, and you move forward in this position. For your opponent, there is an open avenue of attack. When he attacks, you parry with your short sword held in your left hand and immediately move forward to the right, spinning rapidly; then you attack with the long sword held in your right hand.

There are several variants of this technique. The technique called *in ko ran* of the Hozan ryu is an example of one of these. You hold the short sword in your left hand, positioning it horizontally across from your chest on the right. Your right hand holds the long sword with the point directed toward the rear, as in the preceding technique. If the adversary attacks you, you block his sword with the short sword held in your left hand as you move forward to strike with the long sword held in your right hand.

The execution of this technique is nearly the same as that of the preceding one. Why is it called *in ko ran?*

The dichotomy between *in* (yin, negative) and *yo* (yang, positive) is present here. In the art of the sword, *yo to* is the name given to the sword with its point raised to heaven or pointed at the eyes of the adversary. When the sword does not have its point aimed at the adversary or has it aimed at the ground, it is called *in to* or *kage no kurai*, "shadow guard" or "negative guard." For example, the high and middle guard positions belong to the *yo to* (yang, positive) sword, and the low, side, and rear guards belong to the *in to* (yin, negative) sword.

Thus, in the name *in ko ran,* we understand by *in* that we are dealing with the sword of the negative guard *in,* or the shadow guard, but *in* does not indicate the exact position of the sword.

What exactly, then, is the sense of *ko,* which means "tiger"?

To indicate "to the rear" or "behind," the term *ushiro* is used. The ideogram for this is also pronounced *go.* Early on, because of the resemblance of the two sounds, *go* was sometimes replaced by *ko,* with the idea of connecting with the mythical image of the tiger. Indeed, it was believed in Chinese mythology that a tiger could roll up in its tail an object that it could throw as it leaped, or again, that a tiger could strike with its tail. Through this image of a tiger is indicated the rearward position of a sword with which one strikes as one leaps. Thus the two words *in* and *ko* determine the position and function of the long sword, which has the decisive role in this technique. The word *ran* expresses a rapid movement of undetermined direction.

Let us look at another example of an image associated with a technique.

In this technique you extend the short sword held in your left hand toward your opponent at the middle level with your left shoulder forward, and you hold the long sword in your right hand, pointed toward the rear. You move toward the adversary in this position. Your adversary will surely strike at your short sword, which is blocking him. When the adversary strikes, you parry with your short sword, which is not very resistant, since your left arm is nearly fully extended forward. The point of your short sword will definitely be knocked down by your opponent's strike. You let it be knocked down without resisting. As a result of your offering no resistance, the point of your opponent's sword will come down lower than he expected, which will create a gap in his position. At this moment you launch yourself forward off your right foot and strike your opponent's head with the long sword held in your right hand. The oral transmission adds here that you can even let your short sword fall to the ground.

This same technique is called *ryu setsu to* in the Shin gyoto ryu. The characters for the word *ryu* are also pronounced *yanagi,* and mean "weeping willow." The characters for *setsu* are also pronounced *yuki* and mean "snow." *To* means "sword." The image of snow falling from a willow branch, without finding a purchase on it, expresses the movement of the sword falling to the ground without offering any resistance to the adversary's strike.

The Name of a Technique and Its Symbolic Value

In the Enmei ryu there is a technique for throwing the sword that is transmitted under the name *shuriken uchi yo*, "the manner of throwing a sword with the hand."

This is to be used when the adversary adopts a solid guard position and remains immobile. The objective of this technique is not to stick your sword in the opponent's body but, rather, to disturb the solidity of his guard by throwing the short sword and slashing with the long sword. You hold the short sword in your left hand and throw it either from above your left shoulder or from your left side. In both cases your intention is to make your adversary move in order to parry the short sword. To do that, he is forced to move to the left. His left side is then left unprotected and near your long sword. You can then either slash him or stab him.

The Enmei ryu has two instructions for throwing a sword:

1. You raise the long sword high and put forward the short sword, which you rotate in a movement of the shape of a figure eight lying on its side. As you do this, you close in. At the moment you judge optimal, you throw your short sword from your left side toward your opponent's chest, and immediately afterward you strike him on the head from the right, with a big forward movement of your right foot. This technique can be used when your opponent adopts a middle or low guard position.

2. You hold the long sword alongside your hip, with the point directed at your opponent. You raise the short sword above your left shoulder and rotate it as you advance toward your adversary. At the moment you judge optimal, you throw it from above your left shoulder at the adversary's face and move forward to stab him in the chest with your long sword. This technique is particularly effective when your opponent adopts a high guard position.

In all the schools of two swords, these techniques are taught with the same principle, but the names for them are different. Here are some examples:

The first technique is called *hiryu ken* in the Mirai chishin ryu and *hiryu haku* in the Hozan ryu. *Hiryu* is used in both cases. *Hi* means "to fly," *ryu* means "dragon," *ken* means "sword," *haku* means "to move forward."

In the Chinese mythology taught in Japan, the tiger and the dragon are a symbolic pair. The tiger is yin (negative), as we have seen, and the dragon is yang (positive). The tiger symbolizes a sword of shadow, and the dragon symbolizes a sword of light that has a long body and moves in a spiral. Thus in the art of the sword, the dragon symbolizes a sword that is being rotated by one hand. Thus *hiryu ken* signifies a sword being held high and rotated with one hand. *Hiryu haku* means "moving forward with a sword held high that is being rotated by one hand."

The second technique is called *garyu haku* in the Hozan ryu. *Ga* means "to lie down," *ryu* means "dragon," *haku* means "to move forward." The term *ga* refers to the position of the blade of the long sword, which is lying horizontally alongside the right hip.

However, it should be pointed out that in both these schools the technique for throwing the sword is kept secret for as long as possible. In the usual instruction, the short sword is used to parry the adversary's sword. The technique for throwing the sword is applied only at the advanced level. Throwing the sword is a secret technique in all the schools, because its effectiveness is based on surprising the adversary. During the time of the warriors, this secret was kept with the greatest rigor, even among students of the same school.

Why is it that when you go from one school to another, the same technique will have different names? The difference comes from the way the first master of the school visualized the technique in relation to an image. Some names can be more poetic, others more descriptive, but always the words convey an image. The use of ideograms can serve as a camouflage when the richness of an image conceals the precise meaning behind the ambiguity of multiple meanings. By following the threads that bind the specific quality of the image with the meaning of the ideograms that make up a name, the adept can grasp something that has a profound significance for his practice.

In the practice of the warriors, the value of a technique lay not only in knowing how to do it. As long as there was no name associated with a technique, it did not really exist and was not learned. Thus often the final part of a transmission consisted in learning the name of the technique that was considered the most important, the content of which was already known. However, to see this in terms of a dichotomy between the container and the content would not be entirely accurate, because for most adepts, the content did not exist as long as the name had not been given. The word seems to have had a mythical and even magical sense for the warriors of the seventeenth century.

‖ 9 ‖

Musashi Today: The Practice
of a Contemporary Adept

WE HAVE SEEN THAT THE assessment of Musashi in Japan has been far
from unanimous. Studies of Musashi are most often done by literary
critics who know nothing about the practice aspect of the domain they
have entered. Most of the critical views of Musashi are based on senti-
mental judgments built on certain facts. For example, they focus on the
fact that during the fight against the Yoshioka clan, Musashi killed a
young boy, or on the fact that Musashi often used the strategy of turning up late for a duel, and so on. Masters of the martial arts have written little. That is why, if we want to study the art of Musashi from the
point of view of practice, the works of kendo master Morita Monjuro
(1889–1978) are particularly interesting. The judgment he forms of
Musashi is derived from his own practice of kendo, which made of him
one of the great adepts of his time.

Morita Monjuro began his practice of kendo in his childhood. He
received teaching from the most eminent masters of the period and
devoted his life to the study and teaching of kendo. Like all kendo
practitioners, he was interested in Musashi's writings and continued
throughout his life to probe for the deep meaning of the techniques

of this master. He tried to live and realize in his own kendo that which underlay Musashi's technique. Part of this was trying to understand his writings in depth. Through his experiments devoted to raising the quality of his own kendo, he perceived the authenticity of Musashi's art.

We are going to study the work of Morita Monjuro through two of his works (19, 20), published in 1987 and 1988.

The Labyrinth Created by the Way of Holding the Sword

As an adept of kendo, Morita Monjuro developed a problem that was primarily technical in nature. Kendo practitioners hold the sword in two hands, and one of the main techniques of modern kendo is to move forward, with the right hand and the right foot in front, in a series of half steps. This is done in order to remain in the most favorable position for striking with the sword held with the right hand forward and the left hand behind. It was only after long study that Morita realized that this went against the simplest way of organizing the movements of the human body for walking, which consists in making use of diagonal tension by putting forward the right foot along with the left hand, then the left foot along with the right hand.

Morita writes:

In kendo, the difficulties arise from holding the sword in two hands. I was wandering in a labyrinth, trying a variety of methods. I did not succeed in handling the sword correctly and spent my energy uselessly. When you practice kendo using two *shinai,* these difficulties disappear. It seems to me that Musashi understood very early the advantage that comes from a profound principle that is also present in his technique for one sword. I observed this by dedicating myself for long years to Musashi's single-cadence strike. These difficulties tormented me for a long time during my life in kendo, and after having passed fifty years of age, I still had to go through several years of painful research before discovering this principle.

I began studying Musashi's single-cadence strike around 1940. I raised the *shinai,* then I struck. Even if I executed this movement without stagnating, since the two movements of raising and lowering are present, this could not be done in a single cadence but only in two stages. Depending on the skill of the practitioner, he can reduce the time used for the first movement, but the problem is not one of either speed or time. It concerns the nature of the movement. What could Musashi's single cadence be? . . . I observed all the things in life that move. I often watched the movement of the pistons of the trains that passed behind my house. (20, pp. 21, 30)

The Relationship between the Sword and Zen, according to Morita Monjuro

Morita calls *kendo-zen* the kendo that makes it possible to strengthen the *tanden* with every exercise. But he stresses that in Zen there are about seventeen hundred koans, whereas in *kendo-zen* there is only one way: the single-cadence strike, which is the basis of Musashi's art.

According to Morita,

holding the sword with the principle of manipulating it perfectly is synonymous with attuning oneself to the universal principle. The effect is similar to that sought by Zen masters through sitting *zazen* facing the wall. The technique of the sword becomes the practice of the universal principle, and this practice is the equivalent of the koan in Zen. Handling the sword is the way to examine whether one is conforming to this principle.

In his first work, Morita wrote:

For a long time it has been said that "the sword and Zen come together as one," for in deepening one's kendo practice, one reaches a stage where the techniques rely more on the mind than on physical skill. . . . When one practices kendo purely in the physical realm, it is not different from other sports activities. It is only when one goes into it in depth and learns to use the *tanden* in the practice that one can develop one's mind and attain a result that is close to Zen. It is in this way that the sword and Zen come together as one. (19, p. 37)

Before he was able to make this statement, Morita traveled a long, difficult road of practical and theoretical research.

The practice of Zen is certainly good, but a halfway practice of it is useless. If you practice, you have to go all the way, without looking for anything else. . . . I practiced Zen intensively for years, working with the spiritual problem, thinking of life and death. I immersed myself in koan practice and tried to find out what emptiness is. But I do not think that any of these practices was of any use to me at all in kendo. . . . Kendo and Zen do not come together as one. As soon as I saw my opponent facing me, my mind changed. I was no longer the same as when I was meditating peacefully, sitting *zazen*. I found I was much more tensed up than when I was not practicing Zen. My kendo was far better when I was not even familiar with Zen, because I at least knew how to fight in a total, all-out way. I should have realized that the practice of Zen is very long and that if you do not go all the way to the end, the experience of Zen cannot be positive. If you want to practice Zen, you should not seek any other goal than the practice of Zen in itself. . . . If you want to practice Zen in order to make progress in kendo, you are better off just practicing kendo with a good teacher. That is what the Zen master at the Tenryuji temple says. (20, p. 39)

It is difficult to keep in the standing position the power in the belly that you acquired in a sitting position. To achieve this takes a tremendous amount of time and effort. Thus this result is pretty much impossible to achieve in our time.

That is why I recommend practicing the kendo that is carried out via "the *koshi* and the *tanden*."

The practice of standing Zen is also effective. What is called *nio-zen* consists of standing exercises, sometimes with the hands empty, sometimes with the sword. When you meditate standing up in *nio-zen*, the diagonal forces are naturally integrated and the strength of the *tanden* will be assured. (19, p. 67)

The Single-Cadence Strike: The *Tanden* and the *Koshi*

One day, by chance I ended up observing the movements of a dog that was hopping about as it played. I suddenly understood, and my problem of long years was resolved. I understood what Musashi's single-cadence strike means, and I came to a firm resolve about how to hold the sword. . . . From that day on, I have applied this principle to kendo, and everything has gone well. I was able to start practicing kendo tirelessly and with ease. Opponents who were difficult for me to fight I now dominated easily. I discovered the profound taste of kendo that I had never experienced, the real taste of kendo. . . . I said to myself: "How could I have come so far without knowing what kendo really was, after having received the instruction of the greatest of masters? And after teaching kendo at the university on top of it!"

I was fifty-seven years old when I discovered the principle that Musashi seems to have already mastered in his childhood. Musashi must have learned this principle either from his grandfather Shokan or from his father Munisai, both of whom were great adepts of the *jitte*. The *jitte* is held in one hand, and therefore there is no labyrinth as there is in kendo, where one is supposed to wield the sword with both hands. (20, pp. 40–41)

I myself used to talk about striking with the entire body, but I still did not know the real meaning of this teaching. Earlier on, I contented myself with giving a theoretical explanation based on the logic of the lever, on the subtle use of centrifugal force, on movement from a center of gravity, or on the application of the law of inertia. But striking with the body cannot be explained by these simple logics. I realized that there is something much more fundamental.

This has to do with the use of the lower back *(koshi),* through which all kinds of strikes become possible. [The term *koshi* is usually translated as "loins" or "hips," or else as "pelvis," but these translations are approximate. As Morita says, the *koshi* is a zone situated at the base of the back, opposite the *tanden,* which is located in the lower belly.] The *tanden* and the *koshi,* located on opposite sides of the body, constitute a whole in practice. Each exertion of the muscles of the *koshi* is transmitted to the *tanden,* stimulating it by means of pressure, and this activates different parts of the nervous system in a positive way. (20, p. 43)

The musculature of the *koshi* and the *tanden* form a unity, but their roles are not the same. The *tanden* commands the *koshi.* Training of the *koshi* is synonymous with training of the *tanden,* or center of the body, and through this it becomes training of the body and mind. . . . If you conceive of training like this, every technique serves to strengthen the musculature of the *koshi* and the *tanden.* This has pretty nearly the same effect as strengthening the *tanden* by practicing *zazen.* If the practice of kendo remains on the level of mere technical manipulation, the effect cannot be the same. By generating the technique from the *koshi* and the *tanden,* we can strengthen different aspects of our mind and appreciate kendo on the level of the highest subtlety.

Since ancient times, the Japanese have stressed the strengthening of the *tanden* in the various martial arts, because they believed that the force of the *tanden* made it possible to concentrate one's mind and produced an uncanny power as well as indomitable courage. (20, pp. 52–53.)

To strike correctly from the *tanden* and the *koshi,* it is necessary to attain, as Morita puts it, "perfect handling of the body" or "perfect handling of the sword." This involves a movement that is produced by a concordance of the two diagonal forces that go from the right leg to the left arm and from the left leg to the right arm.

Morita gives a definition: "The perfect handling of the sword in kendo is produced by the integration of three elements: the rotation of the *koshi*, the diagonal tensions produced by this rotation, and the movement from place to place of the body."

Perfect handling of the sword is carried out from the *koshi* and requires the strength of the *tanden*. It is in this sense that Morita calls for "kendo done by the *koshi* and the *tanden*," saying that it is only through such kendo that one can shape the mind and body by means of the sword.

> Every practitioner must study and examine the techniques while attentively reading the *Gorin no sho* and applying this principle. Traditional texts on the art of the sword exist, but none compare to those of Musashi, because Musashi attained a completely superior level. This comes out in the simple expression of his phrases, but this could easily go unnoticed if you are lacking in attention.
>
> Many kendo practitioners do not think enough about the general comportment of the body in kendo. They think it is enough to move while holding a sword, but it is not easy to handle a sword perfectly when holding it with two hands. . . . In the art of sumo, you fight without a weapon, and the principle of perfect comportment of the body was discovered a long time ago. . . . Modern kendo is unaware of this principle and many of its adepts run into a wall. I myself suffered for many years before overcoming this problem.
>
> In applying this principle of "perfect handling," I soon discovered that the *tanden* fills with force all by itself. Before that, I tried for many long years to put force into the lower belly by practicing *zazen*. But the problem was that once on my feet, when I began to move, the force in the *tanden* began to diminish. A half hour after starting the kendo session, I no longer had any confidence in the force in my belly. What does that mean? It should not

be that way. This problem tormented me for a long time, without my finding a solution. "Perfect handling" is accomplished by integrating the diagonal tensions of the body that go from the legs to the arms. Applying this principle in kendo, I discovered that the *tanden* was spontaneously filled with force, and my kendo was completely transformed.

In modern kendo, the dominant tendency is to manipulate the *shinai* rapidly with two hands, but you should know that it is impossible to transform oneself truly through superficial techniques. . . . Even if you practice kendo in competition, by training with the principle of perfect handling, it is possible to practice an authentic kendo in which one continues to make progress to the age of seventy and beyond. By mastering the subtle use of the *tanden,* you fill the lower belly, which makes it possible to envelop your body with *ki* and to understand the subtlety of the breath. You can then move and use techniques spontaneously with an adequate outbreath. This is the way you can acquire the eyes of the mind. (20, pp. 55–57)

The Diagonal Tensions

If you calmly practice the single-strike cadence, you should naturally discover the diagonal tensions of the body, and through that you learn perfect handling.

In kendo, the usual teaching is to pull the left hand toward you at the moment of the strike. But if you insist on this movement, you cannot strike properly. Before pulling your hand toward you, it has to be pushed forward. It is strange that this fact has not been pointed out long ago, because this is the most important point.

For example, the direct strike to the adversary's head *(shomen)* should be executed in the following manner: You leap forward feet first, propelled by the movement of the *koshi,* while your left hand is pushed forward in harmony with the right hand in order to raise the sword, and when your feet hit the ground, your hands come down to execute the strike. The movement of the hands does not occur until the last moment. Most of the movements are executed with the whole body, directed by the *koshi*.

You cannot avoid noting a transition between the movements of raising and lowering. But as you learn perfect handling, this separation will disappear. You put your right foot forward, and as the left foot follows it, the striking movement reaches its end. The correct strike is done with the correct movement of the feet, "the movement of yin and yang," as Musashi puts it. Musashi explains: "You do not move just one foot, you must move the right and the left." I understood that by walking in the way Musashi teaches, you become able to strike with the *koshi*. Musashi knew very well that the strike with the body seems slow, but that in reality it is very fast. That is Musashi's single-cadence strike. . . .

In other words, the essence of the single-cadence strike does not reside in the movements of raising and lowering the sword but in the overall comportment of the body. With the yin-yang movement of the feet, the sword moves naturally, following the movement of the body, and the single-cadence strike is accomplished. Raising and lowering the sword is then not two movements but just one. This coincides with the simple traditional teaching "Do not strike remaining on the spot, always strike moving one step forward."

The objective in contemporary kendo is not really to cut a person down, but to learn the way of the sword it is necessary to acquire the ability to do this. Otherwise, it is not possible to understand kendo in the proper way, that is, to handle the sword with the *tanden*. (20, pp. 60, 252–253.)

Through his study of Musashi's single-cadence strike, Morita discovered the principle that brings about the "perfect handling" of the sword and the body. This principle is the integration, through the whole body, of the diagonal tension between the limbs, this integration being produced by correct movements of the *koshi*, directed by the *tanden*.

In addition, the diagonal tensions of the body can be recognized by walking properly, and this leads to a reexamination of the techniques of modern kendo, in which the movements are unilateral and the tensions are not integrated. Morita discovered the meaning of Musashi's text in which he stresses the importance for striking of the ordinary walk. This is the way he integrated Musashi's teaching into his practice.

Morita concludes that by integrating the principle of walking into the technique of striking, you can develop the *tanden,* and by developing the *tanden,* you can also strengthen the integration of the diagonal tensions. Thus it is necessary to strengthen the *tanden* continuously and to practice the techniques with the correct movements of the *koshi,* which is located opposite the *tanden.* By practicing kendo with this awareness, it is possible to understand its true meaning and discover its true value.

Why does the practice of kendo become more profound and more interesting if you integrate the diagonal tensions and develop the *tanden* and the *koshi?*

Telepathy

On the basis of his experience, Morita developed the following hypothesis: Practicing kendo in such a way as to strengthen the *tanden* stimulates and awakens the deepest part of the human brain, which makes it possible to develop premonitory and telepathic abilities.

He takes the example of sumo to illustrate the link between the form of practice he recommends and the ability to intuit the actions and intentions of the adversary.

In sumo wrestling you see perfect comportment of the body, which is due to integration of the diagonal tensions in the techniques. It seems to me that this principle was discovered long ago in sumo, where you work directly with the body without using any instruments. Futabayama attained excellence in this discipline. Even though he was not among the strongest, he had a record of sixty-nine successive wins in his bouts. No one else has been capable of such a performance either before or after him. Listening to his remarks, I think his fighting was telepathic beyond a doubt: "Facing off against an opponent and looking into his eyes, I understand beforehand how he is going to react and thus I am able to fight in a winning manner. When I lost for the first time, I had missed that moment of looking into the eyes of my opponent, which is what caused my defeat." [Futabayama was blind in one eye.](20, p. 251)

I think that telepathic ability and the strength of the *tanden* are closely linked. The functions of the *tanden* and the *sunden,* the point located between the eyes, are linked. In the Itto ryu swordsmanship school, there are frequent references to the *sunden.* So the cause of Futabayama's defeat would be a momentary lapse in the force of the *sunden.* (20, p. 296)

The *sunden* corresponds to the point Musashi refers to when he tells us that, when looking, one must "make a wrinkle between the eyes" by knitting the eyebrows. (20, p. 85)

In kendo, between two persons comes the sword and a distance. This creates an occasion for intuiting the action of the adversary and through this lays the groundwork for the subtlety and diversity of the combat. According to Morita, all the great adepts of the sword in history whose names we know practiced the art that made it possible for them to develop this ability. Musashi was one of them. The secret of their schools was their method of developing this ability. Certain passages in Musashi's writings relate to this.

Musashi divides the functions of the mind in two parts, the surface of the mind and the depth of the mind. In the Scroll of Water he writes, "When the surface of the mind is weak, its depth must be strong so that the opponent cannot perceive one's state of mind."

In the twenty-sixth instruction of the *Hyoho sanju go kajo,* he writes:

Holding and Letting Go of One's Mind
Depending on the situation and the moment, you must either hold your mind or let go of it. In general, when wielding a sword,

you must let go of your will but hold on to the depth of your mind. When you strike your opponent with certainty, you must let go of the depth of your mind and hold your will. These two states of mind, holding and letting go, can take on different forms, depending on situations. This must be worked out well.

When Musashi writes in the Scroll of Water to "intuit the moment in which the adversary does not yet know," Morita's understanding is that this is an application of the text just cited. His idea is that telepathy underlies all the techniques in Musashi's texts.

According to Morita, the voluntary aspect of the mind, connected with the will, corresponds to the recently developed part of the human brain that can be directed intentionally, and the deep aspect of the mind is the more ancient part that governs whatever is linked to our vital functions. This last part controls intuition and telepathic communication.

The ancient brain possesses great sensitivity, and consciousness of it is relatively rudimentary. It is capable of integrating the stimuli that come from the inside of the body with those that come from outside, and also of making us act appropriately without our having a clear consciousness of it. That is why I think "letting go of the mind" refers to the intervention of the ancient brain alone. . . . That which makes it possible to let go of the mind in this manner is the force of the *tanden*. Because through the force of the *tanden,* we can achieve a wholeness or integration of the mind on the basis of which it is possible to "let it go." This is what I think on the basis of my own experiences. (20, p. 190)

It sometimes happens to me that I know the outcome of a bout before I make a move. The adversary moves following my sword, which spontaneously breaks through a gap he allows. There is no stagnation and the strike is satisfying. I have the sensation of having won by means of telepathy.

But during daily training, I am not able to let go of my mind well, whereas I am able to do so during important tournaments.

I think that this is because for me my usual training is giving instruction, and on top of that, I am expecting the exercises to go on for a long time; thus the tension is not the same as during tournaments, where I can engage totally for a few minutes. The same is true when I am training in another dojo with partners I do not know. It will take me another ten years to be able to achieve telepathic combat during daily training, but I am afraid I will no longer be able to lift the *shinai* at that point. [Morita wrote this when he was around seventy.] I began to go in this direction around the age of fifty-seven. This was much too late, especially in comparison with Musashi, who seems to me to have entered this way when he was seven. (20, p. 195)

So this is the way Morita Monjuro ended up doing "telepathic kendo," which he also calls *kendo-zen*.

THE NEN RYU AND ITS LINEAGE

Morita Monjuro combined reflection on his practice with the study of ancient documents on the sword, in which he sought historical material related to the problem he had and the discovery he made. As part of this, he studied the transmission of the Nen ryu, which is based, according to him, on the art of Musashi.

According to the traditional expression, the Nen ryu uses the technique of the past *(kako)* and the present *(genzai)* in order to arrive at the technique of the future *(mirai)*. The technique of the present is composed of techniques for movement. The technique of the past is the technique of the mind—it corresponds to Musashi's "letting go of the mind," which makes it possible to execute the single-cadence strike. The technique of the future is an art of swordsmanship that relies on telepathy. This includes the ability to know the future and see through things. This kind of mental power is called *nen riki* in Japanese, and this is where the name of the school comes from. The goal of the Nen ryu is thus to practice swordsmanship knowing what is going to happen.

The single-cadence strike can really be executed only if it is associated with the principle of walking, which is the basic principle of *kendo-zen*. "The monk Jion [1351–1409], the founder of the Nen ryu, taught six hundred years ago: Strike with the left arm extended. The Nen ryu was the only one to transmit this extraordinary discovery."

Why does Morita say that this was an extraordinary discovery?

We can understand this by returning to the practical problems he talks about. We saw above that the prevailing way of practicing modern kendo goes against the simplest manner of organizing the movement of the human body, which results in a fundamentally mistaken instruction: Extend the right arm at the same time as pulling the left arm in toward yourself. For Morita this instruction is a valid one for cutting a fixed object while remaining stationary *(tameshi giri)* but is disastrous for kendo, because kendo is primarily a practice that involves movement from place to place. Morita tells us that if you apply to swordsmanship the principle of walking, which is an expression of the natural organization of the movement of the human body, the left arm will extend spontaneously. The monk Jion pointed this out six hundred years ago. When executing a strike this way, the *tanden* is naturally strengthened, and thus the single-cadence strike is spontaneously accomplished. According to Morita, the sequence is as follows: The single-cadence strike reinforces the *tanden*, which, in concert with the *sunden*, stimulates and activates the cerebral faculties of intuition and telepathy.

Morita also tells us that when executing the single-cadence strike, the weight should be placed on the left foot (the rear foot). This strike is more effective when the two diagonal tensions of *kendo-zen* extend their power to the right arm.

To explain how transmission of the monk Jion's art to Musashi could have taken place, Morita formulates the following hypothesis: The monk Jion trained fourteen disciples. Tsutsumi Hozan was his twelfth disciple, and he was an adept of the *jitte*. The monk Jion also excelled in the art of jujutsu, which was probably integrated into the *jitte* art of Hozan, who later founded the school that bears his name, the Hozan ryu. However, Jion died before Hozan could learn enough of the "technique of the past," which is the most important for attaining the "technique of the future," but thanks to the art of the *jitte,* he did not run into the labyrinth that is encountered in the art of the sword wielded with two hands. Thus he was able to develop further the teaching received from his master, and he succeeded in attaining the essence of the Nen ryu.

Morita believes it is possible that Hozan or one of his disciples moved to Shimotsuke (today Tochigi) to the west and that he met Musashi's grandfather and transmitted his art of the *jitte* to him. And it is true that this period, the period of feudal wars, was characterized by great mobility among warriors. Moreover, we know that Hirata Shokan, who is considered to have been Musashi's grandfather, did teach the art of the *jitte* at the end of the fifteenth century and the beginning of the sixteenth.

According to this hypothesis, Musashi, who was born into a family of *jitte* adepts, received the transmission of the Nen ryu through the art of the *jitte,* which he later developed when he founded the School of Two Swords.

Even if this lineage connection between the Nen ryu and the School of Musashi did not take place, it is probable that in practicing the *jitte,* Musashi experienced the principle of integrating the diagonal tensions. The separate use of the hands in the art of the *jitte,* in connection with the motion of walking, would have led to the realization of this principle.

In any case we observe in Musashi great intelligence in the use of the body, which is reflected in his instructions on handling the sword and also on the general comportment of the body, notably in connection with colliding or entering into contact with the body of the opponent. When Musashi fought his first duel at the age of twelve, the documents tell us that he first threw his opponent and then struck the death blows. According to Morita, Musashi did not win by brute force but by using the principles for using the body that had been taught to him. He banged into the body of his opponent in a way that applied these principles. Morita views this combat as a proof that Musashi knew these principles from a very early age. And it would have been impossible to have discovered them so early through his own experience. This fact tends to prove that he received instruction from his grandfather or his father.

Strictly observing tradition, the monk Jion transmitted the whole of his art to only one disciple in each fief. A person who reached a high level and wanted to receive the transmission but was in a region where there was already someone who had received it, in order to fulfill these conditions, had to leave the region to receive it himself. Thus the fourteen disciples of the monk Jion continued, each in a different region, to develop and transmit the art they received from their master.

Let us take an example from the genealogy of a branch of the Nen ryu.

The second of the fourteen disciples was named En no Shinmai or Saru no Gozen. His last grandson, Aisu Ikosai (1441–1538), founded the Kage ryu in 1478.

The art of Aisu Ikosai continued in the Kage ryu, and in addition it was transmitted to his son Aisu Koshiro (1518–1590), one of whose disciples, Kamiizumi Isenokami Nobutsuna (c. 1508–c. 1577), founded the Shin kage ryu.

One of Kamiizumi's disciples, Yagyu Muneyoshi (1528–1606), founded the Yagyu shin kage ryu, which became the school of the shogun during the Tokugawa period. Later this school developed and branched out. Of its two principal branches, the Edo school and the Owari school, the first tended to ease off on practice while developing a sophisticated theoretical structure, while the second remained faithful to the tradition of its founder. The school later developed further and its techniques underwent a transformation.

The Lineage Link between the Nen ryu and the Yagyu ryu

In 1984 I had an interview with Master Yagyu Nobuharu, the fifteenth head of the Yagyu shin kage ryu of Owari. He showed me the documents handed down in his family, including the certificates of transmission. Among these documents were various drawings done by Kamiizumi, which illustrated techniques. The positions shown in the drawings are very different from the techniques of kendo that we are used to. The movements are of a much larger scope than those practiced by Master Yagyu Nobuharu today. The master gave me this explanation:

On one hand, there is the difference between the practice of the time when the art of the sword was to be used against heavy armor and the period when this art became part of civilian life. Kamiizumi's period was that of the feudal wars, when people fought in armor. That is why those techniques are relatively simple but very powerful. You had to cut through armor. Whereas after that, the art of the sword developed in the period of feudal peace, where fighting with the sword took place for the most part wearing ordinary clothes. At that point, light and fast techniques could be very effective, therefore subtlety became more important than strength.

Then there is also the difference between the Edo period and our own time. Even though I received the traditional family transmission, the art that is manifested through me is different from that of my predecessors. That is why our position is not the same as what you see in the drawings.

At the time, I was satisfied with this explanation.

A few years later, in 1988, I studied the art of the sword of the Komagawa Kaishin ryu. Among the various schools of swordsmanship I have had the occasion to become acquainted with, this is the one I have found the most convincing, and I have continued since then to practice this art. I did not know the lineage of this school, but in 1991, during a training session, Master Kuroda, the current head of the school, explained to me the lineage connection between his school and that of Kamiizumi. Then suddenly I remembered the documents that Master Yagyu had shown me, because the techniques I was now learning were very close to the drawings by Kamiizumi. The position of the legs, the way the feet were spread, the posture of the body on an angle, the way of holding the sword, the guard position, and so on, were very close to these drawings. I consulted my files on the Yagyu school, and in fact I did find drawings corresponding to one of the techniques I was in the midst of learning. And on one document appeared the name Komagawa Tarozaemon, a disciple of Kamiizumi who was the founder of the Komagawa Kaishin ryu.

Thus this school has survived transmitting quite closely the modalities of training from the time of Kamiizumi, whereas the Yagyu school underwent more development and modified the techniques more. Thus I conclude that the explanation given by Master Yagyu Nobuharu for the evolution of the style of his school had only a limited bearing.

Seeing its connection with the school of Kamiizumi and thence with the monk Jion provided me with a new perspective on the art of the sword I practice. Indeed, this school stresses striking with the arms extended. If you strike with the left arm extended, then the right arm also extends. This leads me to favor the explanation Morita gives of Musashi's single-cadence strike. In practicing this type of strike, I find I achieve more ease by putting force in the *tanden*.

As for telepathy, my experience with the sword does not enable me to give a satisfactory explanation of it. It happens to me only occasionally during practice of bare-handed combat that I clearly perceive the adversary's vulnerable moment. I see an obvious lapse in his state, but I cannot say that this is telepathy or be sure to what extent this sensitivity is connected with the strengthening of the *tanden*.

‖ 10 ‖

Weapons and Ethics in Swordsmanship Training

THE ART OF THE SWORD of Musashi's time can be characterized by saying that it began to aim at something besides a mere technique of combat. Its quest for technical perfection began to merge with a quest for perfection of a religious nature.

In the course of its history, humanity seems to have always felt the need to define the status of arms. A mere sacralization of arms has not been enough for a long time. With the increase in the destructive power of weapons, a moral code for limiting their use has become increasingly important. The use of atomic bombs requires the consent of a number of people, and what they do is constrained by ethics and beliefs. On one level the danger does not reside in the pistol but in the person who carries it. We can only bear witness to the current disproportionate gap between the capacity for and the level of control human beings are capable of.

The technique of the sword evolved from an initial brutal and primitive usage, where force meant everything, toward a subtlety and refinement that is based on premonitory insight into the adversary's approach. In both East and West, when the development of technique

MIYAMOTO MUSASHI, *Floating Duck. Hanging scroll, ink on paper. Okayama Prefectural Museum of Art.*

||||

Having flown across the vast sky,
its wings now forgotten,
this duck sports serenely
as it entrusts itself to the waves
of endless mountain streams.

Under a classical five-line *waka* poem, Musashi has depicted a duck through minimal strokes of the brush. He has suggested the duck's body with washes in varied tones of gray, added emphasis to the head with fuzzing black ink, and slightly exaggerated the beak with firm brush lines. This painting is an example of the "broken ink" tradition of painting, most often utilized for landscapes, a tradition of brushwork that Musashi mastered and created variations upon in many of his scrolls. Here he utilizes the technique to show the compressed energy of a duck swimming in gently flowing water. Similarly, a fine swordsman will concentrate his "chi" in case it should be needed at any instant.

MIYAMOTO MUSASHI, *Self-Precepts.*
Ink on paper. Kumamoto Prefectural
Museum of Art.

||||

PRECEPTS ARE AN IMPORTANT
element in Buddhism, and are sometimes
written out by monks in a series of
columns headed by horizontal dashes.
Here Musashi has written his own code

of behavior, as translated on page 216 of
this book. While he made no effort to
create calligraphy for display, there is a
quiet strength in the brushwork that
indicates how the swordsman-artist has
taken these precepts into his spirit. As
the code of a warrior, the rules he gives
himself include not settling down,
falling in love, or seeking comfort. Like
a monk, Musashi chose a life that
demanded great self-control, in which

he abandoned self-interest. This is not
the same as not having an individual
personality, however. The nature of his
own individual spirit can be seen in the
rhythm of the brushwork, and in this
way his calligraphy can give at least as
good a picture of Musashi as his painted
portrait.

MIYAMOTO MUSASHI, *Goose.*
Hanging scroll, ink on paper. Okayama
Prefectural Museum of Art.

||||

THIS PORTRAIT of a goose shows
how Musashi could take an image
from nature, a moment from
everyday life, and transform it into
a painting of dynamic power. The
goose turns its head to call out,
and the dramatic lines of its beak
are echoed by the twin lines of
brittle foliage springing out from
the cliff above it; the curve of the
bird's neck also echoes the bend
of the cliff to its left. In contrast,
Musashi uses bands of broad and
tonally varied gray wash to
indicate the rocky world in which
the bird must try to survive.
Equally important is the empty
space — more than half the
total scroll — towards which the
goose turns, ready to defend itself
or perhaps just calling out to the
world to witness its life-spirit.

MIYAMOTO MUSASHI, *Daruma
Crossing the River. Hanging scroll, ink on
paper. Tokugawa Reimeikai Foundation.*

||||

THERE IS A LEGEND that the first
patriarch Daruma, after an enigmatic
audience with the Liang emperor in
southern China, crossed the Yangtze
River on a reed en route to the Hsiao-
lin temple to meditate. Actually, the
graph for "reed" once also meant "reed
boat"; in Zen there should be no need
for miraculous deeds. Nevertheless, the
legend gave rise to a number of
paintings of Daruma crossing the river
on a reed, of which this is an
outstanding example. On the face of
the patriarch is a wide-eyed scowl of
single-minded determination, and the
reed is forcefully executed with a few
slashing strokes of the brush. Most
notable however, is the empty shape
outlined by the long strokes of
Daruma's robe. We can follow every
movement of Musashi's hand as he
brought the gray line from center left
up to the right, turned the brush
swiftly at the shoulder and then pulled
the line rapidly downward. A swirl of
the brush across the bottom of the
figure completed this evocative shape,
in which we must imagine the body of
Daruma crossing the waves.

MIYAMOTO MUSASHI, *Kingfisher on a Withered Branch, Hotei Walking, and Sparrow on Bamboo. Hanging scroll triptych, ink on paper. Okayama Prefectural Museum of Art.*

||||

JAPANESE ARTISTS OFTEN painted scrolls in pairs or triptychs, in the latter case usually portraying a figure in the center with landscape or natural scenes to each side. Here we have the happy-go-lucky wandering monk Hotei (see next caption) in the center, flanked by small birds on either side. To the right is a sparrow clinging to an elegantly arching stalk of bamboo, Musashi's version of a theme taken up by Zen painters to show the extraordinary in the ordinary. Nothing could be more common than a sparrow, or more plain than bamboo, and yet in their interaction can be seen the wonderment of the world. Here the sparrow peers down towards the earth while the plant surges upwards into space, creating a subtle compositional tension. In the center scroll, Hotei walks towards us carrying his staff, bag, and fan, full of good cheer. On the left, a tiny kingfisher clings to a dead branch, poised to dive down to catch any unwary fish that might swim to the surface. This kind of alert and attentive equilibrium is that of the swordsman, and also of artists at their finest.

MIYAMOTO MUSASHI, *Hotei Watching a Cockfight. Hanging scroll, ink on paper. Matsunaga Collection, Fukuoka City Art Museum.*

||||

HOTEI IS ONE of the most popular subjects in Japanese painting. In works by Zen masters he represents the legendary ninth-century Chinese monk Putai, who preferred to wander the roads with a smile rather than live in a temple. Merchants saw Hotei as the harbinger of good luck, as his great bag was imagined to be full of goods to sell. To children, Hotei was a jolly playmate who enjoyed their company more than that of serious adults. Musashi, the warrior, here depicted Hotei watching a cockfight. Although the squeezed-together features of Hotei suggest the influence of the Chinese Song-dynasty artist Liang K'ai, Musashi's dramatic expression in this work is one of his own special features. The painter Tanomura Chikuden (1777–1835), commented that "the brushwork is excellent and the ink tones have thoroughly penetrated the paper. How marvelously the eyes pierce the viewer!"

went beyond a certain level, practitioners of arms began to become aware of the state of mind with which they used their weapons.

In Japan, the warriors *(bushi),* specialists with weapons, tried to find a personal balance through the prevailing religion in a way that continued to renew itself as society evolved. An instruction of the sixteenth century commanded warriors who were riflemen to pray to the war god and to Buddha, as did the warriors of the twelfth century who were archers.

We must remember that Musashi lived at the point of transition between the two first periods of the development of the art of combat, at the time when the notion of *bujutsu (bu:* weapons; *jutsu:* techniques) was being formed. The first period, which was that of the development of the technique of combat on the battlefield, ran from the end of the fourteenth century to the beginning of the seventeenth century, when the period of feudal wars came to an end. The second period ran from the seventeenth century to the beginning of the nineteenth century; this was the period of the technical and ideological refinement of *bujutsu.*

Containing the experience of combat in his youth, then the fading away of the need to fight in order to survive and the philosophical development that arose out of this, Musashi's life was a compressed history of the Japanese sword before and after him.

THE STATUS OF WARRIORS

The basis of any form of combat is an interaction between at least two opposed energies. Techniques of defense and attack are an expression of this.

The term *bu* is a Chinese ideogram. It is sometimes interpreted as a combination of the noun meaning "lance" and the verb meaning "to stop." Certain contemporary adepts put forward a philosophical interpretation of the notion of *bu.* They see it as meaning "stopping an attack" and stress the unity in one and the same term of the weapon and its blockage, which requires the overcoming of a contradiction. But this interpretation is uncertain from an etymological point of view. In any case, in the history of the Japanese martial arts, the notion of *bu* has not always been experienced in this way. *Bu,* weapons, have been seen as a fundamental aggressive energy that interacts with the aggressive energy of the adversary.

In warrior society a certain ethic is associated with weapons that countervails their aggressive connotation. Weapons are connected with the sacred, with gods of war and protector gods. Through different historical periods, the use of arms, when considered as a social phenomenon, has usually been justified by association with a divinity or his ideological equivalent. It seems to me that the discrepancy between arms and the reference point used to justify them exists in almost every culture. We need only think of the Christian rhetoric justifying colonialism, the Koran's talk of the sword, or the juxtaposition of the Bible and the revolver in the conquest of the American West. The same has been true in the history of Japan during periods of war.

The unique quality of *bujutsu* during the second phase of the development of the art of combat arises from the fact that this discrepancy began to disappear. This trend was further accentuated later on with the emergence of *budo.* Taking the form of *budo,* the practice of the martial arts contained within itself an internal dimension and depth that played a role as a source of justification equivalent to the sacred external reference points of earlier times. This development reached the point of the negation of arms by arms with the transformation of "the sword that kills" into "the sword that gives life." The study of Musashi helps us to explain the specific quality of this development in the history of the martial arts in Japan.

At the beginning of Japanese history, as in many civilizations, arms were considered sacred. In Japanese mythology the emperor-god was a warrior, and weapons were among his divine attributes. When the emperor himself ceased to practice the calling of a warrior, his reign was justified by his divine lineage, and that functioned as a justification for the military forces that served him. This idea was still in force at the time, around the tenth century, when warriors began to assume political power. Indeed, this ideological conception of the sacred relationship between the emperor and the force of arms has persisted throughout the history of Japan, continually taking on new forms. The actual take-over of political power by the warriors went hand in hand with an evolution in military techniques. The form and technique of the Japanese sword began to transform in the eleventh century with the spread of combat on horseback. The form of the curved sword became established beginning in the twelfth century, and this sword received the name *nihon to* (Japanese sword) to differentiate it from the straight sword that preserved the direct influence of the Chinese. (On the relationships between the techniques of the Japanese sword and those of other countries, see appendix 3.)

The art of Japanese swordsmanship that we practice today has its origins in this period. The history of the development of the various techniques and attitudes of swordsmanship must be understood in terms of the dynamic between the form the sword took on for its use on horseback and the use of this curved sword for combat on foot. The art developed its specific quality through elaborating techniques for slashing with the sword rather than stabbing with it. The evolution in the form and the making of swords went hand in hand with the development of techniques that were becoming more and more remarkable. A great number of schools of swordsmanship developed, the oldest known one dating from the fourteenth century (see page 366).

The feudal wars came to an end at the beginning of the seventeenth century with the establishment of the Tokugawa regime. Japan then lived through a period of feudal peace that lasted for two and a half centuries. The Tokugawa government preserved the peace through strict regulations imposed on the feudal lords as well as the rest of the population. The use and development of firearms were suppressed from the beginning, whereas cutting weapons, and especially the sword, underwent major technical development. The first military decree of the Edo period (1603–1867) dates from 1615 and begins with the following passage: "Warriors should devote themselves primarily to the practice of the martial arts and the practice of letters. Letters are on the left and arms are on the right—this is the way of the warrior from the time of the ancients. The foundations of the warrior family are the bow and the horse."

This passage was written in classical language in order to give it more weight. This classical emphasis explains why the martial arts are symbolized here by the way of the mounted archer *(kyu ba no michi),* which was the way of the battlefield that was displaced when the sword became the principal arm of warriors. With the advent of the feudal peace, martial practice took the form of civilian techniques in which the sword predominated. In 1645 Musashi wrote, "There is no warrior without a sword." Indeed, the *bushi* was never without his sword. Even when he was sleeping, he kept it within arm's reach.

A warrior existed socially through his position in a family, which was itself situated in accordance with the standing of its lord. One of the characteristics of the Japanese feudalism of the Edo period was its reinforcement of the exclusivity of the feudal bonds of dependence. A warrior had, and could only have, one lord, and no matter what the lord's standing was, this bond was exclusive, the devotion expected of the warrior was absolute, and it was expected to provide the orientation for his entire life. Living at the beginning of the Edo period, Musashi was still able to benefit from the flexibility of the relations between Lords Ogasawara and Hosokawa. This flexibility disappeared quickly as the Tokugawa regime became more firmly established.

The relationship of the warrior to his liege lord was situated within a temporality that included his ancestors, and the place in history of the family name and its reputation took precedence over considerations relating to the lives of individuals. The act of voluntary death, which was the extreme manifestation of what the life of a warrior was supposed to be, only took on its full social sense if it took place at the command or with the consent of the lord to whom the warrior owed his life. There are famous examples of the collective voluntary deaths of all the members of a family following the defeat of its head, especially in the fifteenth and sixteenth centuries. Following one's lord into death *(junshi)* was prohibited in 1663.

The way of the warrior was a crystallization of the warrior's conception of the world and his system of values. Codification and ritualization were pushed to an extreme, but the expression and transmission of this way of life took place principally through the body and not through speech. A precise repertory of movements, learned through repetition starting in childhood, manifested and continually reactivated the reciprocal standing of individuals in a chain of hierarchical relationships. In the same way, through the repetition of formalized gestures, death is also brought into the picture—a person may bring about or suffer death (martial arts) or bring death on himself (ceremony of seppuku). For a warrior, carrying a sword was the concrete symbol of his acceptance of death. Musashi writes in the *Gorin no sho:* "Even if you are clumsy, you must persevere in strategy because of your situation. That which a warrior must always have in his mind is the way of death."

We may recall the seppuku of Musashi's adoptive son Miyamoto Mikinosuke after the death of his lord. The son of a warrior knew from the time of his childhood that he had to be capable of killing himself, and he learned the movements of the seppuku ceremony. "Don't cry, seppuku hurts a lot more" was a phrase that used to be commonly said to a young boy who had hurt himself. The sword, symbol of the warrior class, was a concrete symbol of a repertory of movements that was always present in a warrior's life and was the means through which he represented himself.

We cannot overemphasize the fixed character of the lot that, starting in the Edo period, each person found himself faced with from the time of his birth. The path that lay ahead of one already having been traced, it was the way that one followed it that constituted the work of one's social and cultural life. The way of the warrior was a way of committing oneself wholly and profoundly to a path that had been laid out in advance, and doing this in such a way that this commitment flowed into an open universe—the universe of the quest for perfection through the practice of one's art.

Until the end of the sixteenth century, the period of Musashi's youth, warriors could hope to obtain a prestigious position, to realize their social ambition, by means of their weapon. With the establishment of the Tokugawa regime, this potentiality of the sword faded away. Martial arts increasingly became an end in themselves and as such constituted a world without limit. The sword ceased to be a tool of war and became the warrior's soul *(tamashi),* which in and of itself provided a purpose and a reason to exist. From this point on, warriors, living in a closed world, possessed another universe that was profound and without limit, that of the martial arts, in which they could invest all of their energy.

The cosmology of the warrior was organized around two poles that came together in the practice of the sword: death and becoming one with the perfection of the universe. The warrior owed his life to his lord, to whom he was attached through his family line. He was the bearer of his ancestors' honor and also felt responsible toward his descendants. The Buddhist and Shinto religions had assimilated into them the cult of family ancestors. One prayed to one's ancestors every day. One's sword was one's link to one's lord and one's ancestors. It was the sword that forged the warrior's honor and also the honor of his ancestors. The warrior thus owed his life in two directions and also had to be ready to face death.

TECHNIQUE AND THE STATUS OF THE BODY

Musashi's works bear witness to his intense commitment to the perfection of swordsmanship. A general tendency of this sort became firmer and stronger during the Edo period, during which a cultural model for action was elaborated: Profound and complete commitment to an action became one of the most important virtues of the warrior. The accomplishment of any act took on consistency and weight through the precision of movement it required. At any moment of his life, whether asleep or awake, the warrior had to be in a suitable posture. The dividing line between the body and the mind that the West has drawn for so long loses its relevance here. In action or in social relations, it is the whole person, both physical and moral, who is present. Intellectual work cannot be dissociated from the body. Thus calligraphy, for example, is at one and the same time thought, posture, work of the breath, and mastery of movement—all in an inalienable unity. The impetus of energy that carries the movement of the brush is charged with meaning: to read such writing is to pick the words off the page and perceive what is beyond them.

The reference model for daily gestures that is still taught today in Japan, both in school and at home, has implicit in it that a person will be appreciated for the sincerity with which he puts himself into his gestures entirely. This presupposes that an act can be the total expression of a human being, and that it will be well done if it is done wholeheartedly and implies a relationship with others.

The feudal notion of sincerity implied respect for the moral and social order—it was the sincerity with which one accepted one's condition. In the execution of a gesture, a servant would manifest with dignity the respect he had for his master; a woman would show her submissiveness and the propriety of her emotions. To put oneself into a gesture entirely was to manifest to the person to whom the gesture was directed, actually or virtually, the acceptance of and gratitude for the relationship in which the subject found himself with that person. However, such a gesture could not be made unless there was a social consensus underlying it. The range of gestures for each situation was limited; thus they required the greatest attention. The perfection of a gesture was derived from a kind of internalization; it was a matter of finding the total expression of the person within the limits dictated by his position. The idea was that nothing in the person making the gesture should remain outside or alienated from it. The gesture, a technical one or an ordinary gesture of daily life, was received as a total expression of the person making it.

In art, diligent repetition of technical gestures is the means that allows a person to make progress toward the perfection he is seeking. For the Japanese, in the realm of the arts, perfection was human and fundamentally linked with technique. Such a sense of perfection is present in every form of traditional Japanese art, as it is in the martial arts. In a flower arrangement, in the tea ceremony, in a miniature garden, in a painting or a calligraphy, at the moment of the highest perfection, man adjusts himself to the rhythm of the universe that is, as Buddhist thought sees it, present in himself as it is in all things.

"That is the *kami waza!*" (*Kami waza* literally means "the technique" [*waza*] "of the god" [*kami*].) Still today, this expression refers, in Japanese art, to a technique that seems perfect or that is at its very peak. The fact that these two words, *god* and *technique,* can be associated tells us something about the Japanese conception of the technical man. The crucial distinction here is between a conception of technique as objectified and one in which a technique is seen as inseparable from the person who manifests it.

There is a term that corresponds to the notion of objectified technique. This term, *gi jutsu,* came into use at the end of the nineteenth century to translate this Western notion and serves to designate technique in industrial production. (The word written *jutsu* is the same as the one that appears, with its pronunciation distorted, in Western languages in the form of *jitsu,* as in *jujitsu.*) The Western conception of technique sees it as a subordinate feature that serves either art or science. Technique here is no more than a means. The split between technique and science developed as part of the division of labor in the capitalist system of production. The relationship between the realm of ideas (the realm of reason, of science) and the realm of technique (the process of accomplishment, a function of the body) no longer appears here as an immediate or necessary one that can be taken for granted but becomes the object of a mediation and continually has to be reconstituted.

Today, in practice, the distinction between the two senses of the word *technique* is not as clear as it seems it should be on the basis of etymology alone. The term *gi jutsu* is much more prevalent in the current language, but what is understood by *gi jutsu* does not correspond exactly to the Western sense of the word *technique;* and the notion of *waza,* the only term for technique in the traditional language, now has come to refer to some of the things supposedly covered by *gi jutsu,* thus acquiring considerable ambiguity. *Waza,* the older term, is supposed to designate "technique in the realm of the arts." According to the *Kokugo dai jiten,* the term *waza* means "a gesture or act that has a profound meaning or is done with a significant intention; the act of doing something knowingly; a Buddhist act or ceremony; an act that has a precise purpose that has become customary; work, duty, profession; an event; technique, means, capacity; misfortune, something sinister, a curse." (99) In this view of the word, the act, and thus the human being, is within the technique. Moreover, it is not a means of achieving a pre-conceived end.

Technique *(waza)* is connected with the body. Thought and accomplishment by means of the body are hardly distinct, and there is no relationship of subordination of one of them to the other. The process in itself constitutes the goal. The awareness of the conception and the awareness of the act are not detached from one another and remain rooted together in the gesture, that is, in the body in the full, broad meaning of the word. The tool is an extension of the body and no more.

Accomplishment, at least in essential terms, occurs in a moment in which the body and the mind fuse together. Logical reflection is not absent, but it is limited by the mode of accomplishment. For example, an artisan making a sword has the time to reflect and to calculate during the preparatory phase of his work, but when he strikes the steel, his mind must be empty, barring all extraneous thoughts. The moment of tempering the steel or finishing off the blade requires sharp attention. The artisan must seize the moment at which he is at one with the object he is fabricating. The same holds true in calligraphy, in painting, in sculpture, or in pottery—there are decisive and irreversible moments at which the practitioner must be at one with the object. These moments are marked by a particular kind of breathing. The technician's efforts have the effect of fusing thought and action so that they exist as a unity. Divine technique, or *kami waza,* arises from perfect fusion or unity.

Body and Mind

Musashi uses the expression *cho tan seki ren* several times in his work, which literally means "morning" *(cho)*, "to build" *(tan)*, "evening" *(seki)*, "to train" *(ren)*. This expression is often translated "I trained morning and night," but I have translated it "I have continued to train and to seek from morning till evening."

At the end of the Scroll of Water, Musashi wrote: *Sen nichi no keiko o tan to shi, man nichi no keiko o ren to su,* which I have translated as "A thousand days of training to develop, ten thousand days of training to polish."

For those who are seriously devoted to the practice of *budo,* it is obvious that Musashi's training could last through an entire day, without the limits of morning and evening. We know of a number of warriors whose level of training went far beyond anything we can imagine. The moment one's attention is aroused, all of life has to do with training. These warriors even tried to fill moments of flagging attention, such as sleeping, dressing, washing, eating meals, and the like, with a redoubled awareness of the possibility of combat.

Various documents (29, 34, 37, 39, 120) bear witness to the fact that such warriors tried to go to the very limits of physical exertion in order to make progress in their art, as the following example shows.

Hayashizaki temple is dedicated to the master of the same name, who lived in the sixteenth century and created the art of *iai* (the art of drawing the sword). During the Edo period, a great number of adepts spent time at this temple in order to fulfill a kind of vow: to go beyond the bounds of their art by devoting one or several days exclusively to the practice of *iai* in order to honor the gods and make progress by surpassing their own limits. Nakayama Hakudo, one of the greatest masters of *iai* of the twentieth century, spent a day at this temple fulfilling such a vow. In a period of twenty-four hours, he succeeded in drawing his sword ten thousand times. To achieve this, he practiced constantly, without sleeping, only drinking rice congee from a bowl placed within reach of his hand. In the temple's registry, a considerable number of persons are listed who drew their swords between thirty and forty thousand times. The three adepts who went the furthest stayed for seven days and drew more than ninety thousand times, which is to say more than an average of thirteen thousand times a day. If we may go by the experience of Nakayama Hakudo, we can say that these adepts could pretty well not have slept in the course of seven days of continuous effort. Nakayama explains that when he trains in his dojo, he succeeds on the best days in drawing two thousand times, but then the next day he has to put in twice the effort to arrive at the same result. Are we capable of imagining what sort of effort it took for the person who kept up at least this sort of effort for seven days? These facts help us to gauge the gap that exists between our way of thinking and living and that of the warriors. All the traditional techniques that we have inherited in the *budo* tradition were created through this kind of exceptional exertion of energy, which adepts persevered in over several centuries. Following the tradition, they sought fusion of mind and body by going to the limits of physical effort, until they reached the point of having the feeling that it is through the mind that the body is able to continue with its movements.

We have seen above how it may be justifiable to speak of the absence of a distinction between body and mind in the Japanese conception of action. A clear-cut opposition of mind and body is indeed present in Japanese culture, but it does not have the same sense as the Western opposition between those two factors. In the Japanese conception, the mind can be touched only when, in the course of a physical experience, one lets the sensation of the body fall away. This method was developed in the practice of *gyo* (52, pp. 91–103), an exercise that, at the cost of an intense physical effort carried on for a long time in accordance with ritualized forms, makes it possible to attain illumination or a profound realization of the way. The body is thought of at one and the same time as a hindrance and as a means of nourishing the mind so it can reach liberation and full potential. By exhausting the physical element through extreme effort, the mind becomes free. It is only at this moment that its true power emerges. What is attained is not only an intense moment but a lasting state in which the body is reinvested in a mode of fusion with the mind. This experience generates a lasting transformation of one's way of being, with manifest results, for example, in the martial arts. This is perhaps the precise point that makes it possible to grasp the difference between the Japanese and the Western conception of body and mind.

Now we are in a better position to understand the Japanese adage according to which, by looking at a person's body and posture, you can see his state of mind and his spiritual level. This is also the meaning of the assertions that abound in Zen according to which, "if your posture is not right, the right state of mind has not been attained," or again, "it is enough to see someone's posture to judge their spiritual advancement." Since the body furnishes the means to arrive at a complete fusion of body and mind, which is the ultimate stage that is sought after, any discourse on technique, when technique is aimed at perfection, becomes a discourse on the mind.

Integration of the Religious Element into the Art of the Sword

Placed in quite particular circumstances of peace from the beginning of the Edo period, the Japanese art of the sword opened up a spiritual world within itself that was meaningful enough to constitute the equivalent of a belief system or a religion. The way of the sword itself proposed a meaning to life, an existential direction, which, however, did not prevent adepts from being connected with a traditional religion as well. The way of the sword was defined when it began to offer the adept the possibility of bringing his own aggression into balance through the means of a practice. Indeed, the art of the sword gradually came to internalize the two contradictory notions of aggression (kill or be killed) and harmony (accommodating the other). The field in which it operated then changed from that of the sword that kills, which had been the norm, to that of the sword that gives life. Such a transformation in the quality of his art was the first sign of the evolution of an adept devoted to the way of the sword. He began by acquiring the ability to kill effectively with his sword *(setsunin ken),* and then as he grew older he succeeded little by little in going beyond this attitude as he assimilated an art of swordsmanship "that gives life" *(katsunin ken).*

Musashi was an example of this evolution. After having fought sixty life-or-death duels in his youth, he wrote: "At the age of thirty, I reflected and saw that although I had won, I had done so without having reached the ultimate level of strategy. . . . I continued to train and to seek from morning till night to attain to a deeper principle. When I reached the age of fifty, I naturally found myself on the way of strategy."

The Combat of *Kizeme*

From this time on, Musashi stopped killing his adversaries in combat. His main way of fighting became to dominate his adversary in such a way that the latter became convinced of his defeat without having taken a blow.

This kind of combat, which is called the combat of *kizeme* (offense using *ki*) is considered today in kendo to be the most significant kind of combat. Your adversary attempts an attack. You detect this before his will takes shape in the form of an attack, and you stifle it. Each time he tries to attack you, you exercise pressure on his will with your will to attack in such a way that it prevents him from moving. It is as though you were to stifle a fire by extinguishing each new match your adversary lit and in this way preventing the fire from igniting. Thus it is your will to attack that pushes your opponent back. Each time he tries to launch an attack, he thinks, "If I attack, I will be struck before making a move." Thus he will be forced to back away. Making your opponent back away by interdicting, through emanation of your *ki,* any attack on his part and defeating him in this way is called the kendo of *kizeme.*

Kizeme combat is the ideal form of kendo; it aims at personal development through combat. This approach is based on a kind of religious intuition that is characteristic of Japanese thought. According to this line of thinking, a human being must endeavor to perfect himself, and more precisely to train himself to become better, or in other words, to get closer to the state of Buddha. *Kizeme* combat touches upon this idea of perfection. Thanks to combat, both adversaries can affirm themselves, in both their fullness and their emptiness, and in this way improve, or complete, their way of being. The objective of combat has here been radically transformed. The sword becomes a means of personal development.

It is important to understand that this spirituality of the sword emerged as a consequence of a profound study of technique that involved integrating—and not merely juxtaposing or adding on—religious thought. For warriors the sword was an object of daily life that they carried all the time, and the art of the sword was acquired through a way of acting that engaged their entire existence. In this way it was equivalent to a religion. It is this unique trait that is the hallmark of the Japanese sword.

"When I reached the age of fifty, I naturally found myself on the way of strategy. Since that day I have lived without needing to search further for the way. When I apply the principle of strategy to the ways of different arts and crafts, I no longer have need for a teacher in any domain."

Musashi saw in the principle of strategy an opening toward something that included the meaning of human life and a cosmology. By following the way and perfecting himself, a man must approach the state of Buddha, and Buddha could be interchangeable with the various gods. Taking the brush in his hand to write the *Gorin no sho,* Musashi wrote: "I bow to heaven, I prostrate to the goddess Kannon, and I turn toward the Buddha."

The Confusion between Discourse on Swordsmanship and Discourse on Religion

Musashi's text, while developing an original approach of its own, makes reference to the deep kinship that exists between writings on religion and writings on warrior technique. He says that in writing the scrolls, he does not borrow from ancient Buddhist or Confucianist writings, or either military chronicles or the usual examples from the art of strategy. Among his contemporaries, there is a definite confusion between discourse on swordsmanship and religious discourse. As an example, I cite here a few excerpts from the *Heiho* (or *Hyoho*) *kadensho,* a work on the art of the sword of the Yagyu shin kage ryu written by Yagyu Munenori (1571–1646) and handed down in his family. (56) The thought of Munenori on the technique of the sword is strongly marked by Zen and, much more than Musashi's, contains a confusion between swordsmanship and religious belief. In his text, description and explanation of sword technique often come close to philosophical or Buddhistic discourse.

Here are a few passages from this work, selected from the scroll Katsunin to (The Sword That Gives Man Life):

The two cadences, visible and hidden:

It is necessary at the moment of combat to know what is apparent and what is implicit. This teaching is inspired by the law of the Buddha. For the mediocre man knows only what is shown, without knowing how to direct his gaze toward what is hidden.

It is necessary to heed the movements of the adversary down to the smallest details in order to discern his intention, as if you were looking at the palm of his hand. This implies seeing what is visible and what is hidden, and one must act in accordance with both of them. Strike what is visible and also what is not, without waiting for the situation to develop further. That is to say that the visible and the hidden amount to the same thing, as Lao Tsu teaches. (56, pp. 66–67)

The meaning of *shin* and *myo:*

When *shin* exists on the inside, *myo* appears on the outside. For example, a tree flowers and gives off scent; its branches bear green leaves. This phenomenon is *myo,* which is possible because *shin* dwells within the tree. But you cannot see *shin,* even if you take a tree apart. In the same way, you cannot see the *shin* of a man, even if you open up his body. But it is thanks to *shin* that a man is able to act.

Thus it is necessary to have in your sword the *shin* that will produce *myo* in your technique, and your fighting will flourish. Know that *shin* is the master of the mind that acts on the outside. (56, pp. 70–71)

Shin: That which possesses a strange power that governs the universe, religious being that is superhuman, the gods of Japanese mythology; the existence of a strange force that humans cannot fathom; the mind that inhabits the body.

Myo: Excelling in a manner that human knowledge cannot fathom; that which is strange; the strange facts of life that go beyond human comprehension.

Moving the mind:

> Between two strikes of the sword, there must be no interval, even of a hair's breadth. The sword must act without any stagnation, as in the verbal battles of Zen, where the answer must arise immediately, without the slightest temporal gap. (56, p. 85)

After a period in which guidelines for the use of arms was sought in religion and the dominant ethical codes treated as external reference points, warriors progressively moved on to the integration of religion and ethics into the very techniques of the martial arts. This shift manifested first in archery and then went on to the art of the sword.

THE FORMATION OF KATAS

From the moment that the religious element became an intrinsic part of the practice of swordsmanship, the idea of perfection in the practice arose. The practice of the art became inseparable from the adept's way of life. For Musashi, his art became the factor that concretely defined the conduct of his life as well as the perfection he was seeking. The formation, as a cultural phenomenon, of what I have called the model of the kata, a broader and more precise notion than what is understood by this term currently in Japan, can be dated to around Musashi's time. (53, pp. 89–92)

> A kata is a sequence composed of formalized and standardized movements that is underpinned by a state of mind oriented toward the realization of the way *(do)*. To follow the way, in the Japanese culture, is to seek to attain, by means of the realization of a perfect technique, a human perfection that is regarded as ac-

cessible. Although the term *kata* can be translated literally as "form," "mold," or "type," these translations are not adequate renderings of the Japanese term, which designates an ensemble of standardized forms by means of which a broader body of knowledge has been fixed. . . . There are katas in all forms of the traditional Japanese arts, but the martial arts is where examples are found of the most precise and most strictly formalized katas. . . .

A kata can be composed of the formalization of a single technique or of a combination of several techniques. Some katas are brief, apparently simple and precise, such as the katas of karate, and others are much longer. As a first approximation, we could say that in the martial arts, a kata is the standardized expression of a combat between several adversaries. Starting each time from a different initial situation, techniques of attack and defense are sequenced together as responses to supposed movements of the adversaries.

Learning a kata is based on repetition of precisely standardized technical movements. Depending on the discipline and the form of the kata, you train in it alone or with a partner, focusing your attention on the sequences at the same time as trying for technical perfection. During the Edo period, katas were simple movements of technique (for example, the technique for a sword strike), and the number of daily repetitions was several thousand, which some contemporary practitioners continue to do. If complex sequences were involved, daily practice tended to be on the order of about four to five hours of consecutive repetitions.

Repetition entails a progression:

Work on a kata passes through several stages; it extends over a period of several years and can even last an entire lifetime. In learning a kata, the first thing that has to be done is to make automatic a series of technical movements that aims at the perfect realization of forms and movements, but in the martial arts you must also add dynamism and power, which are elements of effectiveness. . . . Comparing the work of the kata to the making of a sword, you could say that it is necessary to achieve at the same time the precise form of the blade and the hardness of the steel, two elements that have to be balanced in the work of the artisan. But the kata is forging the sword, polishing it, and learning to use it—all at once.

Starting with a particular situation, each kata shows the possibility of a development. The kata puts in play techniques of attack and defense in response to the supposed movements and strategies of the adversary or adversaries. Thus at the same time as putting forward certain techniques, the various katas are a process for the learning of strategy. . . . The enrichment that occurs in the course of successive repetitions makes these things possible, because repetition of the same movements is not identical repetition.

The katas that we are familiar with today are not the work of a single person but represent a distillation of traditional knowledge. Musashi founded a school; the techniques and the model of training he developed were repeated and transmitted by his students, who saw in them a means of reaching toward their master's perfection. These students idealized these technical forms, projecting into them the image of their master. The standardization of the katas took place as they sought to fix the knowledge they had received through this idealized model. At the same time, society was entering into a phase of stability and consolidation of feudal values that was conducive to this process. For the later generations that received them, these katas seemed to be models or molds to which it was sufficient to commit themselves in order to be both effective and in conformity with the expectations of society. By investing these models with their experience, successive masters modified them. They accumulated in them the sum of their experiences in the manner of artists who lay down successive layers of paint on their canvases. Thus the kata, which initially comes across as a rigid form, harbors within it the flexibility that allowed it to perpetuate itself. This is the way the School of Musashi has transmitted to the present generation the katas that were formalized by the master's first students.

It remains to explain why the kata, based on repetition, became a model of action that for generations served as a support for an effort of such great intensity.

The kata is the form that has served as a medium and catalyst for the development of the martial arts since the Edo period. The most visible aspects of it are repetition, standardization, and its ceremonial quality. Through this repetition, which appears to be identical, the adept is seeking to acquire perfect technique. This is associated with the image of the master with whom he identifies. The stronger this identification is, the more the intensity of the repetitions increases, because in the kata, the adept comes in contact with this idealized master, whom he wishes to defeat. The degree of identification is then directly proportional to the weight with which the master-rival weighs on his disciple. (52, p. 154) The repetition becomes in a certain way a struggle against the persecution of the imagined master. At the same time, thanks to his assimilation of the standardized sequences, the adept can reach the point of self-forgetfulness, letting himself be carried by the automatized form. This automatized form is a proven technique that guarantees he will be effective. His itinerary has been drawn up in advance, and the adept does not need to expend any energy to try to invent the path. This path is the way.

As Musashi never stops reminding us, the method of the warrior is to follow the true way, and diligent training in technique is the means by which this quest for perfection can be carried out. But this is by no means an abstraction. The kata and the identification with the master make it concrete and tangible for practitioners. Usually it is said that Musashi did not have a master, but I agree with the hypothesis of Morita according to which, during his childhood, Musashi received the instruction of his father, the primal figure of the master. After that he encountered various adversaries, and through fighting and winning, he acquired the essence of his knowledge. His adversary is thus at the same time his master, and for him the complex figure of the master included also his opponents past and future.

But there is more to the explanation of the widespread incidence of intense practice of a martial art on the part of warriors. This model of action was followed also because it was part of the prevailing system of social values. The model of the kata was integrally connected with the social life of a warrior. What I described, in a simplistic fashion, as the figure of the master is in fact a more complex image with which the warrior identified, in which was also blended an anticipation of his own death, his ancestors, and his lord. A warrior was himself going to become an ancestor for his posterity, and his life was experienced as part of the religious context of the cult of ancestors. His ancestors were connected with the service of the lord whom he served himself, and all of this was lived within a temporality where past-future continuity was the key factor. The warrior identified with the complex image of the ideal of the warrior, in which he took his place in the sacral relationship of his ancestors to the lineage of their lords. The more he tried to be a worthy and honorable warrior, the heavier this image weighed. In other words, in deepening his art, the more he identified with this idealized image, the more he was persecuted by it. His perseverance in the repetitions of his daily martial arts practice was a struggle against this persecution. This process tended to generate a flawless regularity in the accomplishment of his duties to his lord as well as in the intensive repetition of the techniques of his martial art.

The martial arts kata was inseparable from this structure of the warrior's life. When the image of the master merges with sacred values, the quest for technique becomes a quest for perfection.

The Emergence of Harmony in the Art of Combat

From the end of the fourteenth century through the fifteenth century, the development of a simple and powerful art of the sword took place. Through the evolution of forms for exercising alone or with a partner, the idea of harmony arose. This was manifested in the act of controlling one's strikes during the training through which one prepared for combat.

During a second period, from the seventeenth to the nineteenth century, the art of swordsmanship developed along with the formalization of katas; it became more refined in quality and galvanized the energy of

Japanese society, which was now closed off from the outside world. Warriors refined their art without using it in real confrontations. In the form of exercises they killed each other daily, but in reality they avoided death. Nonetheless, for them, confrontation in a fight to the death could arise at any time, and this acted to shape their state of mind.

Through the elaboration of technique, the idea of harmony came more strongly to pervade the exercise of arms, the very nature of which is confrontation and destruction. The art of the warriors flourished under various names such as *bujutsu, bugei, kenjutsu, gekiken,* and so on. In all these disciplines, a confrontational energy was dominant, as indicated by the fact that warriors always carried the two swords and thus were continually accompanied by the fundamental idea of "kill or be killed."

The notion of *budo* appeared in a third phase, at the end of the nineteenth century, when the warrior class disappeared and the values of the preceding periods were lost with the birth of the new society. Thus *budo* is realized in an ideal form when its aggressive, confrontational energy of combat is perfectly balanced by the opposite energy of harmony.

||| 11 |||

Budo

THE MEIJI TURNING POINT AND THE MODERN NOTION OF *Budo*

Starting in the middle of the nineteenth century, the closed and autarkic society of feudal Japan was shaken by the menace of the West. During the Meiji period, the conception of the individual's social space expanded: Until then a person's country had been his fief; now it became the state. This expansion of the vision of the world was experienced by warriors as a profound crisis. The model of action that had proved an effective one for them in the preceding period ceased to be valid in its existing form. Commitment to the martial arts had been lent its social value by the way it wove the cult of ancestors and fealty to a liege lord into daily life. This interwoven whole was taken up into the structure of the katas, dynamic sequences that provided a vehicle for warriors to commit themselves deeply to a quest for perfection.

The arrival of Westerners brought about the collapse of the world that had underpinned this context of perfection. The model of action elaborated in the past now had to find a different structure to relate to. Kano Jigoro devised the new concrete model of *budo* when he created judo. In the notion of *budo,* he elaborated a structure that brought together knowledge of Western methods with the model of action of the warriors. The notion of *budo* made it possible to relate to the new larger world in the context of which the Japanese state was under threat. Identification with this threatened state once again provided a raison d'être for the intense commitment entailed by the structure and logic of the kata.

Before this, warriors engaged in the quest for perfection through the martial arts because these arts had a religious and cosmic dimension to them. In the society in movement that Japan now became, the practice of the martial arts, cut away from its system of social support, was no longer the perfect circle that inspired profound engagement and commitment. But then linking the martial arts with the Japanese state in peril forged the perfect circle anew—the new notion of the Japanese state along with its emperor became a modern incarnation of the old profound beliefs in the sacred world. This was the way that the practice of judo reached for perfection. Kano Jigoro connected it with these values by teaching his students that through judo (a physical practice that was closely linked with study) they must become "pillars of the state."

The Creation of Judo, the "Way of Flexibility"

Kano Jigoro drew inspiration for his creation of judo as "the way of flexibility" from the notion of the way *(do),* which came out of the warrior culture, and which he transformed to accommodate the new social conditions. Judo continued the practice and the conception of technique and action developed during the feudal period, in which the technique and the person applying it were one. Judo was conceived of as a teaching vehicle and its objectives were expressed in a standardized form. This makes it possible for us to elicit the way in which it was a continuation of the previous period and the way in which it set itself apart from it.

Kano Jigoro created judo on the twofold foundation of his practice of jujutsu and his training at the university that had just been established in Japan, inspired by Western models. In 1882, fifteen years after the end of the Edo period and after the beginnings of modernization in

Japan, he became a professor of the economic and social sciences and founded the private school Kodokan (literally, "the residence at which the way is taught"). He created judo as part of the general training he provided at this school.

Kano was a small man (only 160 centimeters tall) who was the son of a merchant family. Following confrontations with his fellow students at school, he decided to learn jujutsu in order to defend himself. This was the martial art that had the reputation of making it possible for a small man to defeat those who were bigger and stronger than he. It was one of the martial arts traditionally taught to warriors, the art of bare-handed combat. At the time, in the wake of the abolition of the feudal classes and the special privileges of the warriors, the martial arts were out of favor, and Kano had a very hard time finding a teacher. In 1877, when he was entering the university at the age of seventeen, he became the student of a former teacher at the government institute of the martial arts (Kobusho), Fukuda Yanosuke of the Tenshin shinyo ryu, whose lineage went back to the eighth century. Under this master's direction, Kano studied the katas and *randori* (free fighting with throws, immobilizing holds, and strangleholds).

To give an idea of the traditional training methods and the intensity of training he encountered, we may cite the account Kano gave of this period of his life:

> One day during training, I was thrown by my teacher, and as I got up, I asked him, "What was that technique?"
>
> "Come at me again," my teacher said, and he threw me again.
>
> So I asked him, "In that technique, what are the movements of the hands and feet?"
>
> The master replied, "Come again," and he threw me once more.
>
> Then I asked him, "How do you do that?"
>
> The master threw me three more times and said, "In any case, you won't be able to understand my explanations. Only repetition will teach you. So come again."

And my teacher continued to throw me without ever giving me any technical explanation. (39, p. 40)

When Master Fukuda died, his family offered Kano all the writings on the transmission of the school that he had preserved. Kano continued to study with a master of the same school, Iso Masatomo, who died in 1881, and then with Master Iikubo Tsunetoshi of the Kito ryu. The instruction of this school, which has a great variety of techniques for throws, complemented the teachings of the first school he studied, which put the accent on strangleholds, armlocks, and immobilization holds.

At the university Kano engaged in various sports, notably baseball, track and field, gymnastics, rowing, and long-distance hiking. Looking for the way to build up his body in the most balanced and complete way, he took a dim view of all these disciplines and concluded that from the point of view of strengthening the body, jujutsu was the most effective and balanced method. In 1882, when he founded his school, he made a critical examination of jujutsu, which directly connected with the lifestyle of the warriors and with their ethics, and developed judo. This discipline is a method for training modern people based on physical practice.

Jujutsu (literally: *jutsu,* "method"; *ju,* "flexibility") referred to bare-handed methods of combat used by warriors to overcome and redirect an adversary's strength through techniques based on fluidity of movement and flexibility. However, the term *jutsu* evoked a limited sphere of action purely within the realm of the martial arts, whereas Kano had in mind a universal application of the method of dominating an adversary through the way of flexibility:

Earlier on I was a very angry person, but owing to jujutsu, and also as my body became stronger, my mind calmed and I got myself under control. I am convinced that we can apply the logic of jujutsu combat to other aspects of social life. Moreover, the mental training that goes along with combat training is particularly precious, because it can be applied to all the phenomena of life. . . . The discipline of judo that I have founded consists in discovering the principle that makes one lose or win, a principle that includes technique. Following the way *(do)* of this principle, a method for training the mind is developed. That is why I call it judo: *ju* (flexibility) means not resisting the adversary's force but avoiding impact by making use of his force. . . .

Judo is thus not simply a martial art, it is a great way *(do)* that can be applied to any domain. . . . Judo in essence is neither a martial art nor physical education; it is the universal way *(do)* that can be connected with anything. (39, p. 13)

Kano Jigoro does not precisely explain the meaning of the word *do*, which could be taken for granted in the Japanese society of this period. Conceived in the closed world of the feudal society, the notion of *do* was based on an idea of the order of the universe. Following the way meant putting oneself in harmony with this universal order.

With Musashi, we encountered this same quest for a universal application of the way (in this case, the way of the sword) two centuries earlier. Musashi was interested in the broadest areas of the culture of his time, and using the principle of strategy, he proved himself a master in various forms of artistic expression.

Kano Jigoro also lived at a turning point in the history of Japan. He undertook the same quest and found himself facing a universe whose boundaries had receded but whose order had been shaken by the advent of capitalist industrialization. Stable feudal society had assigned a place to each person based on his family's position. But Kano had to orient himself in a society where ambition and uncertainty were both key factors. In his desire to establish a new order, he looked to tradition. His research led him to the idea of the way, which he once again placed in a position of honor. The essence of the way was seeking conformity with the order of the universe. Thus the principle he sought to revive when he formulated judo was the principle of a universal order. The proof of the validity of this principle was furnished by the effectiveness of ju-jutsu. And indeed the person who rediscovered this tradition found himself able to make use of a vital energy he had not hitherto been aware he possessed that gave him the possibility of defeating an adversary of superior strength.

Kano's new departure involved a process of objectification in which he explicitly proposed a method with universal applications to the Japanese people, who were setting out to conquer the modern world energized by new perspectives of social mobility.

A New Social Form of the Quest for Perfection

Using as a point of departure the warrior's mode of total commitment in which the effort to reach perfection continually led to pushing back one's own limits, Kano expounded the notion of "maximal and appropriate utilization of vital energy" *(seiryoku saizen katsuyo),* a notion that meshed well with the idea of the division of labor that was just coming into prominence. In effect, Kano brought about a breach in the unity of the way, which was a concrete totality inseparable from the person engaged in it. He did this by proposing an analytical method that was in a certain sense an objectification. He drew on the way to produce the object that was his ideal method.

His school of judo (Kodokan), open to boys from secondary school to university age, had as its goal the overall education and development of the human being. It had three main directions: physical education, martial arts (a method of combat), and moral education. This latter was conceived of as study and practice aimed at applying the principles of judo to the whole of life. It was in the school's course on morality and the rules of life that the practice and ideology that the founder of judo was attempting to establish came out most clearly. He formulated the essence of his course on morality as follows:

1. Study and commit and engage yourself completely by setting a goal for your life.
2. Go toward a great future success without letting yourself be disconcerted by the immediate situation.
3. Work with confidence in yourself and keep in mind that the force that is in you is capable of causing the country to advance.

4. Reflect on the position of Japan in international society and become a future pillar of the state.

In these last two precepts, Kano Jigoro expressed the prevailing ideology of the time. The new power, which had arisen from the warrior class in an effort to respond to the threat of the Western powers, was trying to reinvest in the image of Japan, represented by the double image of emperor and state, the potential for devotion inherited from the ancient feudal loyalties. Kano's school was an excellent example of the way in which this ideology was combined with voluntarism and asceticism in the training of future functionaries of the state and business.

To defeat difficulties, whatever they might be, to develop the habit of self-control, of work and effort, to contribute to the welfare of others through a courageous attitude—here in a few words was the state of mind that was demanded of the students who were to build modern Japan. The lives of Kano's students were ruled by strict discipline and asceticism.[1] The rules for life at school centered around the teacher-disciple relationship (39, pp. 40–41), which required total commitment from the student in pursuing the way he had chosen. These rules seem to be more or less a formalization of the first two principles of the morality course cited above. They are connected with the idea of personal perfection, which was a key element in the traditional pursuit of the way. The first step in this was the ability to be master of oneself in action, that is, the perfect practical mastery of technique.

Inviting the student to immerse himself completely in study was a response to the student's own demand—moreover, the strength of determination the applicant was able to show was one of the determining conditions for his admission into the school. Inspired by the training of warriors, the acceptance of discipline took place through a process of identification with the teacher, who himself observed a discipline and presented the image of someone who was further advanced on the difficult path that the student was seeking to tread. The advanced state of the master was a tangible thing; it was manifested by his mastery in the practice of an art in which he dominated the students not by strength but through technique. This was a reflection of the primary principle of the school: maximal utilization of vital force in the way of flexibility.

This process was an extension of Japanese tradition. In that tradition no great boarding schools or other such educational institutions existed, whether for the martial arts, handcrafts, or other disciplines. Everything depended on the presence of a master, who might be aided by assistants who functioned as his representatives. The student's commitment, based on the feudal model, was to this one master who was capable of transmitting his knowledge to him. "Wander for three years in search of a master," the popular adage ran.

THE EVOLUTION OF *Budo* IN THE TWENTIETH CENTURY

With judo, Kano Jigoro aspired to establish a comprehensive training for human beings that conformed with the order of the universe. But he lived in the period in which the Western division of labor was being introduced into Japan, and in his effort to express and transmit his teaching, a tendency toward objectification and instrumentalism appeared. Thus in his teaching for judo, as will be recalled, Kano distinguished three parts: physical education, combat method, and moral education.

Judo, a method of combat expressed in a set of standardized rules, quickly met with success. Kano's analytical tendency and the distinct quality of judo in relation to the other traditional martial arts were a great part of this success. The activity of judo, which to begin with was a total commitment, underwent a modification that allowed partial practice of it alongside other primary activities within the developing framework of the division of labor. The traditional system of conventions introduced into judo made possible effective but limited matches; the standards for judging their effectiveness tended in the direction of external criteria, and this tendency was further expressed in the introduction of many levels of achievement. All this made it possible for judo to fit into capitalist temporality alongside other profitable and quantifiable activities.

Eventually, nearly all the Japanese martial arts being taught today adopted from judo this system of grades or levels of achievement as well as a limiting of techniques that has become narrower and narrower as competitive tournaments have become more widespread. Also derived from jujutsu, but with a mystical emphasis, aikido, in which there are no competitions, also adopted the system of grades or levels. It was following the example of judo that most martial arts changed their names (for example, *kenjutsu* became kendo) in order to lay claim explicitly to the notion of *do*—at the very moment when the practical reality of *do* was fading away.

The Crisis in *Budo*

The notion of *budo* appeared in the Meiji period in an atmosphere dominated by the need to defend the threatened Japanese state. The social practice of *budo* pursued the directions proclaimed for it at the beginning until the end of the Second World War.

In the postwar period a change in direction took place. The practice of *budo* was prohibited by the occupying power but was restored with a radical change in its social orientation. (41, p. 21) In a first phase, *budo* was dissociated, at least in appearance, from all its ideological aspects. This is what made it possible for it to be accepted again, and then only within the framework of physical education and sports. Starting with the end of the 1950s, *budo* began to flourish again, along with the revival of the Japanese economy. In the course of the 1960s, international competitive events multiplied, starting with judo, then followed by karate and kendo.

Today in Japan, practitioners of *budo* have major difficulty in defining their endeavor. One of their key points is that it differs from combat sports or physical education—but what is the difference actually? The answer to this is a confused one. Currently there are two trends in the practice of the martial arts in Japan, both of which claim to manifest the authentic *budo* tradition. One emphasizes an austere approach, which is

violent and even bloody. Effort and even physical suffering are prominent aspects. The other trend links itself with spirituality, with an attitude of transcending aggression, and it criticizes the other trend as being
primitive and unworthy of the name of *budo*. Various other currents os-
cillate back and forth between these two trends, ranging from more or
less traditional practices that accentuate the ritual side to modernist approaches that express themselves in the language of sports. In Europe
the meaning of the word *budo* is still vague, because it tends to include
all Asian martial arts practices, both traditional and modern. Here too
the same two major trends are found, sometimes extravagantly exaggerated, owing to the lack of precise cultural reference points. Here one
encounters a mixture of cultural approaches connected with China,
Japan, Korea, and other southern Asian countries. This is a kind of projection, constructed by Europeans, of an attractive and somewhat mythical image of the Asian martial arts.

In Japan the sense of the word *budo* has also become vague and imprecise at the same time as the disciplines that are part of it have prolif-
erated. In an attempt to demarcate the traditional martial arts from the
others, the word *bujutsu* (*jutsu:* technique) is used. The distinction this
makes is not altogether clear, but *bujutsu* has a more ancient tone to it.
There are different classifications of the particular disciplines that are associated with either *budo* or *bujutsu*. However, from my point of view
the principal difference between the two has to do with the conception
of combat that underlies the practices, and this in turn is connected with
the historical conditions in which these conceptions arose. We have seen
that the ideology and the technique included in the notion of *bujutsu* belong to an earlier period of Japanese history. This combination of ideology and technique served as a matrix for the formation of the notion of
budo, which was a recent reorganization of it.

The creation of *budo* made it possible for the idea of perfection inherent in the traditional practice of the warriors to find a place in Meiji society. This development took place in connection with the awareness of
the Western threat that faced the state. The circle of perfection could be
drawn by identifying the practice of *budo* with service to the state, embodied in the emperor. Today, however, Japan is far from being menaced

by the West. There is a sense of security, albeit somewhat troubled by attitudes critical of Japanese dependence on the outside world and the economic expansionism of Japan, which is coming to pervade the entire world. From the Meiji period to the 1950s, the primary preoccupation of the Japanese was to feed the entire population, whereas present-day Japan is rich with material and cultural abundance. Under these conditions, the circle of perfection inherent in *budo* can be drawn only within the discipline itself on the level of the individual. No contemporary practitioner of *budo* can have the consciousness of becoming "a pillar of the state" by engaging himself deeply in the practice of his art.

Today the intensive commitment and engagement required by the practice of *budo* can be sustained only through a kind of proxy structure. Such a structure has been furnished through hierarchical organization of traditional martial arts groups. The basis of hierarchy is the level of progress an individual has achieved in his art, and these levels of achievement have been institutionalized as grades, the systems for awarding that are sometimes controversial. The system now must turn on itself, for the conditions that existed in previous periods of history that permitted an extension of its vision to an identification with the values of society as a whole are no longer present. Thus currently the discipline tends to take coercive forms that take precedence over the more difficult quest for perfection. In certain disciplines of *budo,* the conformity-demanding aspects of the groups, requiring everyone to fit in, predominate over the search for the way. This is one of the reasons the image of *budo* is often associated in Japan with the political extreme right.

The Thwarted Striving toward Totality

I think that to clarify these points and understand the malaise that is currently affecting the practice of *budo,* it would be worthwhile to undertake a reflection on cultural factors whose roots reach back to Musashi. The knowledge we have of the past that Musashi was part of is not merely abstract. *Budo* is not merely an antique object. It is a discipline that is practiced today, and in my view, by studying it more deeply and developing it in a form that accords with contemporary society, we can find an excellent method of training.

In Musashi's time the martial arts were characterized by a striving for perfection within a framework that included a supra-individual dimension—both divine and feudal. Discourse on technique was not distinct from religious discourse, because the martial arts aimed at perfection, the dimension in which religion is situated. Self-engagement was pushed to the limit because it was animated by the supra-individual dimension that it included. The power of this dimension came from the coexistence of the two ideas of divinity and the feudal lord, which were linked through the cult of ancestors.

Later adepts of *budo* were able to engage and commit themselves so completely because *budo* also included this supra-individual dimension, which *budo* formulated in a new way: Japan under threat, represented by the emperor, corresponded to the feudal lord to whom one owed one's life, and because of the divinity of the emperor, both aspects of the cult of ancestors, the divine and the feudal, were synthesized within him. This activated the missing link in the chain of perfection, and the adepts were able to commit themselves with the idea of becoming pillars of the state. Practicing a *do* meant accepting in advance the great effort that is indispensable for realizing it. It therefore contained an attitude of acceptance toward hierarchy that was intrinsic and thus present even when not supplied externally by an ideology. This attitude could easily be drawn upon, especially during a period of crisis, when an ideology does take shape and creates a perspective requiring conformity and self-sacrifice. The recent history of Japan shows examples of *budo*'s being co-opted in this way by the dominant militaristic ideology. And we have seen that the current crisis in *budo* is to a great extent a crisis caused by the absence of an external reference point.

That is why a politically conservative line of thought has found its way into the modern practice of *budo,* a conservative outlook that places the emperor in the position of God, as during the Meiji period. In the 1960s, in the writings of the novelist Mishima, the following question to the emperor returns again and again in the form of a complaint: "Why did you descend to the human state?" What Mishima was striving for was perfection in the form of an action. (52) He was seeking to achieve this through a return to the warrior tradition, in which there was an immanent presence of death. He practiced various martial arts, but he was unable to commit himself deeply to practice because his primary self-investment was in the written expression in which his physical practice was reflected. He identified with the warriors, but his actual practice of the martial arts was not intense enough to rise to the level of total engagement, so he looked for this in the political realm. "To act, you need an adversary, and I have chosen as an adversary the Communist Party; apart from this, I have nothing against the Communists." But this mythical adversary was inadequate. It was only by placing himself in a circle of action in which existence was under threat that the perfect circle could be realized. The form of the state in which the emperor was God no longer existed, but in the eyes of Mishima, such a form of the state was necessary to provide the ground for the Japanese identity. This structure that he conceived of was in peril, but the defense that was necessary was not against the outside. What had to be defended was the structure as emanating from the emperor, the equivalent of the sacred, by which all action could be perfectly realized. Thus he created for himself a consciousness of the peril of the state that he wanted to establish, and this was enough to justify the sacrifice of his life. Through this he closed the circle of perfect action.

In my view, by taking his action all the way to the level of death, Mishima clearly showed the empty space, the missing link that exists in the realm of traditional action that many are confusedly searching for today in their practice of *budo*. But at the same time, he also demonstrated the impossibility of filling this gap by a return to the past.

What distinguishes *budo* from various sports activities is the quest for perfection. If you adopt this hypothesis today, the following question arises: Is a new framework for striving for perfection possible in a new form of *budo* that does not have a sacred collective dimension integrated into it?

‖ 12 ‖

The Relationship between Adversaries

NOW THAT WE HAVE elucidated the ideology of *budo,* a qualitative analysis of the practice of the martial arts that espouse this approach will enable us to establish criteria for distinguishing *budo* from other similar activities. In contemporary Japanese society, kendo is the practice that is most faithful to the notion of *budo,* even though it too has come to accommodate sports competition. The judo of today has traveled a long way from its original ideal and is now most often thought of as a competitive sport.

In connection with Musashi, I have already described the notion of *kizeme* combat in which the ideal of kendo has taken concrete form. In order to define the practice of *budo* clearly, I will now give a precise analysis of a form of combat that is representative of the kendo ideal in its fullest sense. This example is particularly interesting from the point of view of the relationship between adversaries and the ways in which the quality of combat is judged. It shows the complexity and subtlety of this form of combat as well as the risks of confusion involved in it.

Let us listen to Ogawa Chutaro, a holder of the ninth *dan* in kendo.

In 1987, at the age of eighty-five, he told the story of a historic bout that was a highlight in the annals of kendo at the beginning of the twentieth century. "When I was twenty-seven years old, I witnessed at the Butoku-den of Kyoto a bout between two famous masters: Takano Sazaburo and Naito Takaharu." The best masters of kendo of today place these two masters among the greatest of the modern era and consider it all but impossible to equal them under current conditions.

The points of the *shinai* of the two masters hardly touched each other. Both initially adopted a middle guard position *(chudan)*. Then Master Takano bowed slightly and took the high guard *(jodan),* raising his *shinai* above his head. . . . Master Naito kept his *shinai* in *chudan,* pointing it toward his adversary's eyes. In this position, he continued powerfully emanating his offensive *ki,* while Master Takano also emanated his *ki* from his *jodan* guard position. The spectators made not a sound, and the hall was as silent as the earth moistened with water. The bout continued in silence. Thirty seconds, then a minute passed. All of a sudden, with a dry sound, the *shinai* of Master Takano struck the wrist *(kote)* of Master Naito, who remained immobile, not at all troubled by the blow. Master Takano went back into the *jodan* guard position. Master Naito continued in *chudan.* After feinting a strike at the wrist, Master Takano struck at the head *(men),* then he went on to strike Master Naito five times to the head and the wrist. Each time the dry sound resounded in the hall, but Master Naito remained imperturbable, as though Master Takano's attacks did not exist. After a moment, the judge gave the signal to end the combat, and the two masters separated. Master Naito had not delivered a single blow.

This is a description of a model combat between the two great masters of the period. Takano struck Naito five times on the wrist and the head, while the latter made no attack at all. [Takano actually struck seven times but only five are counted as correct.] Thus it would seem that Takano must have won the victory by a large margin. Let us continue to read Ogawa's account.

During this bout, each time Master Takano wanted to strike Master Naito's wrist or head, Master Naito projected his *ki*. If Master Takano had struck after having put Master Naito in a defensive position by projecting his will to attack, these strikes would have been valid. But each time Master Takano tried to attack, Master Naito quashed Master Takano's *ki* of attack with his own *ki*. That is why all of the latter's strikes failed, even though they touched the adversary. There was no void either in the guard or in the mind of Master Naito. Master Takano struck where there was no void. He merely struck, and his strike merely landed. That is all. If one strikes at random without creating a void in his opponent, this strike is not effective and does not constitute a real strike. In the same way, if one strikes at a moment when one should not strike— and that was the case in this combat—it is the one who strikes who has come down in quality. That is a difficult point in kendo.

Ogawa cites a commentary of Sosuke Nakano, tenth *dan*:

The bout between Naito and Takano was a combat of *kiai* versus technique. Takano fought with his techniques, whereas Naito fought with *ki*. It was a magnificent model combat, beyond all description. I was amazed to see that the distance is so great between combat using the full amplitude of *ki* and combat using techniques.

What is the meaning of this statement?

In truth, as Ogawa says, this is a difficult point in kendo. It is also a point that few young Japanese kendo practitioners understand today— which means that kendo, too, is tending away from *budo*.

THE COMPLEXITY OF COMBAT IN *Budo*

If we had watched this bout as ordinary spectators of a contemporary kendo sports competition, our judgment would be simple. Takano won the victory by a large margin, because he struck five times while Naito remained imperturbable, did not parry, did not attack. But the judgment of the masters of that period was completely different. Why?

In the first place, it must be stressed that this bout was one between masters of the highest level of the period, highly esteemed by their peers. Behind the appearances, the seasoned onlookers saw the unfolding of a battle between the minds and wills of two persons. This is what is called the combat of *ki*.

The high guard *(jodan)* is in principle a position one takes against an inferior adversary. Takano adopted this guard and bowed to his adversary to indicate his respect, and in a certain sense, to excuse himself. Having taken up *jodan,* it was he who should have driven back his adversary, even without striking him. But through the whole confrontation, Naito, with his *chudan* guard position, drove his adversary back with the will transmitted by his *shinai*. He remained imperturbable, even when receiving a blow. Takano was driven back by the will and immanent power of his adversary and he had to strike to avoid backing up even more. He did not create a void in his adversary and then strike, but his adversary forced him into the action of striking. Thus Takano's strike was not an affirmation of the vulnerable position into which he had forced his opponent. His blows were like the movements of the ice axe of a mountain climber who is trying to avoid slipping down a face and not like the axe movements that support an ascent. It should be added that Ogawa, a student of Takano's, leaves out the fact that Takano was backing up when he delivered those blows and that when the judge stopped the bout, he had been driven back all the way to the boundary of the combat area. If his strikes had been valid, he would have been the one who moved forward. Naito forced his adversary into a situation where he had to strike without choosing his strikes, whereas he himself remained in a condition of fullness. It was this character of the way he conducted this combat that the other high-level adepts saw as "magnificent beyond all description."

For an ordinary spectator, Takano's blows might have appeared superb, because they were received unparried, but for the high-level adepts, it was obvious that these blows were not decisive and that it was for this reason—seeing their imperfection—that the adversary remained imperturbable and did not parry. What was important at this level was not the simple fact of landing or not landing a blow but discovering how to dominate the *ki* (the will or energy) of the adversary. If it is possible to annihilate the adversary's *ki,* he will not be able to attack, and even if he does attack, his movement will not be able to be perfect, because the *ki-ken-tai*—the unity of *ki* (will and energy), *ken* (the movement of the sword), and *tai* (the center of the body)—is only imperfectly integrated into his technique. A practitioner who is able to drive his adversary into this situation has no need to strike him with a blow.

However, there remains this question: If Naito dominated his opponent with his *ki,* why did he not strike a blow? If indeed he had succeeded to this extent in driving his opponent back with his *ki,* it seems he could easily have struck him as well. Without a doubt Naito could have entered into the combat on the level of technique and struck a blow, but this combat was an occasion for him to deliver a warning to the partisans of the view that a blow must be landed at all costs, a view that was beginning to emerge at that time. In fact, the force of his approach was felt all the more clearly because it took a paradoxical form. Nevertheless, to appreciate it, a viewer had to have the insight to see beyond the appearances of combat. The fact that the significance of this bout has become somewhat enigmatic today for the majority of kendo practitioners shows that kendo has indeed evolved in the direction that Naito feared.

If we compare this bout to those of Musashi during his final period, we will recall that Musashi always drove back his adversaries without letting them touch him, which left the outcome completely unambiguous. For one thing, the attitude toward combat was different then, and it was de rigueur not to let oneself be struck. In addition, Musashi's level was far superior to that of his adversaries. Here the technical level of the two opponents, Naito and Takano, was almost the same. Appreciation of their combat had nothing to do with assessing a difference in technical competence, since everyone knew they were both on the highest level. Evaluation had to do with the manner in which they fought. Takano fought by deploying his techniques, whereas Naito gave priority to *ki,* while still keeping his technique intact. He was looking for kendo beyond the technical plane, because for him, at this moment at the beginning of the twentieth century, comparisons of technical skill no longer made any sense. For him it was necessary to enter the realm of *ki* combat, thinking that only by taking this direction could kendo retain an authentic value for modern society. Still it remained necessary to train in technique; one had to reach the point in technique where one could trust one's life to it. Nevertheless, when Naito's students won a victory in a tournament through technical virtuosity, he criticized them severely for having won by means of superficial technique. If a student lost but still maintained a correct and worthy attitude, he evaluated positively the way in which he lost. For him, technique had to carry the mind, but it should not flourish by becoming dissociated from the depth of the mind. Facing Takano, his equal in technique, Naito brought to the fore that which goes beyond technique by proposing combat by *ki.* Takano did not enter into this dimension and stuck to a confrontation of technique, but he was driven back by his adversary. In the eyes of the high-level adepts, driving back one's adversary the way Naito did seemed far superior to winning by means of a blow. The difference in level between the two adversaries was not great enough to allow him to drive Takano back without being touched at all.

Until the beginning of the twentieth century, the mastery of the adepts who taught kendo permitted this kind of awareness. Still today, certain kendo masters attach primary importance to combat by *ki,* the emanation of energy and will that precedes an exchange of blows, and they see in this the determining phase of a bout. For them this type of combat represents the ideal or the ultimate stage of kendo. As an example, I cite here an assessment by a ninth-*dan* master of the tournament of 1987:

> In the eighth-*dan* tournament, there was not a good bout this year. However, Master A. fought rather well. With his *ki,* he was able to make an adversary of equal level back up six or seven meters. This is something that is difficult to accomplish. But he still did not

grasp the essence of kendo, because he struck a blow at the end. He should not have struck, because he had been able to drive his adversary back to that extent by dominating him with his *ki*.

This assessment reflects an idea that one encounters frequently in Japan in various formulations: "If he had driven his opponent back to that point, he should not have struck, because the outcome was already obvious." "If you strike, that shows cruelty." "What sense could the act of striking have once you have moved and immobilized your opponent through the force of your *ki?*"

This is precisely the point where kendo and the warriors' art of the sword differ. Once his sword was drawn, the warrior had either to kill or be killed. The importance of Musashi in the history of swordsmanship is to have achieved the combat of *ki* at a time when confrontations were still a matter of life or death. It may thus be said that the prototype of the contemporary kendo ideal began to emerge with him.

The Sensation of Being Dominated

As in the combat we described above, it sometimes happens in the course of kendo training that when facing an adept of a high level, the combatant who strikes a blow that is apparently correct does not have the sensation of having dominated his adversary but, on the contrary, feels dominated by him. This way of conducting a bout is used in teaching by masters of a high level working with students who are capable of understanding the significance of it. In 1990 a seventh-*dan* kendo practitioner described his training to me as follows:

> Master Horiguchi is eighty-five years old now and is somewhat weak. He cannot fasten the laces of his armor by himself. One of his students has to help him get ready each time. That is why, outside the dojo, you could not imagine that he is a kendo master.
>
> But each time that I take my position facing him to fight, I can do nothing. I never succeed in touching him, and he does whatever he wants. It is really strange, but doubtless this is the combat

of *ki*. I do not understand how he manages to strike me so easily. He allows me to touch him only when I succeed in bringing off a good strike. But the rest of the time, I am at the mercy of this old man. When I watch him fighting with others, it is the same thing. He makes light work of the eighth-*dan* people.

Even though masters of this level are rare, this master is not unique in the world of kendo.

Let us examine how and why the sensation of being dominated in this manner comes about. You feel that it is your opponent who has led you to deliver a blow and not you who have created the conditions that made it possible to strike him. He causes you to feel uneasy all the while you have not struck him, and that is how you know that it is he who is forcing you into the movement of striking. You then have to bow to him and thank him for having "struck" you in this fashion. However, as viewed from the outside, it is you who have struck a blow and won the bout.

In reality, what has happened here? Your adversary penetrates into a void in your perception but does not take advantage of this to strike you. Instead he exerts pressure on this weak point of yours with his will and energy *(ki)*. You are forced to back up. But your opponent has another possibility here: If at this point he presents you with a void in his guard and continues to exert pressure on you at the same time, this creates an uneasiness in you that you can dispel only through a striking movement. In such a case, you are not satisfied with your strike because you feel that the integrity of your technical act has been disrupted, that your *ki-ken-tai* (the unity of *ki*, sword, and body) has been troubled. This sense of dissonance arises because your opponent is the one who directed the blow that you struck; thus you feel a lack of fullness in your striking action.

If you are sufficiently advanced in the way, you will then be inwardly convinced of your defeat, even if others think you have won. That is why it sometimes happens that a high-level kendo practitioner, having performed successfully from the point of view of the judges in bouts that were part of his examination to be promoted to a higher grade, refuses to accept the higher grade, saying: "I landed some blows, but I did not have a sense of fullness. Having fought in such an unsatisfactory way, I cannot accept promotion." The awareness that underlies such an attitude is more or less present among kendo practitioners of a high level. Such an awareness develops progressively in the course of receiving teaching and progressing on the way of kendo, and it is indispensable for understanding kendo and, more generally speaking, *budo* in their full significance. In sports competitions in karate or judo, this sort of awareness is very undeveloped, because the combatants tend to experience a victory, even an accidental one, as a feather in their cap. In my view this is one of the principal criteria for distinguishing sports from *budo*.

THE SIGNIFICANCE OF THE QUEST FOR *Kizeme*

The awareness of *kizeme* arises in the context of an adept's search for perfection. We have seen that in the course of the history of Japanese martial arts, the quest for perfection became progressively more important over the course of the Edo period. This quest was structured according to a double polarity—around the social pole and the personal pole of self-perfection through technique. That second pole is what we shall now attempt to define. The schema is the following: Technique blends with a person's overall way of existing during combat, and combat is also prepared and experienced through daily training that becomes an integral part of one's everyday life. At this point the practice of *budo* begins to merge with one's way of life altogether.

When your adversary makes you feel your technical inadequacy on the level of perception in combat, thanks to him you can see and then try to fill in the void in your perception he has made you notice. In *budo* this void is immediately felt as a void in your own being, and experiencing it allows you to progress toward a better way of being. This approach arises from the idea that one should work on oneself in order to become better, an idea that underlies the Japanese conception of the way. Kendo is a means to achieve this.

To fill the void they have felt in their technique, some adepts of the sword have sought in Zen or other forms of religion a means to deepen their study and progress. At the same time, Zen masters have advised some adepts to seek in the practice of the sword a more direct path to Zen.

Shirai Toru (1783–1850) is considered one of the greatest practitioners of swordsmanship of the last two centuries. Katsu Kaishu (1823–1899), a famous statesman of the Meiji period, an accomplished student of both swordsmanship and Zen, describes as follows the impression he had in training with him:

> The way of the sword and Zen are identical, any difference residing only in words and forms. When I was devoting myself to the way of the sword, I had the opportunity to receive some lessons from an adept named Shirai Toru. I learned an enormous amount from him. His art of swordsmanship had a kind of supernatural power. As soon as he took his sword in hand, there emanated from him an atmosphere that was at once austere and pure, then an invincible power surged from the end of his sword that was supernatural. I could not even stay face-to-face with him. I wanted to attain his level and I trained seriously, but to my regret, I was very far from reaching it. I asked him one day why I felt such fear in facing his sword. He then answered me with a smile: "It is because you have made some progress in the sword. Someone who has nothing will feel nothing. See how profound the sword is."
>
> These words increased my awe before the vastness of the way of the sword. (26, p. 118)

Indeed, the outpouring of Shirai Toru's energy in combat was such that adepts of the period said, "Shirai's sword diffuses a circle of light." For Katsu Kaishu, the strange energy diffused by Shirai's sword was the equivalent of the energy that could be acquired through Zen.

"Perfecting oneself" is a very old idea in Oriental culture, which has been taken up in large part into the practice of *budo*. The Oriental idea of self-perfection is based on a kind of intuition of a movement toward fusion with the universal principle. It is an attitude of opening that is conceived of as the ascent of oneself in one's smallness toward the ideal or toward the gods. We have already discussed this in connection with the notion of *gyo*. *Budo*—and this is particularly the case for kendo—is based on an intuition that developed from these foundations and led to the creation of a specific practice. To be able to achieve a perfect strike presumes that one has in oneself the potential to enter into resonance with the principle that rules the universe. This, however, is a potential that it is difficult to master and apply effectively.

To achieve this, the practitioner can make use of techniques that have been transmitted by his master in the form of katas. The idea of perfection in *budo* from the beginning had both an individual and a collective character. It meant living profoundly in the here and now with a *shinai* in one's hand, projecting the totality of one's own existence into a *shinai* and finding a resonance in the reaction of one's adversary, whether he is actually present or one is training alone against an imaginary figure of the master-adversary.

Today, for someone who is capable of seeing in it the distilled experience of his predecessors, the kata represents a privileged means of evaluating the adversary and learning to know oneself. Entering into the experience of one's predecessors in a process of identification that comes from concretely repeating their movements—this process can convey, through a kind of resonance, an intuition of the meaning these movements had for them. In the first phase, a kata serves to instruct; the practitioner finds in it, as though in an alphabet, certain directives that did not previously exist in his repertoire of movements. In the second phase, the adept uses the kata as something to fill with his own experience. While executing sequences of movements that are called kata in the proper sense of the term, the depth and meaning realized and experienced do not depend only on the degree of visible perfection that is achieved but even more on the intensity and amplitude of the psychological state that is lived during this brief moment.

Today a kata is often thought of as a mere sequence of movements, but beyond the forms and the series of movements, the kata points to a way of being: the particular quality of the Japanese form developed in the course of the Edo period. During that time the kata became a way of being because it came to include within it a complex chain of identifications that galvanized energy and had the effect of arousing intense engagement on the part of the practitioner. We have seen by examining the example of Musashi how these katas were impregnated with religious references.

The model of the kata has survived into the modern era with a modification of its external references. To find guidance, the practitioner depends on his master or masters, whose images become fused with a higher ideal image. In other words, a master is he who presents an ideal image to the practitioner by being situated within the dimension of the way. The master guides the practitioner toward the realization that he himself embodies but that is at the same time something that resides in each one of us—and that is the true master, the principle of this universe in which we live and die. To exert oneself to be able to realize a magnificent strike is a way of approaching this principle. Therefore one should work on oneself and attempt to perfect oneself. Ultimately, each practitioner is the judge of his own state and perceives the qualities and deficiencies of the adversary as well as his own. When his strike is satisfying, it is proof that his path is headed in the right direction and that he can advance—advance toward true self-realization—because every practitioner is his own master to the extent that he represents the universe he is a part of.

These comments may help us to understand how the very ancient idea of self-perfection in the culture of the East is fundamentally different from the modern Western notion of developing one's personality, even if, at first blush, they seem quite close. And it is the idea of working with oneself in this deeper dimension that attracts many Westerners to *budo*.

CONFRONTATION AND HARMONY

One point should remain quite clear. Though *budo* arose on the basis of models of combat intended for actual fighting, it is a modern martial arts practice that appeared when the primary need to prepare for such mortal combat ceased to be present. Even if it might be useful in a street fight, it has never been defined on that basis. We have seen that judo provided the ideological side of the *budo* model and kendo the practical side.

During the first years of practice, the student of kendo is mainly concerned with the movement aspects of the techniques he is training in—speed, power, endurance, continuity—because these are the external elements of effectiveness that are immediately accessible. Over time his attention becomes progressively more refined and begins to relate to more subtle dimensions of technique. For example, instead of being content with studying speed and power and with acquiring a great diversity of techniques of movement, the student is led to pay attention to cadences, breathing, the question of the distance to adopt between himself and the adversary, and the question of intuiting the adversary's intentions.

An advance in the level of a student who is searching for the way of kendo thus implies a shift of attention regarding what constitutes the elements of effectiveness—a shift away from those elements that are apparent and obvious toward those that are less visible from the outside. This shift is accompanied by a change in the student's attitude toward his own body and an increase in the acuity of his perception of the adversary. As he passes through the various stages, he inevitably begins to incorporate a form of introspection into his technical work. In this way, in the course of a student's progress, the exercise of combat becomes a kind of calling into question of his way of being.

If he is the victim of an attack that he was unable to parry, he is called into question physically. All kinds of attacks are liable to reach him at any point where his attention is insufficiently present, wherever he does not exist with fullness. Being reached by an attack means for him discovering and confirming the inadequacy that allowed his adversary to penetrate. Thanks to the adversary, he is able to discover the inadequate part of himself that he still has to build up. A successful attack of his is evidence of fullness or emptiness in relation to the adversary—because he must not attack on the basis of an arbitrary decision or a reckless impulse but only when he is certain of having created a void in his adversary. He must learn to intuit what is going on with the other without revealing himself.

Thus the student who wishes to acquire these forms of acuity and power integrates introspective exercises into his training. In the extension of Musashi's instructions, he seeks to develop a sensitivity by means of which the will of the adversary can be sensed as though feeling it on one's skin. He also teaches the practitioner to project his energy to interact with and impede that of the adversary. According to the ideal approach of kendo, in order to project one's will onto the adversary, it is necessary to have an unperturbed mind; to detect the will of the other, one must have a mind that is pure like a mirror that reflects without distortion. During combat, the mind of the adept comes close to a kind of meditation, because his whole space-time is filled by the interactive, confrontational field that forms around his and his adversary's swords. In other words, in this space-time, apart from this field, there is nothing. This field is emptiness, but emptiness as Musashi defines it in his Scroll of Heaven:

> The meaning of emptiness is space where there is nothing, and I also envisage emptiness as that which cannot be known. Emptiness, of course, is where there is nothing. Knowing that which does not exist while knowing that which exists—that is emptiness. . . . He should know that true empty space is there where the clouds of uncertainty have completely dissipated. . . . Think of the void as the way and see the way as the void.
>
> In emptiness the good exists and evil does not exist.
>
> Knowing exists, the principle exists, the way exists, and the mind—is void.

To reinforce this state of mind, some practitioners have had recourse to Zen meditation; others seek it only by immersing themselves in the exercise of combat.

All movement during combat should be the dynamic consequence of the interaction of two beings. In the combat of *budo,* the way the confrontation manifests is therefore determined by the confrontational interaction of the energy of two persons, and the movements of technique appear afterward. In practice, students are invited to acquire the insight necessary to perceive what is going to happen before the technical movements actually begin—in their own combat and in that of the other.

This way of acting, rooted in introspection, is the foundation of *budo,* and it is based on techniques that can put us in a place between life and death.

In *budo* we see a complex structuring of techniques around the concrete phenomena of combat, in both the physical and the mental realms, aimed at conducting combat in the surest possible fashion. The core of this structure therefore remains combat in which the sword kills. However, the appearance of the idea of "the sword that gives life" was the pivotal point of this structure, its origin. For the objective embedded in the structure was no longer to accomplish the primary goal—it was replaced by the means of arriving at that goal without ever really trying to reach it. From the moment where someone succeeds in creating in himself the conditions for defeating his adversary, he no longer has any need to win; it is no longer worthwhile to deliver the winning blow. In this process we see that there has been a reversal of the goal and the means, and also in the way of looking at the adversary. The person facing you is no longer a true adversary; each practitioner himself has become his own most important adversary. The person facing you is only an intermediary who brings this principal adversary to the fore.

This is the specific quality of *budo,* which ultimately can be only a philosophical one, even if this word is rarely employed. More modestly, we might say that the principal objective of kendo is the training and development of the human being as such—this is one of the basic precepts of the teaching of this art.

The ideal image of *budo* constantly refers back to its history. The history of the martial arts is the history of the creation of a culture through combat. Combat, in its simplest sense, is killing each other. Around this primitive act, with the growth of civilization, various developments have taken place.

The best way to grasp the specific quality of the different forms of combat developed in the art of the Japanese sword is to consider it from the point of view of the relationship between adversaries. Three major periods can be distinguished, which were dominated successively by the primitive form of combat, *bujutsu,* and then *budo.* It goes without saying that these forms also coexisted at various times. In the course of time a shift occurred, and in the final stage a reversal, after which the preparation for combat became more important than combat itself. The act of combat was sublimated.

1. The primitive form of combat, the confrontational interaction of energies

In the primitive forms of combat, aggressions collide in the most direct manner. The technique of combat is a direct expression of the destructive impulse. Through technical elaboration, the manifestation of the destructive impulse takes on various forms, but the energies of the two combatants confront one another, exerted unilaterally from each side. In this form of combat, the prevailing idea is that fighting is learned on the battlefield. Preparation in terms of technique is not systematic but random and personal. The ability of a warrior is based on his favorite technique. Techniques are few and development of them is limited to the level of the individual or small group. However, with more refined elaboration of combat techniques, certain forms of harmonization of energies do develop.

2. Bujutsu, the existence of two energies, harmony and confrontation

In the combat of *bujutsu,* technique is conceived of as relating to both body and mind and also as involving a relationship with the adversary. Elaboration of technique extends into the dimensions of space and time (the notion of the *ma*), cadences *(hyoshi),* and foreseeing the actions of the adversary. In addition to the confrontation of energies, there now appears a consciousness of harmonization with the adversary, which is necessary for fighting with certainty. Technique is therefore elaborated in the context of a dynamic rapport between adversaries, where both confrontation and harmonization of energies is present. Let us make clear, however, that *bujutsu* is still characterized by life-and-death combat, because *bujutsu* was a real social function within warrior society.

Thus there was a preponderance of confrontational over harmonizing energy.

At the same time there was a tendency for discourse on technique to become mixed with religious discourse, and this led to a consciousness of the modalities of harmonization with the adversary.

3. Budo, the balance between harmony and confrontation

The warrior practice of *bujutsu* had to pass through a transformation in order to find its place in modern society and take the form of *budo,* a modern cultural activity. This happened at the time when the utilitarian role of the martial arts disappeared. *Budo* became a means of personal training, a method of education, or a leisure activity. The combat of *budo* does not entail real death, but death is internalized in the technique. The idea of death became a means of introspection and was no longer a concrete phenomenon that might appear as a result of combat. The two energies of confrontation and harmonization were balanced in the approach to technique.

However, different tendencies exist in current practice. In some disciplines that are close to *bujutsu,* confrontation is dominant, whereas in others, harmony is more important. In the techniques in which harmony predominates, the practice tends to become milder, and the gap left by the absence of confrontational tensions is generally filled in by a vague sensation of *ki*. In the absence of confrontational forces, students sometimes seek to develop in their stead the strange power of *ki,* and it sometimes happens that a person finds himself driven back or thrown without the other person's having touched him. And it is true that the will directed toward harmony creates and reinforces an unconscious attitude that wants to accommodate the technique of one's partner. When one of the partners uses, for example, a pushing or throwing technique, instead of resisting, the other accepts the execution of this technique and lets himself be thrown or pushed without resistance. At an advanced level, one partner becomes capable of reacting positively to the will of the other, even before the other has initiated his technique. Under these circumstances, if one of the partners is in a position of physical or psychological power, it sometimes happens that the other lets himself be thrown or pushed back without bodily contact. This phenomenon is often explained by the notion of energy *(ki)*. I do not wish to enter into a discussion of *ki* at this point, but it seems we may take for granted that psychological factors play a major role here.

As a counterpoise to this phenomenon, tendencies have appeared in *budo* toward a form of practice in which confrontational tensions predominate. This tendency favors bloody conflicts in which physical condition and aggression play the primary role. Students of this tendency declare that their practice is the real *budo,* contrasting it with forms in which harmony predominates. In reality this is nothing more than a return to the primitive form of combat.

Currently the practice of *budo* oscillates back and forth between these two poles. Kendo seems to be the discipline that integrates the two kinds of energy in the most balanced fashion. Thus it is the form of *budo* that comes closest to the definition that I have proposed. The combat of *kizeme* is its highest fruition, but access to this level is difficult, and young students tend to move toward a more sports-oriented practice in which confrontation predominates over harmony. Kendo requires long years of practice, but in the course of one's personal evolution, with age and advancement in technique, the quest for harmony becomes more and more important.

From my point of view, the practice of *budo* is a vehicle for gaining knowledge of oneself and others, a vehicle that can be developed independently of the beliefs that gave rise to it in Japanese culture. Reflection on and analysis of its various dimensions makes it possible to conceive of *budo* as a means of personal development, self-perfection, that is capable of functioning in its fullest sense outside the culture that produced it.

‖ 13 ‖

One Life, One Art

MUSASHI FOUGHT HIS first duel to the death at the age of thirteen and persevered throughout his whole life in the study of the art of swordsmanship, which he called strategy *(hyoho)*. Endowed with exceptional physical strength, he tread an adept's path that made of him a legendary figure. But when we read the lines he wrote toward the end of his life, "As for me, I have become older and no longer go out much; my condition does not permit me to practice strategy. I have the wish, accompanied by much longing, to see you again once more," we see him once again as a human being and may find ourselves touched by compassion.

In his youth Musashi engaged in many duels to the death, from which he always emerged the victor. Toward the end of his life, a unique approach to combat became second nature to him: to defeat the adversary without striking a single blow. He showed in that way that he had raised his level to the point where he could defeat an adversary simply by overwhelming him with his combative energy. It was a matter not only of a change in his attitude toward combat but also of the evolution of his level of accomplishment and his personal level of being. Indeed, dominating an adversary without striking a single blow implies not only a level of accomplishment far superior to that of the adversary but also a radical development in the concept of combat. The adversary, who for his part has tried to land blows, becomes convinced of his defeat because he has been forced to retreat even though no blows have been aimed at him. Combat is more than a confrontation of technique, it is an overall confrontation between two persons. This conception of combat entails the idea that the art of swordsmanship is an overall expression of the way of being of the person who practices it. With this as a point of departure, a cosmological outlook develops in which, at a given point, discourse on the method of the art of swordsmanship tends to blend with expressions of the swordsman's beliefs.

Musashi's personal evolution over the course of his life seems to recapitulate the historical evolution of the art of the sword.

Swordsmanship began in Japan, as in all civilizations, with techniques that aimed to kill. Around Musashi's time the warriors of Japan, who had experienced bloody combat, began to move toward a new form of the art of swordsmanship, that of defeating without delivering a blow. A few of Musashi's contemporaries reached levels of accomplishment comparable with his.

With the advent of peace, in the course of the Edo period, this way of defeating an opponent became the standard to be reached by students of the sword, but since warriors still had to fight with their swords, it did not become the sole ideal form of combat. In the modern period, when students of the sword no longer fight with real swords, it has become the ideal in kendo.

Nowadays, whether we are talking about Japanese swordsmanship or kendo, combat has become in a certain sense a fiction, but the fashion in which adepts engage in this fiction remains decisive for their work on themselves. The technique of swordsmanship is closely linked with our mental state; scrutiny of our technique refers us back to our state of mind. To increase one's ability with the sword, one must work on technique and one must work on one's mind. That is why some defeats are privileged moments for examining and correcting one's overall attitude. In this way the art of the sword moves in the direction of a way for the development of the human being by means of combat.

Defeating the adversary without striking is a paradox that develops in the realm of awareness. The person who is defeated without having been struck is in reality struck by a sensation of energy that overwhelms him and makes him have a sense of an inner void. The sword emerges as a means of calling into question the manner in which an adept engages in combat; thus it becomes an instrument of introspection. By causing him to engage profoundly with the sensation of his life being called into question, swordsmanship moves away from its primary function—killing—and acquires an educational character. In this way, through the intention to defeat one's adversary without striking a blow, this paradoxical idea appears: the sword that gives life. This is a specific cultural trait of the Japanese sword.

The modern notion of *budo* is primarily based on this idea, currently put into practice through a form developed in kendo. Let us set aside here the problems posed by the rigidity of traditional martial arts groups and their excessive demands for conformity already mentioned above and focus on the fundamental structure of the rapport between adversaries. The adepts of the highest level seek an interaction of energy and mind that exists prior to any technical exchange, which is known as the combat of *kizeme*. In this type of combat, the ancient idea of the sword that gives life merges with the modern idea of human self-development.

In other words, the fruition of combat in kendo is a value that is created by transcending the two opposing vectors of killing and giving life.

From the point of view of technique, this opposition is expressed by aggression and harmony, the energies emanating from the two adversaries. The ideal form of *budo* comes about through achieving a perfect balance between these two vectors, even though this balance is constantly threatened.

From the point of view of training and education, the quest, which is a conscious one, is to form oneself by committing oneself fully and completely to an act. This is how *budo* takes up the quest for perfection in a modern way.

APPENDIX 1

THE TRANSLATION OF

THE *GORIN NO SHO*

The Text of the *Gorin no sho*

The text of the *Gorin no sho* used throughout is from the 1942 edition of the most common version, the one edited by Takayanagi Mitsutoshi. (10) This edition is based on the text handed down in the Hosokawa family.

In making my translation, I compared different versions and different transcriptions into modern Japanese of Musashi's texts. Where these versions presented significant differences, I have so indicated in a note.

Translation of the *Gorin no sho*

In my translation of the *Gorin no sho* I made every effort to render as faithfully as possible the meaning such as it appeared to me from reading the Japanese text and continually referring to the practice of the martial arts. Difficulties in comprehending Musashi's text are numerous, even in Japanese. At the end of his edition of the *Gorin no sho*, Watanabe Ichiro wrote:

> The *Gorin-no-sho* was written by Musashi on the basis of the *Hyoho sanju-go-kajo* in the strained psychological conditions of the end of his life. He did not have enough time to reexamine the text; that is why all through it we see traces of confusion and repetition. Nevertheless, this has the advantage of showing, in the manner of a sketch, the thoughts on the martial arts and on life that he had come to after more than fifty years of practicing swordsmanship. But if we read it from the point of view of the technique and original principles of the School of Two Swords, we cannot help but recognize that it

is too abstract and general, lacks concrete detail, and leans too far toward the psychological aspect. (13, p. 172)

In the epilogue to his work on the *Gorin no sho,* Takayanagi Mitsutoshi writes:

In any event, the *Gorin-no-sho* is a work that is difficult to read. In general, works on art and technique are difficult. . . . It is by knowing kendo that the *Gorin-no-sho* can be fully understood. It must be admitted, therefore, that it is normal for this work to be difficult for us to understand. But considering his time in history, it is admirable that he was able to write with so much clarity.

However, it is not enough for us to establish that the *Gorin-no-sho* is a work that is difficult to understand. It must be admitted that Musashi lacked the ability to organize his knowledge. I do not mean to say that he did not master kendo in an organized fashion; he was able to become an adept of the highest quality because he did master his art in an organized fashion. It is in his way of organizing his knowledge on the art of the sword in a scientific manner that he shows himself lacking in the ability to organize. (10, pp. 96–99)

The difficulties in Musashi's text present themselves all the more acutely when one is translating it. As his critics indicate, repetition, elliptical expressions, and obscure and ambiguous passages are numerous. In a translation into a Western language, because of the logical structure of this language and the precision of its terminology, the risk is double: Sometimes a translation that is too precise, even if it closely follows the text, runs the risk of only partially rendering the meaning; sometimes the meaning is liable to become diluted, giving the impression of very general aphorisms. It is true that Musashi often uses words in a polysemous fashion, but the appearance of empty generality that one can sometimes encounter on a first reading acquires precision, in my experience, when the passage is applied to practice.

The critics just cited seem to have based their remarks on a distortion of the sense of Musashi's work. They consider it as a literary work, the entire sense of which is meant to be communicated by the use of words. In my view, Musashi's text should be understood by seeing its connection to those to whom it was addressed, his students, and by understanding the role its author intended it to play for them—a guide to be used as a complement to shared practice.

At the beginning of the Scroll of Water, Musashi says, "Read this text thinking that it is written for you, do not think that you are reading or learning just written things." As we practice the martial arts, we feel the need to preserve the know-how we acquire, either in writing or through drawings. When we receive an explanation that makes us truly understand an important aspect of a technique, or when we discover for ourselves a new meaning in a technique, we feel the need to note this down. These notes are often composed in a kind of shorthand, and if another person were to read them, they would probably have a hard time understanding them. But if our experience and our sensations, for us, give substance to this simple notation, it will be enough to preserve the sensations we have felt and the knowledge we have gained.

For example, in my practice notebook, I read the following line: "Do not stay frozen after gripping the adversary's wrist." That is a note I took fifteen years ago in Tokyo when I received instruction from Master Kubota, who taught me gripping techniques in jujutsu. *Itsuku,* "frozen" or "fixed," is an expression frequently used by Musashi. This simple note evokes for me a whole series of exercises that I carried out under the direction of this master. It even evokes for me the pain I felt in my wrist, which became swollen and nearly black from the bruising that resulted from continuous gripping exercises. It is accompanied by these various sensations that I recall Master Kubota's precious teaching, which I could formulate in the following fashion:

When faced with a punching attack, you should never think of gripping the adversary's wrist but, above all, think of parrying. Parrying should always be uppermost in your mind. If you succeed in parrying in the right way, following the pattern of movement of your technique, you will naturally succeed in gripping your opponent's wrist without fail. But once you have gripped his wrist, your hand must not remain frozen *(itsuku)* even for a brief instant. If you stagnate, you will not be able to exert the right pressure with the base of your index finger, and you will lose the entire effectiveness of your grip. Staying stagnant is a disease in the practice of the martial arts. You must avoid stagnation in all techniques, especially in footwork. As soon as your feet freeze or stagnate, you become vulnerable, since at that precise moment you can no longer react appropriately to your opponent's attack. Conversely, you should not let the moment escape when your adversary's feet are about to stagnate. That is the moment when you can attack.

For me, this whole series of teachings I received from that teacher arises out of that little note. The way I read it is very different from how I would read a text by someone else. First, in order to grasp the thought of another, we have to try to understand the thread of their logic. Sometimes, then, our own experience might accord with theirs, and in this case only what they have written can acquire for us a body that is richer than the explicit expression. But this is rather rare; whereas for personal notes, a few written words always serve to evoke a sequence of experiences. But it is possible that a few words written by a master can capture an experience he has shared with his students. For example, Master Kubota, after having shown us a number of gripping and throwing techniques, explained to us that to make these techniques more forceful and effective, the essential point was *sakazuki o nomi hosu,* "empty a glass of sake." This description of a movement and the form one's hand takes in executing it summarized in the best manner the way to execute and work with the grip in order to immobilize the adversary. Later, in a booklet intended for his students, he wrote the following brief description: "After having accomplished the hold, if you make the gesture of emptying a glass of sake, your adversary will be hanging by his wrist like a rag." For those who received his instruction, this text is clear and eloquent. The image he used was a guide that would help them to improve their practice.

In the passage from the Scroll of Water cited above, I believe Musashi was reminding his intended readers, who were his close students, that his text should be read in this way and that everything he had written in his book had already been explained in a richer fashion in the course of his instruction. Thus this was not a work intended to make his strategic thought and his techniques understandable to a reader who was discovering them for the first time. In a certain sense the *Gorin no sho* is a synthesis of the notes that Musashi's students might have taken if they had their master's permission and if they had had writing ability comparable to Musashi's. In any case, Musashi's students certainly did not read this work with the feeling of encountering this material for the first time. Thus Musashi was giving them his teaching in the form of a final synthesis, hoping that his disciples had already assimilated it well and that they would read the text as though they had written it themselves.

Thus reading the *Gorin no sho* as a text that stands by itself would represent a departure from this understanding. There are several possible readings of this work and several possible approaches that a translator could take. I chose to understand the *Gorin no sho* on the basis of my practice, first of all to enrich this practice. I tried to apply Musashi's instructions to barehanded combat and also executed the techniques sword in hand in order to understand them well.

In my translation I have attempted to reconstruct the meaning the text would have when being read in this fashion. I have endeavored to remain faithful to the Japanese text, but sometimes the literal translation seemed to obscure or impoverish the meaning. Particularly for those passages that Japanese authors criticize for their lack of organization or their repetitiveness, I tried to bring out the flow of the author's thought. There was an implied reference here to an experience of the strategy of combat that did not need to be made entirely explicit, because of the style of communication Musashi chose in view of the fact that he was addressing his most advanced students. The difficulty arises in part from the fact that Musashi plays on the multiple meanings of words and often uses the same term in different senses. Two examples are *kokoro* and *michi*. I chose, as I explain below, to translate these terms in various ways. One of the major difficulties was to provide an effective description of movements as well as the dynamic that underlies them; this was difficult because of the inherent differences in the way the body and the mind are represented in the two cultures. Since repetitions of words or expressions in one paragraph were frequent, I tried to render the meaning of the text in the best way and avoided repetitions when they obscured it.

All through the translation, I have tried to maintain the contribution to the overall meaning that comes from putting Musashi's instructions into practice, yet I was constantly vigilant to avoid personal interpretations.

In the *Gorin no sho* there are certain terms that appear frequently that pose particular difficulties for translation. It seems to me necessary to offer some explanation of these.

Some Terms That Create Difficulties for Translation

The meaning of the terms *ku, michi,* and *kokoro* is so broad that they are difficult to render in another language, and moreover, in Musashi's writings their sense varies according to the context. Therefore I made the decision to use several translations for each one of these words and give the Japanese word either in parentheses or in a note.

In addition, certain terms that have no equivalent in English recur frequently in the text. They are *hyoho, hyoshi, ri,* and *toku.* Nevertheless, in order not to make the translation too ponderous, I have systematically used an English term to translate each of them. However, I feel it is indispensable to draw the reader's attention to the disparity in meaning between the Japanese terms and their translation.

Hyoho

For *hyoho* I did not find any expression that renders its precise meaning. After having long hesitated over the possibility of simply keeping the Japanese word in the translation, I decided to translate the word systematically as "strategy." Despite this, however, considering the importance of this word in Musashi's thought, I used the Japanese word *hyoho* in the commentaries.

Hyoho (or *heiho*) means "military method" or "strategy." For Musashi it means a way *(do* or *michi)* that determines the direction of one's whole life. This is the way he followed with perseverance, committing himself to it totally. The term *strategy* is deficient in rendering *hyoho* because, though it does indicate an area of interest and activity, it does not include the dimension of "the way" that is present in the Japanese. Moreover, this term also does not include the dimension of the practice of technique, which for Musashi is central to the conception of *hyoho.*

In the practice of *hyoho,* Musashi distinguishes two levels, which he refers to frequently in the text: *daibun no hyoho* and *ichibun no hyoho. Dai* means "great" and *ichi* means "one." Sometimes he uses the words *tabun* instead of *daibun* and *shobun* instead of *ichibun. Ta* means "many" and *sho* means "small."

For *bun* I give here only the senses that are relevant to the use of the term in our context:

1. Separate part or division of a part, a party, social situation, degree of ability.
2. The position or hierarchical place that corresponds to a particular role.

Since Musashi uses these pairs of terms interchangeably, I conclude that *daibun* and *ichibun,* on one hand, and *tabun* and *shobun,* on the other, have the same sense. What they refer to is something relating to a party composed of a single person and something related to a large or numerous party.

I translated *ichibun* and *shobun* by "individual strategy." It was difficult, without a long paraphrase, to render the sense of "small" that goes with *bun* but does not apply to strategy. "Small-scale strategy" was a possible translation. With the words *daibun* and *tabun,* strategy having to do with large divisions or large parties, Musashi refers not only to the art of leading large groups in combat but also to leading groups in all aspects of life. Two translations struck me as possible—either "large-scale strategy" or "group strategy" as opposed to "individual strategy." I decided on the latter, more concise formulation.

Hyoshi

It seems necessary to explain the precise meaning of *hyoshi,* since this notion is quite complex.

According to the dictionary, it has three main senses:

1. A musical term.
   a. Basic element of a rhythm. Division of a melody arrived at by counting the number of rhythmic elements. The break in a melody made by a rhythmic unit.
   b. Unit of time measure in the performance of music. Powerful drum sound that marks a rhythmic unit in traditional Japanese music *(gagaku).*
   c. Musical instruments of Noh theater.

2. Rhythm, cadence, or momentum in things or in musical expression.
   a. Striking a drum or striking two pieces of wood together to give a signal or a warning.
   b. The momentum or cadence with which things evolve or advance.
   c. The texture of the sensation felt in doing something.
   d. The moment or the occasion when something is accomplished.

3. The wooden blinders attached to the two sides of a horse's head. (99)

Even though *hyoshi* is usually translated "cadence" or " rhythm," these words do not render well the sense the term has in the martial arts. For this reason, I summarize below the essential points of the analysis of *hyoshi* I have given elsewhere:

> In combat, for each movement of evading, blocking, attacking . . . there is a cadence, and this is a constraint for us, just as the cadences of the adversary are. No movement is independent of certain rhythms that are at once physical and mental. Even when we are apparently immobile, just from the rhythmic contraction and relaxation of our muscles, of our breathing, etc., we possess a rhythm that is linked to the movements we are making or are about to make. . . .
>
> The relation between two combatants brings into play the whole set of cadences manifested by each of them: movements, facial expressions, breathing, the ebb and flow of muscular tension, mental state. . . .
>
> In combat, we live each moment in waves of rhythm or cadence. The subjective time of the combatant does not flow in a flat, uniform fashion.
>
> The Japanese notion of *hyoshi* refers to the sequence of spatiotemporal, rhythmic intervals produced by the reciprocal relations of two combatants, and at the same time, to the cadence proper to each of them, which is closely linked to breathing and mental state.
>
> In a more general sense, I would define *hyoshi* this way: It is an integrated set of cadences that link as rhythmic factors several subjects and their surroundings within the framework constituted by a cultural activity. This integrated set of cadences comes to fruition in a balance or an overall harmony. (53, pp. 86–87)

Kokoro

Kokoro designates the functions of the mind, emotional and intellectual. This notion is used in opposition to the body and to an object. Five major meanings are distinguished with variations in subsidiary senses. I summarize those relating to Musashi's use of the term.

1. Spiritual and mental activities as a whole.
   a. The basis of a human being's spiritual activities: reason, knowledge, feeling, will.
   b. The true thought that cannot be grasped on the surface, or the original state of thought.
   c. The innate or acquired tendency of a person's spiritual activity, thus personality or character.
   d. The secret conception of a thought or a feeling. The inside of the mind.

2. One of the following areas of activity of the human mind: knowledge, feeling, will.
   a. The psychological activity that permits one to decide on a behavior through thinking things through in an orderly fashion; discrimination or discernment; detailed thought.
   b. Ability to cope with things according to the situation.
   c. Ability to accept that which is contrary to one's own thought.
   d. That. which fluctuates subtly within the subjective process in relation to the external world.
   e. Consideration or feeling with regard to others.
   f. Sensibility that is capable of understanding or giving birth to poetry, literature, or the arts.
   g. Consciousness or feeling that is at the origin of linguistic expression.
   h. Intention.

3. Mental activity that has a profound relationship with human activity, such as religion.

4. Having to do with objects or things by analogy with the human heart.
   a. The essential way of being of things. The central line. The principle of things.
   b. The reason things occur. The principle of things.

5. With regard to the human body or things, the aspect that has to do with the heart or the position that corresponds to the heart.
   a. The center of things.
   b. The heart, the chest. The part of the human body where it was traditionally thought the heart resides.

I have translated *kokoro* by "mind" where it was related to the first group of senses, with accentuations of meaning varying according to the context. I have translated it by "sensation" in sense 2h and in occurrences where it reflected the third and fourth group of senses.

When *kokoro* designated "mind" in a sense in which in the English language there is no distinction between the mind and the person, that is, in cases where mind was indistinguishable from the mere expression of the existence of a subject, I did not use a particular word for *kokoro*.

Ku

Ku presents more than a terminological problem. The difficulty was to render the fullness of the Japanese term in English, in which no equivalent for it exists.

Ku means:

1. Between heaven and earth. Heaven or sky. Space.
2. Emptiness, void.
3. Without foundation.
4. Without interest, without meaning.
5. Buddhist term: all things, from heaven to earth, originate from internal and external causality and are empty of a nature of their own. In reality, *ku* has neither real substance nor natural autonomy. (99)

There are three normal pronunciations of the ideogram *ku*. Pronounced *ku* or *kara,* it tends to mean emptiness; pronounced *sora,* it means heaven or sky, but the two meanings can overlap.

In Musashi's text the ideogram is pronounced *ku,* but Musashi sometimes gives it the first of these two meanings, at other times the second, and sometimes even both at the same time. I have translated this term with one or the other of these two meanings, or else with both at the same time. However, most of the time, especially when it deals with practice and the attitude that underlies it, the sense of the term is "emptiness." In the Scroll of Heaven, the term is taken in its very broadest sense; that is, it takes on the Buddhist meaning.

Michi

Musashi frequently uses the term *michi*.

According to the dictionary, *michi* is composed of the prefix *mi,* "veneration" or "respect," and the noun *chi,* "the god who possesses the way or the road." (99) But this etymology is doubtful.

Michi has two principal meanings:

1. A place where humans pass and phenomena having to do with this passage. In more precise terms:
    a. The line of a journey, road, way on earth; maritime way.
    b. Small road, path (as opposed to a large road or a boulevard).
    c. The region or area one can reach by following a road. The six principal roads (in the *Kojiki*).
    d. The process of a journey or a voyage.
    e. The act of walking or making progress on a road or the route of a journey.
    f. The length of the road or the journey. Unit of measure of the length of a road.

2. The manner in which a person progresses. The guideline for conduct a person should refer to in leading his life. In more precise terms:

a. The line or direction to follow for each person in accordance with his position or situation. The line or the principle in accordance with which things naturally evolve. The principle or reason of that which is normal and just.

b. The way or the road indicated by the gods, the Buddha, the saints or sages. Doctrine, dogma, the way of Buddha.

c. Means, method; way of doing things. The right way of doing things.

d. A particular domain. A particular direction.

e. An area of specialization. A special method. An area of art. From the time of the feudal period, *michi* also began to take on the sense of following the way in order to deepen and expand the quality of being human or to edify and educate the human person.

f. The route or road to take in order to achieve a goal. A process it is necessary to go through in order to attain an objective.

In Musashi's writing, *michi* has several meanings, which vary according to context. For this reason I did not always translate it with the same term. When I translated it by a term other than "way," I have so indicated in a note, or I have given the word *michi* in parentheses after the translation.

Musashi often uses *michi* in sense 2, especially 2b and 2e. In that case I translate it as "way." In several passages in the Scroll of Earth he makes use of the sense of "domain" or "specialization," somewhere between 2b and 2e, to convey the sense of a professional activity. He also often uses sense 2a. In those cases, I translate: "principle *(michi)*."

In descriptions of technique, Musashi frequently uses *michi* in sense 1, especially 1a, 1d, and 1e.

Ri

The pronunciation *ri* corresponds to two ideograms. Musashi uses both of them:

1. Reason, principle.

2A. (a) Very hard-hitting, quite incisive; (b) that which is convenient; (c) effectiveness, utility; (d) the terrain is excellent; (e) victory; (f) interest, advantage, gain. (100)

2B. (a) Interest, gain; (b) interest (on a sum of money); (c) advantage or opportunity, or domination in combat, victory; (d) that which is convenient, useful; (e) function, effectiveness; (f) quite sharp (for a blade), incisive (for the intelligence). (99)

The meaning of the first ideogram does not cause any problems for translation. But Musashi frequently uses the second ideogram but adds to it the sense of the first one (reason, principle). For example, at the beginning of the Scroll of Water, he writes: *"Tatoe kotoba wa tsuzukazaru to intomo, ri wa onozukara kikoyubeshi."*

Musashi is speaking here to his students, presenting to them his whole approach to the Scroll of Water. In this context the sense of "reason" or "principle" seems to be required. For this reason, I translated: "Even if words are insufficient, you should understand the principle intuitively."

Musashi also employs the second ideogram in the sense of "advantage, effectiveness, opportunity."

Toku

Toku means:

1. Expression in the action of mastering the way of human beings.
2. Expression of rightness in action.
3. The personal ability that makes it possible to decide with certainty in conformity with moral principles or a moral ideal. The habit of deciding on and carrying out a right action. One of the most important conceptions in human ethics.
4. Rightness. The way of the good.
5. The force and quality that make someone respected. Virtue.
6. Innate nature. One's personal quality.
7. Blessing. Grace.
8. Wealth.

In this last sense, *toku* can also be written with another ideogram, but Musashi does not use that one. (99, 100)

I translated *toku* as "virtue," the most frequent sense in Musashi's writings. When I used another translation, I so indicated in a note.

APPENDIX 2

SEN—TAKING THE INITIATIVE: A CENTRAL NOTION IN MUSASHI'S PRACTICE

MUSASHI STATES that it is impossible to give in writing the details of the notion of taking the initiative, precisely on account of its difficulty and importance.

The idea of *sen* is one of the central points of the technique of kendo, and also karate, since all practitioners must refine their techniques in relation to *sen*. I think that *sen* is also fundamental for all forms of combat. However, still today the theoretical elaboration of the idea and content of *sen* remains inadequate.

Practitioners frequently content themselves with quoting phrases from Musashi and other adepts of the Edo period. It is to the work of Chiba Shusaku (1794–1855), a celebrated sword master from the end of the Edo period, that they refer most often. His elucidations of the sword techniques that had been transmitted up to that period seem far in advance of his time. He removes the veils of mystification from certain technical instructions and explains them in simple language, based on his own experience.

With regard to *sen,* he gives the following explanation, without ever actually using the term *sen:*

In *kenjutsu* there are three occasions one must not allow to escape. The first is the moment when your opponent is about to attack, the second is the moment when your opponent has parried your attack, and the third is the moment when your opponent's attack has just failed. By taking advantage of the opportunities created by these three situations, you must try to win, without limiting yourself to a single attack. . . . You must strike with certainty just at the moment when your opponent is about to attack. If your opponent has parried your attack, you must never back away in order to start again from a distance. When your opponent's attack has failed, you must never let this opportunity to attack him pass. (82, pp. 16–17)

This passage is frequently quoted today in works on kendo technique in order to explain what *sen* is.

A little further on, with regard to the first of the three opportunities for victory, Chiba Shusaku gives the following further explanation: "To make your strike successful, you must attack the instant your opponent unleashes his attack. That is the instant when he means to attack but his will has not yet taken the form of a movement. If you attack at the same time he starts his movement, each of you will receive a blow simultaneously."

With regard to *sen,* he wrote: "In the other schools, it is sometimes said: *sen-sen no sen.* This refers to the following situation. When you think of attacking, your opponent guesses your intention and attacks first. You execute a parry that succeeds in causing his attack to fail, and maintaining your original intention to attack first, you hit him with an attack to win. The situation boils down to *go no sen,* that is to say, you defeat the adversary after having executed a parry. This is not a complex situation, as some would have us believe."

As Chiba Shusaku tells us, during the Edo period various expressions related to *sen* were used, and as technique was elaborated further, terms continued to proliferate, creating ambiguities that were sometimes the result of an attitude of mystification. We find, for example, in addition to the expressions Musashi uses: *sen no sen, sen-sen no sen, go no sen, sen-go no sen, go-sen no sen.*

Currently these many expressions continue to be used. They are adapted to particular situations but without a clear idea of what is being talked about. I believe that this vagueness results from the fact that the most serious practitioners have tended to content themselves with the explanation that corresponded to their own technical achievement. If through one explanation—even if it was inadequate theoretically—they succeeded in meeting combat situations, they did not go further in their thinking, because their main preoccupation was to raise their own level of practice. Great contempt still persists toward the words of those who have not attained an excellent level of practice. And when it comes to ideas like *sen,* even the words of practitioners of the highest level are given relatively little consideration in comparison with those of the great adepts of history. In the realm of the Japanese martial arts, the prevailing approach is to invest one's energy in a perfecting of practice that has no limits rather than devote even a part of one's attention to theory. In this sense, the attitude of the great adepts of the martial arts is more like that of artisans than that of scientists.

As far as Musashi's text is concerned, I think the problem comes from the fact that he wrote about *sen* purely on the basis of the way he fought and did not describe the overall situation, whereas Chiba Shusaku's text is easier to apply because he explains things in relation to the reactions of the adversary. However, he also does not go so far as to explain why the three situations he describes are important or what an optimal situation for taking the initiative in combat consists of.

If we are able to be clear about what constitutes the basis of an opportunity in combat, we will be better able to understand the meaning of Musashi's and Chiba Shusaku's words as well as the further possibilities that lie within them.

According to my analysis, it is possible to explain clearly the principle that lies at the root of *sen*. The term *sen,* employed in relation to swordsmanship, signifies "to precede one's adversary in a decisive act of combat, that is, to strike the adversary before he strikes you." The point is to assure yourself a victory by situating your attack in the moment when your opponent's mind is detached from his action, that is, in a moment when he would have difficulty evading your attack.

Musashi teaches three main modes of creating such a vulnerable moment in the adversary. Chiba Shusaku's study points out three precise situations. His explanation is not as complete as Musashi's, but it is more concrete and precise. For this reason I will take it as my point of departure.

Why should you attack at the moment when your opponent is about to attack you?

When we carry out an intentional act, there is always a lag between the will and the movement. We are not very conscious of this fact because this lag does not have important consequences in our daily lives. But in the practice of combat, when we execute movements of technique with the utmost possible speed, the lag between the perception of an act and the act itself has important consequences. If we consider the time involved in relation to the speed of the execution of the technique, this small lag can be big enough to constitute a moment of vulnerability. Thus when you want to launch an attack, the will to attack always appears first and the actual movement of attack follows. This will of attack is focused on the point that you want to attack. For example, if you want to strike your opponent's head, your will is directed at his head, and this is what is going to attract the actual movement of your strike. Thus during this lapse of time, the attention you need to protect yourself against an attack is missing. This lag is so brief that ordinarily we are under the impression that the will and the movement occur at the same time.

In general, the stronger the will to strike is, the more clearly the lag manifests. For this reason, in a combat with a beginner in kendo or in karate, the more the tension mounts, the more evident the lag appears. You see that he is going to attack you to the head or to the side, because you feel his attention focusing and fixing on those places. At this moment you also see that he lacks attention for protecting himself. If you launch your attack at this instant, your attack succeeds as though you were stepping through a gap. This gap is bigger or smaller depending on the level of the combatant, because technical refinement is directed toward the diminution of this lag.

The strike of nonthought taught by Musashi in the Scroll of Water is precisely a strike in which the will to attack is effaced to the greatest extent possible. Thus it does not allow the adversary to perceive the point at which your attack begins, and thus it does not present a vulnerable moment that he can step into.

This shows us the way we can look for a vulnerable moment in the adversary at the instant he is about to attack. However, as Chiba Shusaku says, it is already too late if you carry out your movement at the same time as your opponent does. Perceiving the movement of his will to attack must make it possible for you to carry out your attack at the instant his will touches you but when he has not yet begun his movement.

In learning *sen,* this situation when the opponent is about to attack is fundamental, because his vulnerability is at its most evident at this moment. For this reason the process of learning *sen* generally begins with this exercise. In karate the term *deai* (taking the initiative at the moment of encounter) is used to designate the equivalent situation. I shall now explain how the principle I have elicited applies to the other two situations pointed out by Chiba Shusaku.

With regard to the second of those situations, why should we attack at the moment the adversary has just parried our attack?

The attention of someone who is parrying the attack of an adversary is held for a short instant. The more menacing and powerful the attack is, the more it holds his attention. If you launch an attack to the adversary's head, his attention will be concentrated on your weapon and on his own, since he is using it to carry out his defense technique. His attention is held there and is therefore not present for the defense of any other part of his body. That is why Chiba Shusaku adds here, "If your opponent has parried your attack, you must never back away in order to start again from a distance." If you start again from a distance, you let this brief instant of opportunity escape, since the two adversaries then return to combat with a renewed state of readiness.

In bare-handed combat, as for example in karate, where arms and legs are used, this situation is easier to understand. When you throw a punch to the face of your opponent and he parries, his attention becomes fixed on the hand with which he is carrying out his defense. The stronger your attack is, the more threatening it is to him, and the stronger this tension is, the less attention he has available to defend the lower part of his body. If, while maintaining the pressure of your punch, you can execute a kick, this technique will succeed as though you were stepping through a gap. In practice, the difficulty thus consists in launching your kick before your opponent has a chance to withdraw his attention from your punch.

The third situation presents itself when the adversary's attack has failed.

Your opponent launches an attack to your head, thinking he is going to land his blow, but it fails. In this situation his attention and his striking movement, joining together, converge on your head, which he already thinks he has succeeded in striking. He then immediately realizes his failure and will have to renew his attack or revise his strategy. If he attacks you again in the same way as the first time, he will first direct his will to attack at you—with a lag before the actual movement. In addition, at the moment in which he failed in his attack, his will and his movement were joined, not in the manner of simply coming together, but as though stuck to each other. The stronger his will to strike and his certainty that he will succeed, the more stubbornly the will and the movement will stick to each other. In order to start fresh with a new attack or a new technique, he will have to pull these two elements apart. To execute a new attack, your opponent will once again have to direct his will to attack at you and then carry out the attack movement. In reality, these operations take place fast, but the time they require is long enough for you to launch an attack. In this third case, it should be noted that there is a pulling apart of the intention from the movement and then a new fixing of the attention.

In this third of Chiba Shusaku's three cases, we understand that the principle that makes it possible to win without fail is that of inserting one's attack in a gap in the adversary's attention. This allows us to understand that Musashi's text concerns the general approach that can create this kind of opportunity, without going into further details. Chiba Shusaku indicates the three situations in which this opportunity appears most often.

Musashi writes, "Taking the initiative is essential in *hyoho,* because it is through this that a rapid victory in combat will be determined." All through his work, it seems to me, the principle we have just examined underlies what he has to say about ways of winning. For Musashi, victory must not be a random or accidental achievement, it must be the consequence of a strategic principle. I have expressed this through the image of winning in as clearly evident a fashion as if one were stepping through a gap that has been left open.

We saw above that many terms are used to express the notion of *sen,* but we now understand that there is a single principle underlying them all.

How should we interpret Musashi's text on the basis of this principle?

What Musashi calls *ken no sen* occurs when you attack by closing in on your adversary. The main way of creating a moment of vulnerability in him is by acting against him. Musashi does not describe what forms these moments take, he simply says, "All through the combat, preserve an untroubled mind with the sole idea of crushing your opponent; in this way you will gain a victory with a mind that is strong to its depth."

If you act to attack, your opponent will parry your attack. This corresponds to the second situation indicated by Chiba Shusaku. If the action you take is to apply the pressure of a virtual attack without really attacking and if your opponent reacts to this pressure by launching an attack, you can take advantage of the moment of vulnerability that will appear just as he is about to attack in order to take the initiative. This is the first case described by Chiba Shusaku.

What Musashi calls *tai no sen* takes place when the adversary attacks you: "Pretend to be weak and remain without a reaction. At the moment when he approaches, make an ample and vigorous move back, then, with a leap, feint an attack, and the instant he relaxes strike him, straight on and with force." These movements disconcert the adversary at the moment he is about to launch his attack; his will to attack becomes separated from his movement and a hesitancy appears in him. A sort of hollow is produced in his will to attack. This is the instant in which he relaxes, in which his will to attack and his attack movement drift apart from each other. This causes a vulnerability to appear.

Musashi also writes, "When the adversary attacks you, oppose him with the greatest vigor—he will modify the cadence of his attack; take control of him in this moment of change and defeat him." Just when the adversary changes his cadence in this way, a moment of vulnerability appears, for the same reasons as before.

Producing a moment of vulnerability in the adversary is also the objective of the *tai-tai no sen* taught by Musashi.

In his exposition, Musashi does not give a concrete description of the situation but confines himself to saying, "Although you may not necessarily be able to attack first, it is preferable to try to force your opponent to move through your initiative." The point here is to lead your opponent into a situation in which he is vulnerable. To do this, you must provoke a situation in which there is a lag between his will to attack and his actual movement of attack, and as a result of this, an absence of attention for his own defense. It is equally possible to accomplish this by putting him into a state of confusion in which his will to attack stagnates.

On the basis of this principle, let us analyze the *sen-go no sen,* which is the source of the greatest difficulties and confusion on the part of practitioners. *Sen* signifies that you must seize the initiative of attack. *Go no sen* means taking the initiative by acting after the adversary does. This expression is often used to designate a parry made with a counterattack already in mind. Hence the difficulty in interpreting the expression.

As Chiba Shusaku said, the complexity of this strategy is illusory. It is enough to understand that it refers to an application of *sen* to the situation of *go no sen*. Here is my analysis of this:

You attack first when you perceive a moment of vulnerability in the adversary, and then he parries your attack. But you launched this attack thinking that it had little chance of succeeding, and your main purpose was to provoke a counterattack. At the moment when your opponent counterattacks, you take advantage of the lag already described to strike him with a decisive attack. Another possibility is to allow him to attack, to parry this expected attack, and then to counterattack in a decisive fashion.

In these exchanges of technique, the subtlety relates to the parry. The one who seizes the *sen* is the one who is capable of detecting or provoking the lag in the attention of the other. In the sequence of attack/parry/counterattack, either your attention is held by your parry or you parry having detected the gap in the attention of your adversary. You can then counterattack with certainty. Thus an analysis that takes into account only a sequence of movements is insufficient to explain *sen*. If such an analysis is too complex, it only mixes things up further. If you succeed in perceiving how gaps occur as a result of lags between the will to attack and the actual movement, the explanation is clear.

APPENDIX 3

EXTERNAL INFLUENCES ON THE JAPANESE ART OF THE SWORD

IN THE PERIOD when the West began to take an interest in Asia, Japan also began to become aware of the external world. Starting from the thirteenth century, Japanese smugglers and pirates began to plunder the Korean coastline. The Chinese called them *wako,* which means "the Japanese thieves (pirates)." The Chinese Empire under the Mongols established the Yuan dynasty with its seat at Daidu (today Beijing) in 1271. In order to get rid of the *wako* once and for all, on the one hand, and to conquer Japan, on the other, the Mongols twice sent out massive military fleets (1274 and 1281).

The Japanese warriors encountered notable difficulties in their engagements with the Mongols, who used weapons and strategy that were unfamiliar to them, particularly firearms. In October 1274, on the eve of the decisive assault, the Mongol force was driven back by violent winds, rain, and turbulent seas. The Mongols tried for a second time in 1281, but as in their previous attempt, at the end of the month of July, on the eve of their attack, 80 percent of the Mongol forces perished in a typhoon. Even though the Japanese warriors were resolved to fight to the end, their victory was mainly due to the elements. The wind that blew the attacking force away was considered a divine intervention and called *kamikaze,* "divine wind." This idea was revived some six centuries later at the time of the national crisis brought on by the Second World War.

The strategy and weaponry of the Mongols went far beyond what the Japanese military was accustomed to coping with, and the Mongols employed them with devastating effect. The damage was particularly heavy in the southern regions of Japan that were exposed to direct attack.

The depredations of the Mongols had the effect of increasing piracy; the Japanese pirates began heavily raiding the Korean coast, and by the fourteenth century this became significant. Between 1375 and 1388, the southern Korean coast suffered more than four hundred attacks from Japanese pirates, and this was a direct cause of the downfall of the Koryo dynasty. The pirates expanded their activities as far as the Chinese coast. Starting in the fifteenth century, piracy became progressively mixed up with the commercial activities of smugglers along the coasts of China and other countries of southern Asia. The feudal lords of the south of Japan profited from this commerce through complex relations they maintained with the smugglers and pirates. (97, pp. 160–168) The amount of trade that fell under the protection of the feudal lords was directly proportional to the intensity of pirate activity. There was thus a clear complicity between the two.

The Ming dynasty suffered from the invasions of the *wako,* and General Qi Jiguang (1528–1587) was given the responsibility of subduing them. According to Matsuda Ryuchi:

> Qi Jiguang was given the responsibility of subduing the *wako*. First he analyzed their techniques, and then he undertook a survey covering the whole of China of the different martial arts that were practiced there, such as boxing, methods of fighting with the sword, the staff, the lance. . . . He made a classification based on the results of his survey and, in 1584, published a treatise entitled *Ji xiao xin shu*. Qi Jiguang developed effective combat techniques based on the results of his survey and supervised the training of three thousand select troops. He succeeded in driving the *wako* away. . . .
>
> Among the Chinese martial arts, there still exists today, under the name *shuang shou dao,* a transmission of techniques for the sword developed by Qi Jiguang to fight the *wako*. The idea was to use two swords that were finer and lighter than the normal swords of the period. This transmission is still extant in the north of China. (117, pp. 52–53)

Here is a passage from the *Ji xiao xin shu* (124), translated from the Japanese transcription of Matsuda Ryuchi:

> We became aware for the first time of the art of the long sword of the *wako* at the time of their invasion. They move about leaping with their long swords, which throws our soldiers into confusion. The *wako* are so nimble at leaping forward to attack that they can cover more than three meters at a single bound. Since they wield swords of a meter and a half in length, that adds up to a penetration of four and a half meters with a single movement. A lot of our soldiers were cut down with the first blow, since their swords are short, and

when they carry a long weapon, they do not manage to move about quickly. (117, p. 53)

Still according to Matsuda Ryuchi, in 1621 in China Mao Yuanyi published an encyclopedia of the martial arts entitled *Wu bei zhi,* which was the result of fifteen years of work and contained a classification of two thousand documents. According to Watanuki Kiyoshi (32, pp. 29–31), the *Wu bei zhi* contains a reproduction of a Japanese scroll on the transmission of the Kage ryu of swordsmanship, illustrated with images of monkeys wielding swords. Mao Yuanyi indicated that this scroll had been lost by a *wako* during a battle against the army of General Qi Jiguang and that it had been handed over to the general. It is possible that Qi Jiguang used this document to develop the techniques he used against the *wako.*

Aisu Ikosai (1441–1538), the founder of one of the two branches of the Kage ryu, was a pirate in his youth. Legend recounts that he traveled to the Chinese coast several times and accumulated experience in combat there. In 1478, at the age of thirty-six, as he was meditating in a cave in the south of Japan, he had a vision that became the basis for the foundation of his school. (32)

We may thus surmise that if the Chinese developed a combat art drawing on their experience in fighting the Japanese, the Japanese also developed their art drawing on their experience in fighting the Chinese, whereas their experience of fighting the Mongols apparently provoked the Japanese neither to examine nor to study the combat technology of their adversary.

The rifle was introduced into Japan by the Portuguese in 1543. It should be noted that this was not only the time when the Portuguese reached Japan but also the time that the Japanese reached various countries of southern Asia. The road to Japan was in some sense opened by the *wako* and the smuggling trade. Once guns were introduced, manufacture of them quickly followed. This was greatly facilitated by the existing technique for the forging of swords. Guns spread rapidly among the feudal lords, which had the effect of radically transforming the organization of the military as well as strategy and the construction of fortresses.

NOTES

Introduction

1. Ancient Japanese works were written on long pieces of paper arranged as scrolls. These were progressively unrolled and rolled as they were written or read through. Each scroll was conceived of as a complete entity, either a work in itself or a chapter.

Part 1: Introduction to the Life of Musashi

1. Let us recall that in the traditional Japanese system, a person is considered to be one year old at the time of his birth and two years old at the time of the New Year. Therefore, depending on the month of the birth, there could be a discrepancy of one or two years in relation to our present system. To make matters easier for the reader, I have attempted in my own text to adjust the dates to fit the current system. However, in the translation of historical documents, I have kept the figure that appears in them, and this explains the systematic discrepancy of one or two years.

Chapter 1: Childhood and Training

1. Tominaga Kengo bases his point of view that Munisai, Musashi's father, remained alive after 1590 on three documentary references:

   1. In a passage from the *Hyoho senshi denki,* we read: "The master was born in the twelfth year of the Tensho era (1584) in the fief of Banshu. Bennosuke was his childhood name. His father Muninosuke was a sword adept. . . . One day, when he was nine years old . . . Muninosuke flew into a temper and drove him out of the house. At this time, Muninosuke's younger brother was a monk in a nearby temple. The master went there and the monk raised him." (9)
   According to this passage, Munisai would have lived at least until 1593.
   2. The *Tosakushi* reports an event involving Muninosuke dated 1589. If Musashi was born in 1584, he would have been five then.

In 1589 Lord Shinmen ordered Munisai to kill Honiden Gekinosuke, one of his principal vassals, whom he accused of having insulted him. Munisai asked the lord to change his mind, especially since he knew Gekinosuke to be a man of sincerity, and also because he was his student in strategy. But Sokan held to his decision. Munisai had no choice but to accept his lord's command. Once he accepted the mission, he had to succeed in it and devise a tactic. Gekinosuke, who was twenty-nine years old, was strong and Munisai was already old; therefore he had to trick him.

He sent a messenger to Gekinosuke asking him to come to his house the following day, because he wanted to transmit to him the ultimate teaching of his school. Gekinosuke came, quite happy. Beforehand, Munisai had asked the monk Nakatsukasa, his close friend, to give him a hand in accomplishing his mission. The monk accepted.

Gekinosuke arrived. Munisai received him with tea and cakes; then he had him served some sake. After a while, Gekinosuke requested him to give him the ultimate teaching as promised.

"Let's go into the other room," said Munisai and went in first.

Gekinosuke followed him. Munisai then said, "Swords are in the way when it comes to studying technique."

So Gekinosuke removed his swords, and when he put them down in front of the entrance to the room, Munisai took his hands and twisted them strongly.

Gekinosuke, thinking that he was beginning the technical transmission, confined himself to saying, "You're hurting me."

Then Munisai said, "I'm killing you, on the lord's command."

While Gekinosuke, surprised, struggled with his unusual strength to get free, the monk Nakatsukasa stabbed him in the chest with a lance and turned it two or three times. Then Munisai cut his head off. He presented Gekinosuke's head to Sokan. The latter, satisfied, congratulated him. (12)

3. Tominaga Kengo puts forward the hypothesis that Munisai left the village of Miyamoto shortly after killing Gekinosuke and that he lived at least until the eleventh year of Keicho (1607). As proof, he educes the signature on the certificate of transmission that Munisai conferred on one of his students. (8, 12) This certificate ends with the following text:

The certificate of transmission of the Tori ryu . . .

The best in Japan *(tenka muso)*

Miyamoto Muninosuke

The twelfth year of Keicho [1607]

The fifth of the ninth month, Fujiwara Kazusane (signature)
To the Honorable Tomooka Kanjuro

In conformity with the custom of the period, Munisai sometimes uses the name Muni, sometimes Muninosuke, depending on which fits the situation. Fujiwara Kazusane is Munisai's genealogical name. This is comparable to Musashi's rendering of his name in the *Gorin no sho,* where he writes: "I am a warrior, a native of Harima, named Shinmen Musashi no kami Fujiwara Genshin, age sixty."

In addition, there are two other, earlier certificates of transmission conferred by Munisai, which show a great similarity to this one. One certificate is preserved in the Hozanji temple in Ikoma, Yamamoto province (Nara):

Certificate of transmission of the Tori ryu . . .
Miyamoto Muninosuke
The auspicious day of the eleventh month of the second year of Keicho [1597]
To the Honorable Okuda Tozaemon

The other certificate has been preserved by the Yamuba family, formerly Hosokawa vassals:

Certificate of transmission of the Jitte tori ryu of the sword . . .
Founder, the best in Japan *(tenka muso)*
Miyamoto Munisai
Fujiwara Kazusane (signature)
To Mr. Mizuta Moemon
The twenty-fourth of the season of the yellow prune tree (spring), the third
    year of Keicho [1598],
the fifth of the ninth month, Fujiwara Kazusane (signature)

So, if Munisai, who was in his sixties, was driven out of the village of Miyamoto by the hostile atmosphere created by the vassals of the Honiden family, where did he go?

The certificate of transmission that Munisai conferred on Tomooka Kanjuro was preserved by the family of a Hosokawa vassal. Let us note that Musashi lived several times in this fief and spent the last years of his life there.

I would like to suggest the hypothesis that Munisai had a significant relationship with the Hosokawa vassals before the Hosokawa family was transplanted to Kyushu. Before 1600 Hosokawa was the governor of the Tango region (Fukui prefecture), which is not far from the fief of Mimasaka. Did Munisai have students in this fief? It is possible that he traveled to the neighboring regions and had students in different fiefs. In 1600 the fief of Hosokawa was transferred to Kyushu. Munisai could have followed this lord to Kyushu and continued to teach his art there. If this hypothesis is true, Musashi would have had an opportunity to receive instruction in the familial art under his father's supervision.

2. We may cite Funabiki Yoshio: "Takeuchi Nakatsukasa Taiho Hisamori was the lord of Ichinose castle in the Kume region. He had been driven out of this castle once and later retook it. When he was driven out of the castle, he joined the Shinmen clan. He founded the Takeuchi school." (7)

3. The art of the *shuriken* continues to be handed down. Here is a translation of some passages in an article by Shiragami Ikkuken, principal master of the Shirai ryu, which had its origin in the art of Musashi:

> Starting December 1, 1943, a system for recruiting students for the Military School was implemented by all the universities of Japan. . . . At this time young people were resigned to losing their lives by the age of twenty-five. This was reflected in the expression "Life is but twenty-five years." The youths of this time did not think their lot was regrettable. I thought I was going to die soon, but I wanted to put to use all the ability I had acquired in the art of the *shuriken* before I died. . . .
>
> Two weeks before I was to enter Military School, I visited the dojo of my teacher, Naruse Kanji. After giving me a final lesson, just for me alone, the master sat down in the middle of the dojo and said: "You are going to leave soon for the war. I will now teach you the most secret teaching of my school, which is called *kani me no daiji* (the essence of the eyes of a crab).
>
> This expression sounded strange to my ears. I wondered, "What relationship is there between the art of the *shuriken* and the eyes of a crab?"
>
> "So here is that instruction. When, face-to-face with an opponent, you judge that the last moment has come, go forward until the point of your adversary's sword can touch your left hand and look into his two eyes with the whole force of your mind. If at this moment his eyes seem to pop out like those of a crab, throw your *shuriken* at the pupil of one of his eyes. Your victory will be sure. If you do not see his pupils, this is the moment of your death. In that case, you do not throw the *shuriken,* and you must throw yourself at your opponent holding a *shuriken* in each hand in order to pierce his eyes. You will die with your opponent. That is "the essence of the eyes of the crab."
>
> My master, Tonegawa Magoroku, told me: "To be able to realize 'the essence of the eyes of a crab,' you have to have gone through a lot of bloody training; only then can you be certain at a distance of three paces from your adversary about something that you ordinarily practice with confidence at a distance of ten or twenty paces. Do not forget that a water jet that shoots up in a garden has its source in the distant mountains. If you are capable of hitting

a face without fail from ten paces away, you will be able to strike between the eyes at a distance of three paces.

Speaking thus, he presented to me his two favorite *shuriken*. I recall with emotion this last teaching of my master: "When you are committed to throwing the *shuriken,* you hold it in your hands and you yourself become a *shuriken* that will fly into the body of the adversary and die with him." (57)

Chapter 3: Deepening the Way

1. One *koku* corresponded to 180 liters of rice. The income of a warrior was measured by the amount of rice produced by the lands placed under his charge.

2. This way of doing things allowed the Yagyu school to develop quantitatively at the cost of a deterioration in its level of practice. Later on the Yagyu school of Edo developed this tendency, while the Yagyu school of Owari (Nagoya) preserved its traditional stringency. Thus there arose a difference in the quality and level of the Edo and Owari branches of the same school. Yagyu Jubei, Yagyu Munenori's eldest son, wrote in the *Tsuki no sho:*

> My father Munenori used to say that he could teach all his knowledge to his own lord, to his children, to people of great virtue [meaning the rich], and to those with great perseverance. Teaching the totality of the art to those persons is not a problem. If I say that I teach those who pay well, some people will say that I am greedy, but those who study and pay a good price for it never become our enemies, and it will be difficult to get them to divulge the secrets of the school. It is necessary to pay gold for teaching. (9, p. 61)

Chapter 4: "Writings on the Five Elements" *(Gorin no sho)*

1. Even the translation of the title poses a problem. It is written *Gorin sho,* but the custom has been established of reading it *Gorin no sho. Go* means "five," *sho* means "writing"; but translating the term *rin* is more difficult. The Japanese dictionary (99) gives for the meaning of *rin:* "rounded form," "circle," "ring," "wheel," "fully open flower." The underlying idea comes from Buddhist thought. In the same dictionary, for the expression *gorin,* the following explanation is given: *go* is a simplification of *godai,* "the five elements that constitute the universe"; *rin* means "the acquisition of all the virtues." The universe is composed of five elements: earth, water, fire, wind, and heaven or space. Each one of these possesses a complete abundance of virtues, expressed by a perfectly completed circle, with the rounded form symbolizing perfect unity.

The work is composed of five scrolls, each of which bears the name of one of the elements. Neither the word *circle* nor the word *ring* is satisfactory, because the image providing a figurative representation for either of these words *(gorin soto ba)* is composed of a stack of trimmed stones: a square one for the earth, a spherical one for water, one in the shape of a truncated cone for fire, the section of a sphere for wind, and a stone in the shape of a lotus bud for heaven. I have elected to use the word *element*, which corresponds to the general idea but is not completely satisfactory either, because it does not do justice to the idea of perfect unity.

2. Niten ichi ryu: *ni*, "two"; *ten*, "heaven, universe"; *ichi*, "one"; *ryu*, "school." *Niten* has several senses:

   1. Two heavens.
   2. The two heavenly bodies, or the moon god and the sun god.
   3. Another heaven or another universe that is contrasted with the natural heaven or universe in the following sense: When someone receives a very great favor from a person, that person is considered as a heaven or a universe. (99, 100)

We could translate the name literally as "School of Two Heavenly Bodies United" or "School of Two Heavens United." In the *Gorin no sho*, Musashi designates his school by this name only twice. He usually uses *Nito ichi ryu*. Instead of *ten*, "heaven," he uses *to*, which means sword, which I have translated as "School of Two Swords." A more literal translation would be "School of the Unity of Two Swords," but this overly long formulation loses the conciseness of the Japanese expression.

The term *niten* evokes two images. We can understand *niten* as a contraction in which the idea of *to*, "sword," is implicit, and this expression then yields the idea of two swords raised toward the sky—or else the two swords, the long and the short, raised toward the sky—symbolizing the two heavenly bodies, or the sun god and the moon god.

Later on, the expression Niten-sama *(sama* means "lord") was used as a name for Musashi by his admirers.

3. "Way of strategy": *hyoho no michi*.

4. The province of Higo corresponds roughly to the present-day prefecture of Kumamoto.

5. The name of Musashi's father was very likely Hirata Munisai. He was one of the principal vassals of a minor feudal lord of the mountainous region of Sakushu, west of Kyoto. He was a practitioner of the sword and the *jitte*, a small metal weapon with six hooks on it with which it was possible to parry a sword and potentially immobilize it for a moment. (See pages xxxii and 8).

6. The province of Harima corresponds to a part of the present-day prefecture of Hyogo.

7. As far as Musashi's year of birth is concerned, opinions are divided between 1582 and 1584. I have adopted the second date, which seems the more trustworthy (see page 7).

8. The province of Tajima corresponds to the current prefecture of Hyogo.

9. Certain duels Musashi fought have remained famous. One of the best known is that in which, all alone, he opposed the adepts of the Yoshioka dojo, one of the most famous of the eight schools of Kyoto. After successively vanquishing the two principal masters of the school in individual combat, Musashi confronted the entire group of the school's practitioners by himself. His victory over the Yoshioka dojo began to solidly establish Musashi's reputation. This combat took place in 1604; Musashi was then twenty years old. At the age of twenty-one, one year after this combat, Musashi wrote "The Mirror of the Way of Strategy" *(Hyodokyo),* which is composed of twenty-eight instructions on strategy. This shows that from the time of his youth he was trying to arrive at a kind of written synthesis of his art. We find in that work a section whose title ("When One Is Fighting against Several Adversaries") recalls this fight against the Yoshioka dojo.

10. Musashi recognized when he was about thirty that despite all the victories he had won up to that point, he had not attained the ultimate level of his art. These victories were only relative ones, since accidental elements—chance, the inadequacy of his opponents, and so forth—were factors in them. For twenty more years he sought after the immutable essence of his art, and it was not until he was around fifty that he believed he had reached a satisfactory state of insight. He expressed this in a poem, as follows:

> I penetrated so deeply into the mountains in my quest,
> Now here I am, come out the other side, so close to human beings.

11. Four-thirty in the morning.

12. "Warrior families," *buke:* This word literally means "family" or "clan," the *ke* of a warrior, *bu.* Here the term is used to refer to the class of warriors in the context of the education that is appropriate for this social group. The term *ke* is also pronounced *ie* and means "house," "family," and also "clan." Here, by an extension of the sense of "clan," it designates the class of warriors. The terms *bushi,* "warriors" or "samurai," and *buke* should be distinguished.

13. *Suki mono* or *suki sha:* from *suki,* "art of living that includes the art of tea," and *mono* or *sha,* "man." This term is no longer in use today.

14. This sentence, like one that comes a bit further on ("Without learning how to handle weapons, without knowing the advantages of each of them, a warrior is lacking somewhat in education") has a tone that is critical toward the warriors of the time. In Musashi's eyes, very few warriors seem to have been worthy of the name. Musashi declared in a previous paragraph, "But very few like the way of strategy." Thus the practice of strategy does not seem to have been easy, even for warriors of this period.

Musashi's attitude will become clearer and clearer as we advance in the *Gorin no sho*. He is trying to find, by means of what he calls *hyoho*, "strategy," a pragmatic approach that is generally applicable. But his pragmatism is not a technique in the Western sense of the term. There is no mind/technique duality. For Musashi, technique is not distinct from mind. Thus mind must be sought for in technique, and the principle of effectiveness is always included in the essential logic of technique. Musashi considers the *hyoho* he practices to be a great principle applicable to all phenomena. He is himself his techniques; the man becomes one with the techniques he applies. Each of the arts can become a path in life if it is understood as a way.

This manner of thinking was reinforced and refined during the Edo period (1603–1867), when Japanese society cut itself off almost entirely from the outside world. Japan fell back on itself and developed a society in which various cultural models came together in their movement toward refinement and formalization. It is only in societies of this type that it is possible to conceive of a principle that is valid for all phenomena, such as the one sought by Musashi.

15. Kantori is presently called Katori and is located in Chiba prefecture. The shrine of Katori is dedicated to Futsunushi no kami, a god of war. (100)

"Kashima" refers to the shrine of Kashima, located in Ibaraki prefecture. According to the *Kojiki* (122, pp. 65–70), Takemikazuchi no Mikoto conquered the country of Ashihara no nakatsu kuni at the command of the goddess Amaterasu. The Kashima shrine is dedicated mainly to Takemikazuchi, a god of war. Hitachi was an ancient province that corresponded to parts of the two present-day prefectures of Chiba and Ibaraki.

When the *sakimori*, soldiers of eastern Japan, moved down into Kyushu to defend it from the invasion of the Koreans and the Chinese, they went to pray to the god of the Kashima shrine. This ritual at the shrine, which was called *kashima dachi*, became established as a custom in the seventh century. Use of the ritual in connection with the recruitment of *sakimori* was abandoned at the beginning of the tenth century, but the cult of the war god of the Kashima shrine continued. It took on greater importance beginning in the Kamakura era, especially for warriors of eastern Japan. The town of Kashima developed along with the shrine.

The two shrines of Katori and Kashima are located on opposite banks of the Tone river. The water god, the god of the river, and the god of the tides are also venerated there. As far as the practice and culture of the martial arts are concerned, the traditions of the two shrines go back to mythological times. Beginning in the fourteenth century, several schools of swordsmanship were founded by priests of these shrines.

The oldest known of these schools was founded by Iizasa Choisai Ienao, a warrior attached to the Katori shrine. (1-b, 1-c, 32, 42) Choisai was experienced in battle and the study of the sword and lived at the Katori shrine while striving to perfect his swordsmanship. He prayed to the war god of the shrine from morning till night and trained with his sword against the trees. At the end of three years of solitary exploration, he received a revelation from the war god and founded the school of the sword known as Tenshi shoden Katori shinto ryu. This school is presently called Shinto ryu. Iizasa Choisai died at the age of a hundred on the fifteenth of the fourth month of the second year of Chokyo (1488).

The school of swordsmanship called Kashima shin ryu or Kashima shin kage ryu was founded by Matsumoto Bizen no kami Masabobu (1468–1524), a student of Iizasa Choisai. The Matsumoto family had been priests of the Shinto shrine of Kashima for generations. Here in brief is the story of Matsumoto Bizen (15, pp. 9–18; 32, pp. 23–29; 42, pp. 276–292) and his student Bokuden (32) as recounted in various chronicles and legends:

Starting from the teachings of Iizasa Choisai, Matsumoto Bizen developed techniques for various weapons, such as the lance, the *naginata,* and the staff. He transmitted the ultimate technique of his school under the name *hitotsu no tachi,* "the single sword." He fought with the lance on the battlefield twenty-three times and killed and beheaded twenty-five famous feudal lords and seventy-six ordinary warriors. He died on the battlefield at the age of fifty-seven.

Matsumoto Bizen transmitted the *hitotsu no tachi* to Tsukahara Bokuden Takamoto (1489–1571), also the son of a family of priests of the Kashima shrine. Having received the teaching of Matsumoto Bizen, Bokuden studied the art of the Katori shinto ryu with his father. In 1505, at the age of seventeen, he fought his first duel with a real sword and killed his opponent. After this he fought nineteen duels and participated in thirty-seven battles. He was wounded only by arrows, six times. The number of enemies he killed reached 212.

He secluded himself in the Kashima shrine for a thousand days and received a revelation related to the art of the sword. Then, with the teachings of Matsumoto Bizen as a basis, he founded the Shinto ryu, whose technique is a revitalized form of the *hitotsu no tachi.* Bokuden traveled through various regions in the course of three journeys, during which he met adepts of various schools and transmitted and spread the art of his own school. Here is a passage from the *Koyo gunkan* recounting his first journey: "On the journey he took to improve his understanding of strategy, Tsukahara Bokuden traveled on horseback with three spare horses, taking along with him three hunting falcons. Eighty men made up his retinue. Thus, with regard to his study of strategy, lords as well as accomplished adepts treated him with respect. Bokuden was a real adept of the art of the sword." (15, p. 10; 32 p. 24)

In Kyoto Bokuden taught his art of swordsmanship to three Ashikaga shoguns in succession: Yoshiharu (1511–1550), Yoshiteru (1536–1565), and Yoshiaki (1537–1597).

Within the Katori and Kashima traditions, the lineage of Iizasa Choisai, Matsumoto Bizen, and Tsukahara Bokuden Takamoto is the best known. (1-b, 1-c, 15, 32, 42)

The techniques of the schools of swordsmanship that issued from this tradition are forceful and simple, since they were intended to be used on the field of battle, where warriors fought in armor.

In his text Musashi seems to be making an allusion to the manner in which Tsukahara Bokuden propagated his school.

Musashi also wrote that Arima Kihei, his first opponent in a duel, was a practitioner of the Shinto ryu, founded by Tsukahara Bokuden.

16. "The ten talents and the seven arts," *ju no shichi gei:* According to the dictionary (100), *no* and *gei* have the following meanings:

No: (1) The ability to accomplish things; (2) a person who has a talent or who has accomplished things; (3) the technique of an art, ability for technique; (4) effectiveness; (5) Noh theater.

Gei: (1) The technique or the knowledge acquired in a martial science or art; arts, crafts; (2) game technique; (3) technique, work.

17. "Pragmatic domain," *rikata:* Literally, *ri* means (1) trenchant, very sharp; (2) convenient; (3) effective, useful; (4) the terrain is excellent; (5) victory; (6) interest, advantage, gain. *Kata* means "direction," "position," "domain," "means." Thus *rikata* refers to a domain that creates an interest or an advantage and therefore has a concrete usefulness.

18. "The principles," *ri:* Musashi frequently uses the word *ri* in the sense of principle or reason (see appendix 1).

"The sword": *kenjutsu* literally means "techniques of the sword," hence "the sword," "the art of the sword," or "swordsmanship."

19. During Musashi's time, encounters between schools of the sword were for the most part battles fought without mercy, and taking matters lightly or having the illusion of knowledge could result in death. Thus he recommends not pausing over what is not essential. Musashi's own difficulties show through behind this remark—he never obtained a position of responsibility from a great lord commensurate with the abilities he considered himself to possess.

20. "Four ways": The description of the four ways—warrior, *shi;* peasant, *no;* artisan, *ko;* and merchant, *sho*—does not follow the hierarchical order. This might seem a bit incoherent, but it is doubtless connected with the movement of thought preparing the comparison between the *bushi* and the carpenter.

During the Tensho era (1573–1592), in institutionalizing the existing social hierarchy, Toyotomi Hideyoshi established four feudal classes or orders. This system was reinforced by the Tokugawa regime. Its principal aim was to guarantee the power of the governing class of warriors, which henceforth possessed a monopoly on weapons and benefited from various privileges. Above them, but without effective power, were the nobles who surrounded the emperor. Below these four classes, two other classes existed: *eta* and *himin,* which were considered nonhuman. The *eta* performed various impure manual tasks, notably work with animal skins. The *himin* were beggars and at the same time did work connected with the transport and cleaning of corpses.

The feudal classes were abolished in the Meiji era, but they were replaced by new social classes: *kazoku* (new nobles), *shizoku* (former warriors), and *heimin* (ordinary people). This social classification was abolished by the constitution after the Second World War. But the problem of the *eta* and the *himin* was not resolved in a satisfactory manner. Today tenacious social discrimination against the former *eta* and *himin* still exists, even though these classes no longer exist from a legislative point of view.

"For traversing human life," *hito no yo o wataru koto:* To evoke the situation of human life, Musashi uses the image of a ship crossing. He uses this image again in the Scroll of Fire.

21. *Toku* is most often translated as "virtue" (see appendix 1), but it also has the sense of "richness." In this passage, *toku* seems to draw on this second set of meanings and indicate the particular qualities, the richness, hidden in each weapon.

22. "Black cords," *sumigane: sumi,* "ink"; *gane* or *kane,* "ruler."

23. "Noble house," *kuge: ku,* "the emperor's court"; *ge,* "house." This refers to the social system of vassalage. "Warrior house," *buke: bu,* "military person," *ke,* the same meaning as *ge.*

In order to understand Musashi's comparison, it should be explained that in Japanese, the same term refers both to the house as a building and to the family that occupies it. The corresponding ideogram is pronounced *ie* when it is alone and *ke* or *ge* when it is combined with another word. For Japanese thought this is not merely a verbal matter but also expresses the profound sense of identity that exists among members of a family and also solidarity among members of a family down through successive generations, both of these being given material expression in the sheltering form of the house. This notion can be expanded to the level of the clan, which is conceived of as a large family, and can then extend beyond that to the solidarity among clans composing the social class of warriors.

Another extension of the term allows it to designate a school of a traditional art; for here, too, the mode of transmission of the school was based mainly on the system of house and family. The relations between the master and his disciples were patterned on the model of the family relationship of father to children. The system of adoption was often utilized to perpetuate the family name that was linked with the knowledge transmitted by a school in a hereditary fashion. The point was for the head of the family to be able to perpetuate his art and perhaps also direct the school. This tendency became more pronounced with time.

Musashi, for his part, maintained the continuity of his family through adoption, but his school was perpetuated independently of his name. It was often the case during the Edo period, and is still often the case today, that when the leadership of a school is determined by family inheritance, the quality of the school declines. What happens in these cases is that the disciple who takes over the succession is not necessarily the best one but the one best placed within the family.

24. "The Four Houses," *shike: shi,* "four"; *ke,* "house" or "family."

Several interpretations of Musashi's use of the word *shike* are possible. The word could refer either to the four Fujiwara families or to the four schools of the tea ceremony; or else it alludes to both of them. In the first sense, *shike* is an abbreviation of Fujiwara *shike* (the four Fujiwara families), which refers to the four main Fujiwara families of the eighth century. The Fujiwara family exercised a very great influence on imperial policy at that time. This family began its rise to importance at the end of the seventh century. After that it divided into numerous branches, some of which were to play an important role in the history of Japan.

The term *shike* can also refer to the four schools of *cha no yu* or *sa do* (tea ceremony). The four schools are the Omote senke, Ura senke, Mushanokoji senke, and Yabunouchike senke.

I have opted for the first interpretation, based on the first paragraph of the introduction to the *Gorin no sho,* where Musashi gives his name as Shinmen Musashi no kami, Fujiwara no Genshin. The family name taken by a *bushi* was, as Musashi's name indicates, a composite form, and often one of the names it included was a reference to a more-distant clan than the one with which he was immediately connected. Inclusion of this more-distant clan served to link the individual with the period of the emergence of the *bushi* in Japanese history. In using this name, Musashi was indicating a remote derivation of his family line from the Fujiwara clan.

The other name he used, Shinmen, was that of the feudal lord of whom his family had been vassals for several generations; this is a name Musashi's family would have received authorization to use. Musashi used this name when he wanted to clarify his line of descent. The name Miyamoto does not appear here. This was the name of the village where he spent his youth, and it was not necessary to include it in his official name. Genshin is the Buddhist name that he chose as a participant in that spiritual path. The ideograms composing it can also be pronounced Masanobu. Masana would have been a childhood name.

For a *bushi,* genealogy was of major importance. A sense of honor was always attached to the family name. Although the choice of name was sometimes a matter of circumstance and was flexible, once it was determined, a *bushi* lived and died by his name.

25. "School," *ryu:* "Style," *fu,* can also be read *kaze,* "wind." "House" is *ie.*

26. "In this way the chief carpenter": In Japanese, there are two different ideograms that are pronounced *toryo.*

Toryo: (1) post, beam; (2) he who is in charge of a country; (3) chief; (4) master carpenter.

Toryo: (1) ruling all things; (2) he who rules and directs, presides. (100)

Musashi uses the second ideogram to refer to the chief carpenter as well as the chief warrior, thus stressing the comparison. That is why, in this passage, I translated as "chief carpenter" and not "master carpenter," as in the rest of the text.

I translated as "resemble each other" the expression *onaji,* which literally means "the same, identical."

27. Shoji: sliding screens made of stretched, translucent paper.

28. *Tokonoma, toku mawari:* architectural feature at the rear of the main room.

29. "Being vigilant with regard to the surroundings," *monogoto o yurusazaru kato: yurusazaru* is used in the sense of *ki o yurusanai,* "not relaxing one's attention and going into detail."

30. "Knowing substance and its function": *taiyu o shiru.* Musashi writes it *tai yu,* in hiragana.

Authors offering commentaries on the *Gorin no sho* are of different opinions on the interpretation of this term, for which four transcriptions into ideograms are possible with the following meanings:

1. "Great courage" or "courage manifested in the accomplishment of an important thing." (10)
2. "Function, effect, use." (13)
3. "Essential point" (11); Kamata (4) retains the hiragana and gives an interpretation in his commentary that fits with that.
4. "Substance and its application" (Buddhist term).

Musashi's contemporary, Yagyu Munenori, writes: "*Tai yu* exists in each thing; when there is *tai,* there is *yu.* For example, the bow is *tai* and the act of aiming, drawing, and hitting the target is the *yu* of the bow. The lamp is *tai* and the light is *yu.* . . . The sword is *tai;* slashing and stabbing is *yu.* Thus the essence derives from *tai,* and that which arises from the essence and moves toward the outside in order to accomplish different functions is *yu.*" (56, p. 102)

Yagyu Munenori developed a theory of the art of the sword based on the practice of Zen. Musashi also practiced Zen; that is why, in view of Yagyu Munenori's interpretation, I based my translation on the fourth sense of the term.

31. "Ambient energy": I translated the term *ki,* which means "air," "ambience," "vital energy," this way in order to try to preserve the play on the two aspects of the term's meaning.

32. Musashi could in fact have been a carpenter and even a master of this discipline. In the course of his life, he handcrafted works of art as well as weapons and objects of daily usage for a warrior. His wood sculptures and his paintings are well known, but he made a great number of ordinary objects whose qualities are also highly esteemed: wooden swords *(bokken),* saddles, *tsuba* (sword hilts), metal *hunchin* (paperweights for Chinese ink calligraphies), and so on.

The modern separation of art from handcraft did not exist for Musashi. He was an artist and artisan at the same time. At the time of his duel with Sasaki Kojiro, it is said that he made a wooden sword from an oar just before the bout. Later on, when one of his patrons asked him, "What was the *bokken* like that you used to fight against Kojiro?" by way of answer, Musashi readily made on the spot a *bokken* of 127 centimeters in length. This *bokken* is still preserved today. (11, p. 37)

33. Musashi writes this *mendo. Mendo* or *medo* refers to "long external corridors." In the construction of this period, long, raised external corridors linked buildings. To make it possible to enter inner courtyards on horseback, it was sometimes necessary to provide passageways by having a corridor that could be raised in the manner of a drawbridge. This is what was called a *kiri medo* or *medo.* Later on this term came to refer to the long corridors. (99)

Mendo, written in another way, means "problem of detail." The ideogram is derived from the one for the term above. The business of getting the horses by the *medo* was a source of problems, hence the emergence of this second sense, which is more common today. (100) I kept the first interpretation because it fit with the logic of the comparison of strategic qualities to the work of a carpenter.

34. This arrangement might seem puzzling from the point of view of Western logic. It does not have anything to do with an analysis of the techniques. It reflects something that is much more important for Musashi: the state of mind that must dominate

each phase of progress along the way. In truth, for Musashi, swordsmanship is not merely a matter of technique but rather—as we have already seen—a way of life. Nevertheless, in the course of this work, the techniques are described with the greatest precision. For Musashi, man and nature are of the same order, both part of the same cosmic entity; this is what is expressed by the orientation of the Scroll of Water.

The explanation of the meaning of the Scroll of Heaven might cause the reader some confusion. This scroll represents the fruition of the process of the way, that is, emptiness, which is not nothingness but rather the origin of existence.

35. "Principle": *ri.*

36. "Model," *kata,* means "form, prototype" or "model for the plastic arts." It is also the word that designates standardized sequences of movements in the physical arts. A kata in this sense serves at once as an ideal reference point and as a means of transmission of technical knowledge.

37. "Happens in a short time": this idea also refers to urgent situations.

38. The word *wind* has several metaphorical senses. In the common expressions referred to here, different images are evoked. In the reference to the ancient wind and the modern wind, the image is that of fashion. In the expression "the wind of such and such a family," the meaning is "family tradition."

39. "Deviating from the true way": I translated the word *gedo* in this way, which refers to "religions other than Buddhism (for which the word *naido* is used), heresies, dogmas that are in conflict with the truth, an insult."

40. The word *ku* has several senses: "heaven," "sky," "emptiness," and "space" (see appendix 1). In the Scroll of Heaven, Musashi uses it in the full range of its meanings, stressing the sense of emptiness. In the text, after having translated it the first two times as "heaven (or emptiness)," I used one translation or another depending on the nuance that seemed to me to be dominant at that point.

41. "Depth," *oku,* and "surface," *kuchi. Kuchi* literally means "mouth," hence the image of a mouth through which entry is made and thence of an entrance or surface in relation to a depth or core. Usually for the dichotomy of "surface" and "depth," the pair of terms *omote* and *oku* is used.

42. "The principle of the way": *dori.*

43. "High level of ability": *Kidoku,* which today is pronounced *kitoku,* literally means (1) "extraordinary, marvelous, something rare and strange, the fact of particularly excelling, a strange sign, excellent effectiveness, being deserving of praise"; (2) "the strange power of God and of Buddha."

44. Musashi called his school Nito ichi ryu. It is possible to interpret *ichi ryu* simply in the sense of "my school," but in the vocabulary of the martial arts, *ichi* is frequently used with the connotation of unity, the integration of multiple elements. For example, *ichi ban*, "a single occasion"; *ichi nen*, "a single intention"; and *ippon*, whose meaning I describe more precisely below. *Nito* means " two swords." *Ichi* means "one," and *ryu* means "school." To say only "the School of Two Swords," it would be enough to say *nito ryu*. By combining the two words *nito* and *ichi*, Musashi seems to be expressing the state of the *bushi* who knows how to use the two swords as one. Thus the meaning is "School of the Unity of the Two Swords," but so as to stick with a rendering that reflects the concise rhythm of the name of Musashi's school in Japanese, I am reserving mention of this nuance for a note only.

To explain further the sense of *ichi*, I will take the example of the term *ippon* used in all the contemporary Japanese martial arts to indicate a victory. *Ippon* is a contraction of *ichi hon*, *hon* meaning "fundamental" or "essential." In a training session or a tournament, it is customary to count the number of bouts won by each participant. *Ippon* refers to a win obtained through the use of a single technique within a system of conventions where it is recognized that if the particular movement in question had been fully completed outside the conventional system, the opponent would have suffered a blow that would have put him out of combat. In the days when people fought with real swords or with wooden swords, the result of a duel was most often determined by the use of a single decisive technique. During the period of Musashi's youth, the result was death. However, in performing combat exercises within a school, thanks to the conventions that were adopted, the practitioners could engage in combat repeatedly in a series of many bouts. They then counted up the number of victories and defeats in terms of units of *hon (ippon)*. What is sought after in the martial arts is the ideal *ippon*, that is, a victory obtained through a technique that has an integral connection with that which is fundamental to the combat.

45. *Ryo koshi* means "two swords." *Ryo* means "two," and *koshi* is the unit used to count swords.

46. The *naginata* is a weapon with a long handle and a thick, curved blade like that of a scythe.

47. *To no momo: To* is currently pronounced *soto* and means "outside"; *mono* means "weapon." Thus the expression means "weapon meant to be used outside," among other places, on the field of battle.

The ideogram *to* or *soto* is also pronounced *hoka*. In that case the meaning is different: "the realm or world that exists outside the ordinary one; a thing that exists outside normal standards; elsewhere, other than." If we interpret it in this sense, then the sword being the normal weapon of the warrior, the lance and the *naginata* are added on to that. We could then translate: "The lance and the *naginata* are weapons of war additional to the sword."

48. It should be noted here that in Musashi's text, the designation for each of the two swords is not consistent. Sometimes he uses *tachi* and *katana* and sometimes *katana* and *wakizashi*. As he himself explained in the previous paragraph, the two expressions mean "the large sword and the small sword," but *katana* refers to the small sword in the first expression and the large one in the second. In Musashi's time, the names of the swords had not yet become altogether fixed.

49. "It is deplorable to . . . ," *hoie ni aru bekarazu: Hoi* is pronounced *honi* at the present time and means (1) "true mind," "spirit," or "intention" or "intention," "initial intention," "true desire"; (2) true sense, true meaning; (3) that which originally should be, character or manner inherent in a thing.

A literal translation would have been: "It is not in the true spirit to . . . ," but to avoid confusion with the translation of *kokoro*, I decided to avoid the terms *spirit* and *mind*.

50. Clearly there was no idea here of drawing the bow using the left hand alone. What is being talked about is carrying a bow so as to use it at some other moment. It should be noted that in battle, warriors carried several weapons at the same time. In addition to the two swords stuck into the belt on the left side, some warriors carried two or three more on their backs so they could change weapons; and others, as Musashi says, carried a bow, a lance, a *naginata,* and so forth.

51. In spite of what Musashi says, it is extremely difficult to wield a sword easily with just one hand. Even holding a *shinai* (a bamboo practice sword), which is three to four times lighter than a sword, with just one hand, it is difficult to fight with ease.

Nowadays, there are very few practitioners of kendo who use two *shinai*. The difficulty experienced now must have been much greater when practitioners fought with swords in real combat. The fact is that in sword combat, it is not enough merely to swing the weapon, but one must also be able to parry the attacks of an opponent who is using a heavy sword that he is most often holding with two hands and then be able to slash him. It is not possible to evaluate the difficulty involved in this by fighting with *shinai* alone. "It is impossible to use two swords without having the innate strength of Niten-sama" (Sir Niten, or Master Niten, was the title of respect given to Musashi). This is an adage that is often heard in sword circles. To give you an example of Musashi's strength, I cite here a passage from the *Nitenki:*

> One day Lord Nagaoka asked Musashi: "How should bamboo poles for flags be chosen?"
> "Show me the pieces of bamboo you have," replied Musashi.

The Lord had a hundred pieces of bamboo he had ordered for this purpose brought into the garden. Musashi picked up one of the pieces of bamboo, and holding it by the end, made a rapid stroke in the air. He went on to do the same thing with each piece of bamboo. Every one of them broke in half except one, which Musashi gave to the lord, saying, "This one is good."

"That is an absolutely sure way to test them, but it can only be done by you," replied Lord Nagaoka, smiling. (2, p. 181)

52. It might be useful to make clear just how difficult it is to handle a heavy sword. At the present time in kendo, an adult man uses a *shinai* that weighs about 500 grams, a woman one that weighs 420 grams. When practitioners of another discipline, such as karate or judo, use a *shinai* for the first time, they generally have the impression that it is very light. But as they begin to practice kendo, their impression changes very quickly, and they pass through a phase where the *shinai* seems very heavy to them. Practitioners of kendo are very sensitive to the balance and differences in weight of their *shinai,* a difference of 10 or 20 grams being strongly felt. When kendo is practiced using two *shinai (nito),* the large *shinai* weighs about 375 grams and the small one 265. But when doing combat exercises, a *shinai* of 375 grams, held with just one hand, seems very heavy, and very few modern kendo practitioners succeed in handling one one-handed with ease.

The large sword that Musashi talks about weighed between 1,200 and 1,500 grams. Thus it was three to four times heavier than the *shinai* currently used in the *nito* (two *shinai*) combat form.

53. Here I decided to translate *hoi* this way because it seemed to me to have the sense of "initial intention."

54. This sentence explains what the way of strategy means for Musashi. It goes far beyond handling a sword. He makes things that others might seek in religion a part of strategy itself.

One anecdote—perhaps romanticized—tells us that on his way to meet a great number of opponents whom he was supposed to face in a fight in which his chances were very poor, Musashi passed by a Shinto shrine. Suddenly becoming aware that he had started to pray with the intention of asking for the protection of the gods, he straightened up and came to his senses, accusing himself of lacking confidence in his strategy, for he should be trusting his fate only to that. (61) This is the sense in which the phrase of Musashi's found in the *Dokkodo* is usually interpreted: "Respect the Buddha and the gods without relying on their help." In this way he expresses incisively and explicitly a tendency that ordinarily underlies the philosophy of *budo* but is left unspoken. Warriors could be practitioners of different religions, but the religions were more a coloration of the way of the warrior than the other way around.

55. *Hyoho futatsu no ji no ri:* Literally, *ri* means "interest, advantage." Musashi often uses *ri* without distinguishing it from its other meaning, "reason, principle, the logic of things, meaning." Here, in connection with "knowing the *ri* of the two ideograms *hyo* and *ho,*" it seems more plausible that *ri* has more the sense of "meaning" or "principle" than "interest" or "advantage."

56. Musashi uses the term *bugei* to designate the martial arts in general. It is important to note that Musashi makes a point of the demarcation separating *hyoho* from the other terms. That is why I prefer here to indicate the Japanese term he uses each time rather than to translate them all as "martial arts." We have:

> *hyoho sha:* man of *hyoho,* someone who knows how to handle the sword
> *ite:* archer
> *teppo uchi:* someone who shoots a gun
> *yari tsukai:* expert with a lance
> *naginata tsukai:* expert with the *naginata*
> *tachi tsukai:* expert with the long sword
> *wakizashi tsukai:* expert with the short sword

57. "The virtue of the sword," *tachi no toku:* On the meaning of the word *toku,* see page 347. I have translated *toku* as "virtue," but this word can also mean "interest" or "advantage." The nuance of "virtue" seemed to me to be present in the sense in which Musashi employs the term here in relation to the sword.

58. "Persevere": in this sentence Musashi uses the term *migaku,* which means "to polish" and which I have translated "to persevere." Musashi frequently uses the term *migaku* in the sense of "persevere, develop oneself, study in depth," and the like. This expression is frequently used in the realm of the arts.

59. "Appropriately": *ideau* or *deau,* meaning "to meet, to face, to coincide, to adjust to, to suit the situation."

60. "If you compare the two . . . ," *yari wa sente nari, naginata wa ushirode nari:* I rendered Musashi's comparison as I did in view of the following:

- *Sen te* means "precede somebody in an act, do something before someone else, attack before someone else, fight at the head (of a group), take the initiative by attacking first."
- *Ushirode* or *gote* means "the back of a person or a thing." When it is opposed to *sente,* it designates "someone who lags behind, who lets the other take the initiative."

61. The expression *torikomori mono* could also refer to the opposite situation: "when you are attacking one or more enemies who are shut up in a house" or "whom you have encircled and who are on the defensive."

62. "Indoors": This is the translation of *zashiki*. This refers to training taking place in a covered hall. This phrase confirms that in Musashi's time, the quest for technical subtlety began to be a trend. According to Musashi, this takes you away from the practice of effective combat. This trend was further accentuated later on.

63. "They will not be appropriate . . . The bow is appropriate." In both cases, the verb is *deau*.

64. One *ken* equals 1.8 meters; twenty *ken,* the measure given here, is thus equivalent to 36 meters.

65. "The interest is great": This sentence, which is incomplete in the copy that has come down to us, is written as follows: *Sono ri ooshi*. I think this phrase is a copying error, taking the place of *sukunashi*. In that case, the translation would be "This does not have much interest." Indeed, in many transcriptions into modern Japanese, this sentence, which does not fit into the context, is dropped; also some texts adopt the sense of *sukunashi*.

For example, Kamiko Tadashi, in his transcription, omits this sentence from his reference edition of the text of the *Gorin no sho*. (5, p. 60) Kamata Shigeo interprets it in the sense of *sukunashi*. He translates it into modern Japanese as *"Sono riten wa sukunai."*(4, p. 81) Terayama Danchu keeps the expression *sono ri ooshi,* but he attaches it to the next sentence. He has *"Sono riten no ooi nodewa jokaku no naka kara no teppo ni masarumono wa nai,"* which translates as "There is nothing more advantageous than shooting guns from the inside of a fortress." (11, p. 113)

66. As Musashi has already said, generally warriors carried two swords, the long and the short. The size of a pair of swords varied according to personal choice. The size of a sword was normally measured by the length of the blade, but to get a real idea of the dimensions of a sword, it was necessary to take into account the thickness, breadth, curve, and form of the edge, which composed the overall form of the blade, as well as the quality of the steel. Among the different possible sizes of pairs of swords, Musashi advises choosing large sizes.

67. "Cadence," *hyoshi:* The notion of *hyoshi* has major importance in the *Gorin no sho*. The term does not have an exact equivalent in English and poses significant translation problems (see appendix 1).

68. "Musicians with their stringed or wind instruments," *reijin kange: Reijin* means "a person who plays music." This word refers in particular to an officer who is a musician playing the traditional official music known as *gagaku* at the court for the nobles and also in shrines and temples. *Kan* refers to stringed instruments and *gen* to wind instruments.

69. "That which does not have a visible form," *ku naru koto: Ku* means sky, heaven, emptiness, or space (see appendix 1).

70. "The concordant cadences and . . . the discordant ones," *hazu no au hyoshi, hazu no chigau hyoshi: Hazu* refers to the two ends of a bow where the string is attached. It also refers to the notched end of an arrow that fits onto the bowstring. This is called more precisely the *ya hazu*. On the basis of this image, *hazu* also means "that which is thought will normally happen, that which is reasonable, reason." It is also used in the sense of "plan" or "promise."

71. I will try to convey a more concrete notion of these different forms of cadences or *hyoshi*.

- "The striking cadence (or *hyoshi*)": *ataru hyoshi*.
- "The interval cadence," or more precisely, "the *hyoshi* that places you in the interval between actions": *ma no hyoshi*. This term refers to all the rhythmic elements that can develop in an interval or the moment of void, however short it may be, that occurs between two movements or between two phases of the breathing process. Such moments of void occur when a person is in movement as well as when he is not moving, for example, when he is in a guard position. If your level is high enough, you can detect these moments of void in your adversary and at this instant attune yourself intentionally to his rhythms; and you can also become aware of the moments of void in your own actions and fill them with a new rhythm.

    What Musashi means by *ma no hyoshi* will be dealt with later as part of the more general notion of *suki*, which refers to a fault or lapse. In the development of technique in the Japanese martial arts, ways of provoking a fault *(suki)* in one's opponent play an important role. It is not a matter of finding such a fault in your opponent but of creating it in him by exerting various pressures through your own technique and through your will to attack.
- "The opposing cadence," *somuku hyoshi: Somuku* means "to turn one's back on one direction, to go in the opposite direction, to move away" or "to wrong-foot someone." This expression refers to deliberately not matching the other's *hyoshi* in order to forestall an action (either your own or the opponent's). On the simplest level, this means knowing how to break the *hyoshi* of an attack by backing off. If you are capable of applying this awareness to your own actions, you can realize, at the moment of unleashing them, that certain attacks are futile, and you then become capable of dropping them in order to stay focused on something more important.

I find a connection between this notion from martial arts practice and Musashi's fighting style. It is said that Musashi was able to elude the blade of his opponent with great precision, dodging it by a margin of one and a half centimeters. This quality of Musashi's perception is called *mikiri*. However, in the documents that are relatively reliable, we find only a single account that would confirm this capability of Musashi's. In the *Nitenki* we find the following passage from the account of his duel with Sasaki Kojiro: "Kojiro's sword cut through the knot of Musashi's headband, and the headband fell to the ground. Musashi also launched his attack at the same moment and his stroke struck the head of his adversary, who fell immediately." (2, p. 174)

The literal translation of *mikiri* is: *mi*, "to look" or "to see," and *kiri*, "to cut." Hence we may translate the term "to see with cutting minuteness" or "to see all the way with a look"; more precisely, we could say "discerning the state of situations or things with incisive rigor." This incisive rigor is not based just on a static perception of distance, because in the martial arts, distance includes movement—that is why the space of distance becomes fused with cadences. Thus *mikiri* rests on the accuracy of *hyoshi*, especially of the *somuku hyoshi*, which causes the opponent's attack to fail and leads to a sure victory. That is a first dimension of *mikiri*.

According to Musashi's logic, which is now familiar to us, *mikiri* could also be understood on a larger scale. In the course of the numerous combats in which he engaged, Musashi was never once mistaken in his assessment of the strength of his adversaries, which is what made it possible for him to avoid defeat. He never lost a fight and doubtless achieved the highest level of his time. We can also draw the conclusion that if he judged certain opponents to possibly be superior to himself, he avoided fighting with them for as long as he had not succeeded in turning the situation in his favor. For Musashi, discernment of incisive rigor must be the basis of strategy, individual or collective. In the situation of a duel, the *mikiri* of three centimeters determines the *ma* and decides the issue of the bout. *Mikiri* extended to large-scale strategy distills in one word one of the teachings of Sun Tsu: "If you know yourself and you know your enemy, you will not lose one fight in a hundred." This rigorous discernment characterizes the sword of Musashi as well as his artistic expression.

72. "Think of that which is not evil," *yokoshima ni naki koto o omou:* The Japanese expression here contains a nuance of double negation: "Think of that which is not good." Another translation, corresponding to a second sense of the term *yokoshima*, is possible: "Think of that which does not deviate from the way."

73. "Method," *ho: Ho* means "law, rule, manner" or "method, model." It is also a Buddhist term meaning "teaching of the Buddha." In this sentence Musashi uses *ho* to refer back to *hyoho*, thus to his teaching as a whole; that is why I translated this term as "method." A bit earlier he uses this term to refer to the precepts he had formulated. The sense of the term being clearly limited there, I translated it "rules."

74. "You maintain your vital energy constantly . . . ," *ki ni hyoho o taesazu:* A more literal translation would be: "In your *ki,* you do not interrupt strategy." Inversion can serve to reinforce the meaning of an expression.

75. "You have free mastery of your body," *sotai yawaraka nareba:* The more usual reading of the ideograms is *jiyu,* which means "free." But in the text of the *Gorin no sho* handed down in the Hosokawa family, which is today considered to be the one closest to the original and which I use as my basic text, these ideograms, in this passage, are transcribed without annotation, while in another passage of the Scroll of Water they are accompanied by an annotation in katakana: *yawaraka.*

In the *Ihon gorin no sho* by Yamada Jirokichi, this sentence is written differently: *Sotai yawarakani jiyu ni nari.* (14, p. 365) Thus it contains both the words *yawaraka* and *jiyu.* The meanings of these words are as follows:

• *Jiyu* means "pursuing freedom of the mind or thought." In its Buddhist sense, it means "without any constraint."
• *Yawaraka* means "being flexible, gentle, docile."
• *Yawara* is also pronounced *ju.* It is "the art of flexibility," which was the ancient form of judo. (100)

Although in the dictionaries I consulted I did not find any indication of affinity between these two words, their meanings are often used in association with practical explanations of jujutsu. For example, when I was learning jujutsu under the tutelage of Master Kubota Shozan between 1975 and 1980 in Japan, he explained the meaning of the word *ju* by completing it with the meaning of the word *jiyu.* Following his explanations of technique, he often added, *"Ju wa jiyu. Jiyu deareba yawarakai."* ("Flexibility means freedom. If one is free, one is flexible.") I interpret this as follows: The flexibility of jujutsu aims at the freedom of the body that is derived from perfect mastery of the body. If one is free in the body, the mind is also free. It is at this point that one can acquire true flexibility.

Master Kubota did not invent this association of the words *ju, jiyu,* and *yawaraka.* He himself learned it from his teacher. I have also heard this expression on other occasions, in connection with the practice of the martial arts of *kenjutsu* and karate.

Even though these connections are not reported in the dictionaries, I think it should be pointed out that these ideas are transmitted together in the practice of the martial arts. This helps to clarify Musashi's text.

76. On the sole copy of the *Gorin no sho* that has come down to us today, mention is added of a transmission later in 1667.

77. The work is composed in five scrolls, and each scroll is signed and dated in the same way.

78. "As its fundamental model": *mizu o mototoshi*.

79. "A method of pragmatic effectiveness," *rikata no ho:* For *rikata,* see note 17, page 367; literally, it means "method in a pragmatic domain."

80. *Ri.* See appendix 1.

81. "Read this text . . .": Let us recall that Musashi is writing for his students by way of complementing the practical exercises they have carried out under his guidance.

82. In the next three paragraphs, Musashi uses the word *kokoro* twenty-four times. See appendix 1.

83. Musashi here crystallizes his experience of combat in an image, writing that it is necessary to keep one's mind at the center of oneself and at the center of everything, and that the movement of the mind must never stop. When he writes that the mind must not be too much to one side, this means that one must not become attached to anything in a partial manner.

This image translates what he feels at the time of combat, when his body is reacting before any conscious reflection. He is describing a state of mind that permits him to react appropriately to each situation that arises, all the rest being left outside the field of consciousness. This is what we express sometimes in the course of training by saying "Relate to your mind as though you were sleeping"; for at the moment of falling asleep, the various thoughts and preoccupations of daily life that are an obstacle to the emergence of lucidity at the time of combat subside. Ordinary thoughts are like spots on a glass pane—only by wiping them away can we arrive at a clear view. "Relate to your mind as though sleeping" conveys the most accessible technique for attaining this state of mind.

When we attempt to apply Musashi's teaching to the combat situation, we become aware that out consciousness of time changes spontaneously. We move then in a time that is not flowing in a linear fashion but extends out like the universe. This is what I describe as "exploded" or enlarged time. (53, p. 118) This is a matter of perceiving all the aspects of a situation on the same level. The temporality of everyday life in a sense follows the image of speech flowing. Exploded or enlarged time opens one to a multiplicity of simultaneous perceptions and thus distinctly contrasts with the hierarchizing function entailed by speech, which is perpetually classifying, which operates by making the field of consciousness narrower and more precise. The temporality of combat is time during which verbalization (even for oneself) ceases to be a privileged means. The image we use for it has been devised after the fact in an effort to communicate with someone else who has also himself experienced this opening of awareness to simultaneity.

"Situating the mind at the center" describes the attitude acquired in combat of maintaining a sense of direction that underlies consciousness, which guides physical movements. Fixing precisely on an object or an aspect of the situation disrupts the breadth of this opening and puts one back in the channelized structure of everyday time. In this psychic state, neither the body nor consciousness undertakes movements by itself.

84. "Posture in strategy," *hyoho:* The posture that Musashi indicates is close to that used in the standing meditation that is an essential part of certain Chinese martial arts. In these disciplines, practitioners seek through standing meditation to achieve integration of the overall forces of the body and to extend the sensorial field that plays such an essential role in the art of combat. Some kendo masters today practice a similar meditation called *tachi geiko* (standing training) or *ritsu zen* (standing Zen). This posture makes it possible to stimulate and strengthen the various parts of the body and at the same time to enlarge the field of vision. In this exercise they include the instructions Musashi gives on the way of looking and emphasize that to see properly, it is necessary to have correct posture.

In the standing meditation used in the art of the sword, the practitioner tries to arrive at an empty state of mind that augments his lucidity and provides a foundation for exercises with energy. Starting from that, he tries to imagine various movements of technique and movements in the combat situation, without moving. In this way he studies in depth the sensations inherent in the movements so as to arrive at the essence of the movement of the technique. This is the point from which one of the paradoxes of the teaching of *budo* is derived: Speed is not worth as much as slowness; slowness is not worth as much as immobility. To perceive true movement, it is necessary to be immersed in immobility—this is the significance of the exercise of standing Zen.

85. Here Musashi uses the two terms *kan* and *ken,* which I have translated respectively as "looking" and "seeing." *Kan* refers to the "the profound looking that illuminates the essence of things," and *ken* refers to "looking that makes it possible to perceive the surface of things."

86. When we fight with excitement, our eyes are often very wide open. It is not possible to maintain this position for a long time, and we blink. Moreover, when we have our eyes wide open, we do not see distinctly what surrounds us. The way of looking that Musashi describes is close to that of painters who look at objects by squinting. This way of looking in the midst of combat has an influence on our state of mind. By looking in this way, we can curb our excitement and avoid losing our lucidity. Thus it should be understood that this way of looking is the result of the state of mind described by Musashi. That state of mind brings about that way of looking, and that way of looking is conducive to the state of mind of *hyoho.*

87. The term *itsuku* means, in the literal sense, "to establish oneself at the place one has arrived and remain in place there." I translated this as "to become fixed." This term merits an explanation. It is generally used in the martial arts to describe a negative aspect of the accomplishment of a technique. It has to do with the instant that precedes or follows a movement in which either the body as a whole or a leg or a limb or a weapon remains fixed or frozen. As a result of this stagnation, however brief it may be, the technique loses its effectiveness and one consequently runs the risk of creating a moment of vulnerability vis-à-vis one's adversary.

For example, if after having executed a technique, the body, the arm, or the hand remains at the point reached by the last movement, the realization of the following techniques will be hindered, which brings down the level of one's technical execution as a whole. In the art of the sword, it is said that even if one's movements are correct, if the hands are in a state of *itsuku* (fixation), the sword does not cut well. The degree of effectiveness of sword strikes or punches with the fist is often diminished by this form of stagnation.

The phenomenon of *itsuku* comes from a lack of mastery of the techniques and also from a certain psychological state that is inherent in combat.

An anecdote well known in kendo circles illustrates the complexity of this phenomenon. A practitioner who had attained a high level in the art of the sword underwent his first duel to the death. He defeated his opponent, but from the moment when he cut into his opponent's body, a strange sensation remained in his hands and spread to his entire body. As he looked at the slashed body in front of him and saw the blood gushing from a gaping wound, his hands remained clenched for a moment. He said to himself: "It's fortunate my hands tensed up afterward and not before."

He was able to win because his technique was excellent, but this technique had remained partially abstract and there was no way to get beyond this abstraction other than through the experience of real combat. This is why, during a certain period, the experience of killing and slashing a corpse was a part of the training in technique. For the same reason, at the end of the Edo period, dogs were often found that had been killed or mutilated by sword blows. (94, 123)

88. "Jumping," *tobi ashi;* "with a floating step," *uki ashi;* "stomping heavily," *fumisuyuru ashi.*

89. "The essential instruction . . .": Certain masters of modern kendo insist on movement *suri ashi,* that is, by sliding the feet—lifting the heel and always keeping the same foot forward. This is a contradiction of Musashi's instruction.

What approach is closest to the right one? During the Edo period, the art of the sword was refined and developed through training in dojos, buildings designed for practice, where it was not necessary to worry about the quality of the floor, which was usually a smooth parquet. At the beginning of the Edo period, practitioners—

among them Musashi—were preparing themselves for combat on the field of battle. Over time this need disappeared, while at the same time interest in posture and purity of technique increased and developed to the point where they constituted a kind of aesthetic that became a factor in judging a practitioner's progress along the way. Modern kendo took shape as an extension of this system.

Musashi's school developed directly out of his experiences on the battlefield. There the fighting terrain is never even. To move from one place to another, it is indispensable to raise the toes off the ground, because if they run into a stone or a dip in the ground, one runs the risk of twisting one's ankle or falling, which in battle could lead to death.

Also, still today in the teaching of the Jigen ryu, handed down from the seventeenth century to the present day in the fief of Satsuma (which became the prefecture of Kagoshima), a unique method of movement is practiced. Practitioners of this school perform all techniques lifting the foot up with each step. This might appear ridiculous to someone watching a demonstration in an indoor room with a smooth floor if he is unaware of the reasons for the procedure. This mode of movement goes against the grain of the aesthetic of modern kendo. It seems to me it might be interesting for contemporary practitioners of kendo to have a look at their style of footwork with the help of a little historical perspective.

A similar process has occurred in other disciplines. In karate, for example, until the beginning of the twentieth century, training and combat took place outdoors. There were a certain number of foot movements that were intended to throw sand in the face of the opponent or provide stability on uneven or broken ground. Some of these movements have been handed down to the present time and, in the name of tradition, are repeated in rooms with smooth floors without those who are performing them having any idea of their significance. Other movements have been thrown out because they seem irrational to practitioners executing them on a smooth floor without knowing their origin.

For Musashi, the manner of moving the feet is connected to the fundamental basis of strategy and is not merely a technique. Nakazato Kaizan recounts the following anecdote:

> One day a student asked Musashi about the principle that makes it possible to make progress in *hyoho*. Pointing to the edges of the tatami, which were about five centimeters wide, the master told him, "Walk on the edges."
> The student did this. Musashi then asked him, "If the edge were two meters high, would you be able to do the same thing?
> "That seems like it would be a bit difficult."
> "And if it were sixty centimeters wide?"
> "In that case, I could do it."

Musashi questioned him again. "If a footbridge sixty centimeters wide were run between the top of Himeji castle and the summit of Mount Masui-yama [one league away], would you be able to cross that bridge?"

"I would certainly not be able to do that," replied the student.

Musashi nodded with approval and said, "That is the principle of the prac-tice of the sword. You can easily walk on the edges of a tatami. At a height of two meters, your mind would be calm if you were on a plank sixty centime-ters wide. Now, if the footbridge were as high in the air as the top of the cas-tle and the summit of Mount Masui, your mind would not be calm, because you would be afraid of making a misstep. This fear comes from a lack of train-ing. The beginning is easy, the middle is dangerous, and after the middle, the danger increases further. That is why you must have a confident mind; then you will not be in danger. If you learn to walk on the edge of the tatami while strengthening your sensation of vital energy, you will never make a misstep, no matter what the height of the bridge sixty centimeters wide." (23, pp. 76–78)

90. "Substantial positions, . . . circumstantial ones": Here Musashi uses the expression *tai yu,* written in the hiragana alphabet. The three Japanese editions of the *Gorin no sho* present different interpretations in ideograms of the opposition *tai yu* (see note 30, page 370).

Tai means "the body," understood as a substance or entity that supports various functions, or "essence." *Yu* means "to play" or "to move"; written, it means "to use" or "to employ." *Tai* corresponds to essence or substance and *yu* to an application of *tai,* which is circumstantial.

91. "The middle-level guard position," *kamae no hoi nari: Hoi* or *honni* means (1) "true mind" or "intention, initial intention, true desire"; (2) "true sense, true mean-ing"; (3) "that which must be originally, character or manner of being inherent in a thing." I have translated this term as "original."

92. Musashi uses the term *michi* with different meanings. Its meanings include "way, path, discipline, sphere of activity, route, pathway, trajectory, direction, nature," and so on. In this text *michi* seems to have four different nuances. This is why I prefer to express the richness of its meaning by using different terms to translate *michi* while indicating in parentheses that this is the term being translated. All the same, in this passage this term most often signifies the "pathway of the sword" in the sense of the blade's trajectory. Every time I use the word *pathway* here, it is a translation of the word *michi.*

93. "You must move the sword . . .": In the Scroll of Wind, Musashi criticizes the school that recommends striking with power. Here, when he writes "powerfully," he

is talking about the power that results from striking in a sweeping manner while extending and stretching the arms, not from an effort made with the intent of striking with power.

94. It is difficult to imagine today the precision that Musashi has in mind when he speaks of the path or pathway of the sword, but this notion can be illustrated by a few anecdotes.

The following is drawn from the work of Ozawa Masao:

One day Musashi was received by Lord Shimamura at Kokura on the island of Kyushu. In the course of their conversation, a servant came in and announced to Musashi that a samurai called Aoki wished to be received by him. He was brought in. After a polite exchange, Musashi asked him:

"What is your progress in strategy?"

Aoki replied, "I persevere in it constantly."

The conversation continued and Musashi said to him, "You can already teach in most dojos." Aoki was very happy about this.

Just as he was about to withdraw, Musashi saw that he was carrying a *bokken* (wooden sword) in a handsome cloth case to which a forearm guard of red leather *(udenuki)* was also attached and asked, "What is that red object?"

Somewhat embarrassed, Aoki replied, "That is what I use when I am forced to fight in the course of my travels through various fiefs," and he showed him his great stick, to the handle of which the guard was attached.

Musashi's mood suddenly changed, and he said: "You are an imbecile. At your level, you are still far from being able to think about the combat of *hyoho*. I complimented you before because I thought you could be a good teacher for beginners. If someone asks you to fight with them, the best thing you can do is to leave immediately. You are still far from the combat of *hyoho*."

Musashi then had a child called who was beginning his apprenticeship in *hyoho*. He pasted a grain of rice on the child's forehead at the point from which his hair was pulled back into a bun and told him to remain standing motionless. Musashi then stood up, took his sword, and bringing it down sharply from above, he precisely cut the grain in half and showed it to Aoki. Then he repeated the action, three times altogether. All those present were impressed, but Musashi said: "Even with a confident technique, it is difficult to defeat an enemy. It is out of the question, at your level, to talk about combat." (9, p. 226)

True or not, this anecdote illustrates the reputation of the extreme precision of Musashi's sword. The example of the grain of rice gives a more concrete sense of what Musashi refers to in his text as "the pathway" or "the way of the sword." The sword's trajectory had to be extremely precise and allow at the same time for the adjustment of the force employed to the resistance of the object to be cut.

The second point to note here is Musashi's scrupulousness and the seriousness of his attitude toward combat.

In the history of the great practitioners of the sword, there are many anecdotes that illustrate the effectiveness of a strike from a sword or a *shinai*. This effectiveness derives not simply from the force of the strike but precisely, as Musashi expresses it, from its path, speed, and force being in conformity with the nature of the sword.

Thus, according to Omori Sogen, Harigaya Sekiun (1592–1662), a master who was a contemporary of Musashi's, one day received a *bushi* who challenged the effectiveness of his stroke:

> "It is said that a strike from your *shinai* can break a steel helmet. Is this true? I have put on a steel helmet. Please be so kind as to strike me.
>
> Sekiun refused, and the *bushi* insisted, thinking he was not capable of doing it. Finally Sekiun said, "All right."
>
> He went out into the garden and picked up a *shinai*. He calmly approached the *bushi,* raised the *shinai,* and struck the helmet from above. Having taken the blow, the *bushi* staggered as far as the foot of a tree and fell to the ground spitting blood. (26, p. 46)

The following anecdote is frequently recounted by masters of kendo, but I have not been able to find its source.

> In the nineteenth century, Ueda Umanosuke, a practitioner from the Kyoshin meichi ryu, was challenged to a bout by a practitioner named Yoshida, who came from the province of Hyuga. In this practitioner's school, combat was practiced without protective armor. Yoshida said:
> "You can put on protective armor, but I will fight without armor, because my body is as tough as steel."
> Ueda, irritated by these words, said to him, "I will show you that my *shinai* can break a body, even if it is as tough as steel."
> Saying this, he took a particularly thick piece of bamboo armor used to protect the side of the body and attached it to the trunk of a tree. He struck it a blow with his *shinai* and the three thick bamboo strips of the armor were broken. [If you are familiar with kendo armor, you have some idea what this blow must have been like.] Seeing this demonstration, Yoshida paled and also donned a suit of armor.

Finally, in 1887 Sakakibara Kenkichi (1830–1894) performed a demonstration of *kabuto wari* before the emperor. This involved splitting a steel helmet with a sword.

The three most famous sword masters attempted this and only Sakakibara succeeded. He split the helmet to a depth of 11.5 centimeters, and his sword blade remained intact. The blades of the two other masters were deformed in the shape of the curvature of the helmet. (120, p. 135)

In the history of the sword, we can find many similar examples. The effectiveness of a strike depends mainly upon the way of holding the sword as it follows a trajectory that is "in conformity with the nature of the sword."

95. "The Series . . . ," *tsutsu no omote no shidai: Shidai* means "the manner of placement within an order, the order, the degree, to classify in accordance with an order, the movement of a situation, a process, the derivation of things." (99, 100) The meaning here is the first one; the order followed is an order of presentation and not a hierarchical order. That is why, in order to avoid any ambiguity, I have translated the word as *series*. In the title of each form, I attempted to render the nuance implicit in *shidai* by adopting an ordinal number (first, second . . .).

Omote refers to a technical form or formula. This term is frequently used in the various disciplines of the Japanese martial arts. The literal sense of the word *omote* is "surface, exterior, external shape, facade," whence the sense, "that which is seen and shown officially on the outside." The facade is something official because it is, and must be, presentable for the outside world, the public. Thus in the martial arts, *omote* refers to the techniques that are officially recognized as being characteristic of a given school. But in signifying "the surface," the term *omote* always presupposes that which is hidden behind the appearances. To every *omote* there is a corresponding *ura*, "behind" or "the other side."

The transmission of a martial art generally takes place by following both sides, *omote* and *ura*. The main substance of an art cannot be transmitted solely through visible forms and formulas, so the transmission relies on what is not visible from the outside, the *ura*. This same procedure is also valuable in preserving the secrecy of a school. When the external appearance is too revealing or there is a competition between schools, the practitioners of an art set up complex codes of transmission and practice following the *omote* and *ura* scheme.

For example, in karate a technique called *shuto uke* is frequently used in the formalized exercises known as katas. This technique is interpreted as a parry carried out with the edge of the hand—parrying a blow of the fist or a kick by the adversary with the edge of the hand. Using the right hand, the practitioner moves the hand forward obliquely to the right, starting from the left shoulder. That is the technique that is shown, *omote*, and this explanation has become the "official" one; it is the explanation known to most karate practitioners. By contrast, in the hidden transmission, *ura*, the final position of the hand is identical to that described above, but the practitioner does not strike only with the edge of his hand. In accordance with the situation, different ways of striking are studied: One can strike with the base of the index finger (which is located on the opposite side of the hand from the edge), with the palm of the hand, with the back of the hand; and one can also use the fingers, poking them into the throat or the eyes of the opponent.

Another technique, called *nukite,* is done by poking with the fingers according to the description in the shown, *omote,* listing of techniques. In the hidden, or *ura,* version, this technique is not performed using the fingers but with the bony part of the forearm, with which the practitioner applies pressure to the arm of the opponent with a movement that is close to the motion of a saw.

In the sword technique of the Komagawa Kaishin ryu that I myself practice, six series of katas exist that are called *omote no kata.* Kuroda Tetsuzan, the principal master of this school, published a book on the techniques of his school in 1992. One of my French students, who does not read Japanese, was looking at a series of photos presented in the chapter called "Ura no kata" (115, pp. 356–389) and asked me the following question, "These are examples of bad techniques, aren't they?" Although he had been practicing for only two years, he had a keen awareness of the techniques he was learning and was able to discern small differences from them in the movements shown in "Ura no kata." Not knowing about this kind of exercise, he thought these differences represented deformations of the techniques. The *ura* techniques are in fact more refined, but they often appear less elegant to beginners. And for those who have no knowledge of the techniques of a given school, the hidden techniques may look like they are being performed in a sloppier way than the shown ones. Indeed, without an explanation it is difficult to understand the full meaning of these techniques.

Although this duality is customary in the martial arts schools, the notion of *ura,* the hidden part of the art, is often subjected to a kind of mystification for a variety of reasons. With his pragmatic mindset, Musashi shows the essence of his school in this chapter, without mystifying and in simple language. For him the essential can be expressed by means of the *omote* technical form. Nevertheless, as he adds at the end of each section, one must carefully examine and train in what he talks about, because it is impossible to transmit the practice of an art completely in a written piece, even if one is not trying to keep a secret *ura* part in reserve.

The execution of the five technical forms in Musashi's school today: Musashi's five forms are still practiced today under the same name—*itsutsu no omote*—in the school that hands down his art; however, the techniques as practiced at the present time have diverged from the descriptions Musashi gives of them. This divergence can be explained by involuntary changes that have accumulated over the course of time, since this was a series of techniques that Musashi transmitted in practice before giving them the definitive outlines described in the five forms.

Having witnessed the execution of the five forms by Masayuk Imaii, the tenth lineage successor of the main branch of Musashi's school, for purposes of reference I will describe his executions of each of the five techniques as we come to the description of it given by Musashi.

96. The second part of this sentence poses a problem of interpretation: "When he launches an attack, deflect his sword to your right and, pressing on it, make your attack with the point of your sword." In this sentence Musashi uses the word *noru,* which means "to mount or get in" (a horse or a vehicle); thus this passage has often been understood as meaning "to place your sword above the sword of your opponent." A passage from a work entitled "Writings on the Sword Technique of the Enmei Ryu" *(Enmei ryu kenpo sho)* (1-i) clears up this point. This work, sometimes attributed to Musashi, has been handed down in the School of Musashi of Saga prefecture. Although the general lines of the work are those of Musashi, I do not accept it as being a work by him because it seems to me it was probably composed on the basis of excerpts from the *Gorin no sho* by adepts of the School of Musashi, who have added their interpretations. We find the following sentence there: "*Noru* means neither bringing the sword back toward oneself nor parrying but, rather, rapidly directing the point of the sword upward, then crossing the opponent's sword with it."

I have, however, noted the following in practice: In performing the first form as a linked sequence of three techniques through which one is attempting to place one's sword on that of the opponent, it immediately emerges that our movements are hindered between the first and second techniques. For that reason it was necessary to look for another interpretation. In the practice of the sword, the word *noru* does not necessarily have the sense given above. It can also mean "climb onto the occasion that arises," that is, "seize the occasion or the opportunity to take the initiative." In this interpretation, the instruction given by Musashi is not to put one's sword on top of the opponent's but to strike the opponent on the head, the arm, or the wrist, depending on the opportunity that arises. The technical meaning of the sentence would then be: "When he launches an attack, deflect his sword to the right (so that it is left to cut the air) and, seizing the opportunity, make your attack with the point of your sword."

Even though this second interpretation seems to fit, I have kept the first interpretation because of the text of the Enmei ryu.

97. I translated *kissaki gaeshi* as "turning the point of your sword one quarter of a circle." In the *Enmei ryu kenpo sho* we read the following passage: "The way you turn the point of your sword necessitates a close estimate of the distance away from you your opponent is. When you want to strike an opponent who is far away, you execute a large movement, beginning to turn the point of your sword when your hand is at the height of the right side of your neck." (13, p. 52)

In addition to the issue referred to in note 96, I also differ from the usual interpretation of the overall sense of this paragraph. Usually the situations described are interpreted as a linked sequence taking place in the course of a confrontation and as three exercises to be executed successively.

The three situations described are not necessarily linked. The appropriate way of understanding them is that each situation was to be practiced independently and that the linkage with the following techniques occurred only in the case where the riposte did not succeed. On this basis, we can understand that the idea is first of all to practice dominating the opponent with a single movement in each case, but that the combination is also possible when the counterattack does not succeed.

The first situation is a dodging movement to the left, causing the sword of your adversary to cut the air on your right. You can immediately take the initiative by spontaneously striking the spot that is most exposed at this moment. For this reason Musashi does not say specifically where and how to strike.

If your attack has failed, your opponent will launch another attack, but this situation can also occur in other circumstances. There is no necessary link with the first situation. Musashi provides for the situation in which your counterattack has not succeeded by saying, "strike him from above downward, turning the point of your sword one quarter of a circle, and leave your sword in the position it has reached."

Indeed, in the case where your attack has not succeeded, the position in which your preceding movement of attack has left you can become the optimal preparation for a riposte against another attack on the part of your opponent. For this reason there is a more probable linkage between the second and third situations, but if you execute the third sequence by placing your sword in the low position that corresponds to the situation described, your position will be the low guard position of which Musashi speaks a number of times in this work. Thus you can also execute the third technique independently.

In this sense the three techniques become part of a single form because of sharing the same attitude toward combat: Dominate your adversary at the very moment where he strikes you with his sword. The last two techniques can be a linked sequence, but that is not necessary.

98. The first form as demonstrated by Masayuki Imai: Masayuki Imai calls this guard position *enso no kamae,* and he explains that it is a guard to be related to with a broad and calm mind that contains an entire universe between the two swords. *Enso* means (1) "circular form"; (2) as a Zen Buddhist term, "the circle drawn to symbolize the illumination inherent in the human mind"; at times words or signs are inscribed in this circle to express either a function of the mind or the degree of progress toward illumination; (3) "a circle that surrounds the body of Buddha and the gods." (99)

Masayuki Imai holds the two swords horizontally, with the points pointing at the face of his opponent. This is the middle guard position *(chudan)* with two swords. The blades of both swords are turned outward. The opponent attacks with a stroke of his sword from above downward; Masayuki Imai lowers his two swords and, taking a small step backward, allows the sword of his opponent to cut the air. The opponent launches a fresh attack from above downward; Imai Masayuki stops it this time with his small sword held in his left hand, and he slashes his opponent's arm with his large sword held in his right hand, striking on an angle from the lower left toward the upper right.

This does not correspond exactly to the description Musashi gives (see notes 96 and 97).

99. The second form as demonstrated by Masayuki Imai: Masayuki Imai holds his large sword in the right hand, in the high position, *jodan,* over his right shoulder and his small sword in the middle position, *chudan,* pointing at the face of his opponent. He calls this guard position the "fire guard." The adversary attacks, striking from above downward. Masayuki Imai parries with his large sword and extends the parry into a circular movement that moves the opponent's sword downward by pressing the blade of his sword against the back of the opponent's sword. The adversary pulls his sword back and launches another attack, and Masayuki Imai blocks this by crossing his two swords above his forehead. The blades of the three swords cross for a moment at a single point. But this coming together lasts for only an instant, because immediately Masayuki Imai separates his two swords in a broad movement of a quarter circle, forcing the adversary's sword downward and to the left, and without stopping this circular movement of separation, he strikes the head of his adversary with his large sword, held in the right hand.

100. "A passing cadence," *kosu hyoshi:* This expression comes from the verb *kosu,* which means "to outstrip, travel through, cross (a mountain pass), pass, surpass." This refers to a cadence that makes it possible to turn aside the sword that is trying to knock your own down in the same fashion that one would get over a mountain pass—in the air. The technique can be explained as follows: If your opponent parries and attempts to get your sword down by striking it, you twist your sword aside with a passing cadence, with the result that your opponent cuts the air, and in deflecting his sword you cut his upper arm.

Musashi's original text is written in hiragana without punctuation, which leaves room for a variety of interpretations. That is why, in other interpretations of the *Gorin no sho,* this expression is understood as *okosu hyoshi.* The literal translation of *okosu* is "to wake up, to straighten up or raise (something that has fallen)" or "to begin." The translation would then be a "raised cadence" or "initial cadence." However, this translation seems to me to be wrong, because we nowhere find the expression *okosu hyoshi* in the work of Musashi, whereas he uses *kosu hyoshi* a number of times, for example, in the instruction *"Ni no koshi no hyoshi* (p. 36 of the cited edition of the *Gorin no sho)* and in the *Hyoho sanju go kajo.* (9, p. 247)

Moreover, the interpretation of "passing cadence" fits with the practical application. This cadence appears at the moment when, during an attack, you strike, and after having hit your opponent's sword, you stop for an instant; your opponent will be drawn into this pause, then you take advantage of this instant of stagnation on his part to strike him.

101. The third form as demonstrated by Masayuki Imai: In this form, Masayuki Imai holds the two swords lowered and pointing toward the ground. He calls this position *ritsu zen* (standing Zen). There exists a self-portrait of Musashi in this posture.

The opponent strikes from above downward. Imai Masayuki stops this with his small sword. This situation is close to the first form, with the difference that the body of Masayuki Imai is somewhat farther from his opponent and therefore his large sword does not reach the arm of his opponent. The opponent attacks again; Masayuki Imai parries with his large sword and presses it against the back of the opponent's sword, which he forces down. He cuts the opponent's arm with the small sword, striking horizontally from left to right and passing above the two swords—his own large one and the opponent's.

102. "Strike . . . with an upward motion," *shita yori haru*: Literally, this means, "You strike starting from the bottom." The literal translation, however, might give the reader the impression that there is a preparatory movement downward, which does not exist. That is why I translated "with an upward motion."

103. The phrase "If he attempts to knock down your upward moving sword, you follow your intention of striking his wrist in accordance with the way of the sword" could more simply be interpreted: "You receive and parry the pathway *(michi)* of your opponent's sword, which is attempting to knock your sword down." In this case the verb *ukeru* is understood purely in the sense of "receiving something materially," that is to say, here, the sword of your adversary, which in effect means parrying. Following this interpretation, we would understand the expression *tachi no michi o uke* as meaning that the pathway of the sword referred to is that of your adversary and not your own.

I translated as "follow" Musashi's term *uke,* which is an inflected form of the verb *ukeru,* which means "to receive." But here "to receive" is employed in the sense of "receiving the right principle in the act of slashing" (an inflection of the sense of *michi* translated by "the way"). In other words, the motion of the sword, moved by this principle, will follow the right trajectory. Thus, in this phrase, *uke* has a double sense. On the basis of testing it in practice, this interpretation seems to me to be the more accurate one and also the one that fits with Musashi's general idea. Musashi is indicating the principle of the sword that ought to be followed by the practitioner rather than developing this notion in relation to the sword of the adversary.

104. "You extend the stroke obliquely up to the height of your own shoulder": This determines the movement as obliquely upward. However, another interpretation is possible: "You slash obliquely to a point above the shoulder of your opponent." The description is ambiguous.

The problem resides in a single word, written as an ideogram by Musashi. Throughout his text, Musashi indicates the subject, that is the speaker, or "I," by the word *ware*. However, frequently I have translated this word as "you," because this "I" is used by Musashi to refer to the person he is addressing, his reader, his disciple. Thus if this ideogram is read *ware*, it becomes the subject, and we must translate here: "You obliquely slash the shoulder of your adversary"; but if you read it *waga (mon)*, we must translate: "You slash obliquely up to the height of your own shoulder." I adopted this interpretation because it is better adapted to the practical situation that is described.

105. The fourth form as demonstrated by Masayuki Imai: Masayuki's Imai small sword is pointed toward the opponent at the middle level *(chudan)*, and his large sword, held in the right hand, is placed under his left armpit, pointing backward. His torso is almost in profile in relation to his opponent, whom he looks at over his right shoulder. This is a special position that one would take, for example, in a combat situation where obstacles make it impossible to take the usual position.

The adversary attacks downward from above twice; each time Masayuki Imai parries with the small sword at the same time as he strikes horizontally to the right with his large sword, as though drawing it from the scabbard. His adversary backs off from this movement of attack. After his second horizontal movement of attack from the left to the right, Masayuki Imai extends the movement of his sword up to the level of his right shoulder, and from that point strikes diagonally toward the lower left shoulder of his opponent.

106. The fifth form as demonstrated by Masayuki Imai: Masayuki Imai holds his small sword at the middle level and the large sword at his right hip. Both swords are pointing at the adversary, but the large sword is much farther back. This position is used when there are obstacles or in a special situation.

The opponent attacks downward from above; Masayuki Imai dodges by taking a half step backward, and he parries with his small sword, moving his opponent's sword to the outside, leaving it to cut thin air all the way down. Imai Masayuki immediately strikes the opponent's head with his large sword, taking a half step forward.

107. "Through continuously applying the techniques of these five forms in their full depth," *te o karasu:* Here *te* means "technique"; *karasu* means "dry out by removing the water, draw the water till it runs dry," from which comes the derivative sense of doing something thoroughly and fully or exhaustively. I translated here "applying the tech-

niques . . . in their full depth" in order to retain a trace of the image of getting to the very bottom of the spring or well.

108. Problems posed by these five sections: In Musashi's text, the use of two swords is not apparent. It is simpler to grasp the situation by understanding his text as referring to one sword, because there is no description in which the movements of each of the two swords is explained. Indeed, if this text were read without the reader's knowing that it concerned the School of Two Swords, no one would imagine the presence of a second sword. Why do we have this lack of precision and apparent neglect, even though Musashi insists elsewhere on the importance of two swords in his school? The answer is not simple.

In my view, Musashi describes the essential technique for only one sword because even when using two swords at once, it is with one sword that you slash the opponent. Nevertheless, Musashi stresses the importance of becoming accustomed to handling the sword with just one hand, even to the point of naming his school the School of Two Swords. Taking this into account, I think the movement of the other sword can be regarded as variable; Musashi leaves the second sword freedom of reaction as long as the main action is carried out. Moreover, Musashi speaks only of the main action. For the practitioner who correctly uses the main sword as he describes, the movement of the second sword will be determined spontaneously. An overly detailed description would render too fixed and artificial an exercise that is supposed to be a preparation for real situations. All the same, these technical passages are directly applicable to those who practice the sword holding it in both hands, and they are instructive.

109. "The teaching of the guard without a guard": *uko muko no oshie.*

110. "Depending on the openings furnished by your opponent": *teki no en ni yori.*

111. "All that becomes the occasion for you to strike him," *teki o kiru en nari:* En is a Buddhist term meaning "cause, relation between things, object of thought."

112. "Fixate," *itsuku:* See note 87.

113. "A single cadence for striking your adversary" is the translation of *hitotsu hyoshi no uchi.* In contemporary Japanese, *hitotsu hyoshi* is more commonly read *ichi hyoshi.*

114. "Without moving your body": When you strike from a guard position, making a preparatory movement, as small as it might be, is almost unavoidable. For example, starting from a middle-level guard, to strike a blow to the head of your opponent, you will first have to raise the point of your sword, then strike him. In this case the movement of striking is based on two cadences, that of raising and that of coming down. Even if you execute these movements very rapidly, there are still two cadences there.

This is one of the fundamental questions over which a kendo practitioner will pause for a long time. We examine this question in chapter 9 in relation to the work of Morita Monjuro (19, 20), a kendo master who has devoted a great part of his life to resolving this problem.

In the technique described here by Musashi, the pathway of the point of the sword must not show a break into two movements but must describe a curve that forms a circle and does not require two cadences.

115. As I explain in appendix 1, it is not possible to find a single word in a Western language corresponding to the term *hyoshi,* which contains the idea of cadence, but this does not fully encompass its meaning.

Let us briefly analyze the *hyoshi* in question here, the single-cadence *(hyoshi)* strike.

Musashi writes: "You strike very rapidly and directly without moving your body, not letting your will to attack become attached anywhere." And about the opponent he says: "Seizing the instant when he does not expect it, you strike him with a single blow just at the instant when he is not even thinking of pulling back his sword or moving it out of the guard position or attacking."

Thus, in order to execute this technique, it is necessary for you to be able to strike quickly without manifesting in any way your will to attack. In general, when a person launches an intentional attack, a manifestation of his will to attack, as minimal as it might be, precedes the attack movement. The more he is caught up in aggression or in his will to attack, the more marked this manifestation is. For this reason, one of the principal efforts on the part of a practitioner in training consists in getting rid of this gap between his own will and the execution of the technique by learning how to make a movement that arises spontaneously.

Let us look into the second part of Musashi's term. The single-cadence strike is not only the description of the cadence of a movement in which you strike without manifesting your will to attack; it describes at the same time a relationship with the inner rhythm of your adversary that allows you to grasp the instant in which he is not able to react. A highly accomplished practitioner is always attentive to the will to attack of his opponent and is easily able to detect it. Even when facing a very rapid attack, if he is able to grasp the instant of the gap or lag between the manifestation of the opponent's will to attack and his attack movement, he will be able to react effectively with a less rapid movement.

We are talking about a state in which will and movement fuse and the technique produced is accurate. It turns out that to arrive at this state, you must not "want to," because the more you want to, the more the will to attack becomes manifest. What is necessary is for the body to move all by itself, choosing the favorable moment. This is a state in which, before noticing it, you have already struck, without anything's having intervened between perception and movement. On the level of perception, the single-cadence strike comes close to the strike of nonthought presented by Musashi two paragraphs farther on.

The difficulty in translating the term *hyoshi* is now easier to understand. In Japanese it is just one *hyoshi*, but it is not just one cadence, because it is the coming together of two cadences, your own and your opponent's.

"Interval," *ma*: Just as with *hyoshi*, the term *ma* does not have an equivalent in English. Generally this term is translated as "distance" or "gap," but it expresses not only a spatial gap (or distance) between objects or persons and a temporal gap (for example, the moment in music when the rhythm changes) but also the dynamic tension of the relationship between two or several persons. It is precisely because they both or all participate in this dynamic of relationship that the two dimensions of *ma* and *hyoshi* are inseparable.

116. There are several problems in this passage regarding the understanding of the Japanese text:

"In two phases": The title reads *ni no koshi no hyoshi*. In the original text, *ni no koshi no* is written in hiragana. *Ni no* seems to have a double meaning, that of "second" in relation to the preceding cadence, which was *ichi*, "one," and that of "two" in the temporal sense, that is, referring to a cadence in two temporal steps or phases; this one is situated in relation to the previous one as *ni*, "two." Thus two translations are possible: "the second passing cadence " or "the passing cadence in two phases." I decided in favor of the latter because *ni no* is repeated later in the same paragraph in relation to the strike, and in this case the temporal sense is mandatory.

"The passing cadence": The most frequent interpretation is based on the transcription of *koshi* as the hips or the small of the back; this yields the reading *ni no koshi no hyoshi*, which means "the second, the *hyoshi* of the hips or the small of the back *(koshi)*." In most of the texts published today, this interpretation is repeated and seems to have become established. However, if we read this phrase attentively and relate it to other sentences of Musashi's, and especially if we practice this teaching, it appears that this interpretation is false.

In my view there are two possible valid interpretations of this phrase. If you read *ni no koshi no hyoshi*, the term *koshi* need not be understood only in the sense of hips or small of the back but can also be understood as the nominative form of the verb *kosu*, which means "to get past," as we saw earlier (see note 100). Indeed, this ideogram is found in the original text of the *Ihon gorin no sho*, the edition by Yamada Jirokichi (14, p. 358), and in the twenty-second article of the *Hyoho sanju go kajo* (9, p. 247), which confirms this interpretation.

I justify this interpretation on the basis of Musashi's explanatory sentence that comes afterward: *teki no hari te tarumu tokoro o uchi, hikite tarumu tokoro o utsu, kore ni no koshi no uchi nari*. Before discussing the possible interpretations of this sentence, we must pause a moment over the expression *hari te tarumu*. *Hari* comes from the verb *haru,* meaning "to tense up," and *tarumu* means "to relax." The simplest way of interpreting this expression is to apply it to the state of the adversary, who is relaxing after having tensed up, but Musashi frequently uses the term *haru* to refer to one of the parrying techniques. In this sense the expression refers to the moment the adversary relaxes after having made a parrying movement provoked by a feint. This is the interpretation I chose, translating "after having started a parrying movement."

Teki no hari te tarumu tokoro o uchi, hikite tarumu tokoro o utsu, kore ni no koshi no uchi nari: The translation by M. and M. Shibata keeps the sense of "small of the back" for *koshi* and "to relax after having tensed up" for *hari te tarumu*. The result is "Thus the adversary will at first be in a state of tension, but he will relax this afterward. At that moment it is necessary to attack without delay. That is the secondary rhythm of the small of the back." In this translation, as in the other Japanese translations corresponding to it, it is difficult to see the relationship between the small of the back and the logic of the text.

If we translate *kosuhi* as "getting past," the meaning of the sentence becomes "You feint striking him and then actually strike him at the moment when he relaxes after having started a parrying movement *(hari te tarumu)* or after having backed up." If we read *futatsu no koshi no hyoshi* instead of *ni no koshi no hyoshi,* the translation will be "the passing cadence in two phases" or "the two cadences of passing."

Another interpretation of the entire sentence is to read *ni nokoshi* instead of *ni no koshi*. The term *nokoshi* is the nominative form of the verb *nokosu,* meaning "leave out part of something." In this case the sentence would mean "You feint a strike but leave your movement partially incomplete and you actually strike at the moment when he relaxes after having started a parrying movement." I find this interpretation peculiar, and I have not found any other author who shares it. However, during a conversation with Imai Masayuki in 1987, he rejected the interpretation of *koshi* as hips or small of the back and understood the expression as meaning "passing cadence in two phases." When I explained my interpretation to him, he found it as interesting as his own but nevertheless did not withdraw his own.

These two interpretations partially overlap because in both cases a situation is depicted in which you create a void in your opponent by using two *hyoshi* (cadences), which produces a feint in his direction. It is by reading this way that we see the profundity of this technique and we can understand its real relationship with the previous one, which involves a single *hyoshi,* because the second one is created by doubling that *hyoshi*. By contrast, if you go with "the cadence of the small of the back," there is no need to double such a cadence, and we cannot understand what Musashi is describing in a concrete way. In this situation the point is to create a gap or lag in the *hyoshi* (cadences) in which the opponent is at the end of the first cadence, through which his attention and energy have been emptied out creating a void, while you are fully in the midst of the second one. Thus the instruction to double the *hyoshi* (cadence) is clear in the last two interpretations.

I had this passage read by ten advanced practitioners of the Japanese martial arts of kendo, aikido, and karate. All of them at first interpreted *koshi* in the sense of small of the back or hips. I explained my analysis to them and then asked them to read the text attentively again. After due reflection, all of them, without exception, rejected their first interpretation and then hesitated between the two interpretations I proposed.

In conclusion, in this passage and the preceding one, Musashi places first the different striking techniques that each recquire a single *hyoshi* and then second those that require a *hyoshi* in two phases. This is an example of the ambiguity produced in Musashi's text by the syllabic form of writing. This leads to divergences in interpretation that can be worked out only through a thorough reading of the text in association with actual practice. From the literary point of view, all three interpretations are possible, but from the point of view of actual practice, one is wrong and the other two are possible. This long explanation is justified by the fact that this wrong interpretation has come to be almost systematically accepted in contemporary Japanese publications.

117. "The strike of nonthought," *munen muso no uch: Mu* is "negation"; *nen* means "thought, consideration, what is in the mind, memory of past experience"; *so* means "idea, representation of perceived phenomena." *Munen* is a Buddhist term meaning "without thinking anything, penetrating into the state of nonego." *Muso* as a Buddhist term means "having no form, not being conditioned by form." *Muso* signifies "to empty of all thought, have nothing in the mind." This ideogram is also used in connection with *muso*.

These two ways of writing *muso* used in association with *munen* mean ostensibly the same thing: "not thinking of anything, becoming detached from any idea or thought." I translated this expression as "nonthought."

In practically all schools of the sword, a spontaneous strike is considered the right kind of strike and is a central element in sword technique. It is a strike that arises unconsciously and leads to a positive result. It occurs when your mind, because it is empty, is able to allow itself to be impregnated by the situation and the body comes up with a spontaneous and accurate movement.

To elucidate the idea of striking with an empty mind, I refer to the work "Explanation of the School of Two Swords" *(Nito ryu o kataru)* by Yoshida Seiken: "The term *munen-muso* is widely known, and it seems that one can cut down any opponent if one strikes in this manner. But it should be understood that this strike is viable only under certain conditions. It is viable when you and your opponent are both waiting for the other to attack. During this situation of reciprocal waiting, your strike arises spontaneously if your body and mind are integrated in an attitude of attack." (35, p. 66)

As Musashi says, practitioners often encounter this type of strike, which takes the form of punches and kicks in karate and throwing techniques in judo. In certain sword schools it is one of the ideal goals of technique. Musashi underlines the importance of studying it and training in it consciously. It seems to me that he is emphasizing that to succeed in executing spontaneous and unconscious technique, it is necessary to train in it in a highly conscious fashion.

Apropos of the strike of nonthought, adepts of the martial arts frequently refer to the story of Satori. I will pass on the account of it given by Chiba Shusaku:

> Here is an anecdote. Once when a woodsman was trying to cut a tree in a deep forest, an animal named Satori appeared. The woodsman wanted to catch it, because this animal is rare. Satori then said, "You were thinking about catching me." The woodsman was terribly surprised to hear this. Satori then said, "You are surprised because I know what you're thinking." The woodsman was more and more astonished and thought secretly of killing it with the axe he had in his hand. Satori then said, "You were thinking of killing me." The woodsman thought, "It has the ability to know what I'm thinking. There's nothing I can do." And he went back to cutting the tree. Satori said, "You were thinking that there's nothing you can do against me."
>
> This time the woodsman continued to concentrate on cutting the trunk of the tree, without concerning himself with this animal. The blade of his axe then accidentally came off and planted itself in Satori's head, and Satori died without saying a word. (82, pp. 42–43)

This parable teaches us that even satori can be struck by an axe of nonthought. In *kenjutsu* also, if you are confronting a very advanced practitioner, he will detect your actions as soon as you even think of them. Therefore it is necessary to develop techniques that arise without thought. You must train in this well.

118. "The flowing-water strike": *ryu sui no uchi.*

119. "That seems to be stagnating," *yodomi:* The image is that of flowing water that seems to slow down and stagnate as it passes over a deep spot.

"You strike broadly": This formulation might seem paradoxical. It does not really mean to strike slowly but rather to create a cadence that gives the impression of stagnating. This sentence has to be understood in conjunction with the preceding one, where Musashi asks the practitioner to expand his body and mind. This subjective expansion contains the same latent power as the current when it is passing over a large deep area.

120. "The level of your opponent," *teki no kurai: Kurai* means "position, state, quality, capacity." Thus two translations are possible: "the level of your opponent" or "the position of your opponent." I chose the first because the technique described by Musashi can be carried out only against an opponent whose level is inferior to your own. In sword combat, the result of a bout is not always determined by a difference in level. If his mind is slack, a great master can be killed by a beginner who is determined to die. Musashi's techniques take this fact into account.

121. "The chance-opening blow," *en no atari:* I translated the term *en* as "chance-opening." This term is of Buddhist origin and has four main meanings:

- the secondary cause of a phenomenon or the contingent factors that work in the same direction as the direct cause of the phenomenon
- the relationships between things and phenomena or human actions
- the occasion or the chance of a relationship's arising
- the surroundings of an object

Here I went with the first sense. In Buddhist thought, even when there is no apparent cause, the interdependent links of a cosmic dynamic constitute the hidden cause. In the course of combat, whether this chance that is always there is grasped or allowed to escape will depend on the practitioner's ability. When an opening is offered by chance, if your ability is insufficient, you let it get away. If you have the ability, you can use it. Musashi's teaching here is not to let a chance pass but to transform it into a chance that has been given to you. For someone who does not see, there is in effect no opening for a strike. Being available so that you can grasp the opening is an important ability in *hyoho*.

122. I translated *atari* as "hit" or "blow," *uchi* as "strike." In fact *atari* does contain a nuance of chance. In the title of this section, Musashi uses the term *atari,* but at the end of it he uses *uchi*. Thus he is conveying the idea of transforming a chance situation into something quite clearly evident.

123. "The blow like a spark from a stone": *sekka no atari*.

124. "You must strike quickly . . . ," *ahi mo tsuyoku, mi mo tsuyoku, te mo tsuyoku, mitokoro o motte hayaku utsu beki nari:* This literally means "legs as strongly, body as strongly, hands as strongly, strike quickly with these three parts."

In translating this passage I tried to take into account the logic of Musashi's thought. In fact, the instruction given just before this by Musashi ("strike extremely hard without raising your sword at all") is equivalent in karate to "deliver a powerful punch, beginning your movement just a few centimeters from your opponent's body." So there is no distance for the strike to accelerate in, and it is a very difficult strike to execute. Therefore it is necessary, as Musashi writes here, to mobilize simultaneously the three combined forces of the legs, the body, and the hands and integrate them into one.

125. "The crimson-leaves strike," *momiji no uchi*: *Momiji* in general refers to a kind of maple that turns crimson in the fall, which is also called *kaede*. In a broader sense, *momiji* refers to leaves that turn color in the fall. But here, in my view, it refers to the leaves of the *momiji* tree that color the Japanese countryside with their magnificent purple hue. These leaves fall readily with the first winds of winter. Here the leaf that falls is a crimson leaf, which also evokes the color of the opponent's blood. Musashi seems to be bringing together these two images in his description of this technique.

126. "You extend the force of your strike," *nebaru kokoro nite:* The term *nebaru* appears several times in Musashi's writings. The primary sense of this verb is "to stick or paste," and the next sense is "to persist." What Musashi is expressing here is a force that persists in its effect as a paste does. This image crops up in most of the Japanese martial arts, with the sense of improving a technique, that is, of making it flexible so it can be more resistant and so its effectiveness can persist or penetrate more deeply.

For example, in sumo, force and the capacity for resistance in the lower part of the body are essential. The term *nebaru* is used as a positive description of this. In judo and in sumo, you resist an attempt on the part of your opponent to throw you with a "small of the back that is sticky or flexible," *nebari goshi.* Conversely, when your opponent attempts to resist your throwing techniques, you can throw him nonetheless because of your flexible or sticky small of the back. In karate the action of sticking *(nebaru)* with the hand is emphasized for parrying techniques that make it possible to absorb the impact of your adversary's attack and repulse it.

127. "The body replacing the sword": *tachi ni kawaru mi.*

128. "A strike and a hit," *utsu to atari:* Throughout this text, I have translated *atari* as "blow" or "hit" and *uchi* as "strike," for *atari* contains a nuance of chance. In this passage Musashi stresses this distinction. That is why, to make it clearer, I have translated *atari* in the sense of a chance hit and *uchi* in the sense of an intentional strike.

Musashi's technical ideas come out clearly here. If one wishes to make progress in the way of *hyoho,* it is indispensable to distinguish a controlled strike from one that is produced by chance. Nevertheless, training must be carried out in such a way that even a chance hit will be sufficiently effective. For someone seeking to make progress in a martial art, it is indispensable to understand why he has won or lost. The attitude here differs fundamentally from that of sports competition, where the result is what counts, even if it is fortuitous. A win is not necessarily indicative of the level a person has attained. Let us recall what Musashi wrote right at the beginning of this work: "I have fought more than sixty times, but not once was I beaten. All that happened between my thirteenth and my twenty-eighth or twenty-ninth year."

Winning by means of a chance blow does not constitute an objective in training; Musashi by no means excludes it, but he does not accept it as a real victory. What form of victory is he looking for then? That is what he describes next:

> At the age of thirty, I reflected and saw that although I had won, I had done so without having reached the ultimate level of strategy. Perhaps it was because my natural disposition prevented me from straying from universal principles; perhaps it was because my opponents lacked ability in strategy.
>
> I continued to train and to seek from morning till night to attain a deeper principle. When I reached the age of fifty, I naturally found myself on the way of strategy.

His objective is to win deliberately, by creating the incontrovertible conditions of victory. The distinction between the conscious strike and the chance hit is at the root of this quest. This idea is summed up in one of the key maxims of modern kendo: "Strike after having won, don't win after having struck."

129. "The autumn monkey's body," *shuko no mi:* Two interpretations are possible:

- "The autumn monkey's body": In the fall the monkeys come together to warm each other and huddle together, keeping their hands squeezed tight against their bodies; hence the name of the technique.
- "The short-armed monkey."

130. "Getting . . . close," *hairu* or *iru:* Literally, this means "enter into." In connection with combat, the idea is to enter inside your opponent's range of protection, which is that distance apart at which he can attack you. In the martial arts, this verb is commonly used to indicate the idea of crossing this boundary (either going in or coming out). That is why I have translated it as "getting in close to your opponent" and not "entering into your opponent." On the inside of this range, the closer you get to the adversary, the more the idea is present of entering into his body, *tekini mio iruiru,* to use Musashi's expression, which means to attack him.

131. "Distant": This comes from the verb *tonoku,* which literally means "to move away." The idea expressed here is that if you think of moving your hands forward, which is understood to mean "to execute a technique," the body tends to remain behind, distant from the adversary.

132. "Distance," *aida:* The ideogram can also be read *ma.* It can be interpreted either as a spatial or temporal interval. Therefore two translations are possible: either "at a distance at which" or "at the moment when."

133. "When you are at a distance . . . ," *te nite ukeahasuru hodo no aida niwa:* In this sentence, Musashi uses the word *te,* which means "hand," to refer to the hands holding the sword. This is why the translation is not literal, and the distance is not that at which the hands of the two adversaries are touching but rather that at which the two swords they are holding in their hands can touch each other and exchange blows.

In combat our perception is subject to the pressure of the particular situation, dominated by fear and excitement, especially in sword combat, where a single blow can be fatal. The first adversary is within ourselves, since attachment to life hinders our movements because of our unconscious reaction of fear. Thus the technique of a martial art cannot be related to movements alone. If there is not a psychological foundation sturdy enough to face the situation, no movement will be viable. If a bird is paralyzed, it cannot fly away. His apprenticeship and his study of techniques that basically revolve around the notion of death move the student of *budo* in the direction of introspection. However, this introspection is not metaphysical; rather, it passes through the body. Thus the philosophy of *budo* resides in the technique, in the daily practice of the art.

In the combat situation, the discrepancy or gap between perception and reality is considerable. Consequently, we should not consider the technique of *budo* to be simply technique concerned with movement. Because of this gap, instructions of the following type are given: "If you want to cut down your opponent, think of delivering a blow with your guard position; do not think of slashing with the blade of the sword, think of striking with your guard." These instructions guide the student's subjective sensations and compensate for the gap by shifting perception forward in time; thus an adjustment to the combat situation comes about. Warriors are familiar with this gap and see fear as their greatest enemy.

In this connection, here is an anecdote recounted by Nakazato:

> One day a young boy came to see Musashi to ask him for his help. "I asked my lord to allow me to engage in a duel to avenge the honor of my dead father and I have already received his permission. Everything is ready and the dueling site has already been enclosed with a bamboo fence. The duel will take place tomorrow. I would like to ask you to teach me how to win the duel."

In those days, to engage in a duel motivated by vengeance was considered a normal and honorable act, and even a necessary one, in *bushi* families. Sometimes the decision to seek vengeance was up to the discretion of the head of the family; sometimes it was obligatory. For this kind of duel, one had to ask permission of one's liege lord. If a journey was necessary in order to meet one's enemy, someone who took on this duty could forgo providing his services as a vassal for years on end without losing his position. But if he failed to accomplish his initial objective, he was considered unworthy as a *bushi* and risked having his standing revoked. The vengeance duel was thus sometimes essential for both parties.

Musashi replied, "I am touched by your sense of duty. I will teach you a secret technique that will make it possible for you to win without fail. Hold your knife *(tanto)* in your left hand in a horizontal position, and hold your large sword in your right hand. Advance in your opponent's direction quickly, and the instant you meet his attack with your knife, pierce his chest with the sword held in your right hand."

The boy practiced during the night and succeeded in basically learning the technique. Observing the way he executed the technique, Musashi complimented him and added: "Your victory is certain. Also tomorrow morning when you arrive at the place of the duel, take a good look beneath your seat when you sit down; if you see any ants, this will be a sign of victory. I will stay here and pray for you to win, so you will be protected from all sides. Don't worry about a thing."

The following day the boy saw a great number of ants around his feet, and he was greatly encouraged. Confronting his adversary, he did exactly as Musashi had taught him, and he succeeded in killing his enemy, who was quite powerful. He was thus able to fulfill his most weighty obligation. (23, pp. 82–83)

It is worthwhile to analyze the subtlety with which Musashi taught the technique of the autumn monkey's body here. If one of his disciples had been in this situation, Musashi would not have done it this way. It would have been enough for him to say, "Don't forget the autumn monkey's body." That would have been enough to get his disciple to understand the approach he had to take in the duel. Here, by contrast, he was dealing with a young boy for whom the task ahead was an overly heavy one and to whom, moreover, he had to teach a technique that he could apply the following day.

The first thing Musashi tells him is to hold a knife in his left hand, not a *wakizashi* (a small sword about sixty-five centimeters long) but a knife *(tanto)*. The technique consists in parrying with the knife, which measured about forty centimeters, which is not easy, but if this succeeds, the distance between the boy and his opponent will be short enough for him to stab him with his large sword. If the boy can get inside his opponent's attack zone, first using only his knife, he will execute the technique of the autumn monkey's body without realizing it.

To get inside his opponent's attack range in this fashion, using only a knife, would be possible only if he was without fear. The technique itself (concentrating on the parry with the knife) helps him to keep from thinking that he is crossing the boundary of his opponent's attack zone, which is the most difficult thing he has to do and the most frightening.

Musashi observes the results of the boy's practice session and comes to the conclusion that he has a chance of making good on his accelerated teaching. At that point he tells him, "Your victory is certain." This statement on the part of the celebrated Musashi does not fail to encourage the boy. Next Musashi speaks of the ants. This connection of the ants and victory in combat is all the more amazing because the boy really does find a lot of ants around his feet—thus Musashi appears to have premonitory power. Now, in fact, Musashi could be certain that the boy would find ants, because except in the winter, in Japan you find ants everywhere. What counted was that the boy was able to see those little ants, the perception of which would elude anyone who had lost his head in the moments before combat. Thus the important thing was not that there were or were not ants but whether he saw them or not. The boy, guided by Musashi's suggestion, put his attention on the ants, and he found them. Finding them, he was reassured once again. On top of that, lowering one's glance to one's feet makes possible stabilizing one's physical equilibrium. Musashi raised his confidence level yet another notch by telling him that at the time of the duel, he would be praying for him.

This kind of skill in teaching was also, for Musashi, part of the way of strategy.

134. The body of lacquer and paste": *shikko no mi.*

135. "Comparing heights," *take kurabe:* The contemporary expression is *sei kurabe.* In Japan it is traditional to measure children's and teenagers' heights periodically, often by drawing a line on one of the posts of the house. This measurement frequently takes place on Boys' Day. In this comparison with their contemporaries, it is important for them to show how much they have grown since the last measurement.

136. "Making your movements stick," *nebari o kakuru,* from the verb *nebaru* (see note 126). Making one's sword stick to one's opponent's is an important technique in various schools of swordsmanship. In the old Kashima school, the Kashima shin ryu (Kashima School of the Gods), this technique was practiced and transmitted under the name *sokui zuke* ("to stick with rice glue"). This technique consists in making your sword stick to your opponent's in a subtle fashion. When he wants to attack, you deflect his sword without letting it come unstuck from yours. When he wants to pull his sword back, you also follow him, not letting the two swords come apart. In this way your adversary will lose the fight. To reach this level, of course, one must be a truly accomplished swordsman.

We could think of the *sokui zuke* technique as a more subtle elaboration of the technique described here by Musashi. A similar technique has been developed in the bare-handed martial arts.

137. "Banging into your opponent," *mi no atari:* The word *atari* is the nominative form of the intransitive verb *ataru,* "to collide with," or the transitive verb *ateru,* "to hit." When the impact is delivered by the whole body, as in this passage, I have translated this as "bang," "knock," or "bang into." When it involves a person using an object, a sword, to hit someone, I have translated *atari* as "blow" or "hit" (for example, *"en no atari"* or *"sekka no atari"*).

138. When you are using just one sword as in modern kendo, the bang is delivered by the right shoulder, which is closer to the opponent, because you are holding the sword with two hands, the right hand forward. But in the School of Two Swords, the bang is delivered as described by Musashi, with the left shoulder, because generally you hold the small sword with the left hand and take the guard position with the left shoulder forward. Regarding this position, Yoshida Seiken writes: "When your opponent attacks on the left side, you parry with a quick movement of the short sword. This parry is very effective, and you slash immediately with the long sword in your right hand. Indeed, for an adept of the two swords, there is no better situation than that in which the adversary launches his attack on the left side. It is as though the adversary were coming to get cut down. That is why those who are familiar with the particulars of the two-swords style do not readily attack on the left side." (35, p. 79)

139. "A cadence of concordance with the breath," *iki au hyoshi:* It is also possible to read *iki ai;* in that case the expression means "with a bound."

140. "Two or three *ken*": 3.6 to 5.4 meters. A *ken* measures about 1.8 meters.

141. "The three parries": *mittsu no uke.*

142. "Stabbing," *tsuki:* This is the nominative form of the verb *tsuku,* "to stab or pierce with a pointed object with a violent movement." In the Japanese martial arts, *tsuki* refers, in the art of the sword and kendo, to the movement of stabbing the adversary with a sword. In the bare-handed martial arts (jujutsu, karate), it refers to the movement of punching. It is difficult to translate this word into English with a single word that would designate both techniques. That is why I have translated it "stabbing" when the context was using a sword, and as "punching" in the second part of this text segment, where Musashi explains that the movement is executed with a closed left hand.

143. "For this third parry," *kore mittsu no uke nari:* Because of the last word, *nari,* this expression would normally mean "These are three parries." But what follows ("you should think that you are delivering . . .") would then have no relevance, since according to Musashi's text, it is clear that the first two parries are executed with the large sword held in the right hand. That is why I think we have a transcription error here, and the word *nari* was added by mistake. If we do not take this word into account, which is the choice I have made, then the sense is coherent.

144. Let us look a little more closely at Musashi's description. For the first parry, you take the blade of your opponent's sword on the back of your large sword, and with a movement directed as though to stab him in the eye, you move your sword forward by slightly lifting your wrist, causing his sword, as it slides along the back of your sword, to pass above your right shoulder. This technique can be used even if you are holding your sword in two hands. You can also apply the principle of this technique in the bare-handed martial arts. In karate this technique is called *tsuki uke* or *sashi te*.

The difference between the second parry and the first is that you parry your opponent's attack with the flat of your small sword held in your left hand, pushing slightly downward. The side of your blade will then be resting on the back of his sword. At the same time, you make the movement of stabbing your adversary's right eye, and you will then be in a position where the back of his sword will provide yours, in the manner of a lever, with a support for cutting the right side of his face. You then direct the blade of your sword toward his throat. Thus this parry contains an attack that might be a decisive one. If not, you follow it immediately with an attack with your other sword.

This technique is also applicable when you are holding your sword with two hands and in karate combat. However, in the kendo matches of the present time, very few practitioners are aware of the position and direction of the blade of their sword, because they are accustomed to fighting with a *shinai* (bamboo sword). Since the *shinai* has the form of a round stick, it is difficult to make out the direction and position that the strike would have with a real sword. Let us recall, however, that until the beginning of the twentieth century, the most highly accomplished practitioners of kendo distinguished between false and real victories by determining through the movements of the *shinai* what the direction and position of the blade of a real sword would have been. Such rigor is still necessary today if one wishes to approach through the practice of kendo that which represents the way of the sword in terms of technical precision as well as in the orientation of the mind.

The third parry is more an attack than a parry. In any case, for Musashi no such thing as a parrying technique intended only to achieve a parry exists. We have seen in the instruction of the guardless guard that, for him, a parry is never just a defense but always an opportunity to achieve victory. In this third parry, when you press in as though to stab your opponent's face with your small sword, this technique is not a mere matter of know-how. It also involves the perception and the force of decision that makes it possible to cross the attack zone of your opponent without being overly concerned with the idea of parrying. If you find yourself in a position to stab the face of your opponent with the small sword held in your left hand, the large sword held in the other hand will be in a favorable position to attack.

145. "Piercing the face," *omote o sasu: Sasu* means "causing a pointed object to pene-

trate." What Musashi means by "piercing the face" has been passed down in kendo practice and is expressed today by the terms *seme* and *kizeme*. *Seme* consists in aiming the point of the sword toward the center line of the opponent's body, between his two eyes or in the direction of one of the eyes. During the combat you must try at every moment to strike or stab the adversary. When this clarity of the will is underpinned by real technical ability, the adversary will feel a painful pressure. Projecting toward the adversary the will to stab, prior to any manifestation of technique, is the objective of the teaching on *seme*.

When practitioners of a superior technical level have acquired the ability to project this will and perceive sharply the will of the other, the major part of the combat consists in the confrontation of *seme*.

A high level of mastery of *seme* is called *kizeme*. Thus a high-level combat consists of the interaction of two wills that have taken on a technical form. The two adversaries assume guard positions, and then one of them is repelled without having been able to make a move. The other will already have won before striking—if in this situation a blow is delivered, the victory will be total. Sometimes the bout ends without a blow ever having been struck, but with the result being perfectly clear to practitioners of the same level. It is in this way that the tradition is preserved, and it is also in this way that it is increasingly at variance with today's tendency toward spectacular combat sports.

146. "To repulse," *norasuru:* This is from the verb *noru,* which means (1) "to stretch, elongate"; (2) "to twist, bend over backward"; (3) "the body stretches out to the point of leaning over backward."

The situation depicted by Musashi can be described in the following manner: In taking your combat posture, your body leans slightly forward. When you drive your adversary back, first he stretches his torso upward and loses the stability of his stance, and then if the pressure continues, he leans his torso backward and is then forced to back up.

147. "Piercing the heart," *shin o sasu:* In the transcriptions of this text (4, 11, 13), the authors give the pronunciation *mune* for this ideogram instead of the usual pronunciation *shin,* which is what I have used.

Shin or *kokoro* means "chest, center" and also "heart" or "mind." In Musashi's text, the idea of chest is often equivalent to the idea of the center of the body. In fact, the technique he is describing is usually associated, in the teaching of kendo and swordsmanship, with aiming at the central line of the adversary's body. *Shin* is often used to refer to the central axis, as in a toy top. Here I have translated *shin* as "heart" in order to differentiate it from the expression employed a little farther on, *mune o tsuke* (see note 149).

148. "The back of your sword," *tachi no mune:* Here *mune* means "the back of the blade," that is to say, the part located opposite the edge.

149. "Stab him in the chest," *mune o tsuke:* To designate the chest, Musashi uses the word *mune*.

150. *Katsu-totsu:*

Katsu! This word, pronounced with a very heavily stressed open *a,* is a cry that is used in Zen, sometimes to communicate a function of the mind difficult to express in speech, sometimes to encourage the disciple or to strike him with an intuitive criticism. It is also used to guide the mind of a dead person to the way of Buddha.

Totsu! This word is pronounced with a short stressed *o* and is an exclamation expressing displeasure or the command to stop. But here the word is used as an echo of *katsu!* Musashi uses the sound of the two exclamations to express the immediacy of the linkage of the two movements that form the technique. What is actually pronounced is *ka-tot,* which mimics the resonance of a sound bouncing off a wall.

These sounds, which come from Sanskrit through the intermediary of Chinese, produce an evocative image for the Japanese. When they are used by Western practitioners of the martial arts or Zen, who know them through a retranscription, the sounds are deformed and lose their evocative force and their rhythm. In that case, they can become a braking force on a movement, because the cry associated with a martial arts technique is generally a single syllable, and when there are two syllables, one is dominant and the other almost swallowed.

151. "The parry with the flat of the sword," *hariuke:* Hari comes from the verb *haru,* (99) which means (1) "to stretch a thread, a cord, a piece of cloth, or a net so that there is no fold in it"; (2) "to paste something that is flat"; (3) "to stretch by expanding the elbow, arm, shoulder, or chest"; (4) "to strike with a horizontal movement with the palm, the open hand."

The verb *haru* is used here in senses 2 and 4. The idea expressed is parrying with a slap of the side of your sword, which plays the role of the hand in sense 4 of the term, by pasting it against the side of your opponent's sword (in sense 2 of the term).

At the end of the text, *haru* is used in the expression *haru kokoro areba,* which I translated "with the sensation of stretching your arm," since the verb *haru* applies here to a person and therefore expresses sense 4.

152. *Totan-totan* is an onomatopoeic expression used by Musashi to express the *hyoshi* (cadence) in a situation in which the attacks and parries of two combatants have become repetitive and in which the combat situation has stagnated.

153. To parry a rapid and powerful attack on the part of your opponent, you need not necessarily employ as much speed and power—on the condition that the force applied is sufficiently flexible and powerful to absorb the shock at the moment of tak-

ing the strike, because you can back off slightly without letting yourself be driven back completely. This works both for sword and bare-handed combat. The force applied in this parry should not be confused with that of a simple rigid contraction. It implies suppleness and flexibility at the same time as force. It makes it possible to catch and control the adversary's strike and render it ineffective, and he will find himself for an instant with a disconcerting sensation that will place him in a position of vulnerability. Taking the initiative by means of this parry means forcing your opponent into a situation where he momentarily loses the cadence of his movements.

154. "Conduct against many adversaries," *tateki no kurai:* Musashi fought against more than one opponent a number of times. This passage evokes his combat against the Yoshioka clan, where for the first time, other than on the battlefield, he had to confront a large number of opponents. The number of the Yoshioka clan that he faced alone varies, depending on which document you rely on, from tens (*Nitenki,* 2) to several hundred (*Kokura hibun,* 17; *Honcho bugei shoden,* 1-b). Musashi was then twenty years old (1604).

According to the *Hyoho senshi denki:* "When a large number of students of [Yoshioka] Kenpo surrounded the master, sword in hand, to kill him, the master drew both his swords, and cutting down his opponents, he escaped by getting over a hedge. He fought with great courage, and on the basis of this experience, he elaborated his school's strategy for fighting many adversaries." (9, p. 225)

155. "The principle of combat," *uchiai no ri: Uchi ai* means "to strike each other," which expresses the notion of combat in a concrete manner. In Japanese the idea of combat is expressed by various terms:

- *shobu:* "the idea of victory or defeat"
- *tatakai:* "the idea of fighting or confronting one another"
- *uchi ai:* "the idea of exchanging blows"
- *shiai:* "the idea of a mutual confrontation testing skill or art. Today this word is frequently used to refer to a martial arts tournament or sports competition."

Ri means "advantage" or "profit." Here Musashi uses the ideogram *ri* in the sense of "principle, reason."

156. "Transmitted orally," *kuden:* Written transmission plays only a very minor role in the martial arts. In this respect, Musashi's work is an exception. Often it was even prohibited to take notes during teaching.

157. "The single strike," *hitotsu no uchi:* What Musashi describes here is the original form of the notion of *ippon,* which is present today in most of the Japanese martial arts. *Ippon* means "a single essential blow." It is a contraction of *ichi,* "a single one," and

hon, "origin, root, essence." *Ippon* has become the criterion for a win in competition in martial arts such as kendo, judo, and karate. In that context it has the sense of the decisive point that puts an end to a bout and qualifies a technique as successful. It is in kendo that the application of the notion of *ippon* is least removed from its origin. In kendo the practitioner seeks a victory through a blow that "resounds in the heart of the mind that receives it and also the mind that delivers it." We find this expression in almost every book on the practice of kendo published in Japan.

This notion originally corresponded to the state of mind, described by Musashi, that has as its aim to achieve victory through a single technique. It is this state of mind that guides the search for development and perfection in the Japanese martial arts. All the mental techniques described by Musashi converge toward this state of mind. For example, in order to "stab your opponent in the face," it is essential to seek to win by "a single strike."

158. Direct communication," *jiki tsu no kurai:* The term *jiki tsu* is problematic, and its use seems to be restricted to Musashi alone. It is most often understood in the sense of "direct communication" or "penetration of mind," but these interpretations leave room for ambiguity.

Both of these words has several meanings. I have chosen the ones that are most compatible with Musashi's text. *Jiki* means "direct, straight, honest, rapidly, immediately, communication, quite soon." *Tsu* means "communication, without any stagnation, capacity for supernatural energy, supernatural, to be informed."

An important key here is found in the oral transmission of the *jiki do no kurai* of one of the branches of Musashi's school, the Enmei ryu. According to Yoshida Seiken, the content of this oral transmission *(kuden)* is as follows:

> Your guard position must arise in response to your opponent. That is why, if you take up a guard position, it is based on your opponent, and your guard position is formless like water. Once you are face-to-face with an opponent, a guard position appears spontaneously in accordance with that of the other. For example, if he assumes a high guard, you are in a middle-level guard, and if he is in a middle-level guard, you are in a high guard or a middle one. Thus your guard is the one that makes it possible to naturally dominate the other. You must learn through diligent training to discern the guard position of the adversary so that you can take up a guard position that is suitable and consistent. It is in this way that you will be able to attain direct communication. (35, p. 103)

Based on these elements, I interpret the expression *jiki tsu* in the sense of "direct communication that leads to victory." In my view this involves not only a guard position determined in an effective manner by responding to that of the adversary but also a way of being in combat that is linked to the perception of the adversary and to what Musashi made his adversary feel that permitted him to have direct access to victory.

Yoshida Seiken puts forward another explanation: "The sense of *jiki do no kurai* is a direct path in the mind, that is to say, a state that makes it possible for us to turn ourselves toward the direct way. In other words, it has to do with our own guard position responding directly and correctly to the guard position of the adversary in order to defeat him. I think it would be more appropriate to call this state *jiki do* rather than *jiki tsu,* as Musashi does." Thus, for Yoshida, the two terms *jiki tsu* and *jiki do* express the same state.

Let us note that the reason the teaching of *jiki do no kurai* exists in the Enmei ryu is that Musashi used this term. In the thirty-fifth article of his work *Hyoho sanju go kajo,* he writes, "In my school there exists an ultimate technique that I call *jiki do.*" Given the very close meanings of the two phrases, we can either surmise that Musashi uses the two closely related ideograms *do* and *tsu* interchangeably or hypothesize a copying error, since, written with a brush, these two ideograms resemble each other a great deal.

159. "Even if you gain victory . . .": This sentence refers directly to the beginning of the Scroll of Earth. The principle of victory that Musashi is seeking is the principle of *hyoho.* Victory must proceed from this principle, which extends to all domains. In this way seeking victory in combat leads to philosophical reflection.

160. "This scroll of fire": *hi no maki* or *ka no maki.*

161. "An area of the wrist . . . ," *tekubi gosun sanzun:* Literally, this means "five or three *sun* (fifteen or nine centimeters) of the area of the wrist." This is a reference to the flexible area of the wrist, which corresponds roughly to this length. The numbers express the idea of the ridiculously trivial aspect of things and have no importance as actual measures.

162. "*Shinai*": Kamiizumi Nobutsuna (c. 1508–c. 1577) invented the bamboo *shinai* as a weapon to be used for exercises. (15, 32, 41) Until that time, training in swordsmanship was carried out mainly with the *bokken* (wooden sword). However, exercising with the *bokken* involved a great number of accidents once training took on a form close to that of the duel. The story of Musashi is an illustration of this—in the majority of his duels, using only a *bokken* himself, he fought an opponent armed with a real sword whom he vanquished and often killed.

Kamiizumi Nobutsuna, wishing to avoid accidents, devised the *fukuro shinai,* or *hikihada shinai,* which is composed of a piece of bamboo left whole at the grip, split into thin strips in the area corresponding to the blade of a sword, and sheathed in a scabbard of lacquered leather. The lacquer reinforced the leather and made it shrink, giving it the appearance of a frog's skin scabbard, hence the name *hikihada shinai.* The length of the *shinai* was the same as a sword's. This *shinai* is still used today in the traditional Yagyu shin kage ryu. The commonly used *shinai* is also derived from it.

With the *shinai* one could exercise with less concern, and this made it possible to develop technical subtleties. Musashi criticizes this tendency, seeing it as a superficial development. In Musashi's time, most of the schools of swordsmanship used wooden swords for training. Toward the middle of the eighteenth century, practitioners of various schools introduced the use of the *shinai* along with protective armor. The best-known of these innovators are Yamada Zaemon and Naganuma Shirozaemeon of the Jiki shin kage ryu and Nakanishi Chubei of the Itto ryu. Sword training with a *shinai* and protective armor is called *shinai uchi kenjutsu* or *gekiken* or *gekken*. With this form of training, which became dominant in the course of the nineteenth century, technique diversified and became more subtle.

163. "The meaning of the edge and the back of the sword," *katana no hamune no michi:* Literally, this means "the way of the back and edge of the sword," which refers in concrete terms to exact trajectories of the blade and precision of technique related to that. It is impossible to slash properly without mastering with precision the pathway of the blade and therefore without having an awareness of the back and edge of the sword.

164. "Armor," *rokugu:* In the *Ihon gorin no sho,* this is rendered by the term *hyogu.* (14)

165. "The way of my strategy . . .": In this sentence, the term *michi* is used twice, the first time in the sense of "way"; the second time it is applied to that which makes it possible to attain victory. In that case I therefore translated it "principle."

166. "The principle of the way," *dori:* This has the sense of principle, but to distinguish it from the terms *do* or *michi* or *ri* (which Musashi uses alone in the sense of "principle"), I have translated this expression "the principle of the way."

167. "To win against any person," *ban nin ni katsu: Ban nin* literally means "ten thousand men." In this context, the sense is "all persons, whoever they might be, anybody."

168. "Direct communication," *jiki do:* See the last section of the Scroll of Water ("Direct Communication").

169. "Supernatural power," *tsuriki fushigi: Tsuriki* is a Buddhist term meaning "subtle and excellent force or power which is free and effective and applies to every thing and every phenomenon"; *fushigi* is a Buddhist term meaning "that which is unfathomable, that which is beyond the capacity of human thought and reason."

Musashi is considered to be highly pragmatic. In his writings he confines himself in general to the realm of the tangible, but here he mentions a "supernatural power." In the anecdotes about Musashi, we find a number of descriptions of "supernatural abilities," which might be interpreted as an exaggeration. Nevertheless, still today in Japanese martial arts circles, "supernatural" phenomena are spoken of, that is, phenomena that are difficult to explain, such as causing opponents to fall down from a distance or communicating by telepathy.

In the course of my practice, I have had a few experiences of this nature. For example, a master caused me to feel a strange pressure in the course of combat exercises, as if the air were pushing me backward. I felt this physically, but I was able to resist this pressure because I refused to enter into collusion with the energy of it. His regular students were thrown spectacularly without the master's ever touching them. I concluded from this experience that emanation of a strange energy does indeed exist. In this particular case, this energy did not seem sufficiently strong to throw someone without there being a master-student relationship to create and hold a certain psychological synchronization. If the energy emanated in this way were stronger and the person emanating it were capable of imposing this kind of synchronization on his opponent, then it would be possible to understand the accounts relating to the end of Musashi's life in which he drove opponents back or made them collapse without touching them. (See page 319.)

170. "Vital essence," *iki:* literally, "breath."

171. "Regarding the place of combat," *ba no shidai.*

172. With two swords, the most advantageous situation is to have your opponent on your left and avoid being attacked on the right, because the longer sword, held in the right hand, is always ready to attack.

173. Musashi uses the term *kamiza,* which literally means "the high place." In traditional architecture, the *kamiza* is situated at the rear of a room. The most important person or a guest is placed there. At a gathering, the places people receive are hierarchically arranged starting from the *kamiza.* In general this is the location of the *tokonoma,* a small, slightly elevated alcove in which an ornamental arrangement of some type is placed.

174. "Three ways of taking the initiative," *mittsu no sen:* The term *sen* is often used in teaching techniques of swordsmanship. *Sen* means "to precede." Here the term indicates the need to act first in situations of combat, that is, to take a step forward and thus to take the initiative.

175. *Ken* means "attack, assault." Musashi employs this term in the sense of "connect the will to attack with your own mind," that is, "prepare to attack." *Ken no sen* can thus be translated, "to take the initiative in a situation where you attack first or in which you are in a position to launch an attack." In this case it is your initial disposition that

determines how the combat unfolds. In an attempt to conserve the brevity of the Japanese formulation, I have translated *ken no sen* as "attacking before your opponent."

176. "As soon as you near . . . ," *hayaku momitatsuru sen:* This passage contains an ambiguity. In general it is read *hayaku* (fast) *momitatsuru* (to attack), and then translated "to attack fast." However, this passage can also be read *hayakumo* (fast) *mitatsuru* (to discern), the verb then being *mitatsuru,* "to discern." The word *mitatsuru* is connected with the term *mikiri,* often used to refer to the particular sharpness of Musashi's perception. Both interpretations are compatible with the combat situation.

177. "An untroubled mind," *kokoro hanatsu:* Literally, this means "to let go of the mind." In a synoptic text, *Nito ichi ryu gokui jojo,* written up from his notes by a student of Musashi's, we find the following sentence: "What is called 'letting go of the mind' is part of the domain of mental techniques; it means to cut and clear away various thoughts, troubles, hesitations, fear or hate, and so forth, in order to be able to establish a serene and immutable mind." (6, p. 31)

Kokoro hanatsu is often simply translated "to let go of the mind" in the sense of "to relax"; however, here the text permits us to home in on the meaning more precisely. Hence the translation "preserve an untroubled mind."

178. The term *tai* means "to wait." *Tai no sen* therefore means "to take the initiative, having waited for the attack of the adversary," or more simply, "when the adversary attacks." For the sake of keeping the brevity of the Japanese formulation, I translated *tai no sen* as "taking the initiative at the time of an attack."

179. It should be noted that the term *tai* has two distinct meanings. Musashi writes *tai* in the syllabic alphabet (hiragana) to express it in the sense of "to wait" and *tai-tai sen* in ideograms to express the sense of "to clash" or "to oppose." *Tai-tai* expresses a situation where two adversaries are ready to attack each other. For the sake of keeping the brevity of the Japanese formulation, I translated *tai-tai no sen* as "taking the initiative at the time of a reciprocal attack." The sense of *tai* as it is used here is therefore different from the previous use. This explanation is necessary for a Western practitioner who might tend to draw a conclusion about the sense of the word on the basis of the phonetic system of the language. In fact, differences in linguistic systems are often the cause of errors of understanding and communication for Western practitioners of the Japanese martial arts. Musashi uses three words here: *ken, tai,* and another *tai.* The sense of the third term, *tai,* is more or less the same as that of the first term, *ken.* Thus Musashi could have written *ken-ken no sen* instead of *tai-tai no sen,* which would have made it possible to avoid confusion here, even for Japanese practitioners.

180. On *sen,* see appendix 2.

181. "Holding down on the headrest," *makura o sayuru:* The image is to prevent a movement beginning with the head, that is, from the moment it starts.

The usual sense of *makura* is "headrest," but this term also means "he who is at the origin of things, the preface or the prologue of a story or tale." Thus another image is possible—that of exercising a pressure that prevents someone from getting started on the main story.

182. Musashi indicated in this passage, as though it were obvious, that it is necessary to perceive the will of your opponent. However, trying to perceive the will of an adversary before he makes a move is one of the most important and difficult points in the practice of the martial arts. In all the schools, the most secret teaching revolves around how it is possible to acquire this ability.

Musashi is writing for someone who may have acquired this ability. It is for such a person that the instruction "holding down on the headrest" takes on meaning. In practice, it is incomprehensible for those who have not mastered sufficiently the technique of a martial art. More than anything else, this fashion of expressing himself bears witness to the very high level of Musashi's martial arts practice, and this text, for me, evokes an emotion of a different order from the kind of emotion that can be aroused by literary images.

An equivalent attitude is expressed in kendo today by the expression "giving your opponent a train ticket." That means that you know what station he is going to get off at and you are waiting for him at the exit, holding your *shinai* over your head. You strike him a blow before he can even take a step toward the outside.

183. "Getting over a critical passage": *to o kosu.*

184. "Traversing life," *hito no yo o wataru koto:* To evoke human life, Musashi uses the image of a ship crossing. He has already made use of this image at the beginning of the Scroll of Earth.

185. "This event is unique," *ichidaiji:* This is a term of Buddhist origin that means "a great event, the birth of the Buddha; a thought of unique importance, an affair of great importance."

186. "Realizing the situation": *keiki o shiru.*

187. "Have knowledge . . . ," " *teki no nagare o wakimaru: Nagare* (current), which can also be pronounced *ryu,* comes from the verb *nagareru,* which means "to flow." A school of an art is expressed as a current of water that perpetuates itself by traversing time from the past to the present to the future. It is on the basis of this image that *ryu* became a suffix that is frequently added to the name of a school.

188. "Use tactics . . . ," *teki no keshiki ni chigau tokoro o shikake:* Another possible translation of this phrase is "Use different tactics by following his reactions." In fact, the term *keshiki* means (1) "the external form of things, the sensation that one feels based on a vision of things or a situation, a facial expression; (2) the movement of the mind that it is possible to observe from the outside, the confidential expression of a secret thought."

I chose the first sense, since it corresponds best to the overall sense of the paragraph and to Musashi's strategy.

189. "Crushing the sword with your foot," *ken o fumu:* Musashi uses here the term *ken* to mean "sword," but this term also expresses an allusion to another word *ken,* which means "a place difficult to get past," or "difficulty."

Fumu means "walk on, bring the foot down from above and pressing down on the top of something; pressing on the ground with the foot in order to walk."

I translated *fumu* "crush with the foot," although it literally means "to walk on." I rejected "stamp" and "trample," because the sense is that of a single powerful act and not of a repetition. "Crushing the sword with your foot" designates an attitude that consists in facing a situation of combat and directly confronting the decisive moment. This moment represents a difficulty that is such that if you dominate it, you can win as though you had broken the sword of your opponent with your foot.

The image of treading on something evokes power in combat. The more serious the combat is, the more we tend to make the tension rise toward the upper part of our body and lose the strength in our legs and feet. The teaching of breaking with the foot contains the instruction to stabilize your force during combat.

190. "Repetition of the same cadences": This is the way I translated the ono-matopoeic expression *totan-totan* that Musashi uses to express a technical exchange carried out according to a repetitive cadence that has led to a situation where the combat stagnates (see "The Parry with the Flat of the Sword," page 165).

191. "Crush *(fumu)* with your body": We have seen that the term *fumu* has to do with the state of mind of combat and indicates the force rather than the concrete technique of crushing with your foot. Thus Musashi uses this expression with regard to the body, the mind, and the sword to express the attitude in which one places the totality of one's body above the object to be crushed. Therefore in this sentence I translated the word *fumu* as "crush" rather than "crush with the foot."

192. "You act at the same time . . .": I propose the following interpretation of this sentence. In order to crush the sword of your opponent, that is to say, to crush the action of his technique, it is necessary to act at the same time as he does and not after, but this does not mean knocking into him, because if you collide with him, he will be thrown backward. On the contrary, you meet him at the same time that he is ad-

vancing, and without pushing him back, you act as though to absorb the impact of the encounter with the sensation of following his action. This will allow you to crush him rather than throw him backward.

193. Recognizing the instant of collapse": *kuzure o shiru*.

194. Let us recall that *hyoshi* is the entire set of cadences that constitute a phenomenon. To replace this term with a single word such as *cadence* necessarily involves a shift in the meaning (see appendix 1).

195. "This strike that causes the blow to carry a long way," *uchi hanasu: Uchi* means "a strike"; *hanasu* means "to separate two connected things, to move away, to distance oneself, to free."

According to the dictionary, *uchi hanasu* means "to kill by cutting down forcefully." (99) However, when the dictionary uses this term to describe a technique, it does not indicate killing but rather describes a technique that, when it is applied to the utmost extent, is capable of killing. That is why I settled on the translation "strike that causes the blow to carry a long way."

We are talking here about a way of striking whose effect on the adversary goes well beyond the direct impact of the landed blow, and this increases the effect of the blow. Even if your opponent resists, he will have trouble pulling himself back together in order to riposte. The sensation is not that of striking powerfully or fully but of striking in such a way that your force carries a lot farther than the spot you hit. Your opponent has the impression that the power of the strike covers his whole body and goes beyond that. In this situation, even if there is no repetition of several strikes, he has the impression of being under the pressure of an ongoing series of strikes. Your opponent will then have the impression of being dominated by a force that is greatly superior to him.

196. "If you do not put some distance . . .": *hanare zareba shidaruki kokoro ari*. Another translation is possible: "If you do not drive your opponent back with this strike, the combat will be in danger of stagnating." The first translation makes more sense in connection with the whole technique. When executing it, one realizes that it is a necessary step to place oneself at a certain distance from the adversary.

197. "Becoming your opponent": *teki ni naru*.

198. "Undoing four hands," *yotsu de o hanasu:* This expression is still in use today in traditional Japanese wrestling, which is called sumo. *Yotsu ni kumu,* "to take a four-hands position," refers to the situation in which, in full body contact, each of the two combatants has grabbed hold of the belt of his opponent with both hands. In sumo, the two wrestlers begin by pushing each other or banging into each other, and sometimes one of them wins the victory with these techniques. But if the two wrestlers

move on to putting holds on each other, the combat has passed into another phase. The four-hands position, *yotsu,* is a position from which new exchanges of technique can begin.

In contemporary Japanese speech, the expression "to take a four-hands position" means "to fight on an equal footing."

Musashi's expression is easier to understand if we keep the sumo idea in mind. Sumo has long been one of the foundations of the physical education of warriors, and thus it underlies all the techniques of the martial arts. For example, Chiba Shusaku (1794–1855) took the classification of sumo techniques as his point of departure when in the nineteenth century he systematized the technique of swordsmanship into sixty-eight techniques *(kenjutsu rokuju hatte).* (82, pp. 47–63) Sumo is also a popular pastime, and sumo matches take place on holidays. Musashi, raised in the country, certainly practiced sumo from the time of his childhood. In the West, sumo evokes the image of enormous wrestlers, but those are the professionals. It should be pointed out that until quite recently, the nonprofessional practice of sumo was widespread in Japan.

Musashi, who created his school on the basis of his own experience, is using an expression here whose significance is plain to anyone who has practiced sumo. What he means to indicate is that one must avoid placing oneself on an equal footing with one's opponent.

In my experience, if a practitioner trains in combat only within a confined group, his way of fighting is relatively limited because of the small range of adversaries he faces. When he fights a new opponent, he might well not defeat a person of inferior ability, because he is thrown off by a style of combat he has not yet encountered. He will have an impression of an absence of synchronization, for example, that the two adversaries are attacking and backing off at the same time. He might well lose a bout if his opponent, even one of lesser ability, surpasses him in fighting spirit. By contrast, someone who is accustomed to fighting with a variety of opponents will be able to get out of this kind of situation more easily by modifying his techniques and his cadence.

199. "Moving your shadow," *kage o ugokasu:* What Musashi is referring to in this description corresponds in part to what is practiced in modern kendo under the name of *seme.* At the simplest level, this means a feinted attack used to make an opponent who has taken up a solid guard position make a move. When he reacts to your feint, he reveals his hidden intentions and he has a moment of vacillation that renders him vulnerable.

At a higher level, a practitioner, without making any visible movement, emanates a threat of attack in response to which his opponent is forced to reveal his veiled intentions. This is the moment to launch your actual attack.

If the disparity in ability is considerable, hindered in his action, the adversary will be disconcerted and forced back away from this implicit threat. This situation is an example of the combat of *kizeme*.

200. "Effective means," *ri: Ri* is understood here in its second series of senses: "effectiveness, advantage, interest" (see appendix 1). I usually translate it "advantage," but in this context the idea of effectiveness seemed to be dominant.

201. In Musashi's time the schools of swordsmanship had not yet stabilized, and there were certainly guard positions in use that today's practitioners cannot even conceive of. Today in the practice of kendo, we cannot find an equivalent of taking up a "guard position with his sword held back." The way of moving the feet and the places to which strikes are directed are considerably different from what they were in Musashi's time. In the practice of swordsmanship *(kenjutsu),* there is in use today a side-guard position called *waki gamae.* This is a guard position that is taken to the right side with the right foot back, the torso turned sideways—nearly in profile—and the point of the sword directed downward and back. With this guard the adversary is unable to get an idea of the length of the sword, and when the sword is held completely back, he cannot even tell what the nature of the weapon is.

202. "Constricting the shadow": *kage o osayuru.*

203. "Taking the initiative . . .": The term used by Musashi, *ku,* means at the same time "emptiness," "sky or heaven," and "space." The sense here is "emptiness," designating a state of mind that is undistorted, that reflects a spontaneous wisdom. This notion is close to that of nonthought in Zen. We find this idea explored more deeply in the Scroll of Heaven.

204. "Infecting," *utsurakasu* (transitive), *utsura-kasu: Kasu* is a suffix that strengthens the transitive sense of a verb. The meaning of this word is almost the same as that of *utsuraseru,* which is used more often. (99) It is the transitive form of the intransitive verb *utsuru,* which means "to transfer, change position or situation" for an object or a person. From this three meanings are derived: (1) "to be contagious" (for an illness); (2) referring to time, "to pass, pass by"; (3) "change in the situation or character of a thing."
     Here Musashi plays on a double meaning of the word. Written with another ideogram, which develops its main sense, *utsuru* means "to reflect" in the sense of the shadow or the light of a thing resting on another—its form or its shadow being reflected on something. In this passage Musashi plays on senses 1 and 2 of the term. Several times already we have encountered Musashi playing on a single pronunciation attached to different ideograms that have different meanings in order to give an idea more texture and relief. His play on its pronunciation extends a term's field of meaning.

If a disposition or a sensation is transferred to another being, that is "infecting." If time moves on from one instant to the next, it passes. The time of combat contains all these dynamics—that is why Musashi introduces time in his first list of examples in this section.

205. "And this goes for time too": *toki no utsuru mo ari.*

206. "Irritating your adversary": *mukatsukasuru.*

207. "Before their minds . . . ," *teki no kokoro no kiwamarazaru uchi ni:* Another possible translation would be "before they realize what the situation is."

208. "Without slacking off even to the slightest extent," *iki o nukasazu:* Another possible translation would be "without letting your adversaries breathe for an instant."

209. "Frightening," *obiyakasu:* literally, "to frighten by means of a threatening act."

210. "Coating," *mabururu:* This word comes from *mamireru,* which means "to dirty the whole body with blood, sweat, mud, or dust." The contemporary form is *mabusu,* which is often used as a cooking term, referring, for example, to rolling a fritter in flour.

211. "Hitting a corner," *kado ni sawaru:* In combat position, knees and feet are among the protruding "corners" Musashi is talking about. In modern kendo, only four parts of the body are attacked: the head *(men),* the side *(do),* the wrist *(kote),* and the throat *(tsuki).* Attacks directed at other parts of the body do not count. Matches with adepts of the *naginata* (mainly women)—a discipline in which the shins are also attacked— show plainly the major difficulty encountered by practitioners of kendo resulting from attacks for which they are not prepared.

At the end of the Edo period, the sword had attained a very high level, but at the same time, a certain standardization had distanced the art from situations of combat. When warriors once again found themselves involved in a period of sword combat, between 1850 and 1870, the Ryugo ryu was greatly celebrated for its effectiveness, which resulted from attacks to all parts of the body, notably the shins.

212. "Troubling": *uromekasu.*

213. "The three types of cries," *mittsu no koe:* Left over from the wave of karate and kung fu films is the expression "the cry that kills." And if you attend a competition or a training session of these disciplines, you will certainly hear cries, but they are far from killing; rather, they approximate the cries of animals, accompanied by grimaces.

Musashi clearly says: "Do not sound a great cry at the same time as you strike with your sword."

This teaching differs from the custom that has become the usual one in kendo, of crying out *kiai* and announcing the part to which you are delivering your blow (*men, do, kote, tsuki*) at the same time as you strike. This custom has been inherited from training sessions of former times, where a wooden sword or sometimes even a real sword was used, during which, to avoid accidents, the attacker called out what part of the body he was about to strike. The controlled movement of attack followed immediately after. With this method, the attacker sought to score a sure victory, that is, to attack when he was sure his strike was going to hit home. This is what is called *ki-ken-tai,* which means the simultaneous coming together of *ki,* the sword, and the body at the moment of the strike. In kendo this is a way of ruling out a win by a chance blow and of trying for fullness, a kind of existential sensation, in the act of striking.

The difference between this and the swordsmanship of Musashi is clear. Musashi situated himself first and foremost within an overall strategy of combat in which the life of the combatant was at risk. In modern kendo, defeat can be a challenging moment that can lead to progress. In this context it is necessary to have many experiences of defeat in order to make progress, whereas for Musashi, a single defeat meant death. Another attempt was thus not a viable notion.

214. "As loudly as possible," *ikahodo mo kasa kakete:* This literally means "exaggeratedly, to an unimaginable degree." The expression is composed of

> *ikahodo:* (1) "how much, to what degree"; (2) "the degree, the quantity, and the value are so great that they cannot be assessed"
> *kasa:* (1) "dimension, height, size of superimposed objects; quantity of things"; (2) "height, high part, upper part"; (3) "weight, dignity, talent"; (4) "energy that repels the adversary"
> *kasa o kakeru:* to express exaggeratedly, multiply the dimensions

215. According to Yoshida Seiken, in Musashi's time the two series of cries that were most common in the schools of swordsmanship were *ei, o, to* and *ei, ya, to.* (35, p. 130) Tominaga Kengo writes:

> In the practice of the Niten ryu, different cries exist. During training, most often these three cries are used: *ya, ei, to.* Some groups use *shi, ei, to, ho, yo, ya,* and sometimes another cry is added: *sore.* According to an ancient teaching of this school, the cries are defined by the seven sounds: *ei, to, shi, ho, yo, ya,* and *sore,* and there are no others. Today in the Niten ryu there are masters who use cries and others who do not. Some use a long cry: *u, to;* and others: *ei, ha, to.*
>
> In certain schools it is said that at the moment of a fight to the death, it is not possible to emit a cry, and therefore, it is better not to train in this. In other schools full cries and empty cries are distinguished, with the empty cries considered to be bad and the full cries to be good. In the Jigen ryu they have just one cry: *chie.* (12, p. 205)

216. "Cries of before and after": *sen go koe.*

217. "Concealing yourself," *magiruru.* This comes from *magireru,* which means (1) to blend in, become lost by mixing with a large number; (2) difficult to distinguish because of their resemblance; (3) to hide oneself, conceal oneself; (4) to try to remain unseen; (5) to clutter up.

218. "Zigzagging down a slope" is expressed by *tsuzura-ori,* which means "a road going down a slope in zigzags." This term is also used in Japanese equitation to refer to the technique that is used to go down a slope in a zigzag fashion on horseback.

219. "This strategy can also be applied . . .": Musashi does not give any further explanation of this point. I interpret this sentence in the following way: When your opponent is powerful, you must not have the slightest thought of backing off and must attack with force, varying your attacks from the head down to the feet of your opponent. In this way you can create an opportunity to defeat him without sticking to a particular technique; for if your opponent is strong, he will be able to counter any definite technique. Thus it is important for you to create a diversion at the moment of each of your attacks, continually varying your techniques. This is what Musashi calls "concealing yourself," that is, concealing your intentions behind your acts.

220. "Smashing": *hishigu.*

221. "Determinedly considering him . . .": We find the same sort of teaching in the Chinese method known as *da cheng quan,* which is based mainly on standing meditation. In this method the practitioner practices various bodily sensations, guiding himself with various images. In the course of my practice of this, during a visit to China in 1991, I received from Master Yu Yong the following instruction: "You imagine yourself as a powerful giant while imagining your opponent and everything that surrounds you as small. You are infinitely larger and stronger than they are and you dominate them." The point is to create a psychological state that increases your combativeness.

222. "Starting with the head . . . ," *kashira yori kasa o kakete:*

- *kasa:* (1) "dimension, height, size of superimposed objects; quantity of things"; (2) "height, high part, upper part"; (3) "weight, dignity, talent"; (4) "energy that oppresses the adversary".
- *kakeru:* (1) to hang; (2) to put on top of, to cover; (3) add force or quantities.

The expression *kasa o kakeru* means "to express exaggeratedly, multiply the dimensions." I translated it more literally as "adding *(o kakete)* an oppressive burst of energy *(kasa)."*

223. "Change from the Mountain to the Sea," *san kai no kawari:* Musashi seems in this

title to be making a little play on words. *San* means "mountain," and *kai* means "sea," but another pair of ideograms also pronounced *san* and *kai* mean "three" and "times," which makes "three times." This expression is also used in this sense in the text.

224. "Ripping out the bottom," *soko o nuku:* The image is that of a full barrel from which one brutally removes the bottom. The liquid will completely run out of it; that is, the adversary will feel himself to have lost completely, as though he had been emptied of his contents. This image contains the violence of combat, which is why I translated as "ripping out."

225. Musashi uses the preceding image here again: "he feels completely defeated," *soko yori makuru kokoro ni.* Musashi seems to have used this manner of "ripping out the bottom" as a criterion of victory in his duels. He did not consider himself to have won a bout until he had struck his opponent a blow of his sword in the middle of his forehead, between the brows, which generally brought about his death. If not, this way of striking at least ripped out "the bottom," and his adversary was no longer capable of putting up a fight.

226. "Renewing yourself": *arata ni naru.*

227. I understand this passage from my experience in karate combat. In the beginning, when the development of a combat stagnated, my tendency was to make an all-out effort, straining to the point of exhaustion. In such a situation I had the impression of letting myself slide down a slope, slipping lower and lower. I then had to climb back up at any price, like someone who is drowning. In a case like that, even if I did end up with the win, I expended a great deal of energy and felt exhausted. Around the age of twenty-seven, with the help of this passage in the *Gorin no sho,* I learned to renew myself when the combat was stagnating. It seems that it is necessary, in order to learn to renew oneself in combat, to have accumulated concrete combat experiences and also to have observed a large number of bouts. Otherwise, even if you understand this passage intellectually, you will not be able to put it into practice, because you will not be capable of assuming the necessary distance from your experience of the moment, from your own sensations. In combat you are doubtless caught up in a particular field of tension, and renewing yourself means resituating yourself in a different type of field of tension. To do this it is indispensable to detach yourself from the initial tension, and this requires a maturity that has been enriched by experience.

228. "A bull's neck," *soto goshu:* I translated the ideogram that appears in both copies of Musashi's text as "bull." This ideogram, pronounced *go* or *uma,* means "horse." The related ideogram is pronounced *go* or *ushi* and means "bull" or "ox."

In practice in the schools that have issued from Musashi, the image comparing the bull and the mouse is one that is used by the masters. Moreover, in the training of warriors, the following aphorism has been in use: "A warrior must have the meticulous attention of the mouse and at the same time the courage of the bull." Thus all commentators adopt the second interpretation, with the idea that some change has occurred in the original ideogram. I follow the same approach.

229. "The general knows his soldiers": *sho sotsu o shiru.*

230. To put this teaching into practice, one has to be a very highly accomplished practitioner. All the same, this teaching can serve as a guide in combat exercises for the state of mind of practitioners who have attained a certain level. This also involves trying to take the initiative, which is a central point in Musashi's strategy.

231. "Letting go of the sword handle," *tsuka o hanasu:* At first blush, this phrase communicates the notion of combat techniques that do not use the sword, but it should rather be understood as an instruction on the state of mind of combat. Even if one is fighting with a sword, one must not be attached to one's weapon. It is important to let go of the sword handle mentally, while still using it. Detachment of this kind makes it possible to free the mind and to expand one's vision in the midst of combat.

To refer to my combat experience in karate, when I am close to my opponent, it sometimes occurs that I become detached from the techniques even as I am using them. The point is that in combat, when you become attached to your techniques, sometimes they become a kind of barrier between the two opponents. If you are using a sword, it is the sword that becomes this kind of block; if you are fighting bare-handed, it is your fists, your arms, your legs. When I succeed in detaching myself from my techniques, I have the impression of being able to penetrate directly into the mind of my opponent, and that it is the force of my mind that makes it possible for me to win. Even though it is through the techniques that you gain the victory, attachment to the techniques hinders this mental effort. Nevertheless, you must realize that it takes an enormous amount of work and accumulation of technique to detach yourself from your techniques in a way that is not haphazard or by chance. I think this is the meaning of the notion widely taught in the Japanese martial arts that it is necessary to go beyond technique.

232. "The body of a rock," *iwao no mi:* Musashi explains in his work "Thirty-five Instructions on Strategy" *(Hyoho sanju go kajo)* (see page 208): "The body of a rock is a great and powerful mind that is completely unmoving."

Here is an anecdote about the body of a rock:

One day Lord Hosokawa was asking Musashi about the body like a rock. Musashi asked him to send for Terao Motomenosuke, one of his vassals who was a disciple of Musashi's.

As soon as Terao arrived, Musashi said to him, "Terao Motomenosuke, by your lord's command, you will kill yourself by seppuku here and now!

Terao greeted him calmly and said: "I thank you for this order. Kindly give me just the time to make preparations." Then he withdrew calmly into the next room to prepare to die, without showing the slightest disturbance.

Looking at the back of his disciple who was walking as though nothing had happened, Musashi said, "My lord, that is the body of a rock." (5, p. 180)

That is the end of the story, but we should add that the order given to Terao was immediately withdrawn.

This anecdote shows that "body of a rock" expresses the attitude of a *bushi* who has passed beyond attachment to life and death. This refers to a way of existing without moving body or mind even if "the earth shakes and the sky falls." The body in question here could be better understood as a state of mind, but it is significant that Musashi expresses this attitude by "the body of a rock," which naturally also includes the mind.

"The body of a rock," which characterizes the strategy and the life of Musashi, is the last instruction in the Scroll of Fire.

233. "The Scroll of Wind": *kaze no maki* or *fu no maki*.

234. "Surface training and depth training": This translation relates to the opposition *omote/oku,* literally meaning "entry" or "surface" or "facade" as opposed to "depth" or "core." The opposition surface/depth corresponds to an image in the English language, but this image does not properly take into account the Japanese image of an entry as opposed to an interior depth, which in the case of the martial arts, also contains a reference to that with which one begins as opposed to that which is more profound (see the more detailed note on the last article of this scroll, "Schools That Distinguish between Depth and Surface").

235. "The art of the sword": *kenjutsu*.

236. "My School of Two Swords": *nito ichi ryu*.

237. "A particularly long large sword," *okinaru tachi:Tachi* designates "a large sword"; the literal translation would be "a large large sword."

238. "The longer one's limbs are, the better it is," *issun te masari:* Literally, this means, "a hand longer than one *sun*." *Masari* means "that which is superior or which is dominant." Since *masari* here has the double sense of "longer limbs" and "that which is superior," I gave this idea twice in the translation.

239. "A small sword," *wakizashi:* Musashi uses two names to designate the small sword: *kowakizashi* and *wakizashi*.

A warrior customarily carried two swords: the large sword, a long one, and another that was shorter. In general the blade of the long sword measured 80 to 90 centimeters and that of the small sword 50 to 60 centimeters. Toward the end of the Edo period, the length of swords diminished, with the blade of the long sword varying in the area around 80 centimeters. One of Musashi's swords has been preserved, and its blade measures 93.3 centimeters, which is within the normal range for his time. During the period of feudal wars, some warriors used swords that were 2 meters long. (41, p. 6)

In the handling of swords, a difference of a few centimeters is significant. Today practitioners of *iai* (the art of drawing the sword) practice with swords whose blades usually measure 75 centimeters (2.5 *shaku*) for practitioners who are 1.7 to 1.8 meters tall. The difficulty of the practice increases considerably if the blade is 1.5 centimeters longer. Today practitioners of *iai* capable of using a sword greater than 80 centimeters long are rare.

240. "The sword with brute force": *tsuyomi no tachi.*

241. "If you try to cut through . . .": Musashi is saying that the cutting quality of the sword is not directly proportional to the strength or weakness of the strike. There is a common expression for denoting the quality of a blade, *kire aji,* which means "cutting quality." As we saw in the Scroll of Water, implementation of this quality belongs to a domain that is quite different from that of brute force. For example, kendo practitioners practice repetitive strikes in the air with a heavy wooden sword in order to gain mastery of their normal sword, which is much lighter. They must also practice striking with a light wooden sword as though it were heavy. And indeed, when you take a *shinai* blow from a truly accomplished practitioner, even if the blow appears to be light and slow, you feel the impact of a strike delivered with a heavy object. This does not result from the mere force of the blow but from the fact that the practitioner has struck you holding the sword correctly and following the correct blade path. This is what is usually described as *te no uchi.*

242. "A mortal enemy," *kataki: Kataki uchi* denotes an act of vengeance against an enemy who has killed a warrior's lord or a member of his family. During the Edo period, even though duels based on personal conflicts were prohibited, those that were regarded as acts of vengeance were encouraged and were part of the ethics of a warrior. Such acts of vengeance were carried out on all social levels. They were then prohibited at the beginning of the Meiji period, in 1873.

243. "If you slap . . . forcefully in making a parry . . .": The verb I translated as "slap" is *haru;* it is connected with *hariuke,* "a parry effectuated by slapping with the flat of the sword" (see note 151, page 410).

244. "Your sword might break in two": This passage poses a problem. In the text that I use as my reference standard (10), it is written *okuretakuru*. Takayanagi Mitsutoshi points out that another reading is possible: *okuretagaru*. In this case the sense would be "your sword will have a tendency to lag behind."

In the *Ihon gorin no sho* (14), this word is written *orekudakeru*, which means "to break in pieces."

Even though Watanabe Ichiro (13) uses the same original text as does Takayanagi Mitsutoshi, he writes *orekudakeru* as in the *Ihon gorin no sho*. Following the logic of the text, I also adopt this interpretation.

245. "The principle of the way": *dori*.

246. "In the way of my school": In the copy of Musashi's text (10), there is a gap, a word missing, that I fill in with "way." My supposition here is based on the *Ihon gorin no sho* (14), which in this passage has the ideogram *michi*.

247. "The short sword," *mijikaki tachi*: Farther on in this passage, Musashi speaks of *tachi* (translated as "large sword") and *katana* (translated as "small sword"). In Musashi's time, the names of the large and small swords were not rigorously fixed; the distinction was nevertheless indicated by using *tachi* for the large sword and *katana* for the small sword, or by using *katana* for the large sword and *wakizashi* for the small sword.

In general, *tachi* referred to a sword whose blade measured more than 3 *shaku* (ninety centimeters). The *katana* measured 2 to 3 *shaku* (sixty to ninety centimeters), and the *wakizashi* less than 1.8 *shaku* (fifty-four centimeters).

248. "*Naginata*": In the most widely used version (13), the term used is *nagatachi*, literally, "particularly long large sword." In another version (14), the term is *naginata*. In view of the context, *naginata* is the right choice.

249. "Submitting to the initiative of the other," *gote* or *ushirode*: These ideograms, when pronounced *gote*, mean "put oneself in a passive situation," because one has let the other take the initiative. This term is the contrary of *sente* (on *sen*; see note 174, page 415, and appendix 2). These ideograms can also be pronounced *ushirode*, the sense then being "that which is behind" or "the back of things."

250. "When facing many opponents," *taiteki no naka*: *Taiteki* has two senses: (1) a formidable adversary; (2) many adversaries. *No naka* means "in." The whole expression means "in the number of the adversary," hence my translation.

251. "Close enough": In the practice of the small sword called *kodachi*, one holds the handle of the sword with one hand. Sometimes one grabs hold of the wrist, the

sleeve, or the collar of one's opponent as one comes in quite close in order to use one's small sword more effectively.

252. "Driving them back all of a sudden," *yaniwani shioshi:Yaniwani* means "all of a sudden." For *shioshi* or *shihoshi,* Takayanagi gives the ideograms that mean "way of doing" or "method." (10) Watanabe gives two other possible ideograms that mean "push" or "drive back" and "encircle the four sides." In view of the logic of the text, I translated "driving back."

253. "Your mind will be steered by these ways of doing things *(michi),*" *kokoro nichi ni hikasarete:* The term *michi* (in senses 2 and 3, see appendix 1), means "way of doing." In this case, it refers back to the list that precedes it; hence the translation "these ways of doing things."

254. "A large number of sword techniques," *tachi kazu ooki:* Musashi's critique is directly applicable to the martial arts of the present period. Let us cite, for example, a passage from a book written in 1963 by So Doshin, founder of a martial art called *shorinji kenpo,* which has many practitioners in Japan: "One of the technical particularities of *shorinji kenpo* is the aesthetics of its style and a speed of execution that can be found in no other discipline in the realm of *budo.* You will appreciate the thrilling charm of its highly refined techniques, which are derived from tradition. Moreover, the number of its secret techniques comes to well over six hundred. Thus you can continue to train for a long time without losing interest." (51, p. 37)

Ueshiba Kisshomaru, the successor of his father, Ueshiba Morihei, the founder of aikido, wrote in 1972: "The founder of aikido, Ueshiba Morihei, mainly practiced the jujutsu of the Daito ryu, which includes as many as 2,664 techniques. In addition to this, Ueshiba Morihei practiced the jujutsu of the Shin kage ryu, Aioi ryu, and other schools, and he developed his own techniques on the basis of the secret techniques he had learned. That is why the techniques of aikido today are innumerable." (55, p. 21)

He wrote in another work: "There are several thousand techniques in aikido, and they can be classified into three categories: throwing techniques, immobilization techniques, and techniques of immobilization following a throw. In addition, there are two ways—*omote* and *ura*—of performing each technique." (54, p. 57)

Making a display in this fashion of a large number of techniques is a fitting target for Musashi's criticism; however, in the Daito ryu, this was also a way of discouraging potential novices at the beginning, so that they would end up having to accept only people of great determination.

The techniques in any *budo* discipline are innumerable, but at the same time it could be said that they are few. It all depends on one's point of view concerning technique. For Musashi, who attempts to discern and teach the essential, the fundamental techniques are not numerous. At the same time, he could have said that there were thousands of techniques in his school, since if you count up all the technical variations, they are indeed innumerable in every *budo* discipline, and the School of Musashi was no exception. From the point of view of teaching, the important thing is to distill the essence from the complexity of the techniques in order to provide a structure for the learning process and not to proliferate names of variations, which only creates confusion. As to the essence, the techniques are neither complex nor numerous. What is needed is to develop the insight that can perceive what is essential in a phenomenon whose appearance is complex, and then to teach this. Just through modifications of a single striking technique, one can produce scores of different techniques. However, as a working method, rather than studying scores of variants of a technique in order to get at the primary technique, it is more effective to work on a main technique and study its variants afterward. It seems to me that Musashi's approach is close to this.

255. "Pulling back," *hiraki:* from *hiraku,* which means "moving the body backward while taking up a guard position," or "dodge by means of a movement of the body," or "to flee" (99)—all in response to an attack by an opponent.

256. "Guard position in the art of the sword," *tachi no kamae.*

257. "In this world . . .": This sentence and the next one mean "one does not establish laws except when society has become stable." One does not establish laws in the midst of important events; it is after the fact, in retrospect, that society establishes customs and laws. A society that is looking back in this way is not in the heat of facing the event. For example, in Japan certain measures have been taken to deal with earthquakes, lightning, and fires. These measures were taken in periods of calm. They thus represent a guard position that was assumed at a time when there was no adversary.

In the art of combat, this sort of distance and looking back is not possible because the temporality involved is of another order. It is therefore not possible, as Musashi makes clear all through the text, to rely on a guard position worked out in a rigid fashion, in the manner of a law. In combat, as he explains in the Scroll of Water, fundamentally the guard is made up of positions that enable one to respond in the best way to any form of attack one's opponent might make. This is the idea of the "guard without a guard" recommended by Musashi.

258. "The guard without a guard," *uko muko:* This has been literally translated.

259. *"Naginata":* In the most widely used version of the *Gorin no sho* (13), the term used is *nagatachi,* literally, "particularly long large sword." In Yamada Jirokichi's version (14), the term is *naginata.* In view of the context, *naginata* is the right choice.

260. "Moving a lance or a *naginata* about in such a way as to set up a barrier," *saku ni furitaru: Saku* means "a fence made of bamboo or wood." Kamata Shigeo (4), Terayama Danchu (11), and Watanabe Ichiro (13) interpret this: "to use the lance or the *naginata*

across a barrier." Kamiko Tadashi (5) has: "That comes to the same thing as setting up the lance and the *naginata* rigidly as a barrier." For my part, I interpret *saku ni* as an adverbial phrase expressing the movement of the weapons that continues the sequence expressed in the previous sentence.

261. "Particular ways of gazing": *metsuke*.

262. "Someone playing ball": This refers to an ancient game called *kemari*, from *ke*, meaning "kick," and *mari*, meaning "ball." It was initially called *kumaeri* or *marikoyu*, and then later the name *kemari* was established. The same ideogram can also be pronounced *shukiku*.

This game was initially played by the nobles at the emperor's court. The ball was made from stag skin, and its diameter was about twenty-one centimeters. (99) It was played with eight players, and the players wore leather shoes. The game consisted in striking the ball with the instep. Sometimes a player tried to pass the ball to his partners, sometimes to keep kicking it as long as possible without letting it touch the ground. In this game, elegance of form in body and movements as well as in the curve of the ball's trajectory was sought after. The playing field was a square of approximately fourteen meters on a side. At each corner of the field a tree was planted (a cherry, a willow, a pine, and a maple). The rules of the game were systematized during the Kamakura period (1185–1333), and several schools were founded. The game was played regularly until the Edo period. (99, 104)

263. "Stroking his temples," *hinsuri* or *binsuri*: *Bin* refers to "the hair growing near the ears"; *suru* means "to rub" or "to stroke." Literally, the phrase means "to stroke the hair near the ears."

264. "Acrobat": the translation of *hoka; hokashi*, "magician," "acrobat." *Hoka* means (1) to throw something; (2) "to drop"; (3) an art practiced in the Middle Ages, mainly by monks, which consisted in singing while dancing and performing acrobatics and magic tricks.

265. "While balancing a door over his nose," *tobira o hana ni tate:* literally, "while resting a door on his nose," in fact, on the lower part of the forehead.

266. "In strategy you place your gaze . . .": Certain schools or certain masters placed great importance on fixing the gaze and on the places it was considered suitable to fix it. For example, Chiba Shusaku (1794–1855), the master who founded the Hokushin Itto ryu, taught two ways of gazing, defensive and offensive. (82, p. 17)

The defensive gaze, according to his teaching, should be fixed on the point of the adversary's sword and on his fist simultaneously. He explains: "Imagine a keg of sake. If the cork is missing from the tap, it is difficult to keep the sake from running out. It suffices to stop up the tap to block this flow." According to Chiba, keeping the gaze simultaneously on the sword point and the fist of the adversary is equivalent to stopping up the tap of the keg.

For the offensive gaze, he teaches that the gaze should be placed *obi no kane,* literally, "one measure from the belt sash." If the opponent is of a superior level of accomplishment, instead of looking at his eyes, one should look at his belt, which will make it possible to camouflage one's own intention of attacking.

According to the teaching of the Nen ryu, one should look simultaneously at the face and the fist of the adversary. The Yagyu shin kage ryu says one should look in one direction at the same time as looking in another, *futame tsukai,* and also look slyly while pretending to look at something else, *chugan.*

Musashi says, "In strategy, you place your gaze on the mind of your opponent." The different techniques of gazing I have referred to above represent reference points for discovering the mind of one's opponent. Thus Chiba Shusaku explains that all the gazes he describes should be executed by the eyes of the mind *(mokushin).*

In order "to look at the mind of one's adversary," it is necessary to have a mental gaze directed on oneself. Under the influence of Zen, this idea has increased in importance all through the history of the Japanese sword. The ability to perceive the essence of phenomena is called *shin-gan* ("the eyes of the mind").

267. "Looking and seeing": See the Scroll of Water, "The Way of Looking in Strategy."

268. "Various kinds of footwork": *ashi tsukai.*

269. "Floating foot," *uki ashi:* You keep one of your feet, most often the front foot, floating, touching the ground only with the base of the toes, the heel slightly lifted. You can almost move the foot forward in a floating manner as you look for the right distance from which to attack.

"Leaping foot," *tobi ashi;* "hopping foot," *hanuru ashi;* "stamping foot," *fumit-sumuru ashi.*

"Crow's foot," *karasu ashi:* Terayama gives a brief commentary, without citing any source, on this kind of movement, describing it as "moving with small steps." (11) In the documents I consulted, I found no further description of this kind of movement. I questioned several sword masters, but none of them could give me an explanation of this expression. I think this was a term used in Musashi's time that did not continue to be used later on.

270. "A movement to dampen the impact . . . that holds the body back": *tobi te itsuku kokoro ari.*

271. "It involves a wait," *tai no ashi:* Literally, this means "feet in a waiting attitude, an attitude that puts you on the defensive."

272. "In my strategy . . .": We are reminded here of a passage in the Scroll of Water:

"To move from one place to another, you slightly raise your toes and push off your foot from the heel, forcefully." Here Musashi stresses again: "In my strategy the way of moving is no different from normal walking on a road."

Movements from place to place in modern kendo differ from Musashi's description. In kendo, in general the movement used is one in which the right foot is kept forward and the left foot back, with the heel slightly lifted off the ground.

Musashi also writes in the Scroll of Water, "You should not move just one foot. . . . You must always move the right and left feet alternately. You must never move only one foot."

The principle of not moving one foot alone is respected in modern kendo but in a different form, since at the end of each movement from place to place, the distance between the feet remains the same. Thus you move right-left or left-right, but without alternating the front foot.

Today the principal of moving the feet described by Musashi is applied primarily in the schools of the ancient art of the sword. These schools transmit the classic art of swordsmanship. Very rarely, some contemporary kendo masters use this type of movement.

273. "If your steps are too slow," *ashi bumi shizuka nite wa:Ashi bumi* means "step, gait."

274. "Stress speed": *hayaki o mochiiru.*

275. "A lag has occurred," *ma ni awazaru:* "Lagging behind" is expressed by *ma ni awanai,* literally, "not adjusting to the *ma*" (temporal, spatial, or psychological interval). For Musashi, speed and slowness are produced by a deviation in relation to the proper cadence.

276. The art of Noh drumming is extremely difficult. During a visit to Japan, I was struck by an interview with a young woman of twenty-three, the descendant of a family of traditional Noh theater drummers. She said: "I have been practicing the drum since I was three years old. For a long time I was not considered to be someone who really played. When I was twenty, my father told me with a satisfied expression, 'You have finally become bad.' Before that my level was such that I could not even be considered."

277. "Oimatsu" is a Noh theater song composed by Zeami (1363–1443)—the spirit of an old pine tree appears in order to celebrate springtime in a peaceful world. Later on, the music of this piece was adapted to be played at wedding celebrations or other happy events.

278. "Takasago" is also a song composed by Zeami. Its subject is the journey of a Shinto priest who is traveling from a province on the island of Kyushu to Kyoto. As he is admiring the countryside near the bay of Takasago (in Hyogo prefecture), two old

men appear and recount the story of two old pine trees, of which one was located here, at Takasago, and the other at Sumiyoshi (Osaka). These two pines were called *aioi no matsu*, which means "the pines of Aioi" (the name of a place); but at the same time, through a pun, it also means " two pines *(matsu)* getting old *(oi)* together *(ai)*." After telling him this story, the two old men disappear. When the priest gets to Sumiyoshi, the spirit of a god appears and does a dance in honor of the emperor. Today "Takasago" is a classic song played at weddings.

279. "What is meant by . . .": The opposition here is between *oku* and *omote,* as in the title of the section.

280. "The depth from the entry," *oku guchi:* A possible translation is "the entry door that opens to the transmission of the depth"; however, it seems more accurate to separate *oku* and *guchi* and thus to translate the two words separately.

281. "The ultimate teaching," *gokui;* "the secret transmission," *hiden:* In the text, the two terms are connected *(gokui-hiden)* to form a whole, since the ultimate teaching is generally transmitted secretly.

282. "The degree of their advancement," *kokoro o hodokuru: Hodokuru* is an ancient form of *hodokeru,* which means (1) a knot that is coming undone, (2) capable of understanding, (3) softening the feeling. The sense here relates to the knot of the mind coming undone, which means that the capacity for understanding increases. Thus I translated as "the degree of their advancement," which fit with the meaning of the previous sentences.

283. "Mountains": Musashi uses the term *yama,* which is translated as "mountains." But in Western terms, the mountains mentioned here would be regarded as wooded hills. The situation described by Musashi is similar to one in which someone taking a walk penetrates into the midst of a forest and ends up coming out on a different side, a way out that could also be a way in.

284. "It might turn out . . .": Musashi is opposed to a rigid distinction between *oku* and *kuchi.* Different levels were distinguished among students of schools of the martial arts, generally: beginners, intermediates, advanced students, and ultimate-transmission students. In the course of the Edo period, these divisions increased in number, and at each promotion to a higher level, the students had to pay the master something.

In Musashi's school there was also a distinction between depth and entry, but he was opposed to systematizing the teaching in terms of levels.

It is possible to teach the same technique at a rudimentary level or a more advanced one. In the beginning the accent is placed on the correct assimilation of different parts of the movement, which tends to get divided into several sequences.

With more advanced students, the component elements of a gesture must be fused together, and the movement is executed in a more fluid manner. Thus, with the same technique, there is a change of cadence as it is executed in a more and more advanced style. When a technique becomes fixed in the form of a kata, these two forms of execution are designated *omote no kata* and *oku no kata*.

With regard to the ultimate transmission and the secret teaching, the transmission of what is most important is often accompanied by poems. Here are three such poems that are part of the tradition of swordsmanship and are quoted in several schools, though the authors are unknown:

> The ultimate transmission is like your own eyelid,
> It is so close, but you don't see it.

> The ultimate teaching is just below the surface,
> Why push yourself to look for it so deep?

> Sea wind, powerful waves on the beach,
> The moon is one, its reflections appear many and
> violently agitated. (9, pp. 88–89)

In the last poem, the agitated mind of the practitioner prevents him from discovering the essence. His mind is refracted into multiple reflections, like the image of the moon on a choppy sea. All that is necessary is for the waters to become calm for them to reflect the single image of the moon. In the same way, a calm mind can reflect the essence of the teaching.

285. I do not have written oaths . . .": Musashi refers here to the custom, common in schools of martial arts during the feudal period, of taking an oath at the time of admission. The oath document often had on it, next to the signature, a fingerprint of the student in his own blood, which signified that he was committing himself to keep this oath at the price of his very life. In the text of the oath it was common to mention the penalties that could be imposed by the other members of the school and to make reference to the gods or other supernatural powers with whom the master was associated.

Oaths were generally also found on certificates of transmission. The master pledged before the gods to have communicated the essence of his school. It was customary to add: "He who has studied in my school must never study in another school." The student swore never to reveal the secrets of the school to anyone, not even to his parents or his brothers.

286. "The five or six bad ways," *godo rikudo: Godo* is written *go,* "five," and *do,* "way." *Rikudo* can also be pronounced *rokudo* and is written: *riku,* "six," *do,* "way." Both terms

come from Buddhism. The first refers to the five different worlds into which a living being can fall after his death. These are hell *(jigoku)*, the world of the hungry beings *(gaki)*, the animal worlds *(chikusho)*, the human world *(ningen)*, and the world of heaven *(tenjo)*. The second term, *rikudo,* denotes the five worlds of *godo,* and in addition, another world in which the titans, the enemies of the gods *(ashura),* live.

Musashi's expression is ambiguous. One might think he is using this image in an ironic sense, connecting the many schools with hell and the other lower worlds. At the same time, this imagery borrowed from Buddhist thought reminds us that Musashi conceives of his strategy as a whole that contains both good and evil, and he stresses the importance of doing away with the evil in order to attain the ideal of strategy.

287. "Scroll of heaven," *ku no maki:* In the title, I translated the term *ku* as "heaven," in view of the preceding scrolls each being named after one of the five elements: earth, water, fire, wind, and therefore heaven. However, the term *ku* has a much more complex meaning. Its principal senses are "heaven" (or "sky"), "emptiness," and "space." This ideogram has three common pronunciations. Pronounced *ku* or *kara* it tends to mean "emptiness"; pronounced *sora* it means "heaven" (or "sky"). However, these two meanings (emptiness and heaven/sky) can both be present at the same time. In Musashi's text this ideogram is pronounced *ku,* but Musashi at certain times gives it any one of the three meanings (heaven/sky, emptiness, space) and sometimes all three meanings at once.

In this passage I have translated it by one or another of these terms, depending on the sense of the text. At the end of the text, *ku* seems to be used in a more philosophical sense, thus I translated it as "void."

288. Musashi finished composing the *Gorin no sho* during the second month of the same year, and in anticipation of his death, he gave it to his disciples. The original of this work has never been found. We know it today through a copy made by Furuhashi Sozaemon, one of Musashi's three closest disciples.

Why was Musashi's own manuscript not handed down from generation to generation?

One week before his death, Musashi bequeathed the *Gorin no sho* to one of his disciples, Terao Magonojo. The two names that appear at the end of Musashi's text (Terao Magonojo and Terao Musei Katsunobu) refer to the same person. The first is a commonly used name—doubtless this was the name by which Musashi called his disciple. The second is an official warrior name. Terao signed with his official name to formally bestow the *Gorin no sho* on his disciple Yamamoto Gensuke. "Musei Katsunobu" corresponds, for Terao Magonojo, to "Fujiwara no Genshin" for Miyamoto Musashi.

Musashi led a settled existence the last ten years of his life. When he moved into the cave called Reigando, he doubtless knew that his life was drawing to a close. Indeed, he fell ill several times in the course of composing the *Gorin no sho.* He spent the last two years of his life partly at Reigando, partly at his house in town. Musashi died three months after completing this major work.

This scroll appears as the conclusion of the *Gorin no sho*. Translating and interpreting its meaning are particularly difficult.

Takayanagi Mitsutoshi, a contemporary man of letters, gives the following analysis of the *Gorin no sho:*

> Musashi . . . was able to become a practitioner of the highest quality because he mastered his art in an organized manner. . . . We must admit that Musashi lacked the capacity to organize his knowledge. . . .
>
> His text is organized in the following manner: the main outlines in the Scroll of Earth, his own techniques in the Scroll of Water, combat in the Scroll of Fire, the other schools in the Scroll of Wind, and the conclusion in the Scroll of Heaven.
>
> For Musashi the Scroll of Earth comes first because he is preparing the ground on which he can plot a straight way. The Scroll of Water comes second because water follows the form of the vessel, square or round: it is a drop, it is also an ocean; the color of the deep is pure green. He says that he wrote this scroll on the inspiration of the purity of water. In third place comes war, in the Scroll of Fire, because fire symbolizes the fiery spirit. In fourth place comes the Scroll of Wind, written on the subject of the other schools, following the traditional expressions, the old wind, the modern wind, and the wind of such and such a family. Within an organization such as this, the need to classify one's thought into five parts and call them *Gorin* is not imperative. It is entirely a religious way of proceeding. The name *Gorin* contains within it a religious attitude. The text of the Scroll of Heaven, the fifth, is entirely religious and is without any scientific character. But we must accept this fact, for we are dealing with the work of a person who lived during a period in which there was not an adequate distinction between religion and science. . . . I think this is the main reason the text of the *Gorin no sho* is difficult to understand. (10, pp. 98–99)

This assessment of the Scroll of Heaven is debatable. It seems, rather, that in this brief text Musashi is sharing with us his deepest thoughts on the notion of emptiness. Put in the final position, this scroll appears as a conclusion. What is in question here is the practice of strategy, which advances ever further into a dimension of increasing profundity the more one progresses in it. The method here is different from that of a theoretical or scientific work, where we are accustomed to a progression in which, the further we go, the more precise the vision of the domain in question becomes, and the more definite the objective of the inquiry becomes.

In the way of the martial arts, by contrast, we go forward by a process of learning a body of technique that is composed of precise and concrete movements. But the further we advance, the more the vision of the practice comes to include a broad area of life that tends to become inseparable from a vast ungraspable space. This is because through the technique we learn to see ourselves and others, and then the world that surrounds us. According to the logic of the Japanese martial arts, the principle in accordance with which we create technique for ourselves must coincide with the principle of the universe. Starting with technique, Musashi studies and comes to a deeper understanding of this idea, and he writes this down in the last scroll. Thus Musashi's procedure is a logical one, but this is not the logic of science.

The conclusion is the part that appears the most confused. All through the *Gorin no sho,* Musashi organizes his writing on the basis of concrete things, and in this last scroll, he ends up with an abstraction. This process is comparable to the process of a painter who begins with concrete and precise drawings and in the course of a work's evolution and development, introduces elements of abstraction that, in some cases, are all that is left in the final picture.

Musashi sometimes gives up on the writing process, saying it is not possible to give the details in writing. He knows the limitations of words when it comes to conveying meaning about bodily technique.

In its method of explanation, the Scroll of Heaven offers an example of a different approach to writing that might be a little bit perplexing for us today. Here the role of words is to point out a distinct placement within a great space that is emptiness and also heaven, or the sky. Its words form a constellation if we are capable of connecting them in the empty space that separates them by filling it with our imagination and our intuition. This method would have been an obvious one for the disciples of Musashi to whom this text was addressed.

Musashi's poems are part and parcel of this kind of communication. They are transmitted in his school as an accompaniment to the teaching of his art.

> Under the raised sword, it is hell,
> If you go one step forward, it is paradise.

> After having recognized all the principles, comes the
>   clarity of the light of the full moon,
> I was ignorant of it before; I had nothing.

> The current of a river in winter reflects the moon,
> Like a mirror, it is transparent.

> If you see the earth and the universe as you see a garden,
> I live outside this universe. (9, pp. 88–89)

Chapter 6: Notes of Musashi's Disciples on the Practice of His School

1. A sword that has no protective hilt *(tsuba)* on the handle.

Chapter 7: The School of Musashi

1. A great number of martial arts masters, particularly in kendo, talk about Musashi, especially about his strategic philosophy and his techniques. I have received many helpful teachings from such masters; however, little by little I discovered that the knowledge they attributed to Musashi came more from their own experience than from any precise knowledge of Musashi's thought and technique. And they had even less historical knowledge concerning his life and training.

I undertook a quick general survey of fifty Japanese martial arts masters, aged forty-five to sixty-five, who taught different disciplines. I learned that few among them had attentively read the *Gorin no sho,* but nearly all of them had read passages from it. As to the *Hyoho sanju go kajo,* only a few had read fragments and nearly 40 percent did not know it existed. The majority of masters were unfamiliar with the *Dokkodo* and only one knew that the *Hyodokyo* existed.

A few passages from the *Gorin no sho* are well known, especially in kendo circles. They are mainly the following articles:

Cadences in Strategy (Scroll of Earth)
State of Mind in Strategy (Scroll of Water)
Posture in Strategy (Scroll of Water)
The Way of Looking in Strategy (Scroll of Water)
The Way of Holding the Sword (Scroll of Water)
The Way of Moving the Feet (Scroll of Water)
The Strike of Nonthought (Scroll of Water)
The Chance-Opening Blow (Scroll of Water)
The Blow Like a Spark from a Stone (Scroll of Water)
The Three Ways of Taking the Initiative (Scroll of Fire)
Holding Down on the Headrest (Scroll of Fire)
Moving Your Shadow (Scroll of Fire)

These are primarily articles that are directly applicable to the contemporary practice of the martial arts, especially kendo.

If we look at these articles more closely, we will see that all of them, from a slightly different angle, contribute to an orientation they all share. If a practitioner studies any one of these instructions thoroughly, he will be able to develop his particular qualities. This would be more than enough for most of the practitioners of today. Anyone who has worked hard enough on any of these techniques will at the same time acquire the technical abilities explained in the others.

If we view the *Gorin no sho* as being a treatise on method, what Musashi teaches in his work is much too vast, given our conditions of life, for any one person to be able to put the whole of the technical part of it into practice. Even the study of a few paragraphs will be sufficiently rich to orient the applications of technique of a martial arts practitioner of today. In the course of my inquiry, I learned that the majority of masters who had studied Musashi's strategic thought in depth and related it to their own practice did not feel the need to study the entirety of his work. Partial study, carried out thoroughly and fully, was more than enough for them. This shows the richness and relevance of Musashi's teaching, and thence the greatness of his level of accomplishment. This is why some masters of kendo are able to speak so well and so profoundly about technique by connecting it with Musashi's thought without knowing the whole of his work or the story of his life.

Chapter 11: Budo

1. Rules of life for the students of Kano Jigoro's school:

- Get up at 4:45 A.M.; go to bed at 9:30 P.M. [Each student has to take turns waking all the others, in accordance with Kano's belief that a man should be capable of waking up by himself at a chosen time.]
- Immediately after wake-up, the students clean up the dormitory room and the garden.
- Training in judo is daily and mandatory.
- Hours of study, training, and rest are precisely fixed.
- As they study, students must continuously maintain the classical correct posture: seated on their heels with the torso upright.
- Mandatory dress is a simple traditional garment that is to be worn until it is entirely worn out.
- Treatment of students is the same whether their families pay or they receive free tuition.
- Individual leave is prohibited; however, students whose families live in Tokyo are allowed to visit them twice a month. Group outings are carried out under the supervision of the oldest students, who are responsible for the group. In this capacity, they have the right to carry pocket money [prohibited to individuals].
- Students take turns serving meals to their teacher in order to have the opportunity of a direct conversation with him.
- Every Sunday morning at six, Master Kano gives a lecture on morality to an assembly of the student body. (39, p. 44)

GLOSSARY

The Kanji for each of the following names and terms appears in the French edition of this book, published as *Miyamoto Musashi* (Éditions Désiris, 2000)

Names

Aioi ryu: A school of swordsmanship.

Aisu Ikosai (1441–1538): A sword master of the Kage ryu.

Aisu Koshiro (1518–1590): The son and successor of Aisu Ikosai. He transmitted the Kage ryu to Kamiizumi Isenokami Nobutsuna (c. 1508–c. 1577), who founded the Shin kage ryu.

Akamatsu: The Akamatsu feudal clan appeared in the thirteenth century in the Harima region and flourished there. The continuity of the Akamatsu clan was broken at the battle of Sekigahara in 1600. The family of Munisai was attached to this clan.

Akashi: A town in the prefecture of Higo.

Akiyama: An adept against whom Musashi fought at the age of sixteen.

Aoki Jozaemon: A student of Musashi's, the founder of the Tetsujin ryu (School of the Man of Steel).

Aramaki: A shrine frequented by Musashi in his youth.

Arima Kihei: An adept with whom Musashi fought his first duel, at the age of thirteen.

Asano Denemon: A seventeenth-century sword master, one of the three disciples of Takemura Yoemon, Musashi's third adoptive son.

Ashikaga: Starting with Ashikaga Takauji (1305–1358), who became shogun in 1338, the Ashikaga family occupied the position of shogun for fifteen generations. In the sixteenth century the following members of the family succeeded each other: Ashikaga Yoshiharu (1511–1550), Ashikaga Yoshiteru (1536–1565), Ashikaga Yoshiuji (1541–1582), and Ashikaga Yoshiaki (1537–1597), who was driven out of Kyoto in 1573. This ended the Ashikaga shogunate.

Banshu: A region of Hyogo prefecture of which Musashi was perhaps a native.

Bessho Shigeharu (sixteenth century): A feudal lord of the Banshu region.

Chiba: A prefecture in the Kanto region, in the neighborhood of Tokyo.

Chiba Shusaku (1794–1855): A master of the sword, founder of the Hokushin Itto ryu.

Chishin ryu: A school of swordsmanship founded in the seventeenth century, based on the teachings of Musashi.

Chujo ryu: A school of swordsmanship founded by Chujo Hyogo no kami in the fourteenth century.

Daito ryu: A school of jujutsu, the founding of which can apparently be traced back to a warrior named Shinra Saburo of the eleventh century. This school was practiced for a long time in the fief of Aizu as a secret art. This art was presented in public for the first time by Takeda Sokaku (1860–1943) under the name of the Daito ryu aiki jujutsu. The art of aikido was originated by Ueshiba Morihei on the basis of Takeda's teaching.

Dokkodo: Twenty-one precepts written by Musashi a week before his death.

Dorin: A Buddhist monk. According to Nakanishi Seizo, he was Musashi's uncle, who took charge of Musashi's education during his childhood. (8)

Edo: The Edo period (1603–1867).

Enmei ryu: One of the names used by Musashi to designate his school of swordsmanship.

Fujiwara: Beginning at the end of the seventh century, the Fujiwara clan began to exercise a major influence over imperial policy. This clan divided into a number of branches, some of which played an important role in the history of ancient Japan.

Fujiwara no Genshin: One of Musashi's names.

Fukuda Yanosuke (nineteenth century): A jujutsu master of the Tenshin shinyo ryu. Kano Jigoro was his student.

Fukuoka: A town in Fukuoka prefecture in Kyushu.

Funajima: The island where Musashi fought against Sasaki Kojiro in 1612; also called Mukojima or Ganryu-jima.

Furuhashi Sozaemon: A vassal of Lord Hosokawa. One of Musashi's three best disciples toward the end of Musashi's life.

Fushimi: A castle constructed at the end of the sixteenth century in Kyoto. Today it is the name of a Kyoto neighborhood.

Futabayama: The most famous sumo wrestler of the 1930s. He established a record of sixty-nine consecutive victories that no one has yet surpassed.

Ganryu: "School of Rock," the name of a school of swordsmanship founded by Sasaki Kojiro.

Ganryu-jima: *See* Funajima.

Genshin: *See* Fujiwara no Genshin.

Gunma: A prefecture of the Kanto region in which Tokyo is located.

Harigaya Sekiun (seventeenth century): A master of swordsmanship.

Harima: A region generally corresponding to the present-day prefecture of Hyogo.

Hatano Jirozaemon (*also* Jirosaemont) (seventeenth century): An adept of the sword, a student of Marume Mondo of the Ichiden ryu. Receiving Musashi's teaching led Hatano to found his own school, the Itten ryu. He then took the name of Hatano Soken and became a monk.

Hayashi Razan (seventeenth century): A warrior and scholar.

Higo: A fief corresponding overall to the present prefecture of Kumamoto.

Hikosan: A mountain situated in the north of Kyushu.

Himeji: A fief situated in the Harima region.

Hinatsu Shigetaka: A warrior and author of the *Honcho bugei shoden* (Little Tales of the Martial Arts of Japan), published in 1715.

Hioki Juemon (seventeenth century): An adept of the sword and one of the three disciples of Takemura Yoemon, Musashi's third adoptive son.

Hirafuku-mura: A village in the region of Harima (Banshu), on the border with the region of Mimasaka (Sakushu).

Hirao Yoemon: An adoptive son of Musashi, also known as Takemura Yoemon, an adept of the sword and vassal of Lord Owari (*see also* Takemura Yoemon). Hirata: The name of the family that Musashi's father was descended from, according to certain scholars.

Hirata Jirotayu (1578–1660): Considered to be Musashi's older brother.

Hirata Muni: Considered to be Musashi's father. *See* Miyamoto Munisai.

Hirata Ogin: Considered to be Musashi's older sister. Later married to Hirao Yoemon.

Hirata Shokan: An adept of the sword and also of the art of the *jitte;* principal vassal of Lord Shinmen. He is considered by some to be Musashi's grandfather, but this hypothesis is in doubt, especially in view of the date of his death, in 1503.

Hitachi no kuni: A region corresponding to the greater part of the present-day prefecture of Ibaraki.

Hokuriku: A region composed of the prefectures of Fukui, Ishikawa, Toyama, and Niigata.

Hokushin Itto ryu: A school of swordsmanship. *See also* Chiba Shusaku.

Homan-zan: The name of a mountain in the Himeji region.

Honcho bugei shoden: See Hinatsu Shigetaka.

Honiden Gekinosuke (sixteenth century): A warrior, vassal of Lord Shinmen, student of Miyamoto Munisai; killed by the latter on the order of Lord Shinmen.

Hosokawa Mitsumasa: The son and successor of Hosokawa Tadatoshi.

Hosokawa Tadatoshi (1585–1641): Lord of Higo Kumamoto. He received Musashi into his fief in 1640, not as an ordinary vassal, but as his guest. Musashi spent the last years of his life in Hosokawa's fief.

Hozan ryu: A *jitte* school founded by Tsutsumi Hozan in the fifteenth century. *See also* Tsutsumi Hozan.

Hozoin: The name of a Buddhist temple of the Nichiren sect situated in Nara. At the end of the sixteenth century, the monk Inei studied the art of the lance there under the direction of Narita Daizendayu. After having completed his accomplishments by studying the art of swordsmanship of Kamiizumi Nobutsuna, he founded a school of the lance by the name of Hozoin ryu.

Hyodokyo: "The Mirror of the Way of Strategy," a text on strategy written by Musashi when he was around twenty-one years old.

Hyogo: A prefecture corresponding overall to the former region of Harima.

Hyoho sanju go kajo: "Thirty-five Instructions on Strategy," a work written by Musashi in 1641.

Hyuga no kuni: A region of Kyushu, corresponding overall to the prefecture of Miyazaki.

Ibaraki: A prefecture corresponding overall to the former region of Hitachi.

Ichiden ryu: A school of swordsmanship transmitted by Marume Mondo, a sword master of the sixteenth and seventeenth centuries.

Ichijoji: A Buddhist temple of Kyoto. According to the Nitenki, in 1604 Musashi fought the Yoshioka clan near the large pine tree that was next to this temple.

Iga no kun: A region corresponding to northwestern Mie prefecture.

Iijima Gentazaemon: A seventeenth-century sword adept, one of the three disciples of Takemura Yoemon, the third adoptive son of Musashi.

Iikubo Tsunetoshi (nineteenth century): A master of the Kito ryu, a school of jujutsu. Kano Jigoro was his student.

Imai Masayuki: A contemporary sword master of the Hyoho niten ichi ryu, the tenth successor of the School of Musashi.

Inei: A monk and the founder of the Hozoin ryu, a school of the lance. See also Hozoin.

Ise: A famous shrine in Mie prefecture.

Isenokami: The warrior name of Kamiizumi Nobutsuna.

Ito Ittosai: A sword master of the sixteenth and early seventeenth centuries, founder of the Itto ryu, the style of which is dominant today in the practice of kendo.

Itosu Anko (1830–1915): Karate master from the island of Okinawa.

Itten ryu: A school of swordsmanship founded by Hatano Soken in the seventeenth century. See Hatano Jirozaemon.

Itto ryu: A school of swordsmanship founded by Ito Ittosai.

Iwama Rokubei (seventeenth century): A Hosokawa vassal who played the role of intermediary between his lord and Musashi when the latter was invited to take a position in the Hosokawa fief.

Iwato: A mountain near the town of Kumamoto. Reigando cave is on this mountain.

Jibuzaemon: Toda Jibuzaemon, a sword adept of the seventeenth century, master of the Chujo ryu, younger brother of Toda Seigen. According to Ozawa Masao (9), his real name was Jirozaemon, Jibuzaemon being a transcription error in the *Nitenki*.

Jion: A legendary sword master, the original source of the transmission of the Nen ryu.

Jokyoji-mura: A village in the Echizen region (Fukui prefecture) of which Sasaki Kojiro was a native, according to the *Nitenki*.

Joshu: A region corresponding to the present-day prefecture of Gunma.

Kage ryu: "Shadow School," a school of swordsmanship founded by Aisu Ikosai. *See also* Aisu Ikosai.

Kageyama ryu: A swordsmanship school of the Edo period, practiced principally in the regions of northern Japan. In this school the short sword is used, at the propitious moment, as a throwing weapon.

Kaishin ryu: A school of swordsmanship founded by Komagawa Tarozaemon at the beginning of the seventeenth century on the basis of the teaching he received from Kamiizumi Nobutsuna.

Kamakura: A town; the period during which the seat of the warrior government was at Kamakura is called Kamakura-jidai (1185–1333).

Kamiizumi Nobutsuna (c. 1508–c. 1577): A master of the art of the sword, founder of the Shin kage ryu. He perfected a method of training using bamboo swords *(shinai)*.

Kanawa Goro: A sword adept of the nineteenth century, at the end of the Edo period.

Kanbun: The Kanbun period (1661–1673).

Kanei: The Kanei period (1624–1644).

Kanemaki Jisai: A sword master of the sixteenth and seventeenth centuries. He learned the art of the sword of the Chujo ryu under the direction of Toda Seigen, a master of the art of the short sword *(kodachi)*. Kanemaki Jisai developed the use of the sword of middle length *(naka dachi)*. He was the master of Ito Ittosai.

Kano Jigoro (1860–1938): The founder of judo and a university professor; contributed to the reformation of the educational system of the Meiji period.

Kantori: The former name of Katori, a town famous for its shrine.

Kanzeon: Kannon, a Buddhist goddess.

Kashima: A town famous for its shrine.

Katori: *See* Kantori.

Katsu Kaishu (1823–1899): A sword adept and statesman of the end of the Edo period.

Katsunobu: The warrior name of Terao Magonojo. *See* Terao Magonojo.

Kishu: A region formed from the prefecture of Wakayama and the southern part of the prefecture of Mie.

Kito ryu: One of the two schools of jujutsu studied by Kano Jigoro. This school puts the accent on strangleholds, locks, and immobilization.

Kobayashi Tarozaemon: A wholesale merchant of the town of Shimonoseki at whose house Musashi stayed the night before his duel with Sasaki Kojiro in 1612.

Kobusho: The institute of the martial arts founded by the Tokugawa government in 1855.

Kodokan: The name of the judo dojo founded by Kano Jigoro in 1882.

Kokura: A town in the north of Kyushu where the main castle of the Ogasawara fief was located. Iori, one of Musashi's adoptive sons, became the chief vassal of this fief. A monument to the memory of Musashi was erected by Iori in this town. The monument is known by the name of Kokura hibun.

Komagawa Tarozaemon: *See* Kaishin ryu.

Koyasan: A sacred Buddhist mountain situated on the peninsula of Kii (Wakayama prefecture).

Kubota Shozan: A contemporary karate master.

Kumamoto: A town in Kumamoto prefecture. Kumamoto castle, where Musashi spent the last years of his life, was the main castle of the Hosokawa fief.

Kurama: A Buddhist temple located in Kyoto. Mount Kurama has been connected with legends of the martial arts since the ninth century.

Kyoto: The former capital of Japan.

Kyushu: The southernmost of the four principal islands of Japan.

Marume Kurando: A sword master of the seventeenth century, founder of the Taisha ryu, propagated principally on Kyushu.

Maruoka Yuzaemon: A warrior of the seventeenth century.

Masana: One of Musashi's warrior names.

Masanobu: The ideograms making up Genshin, one of Musashi's warrior names, can also be read Masanobu.

Matsudaira Naomasa: Lord of Izumo; around 1638 he fought against Musashi before becoming the latter's student.

Matsumoto: A town of present-day Nagano prefecture.

Meiji: The Meiji period (1868–1912).

Mimasaka: *See* Sakushu.

Minamoto Tokushu: A sword master of the nineteenth century, a vassal of the Okayama fief. He wrote numerous works on the art of swordsmanship, among others the *Gekiken sodan* (*see also* 1-f under "General Works on the Martial Arts" in the bibliography).

Mishima Yukio (1924–1970): A famous contemporary writer whose death by seppuku made a big impression on Japanese public opinion.

Miyake Gunbei: An adept of the sword, vassal of Lord Honda of Himeji. He fought Musashi in 1620 and became his student after Musashi defeated him.

Miyamoto: A village located in the region of Mimasaka (Sakushu), supposed to be the place where Musashi was born.

Miyamoto Iori (1611–1678): One of Musashi's three adoptive sons. He became a vassal of Lord Ogasawara. Miyamoto Jirotayu (1578–1660): Supposed to be Musashi's elder brother.

Miyamoto Mikinosuke: Also called Muni or Munisai. One of Musashi's three adoptive sons; died by seppuku in 1626, following his lord, Honda Tadatoki, into death.

Miyamoto Munisai (sixteenth century): The father of Miyamoto Musashi, adept of the art of the sword of the Tori ryu, vassal of Lord Shinmen.

Miyamoto Musashi (1584–1645): A sword master of the seventeenth century, founder of the Hyoho niten ichi ryu.

Mogami: The lord of the Dewa region, driven out in 1622 by the Tokugawa regime.

Moriiwa Hikobei: A childhood friend of Musashi's.

Morita Monjuro (1889–1978): A twentieth-century kendo master.

Mukojima: The island where Musashi fought Sasaki Kojiro in 1612. This island, also known as Funajima or Ganryu-jima, is part of the present-day prefecture of Kita-Kyushu.

Muni: *See* Miyamoto Munisai.

Munisai: *See* Miyamoto Munisai.

Musashi: *See* Miyamoto Musashi.

Mushanokoji senke: One of the three main schools of the tea ceremony.

Muso Gonnosuke: An adept of the art of the staff who, having drawn instruction from his defeat in combat with Musashi, founded the school of staff combat called Shinto Muso ryu.

Myoshinji: A Zen Buddhist temple.

Nagaoka Sado (seventeenth century): A principal vassal of Lord Hosokawa.

Nagato: A region of the extreme south of Honshu, the largest of the islands composing Japan; corresponds to the present-day prefecture of Yamaguchi.

Nagoya: A city in Aichi prefecture.

Naito Takaharu (1862–1929): One of the most important kendo masters of the twentieth century.

Nakamura Ichiroemon (seventeenth century): An adept of the lance of the Hozoin ryu.

Nakanishi Seizo: A contemporary author who has written studies on Musashi.

Nakatsukasa (sixteenth and seventeenth centuries): A Buddhist monk, jujutsu adept of the Takenouchi school, and friend of Miyamoto Munisai.

Naokata: The warrior name of Yoshioka Kenpo. *See* Yoshioka Kenpo.

Nara: The most ancient capital of Japan. The Nara period was from 710 to 784.

Narita Daizendayu: A sixteenth-century master of the art of the lance.

Naruse Kanji (nineteenth and twentieth centuries): A master of the art of the *shuriken* of the Shirai ryu.

Negishi ryu: A school of the art of the *shuriken*.

Nen ryu: A school of swordsmanship founded by the monk Jion at the beginning of the fifteenth century.

Nitenki: "Writings on the Two Heavens," an account of the life of Musashi written by Toyoda Seigo in 1712.

Niwa Orie Ujihari: An adept of the art of the *shuriken* of the Chishin ryu.

Niwa Tadaaki (1658–1741): A warrior and the author of several works on the art of swordsmanship under the pseudonym of Itsusai-chozanshi. His most widely known work is *Tengu geijutsu ron,* a discourse on art by the god of war.

Numata Nobumoto: The principal vassal of Hosokawa, lord of Moji castle when Musashi fought Sasaki Kojiro. Later he took the name of Nagaoka Kageyu-zaemon.

Ogasawara Tadasane: The lord of Akashi in 1617. Musashi taught him the art of the *shuriken*. In 1632 he became the lord of Buzen Kokura on Kyushu. Iori, Musashi's adoptive son, became his principal vassal.

Okuzoin: A subsidiary temple to Hozoin temple in Nara. The name also refers to the principal monk of this temple, whom Musashi fought around 1604.

Omasa: Supposed to have been Musashi's mother.

Onko chishin ryu: Literally, "the school in which the new arises on the basis of ancient knowledge." One of the branches of the School of Musashi.

Ono Jiroemon (1560–1629): A sword master of the seventeenth century, one of the two sword masters to the shogun. He was a successor of Ito Ittosai and a head of the Itto ryu.

Osaka: A city in Osaka prefecture.

Oseto Hayato: A sword adept of the Yagyu ryu, defeated in a duel by Musashi.

Oshu: The northern region of Japan corresponding to the present-day prefectures of Fukushima, Miyagi, Iwate, and Aomori.

Owari: The present-day prefecture of Aichi.

Ozawa Masao: A contemporary author and kendo adept who has done studies of Musashi.

Reigando: The cave where Musashi spent most of the last two years of his life.

Rendaino: The field, located in Musashi's time on the outskirts of Kyoto, where Musashi fought against Yoshioka Seijuro.

Ri Sangan (sixteenth and seventeenth centuries): A student of Yoshioka Kenpo. He taught his sword master the techniques for dying cotton.

Rioin (1584–1652): The wife of Tahara Hisamitsu, Musashi's older brother, according to the theory of Harada Mukashi. (17)

Sakakibara Kenkichi (1830–1894): A sword master of the Jiki shin kage ryu.

Sakazaki Naizen (seventeenth century): The principal vassal of Lord Hosokawa.

Sakurai Yoshikatsu (sixteenth and seventeenth centuries): A sword master of the Shinto ryu whose warrior name was Osuminokami; teacher of Muso Gonnosuke.

Sakushu: A region corresponding to northern Okayama prefecture. A more precise name is Mimasaka no kuni. Musashi spent his childhood here.

Sasaki Kojiro: An adept of the sword who fought Musashi in 1612 on the island of Mukojima and was killed.

Sasamori Junzo (1886–1976): A contemporary master of the Itto ryu school.

Sekigahara: The location of a battle that took place in 1600.

Sendai: A town in Miyagi prefecture.

Shibata: A contemporary author.

Shimabara: A fief located on the peninsula of Shimabara on Kyushu. The siege of Shimabara (1637–1638), which followed an insurrection of Christian peasants and warriors, shook the Tokugawa regime.

Shimane: A prefecture.

Shimonoseki: A town of the Nagato region, today in Yamaguchi prefecture.

Shimotsuke: A region of Kanto, north of Tokyo, corresponding to the present-day prefecture of Tochigi.

Shin kage ryu: A school of swordsmanship founded by Kamiizumi Nobutsuna.

Shinmen: The feudal lord of Musashi's family for several generations.

Shinto Muso ryu: A school of the art of the staff, founded by Muso Gonnosuke.

Shinto ryu: A school of swordsmanship founded by Tsukahara Bokuden.

Shioda Hamanosuke: A seventeenth-century master of the art of the staff. He was a vassal of Lord Hosokawa. After being defeated by Musashi, he became the latter's disciple. Musashi, having studied the art of the staff with Shioda, included this art in his school.

Shiragami Ikkuken: A contemporary master of the art of the *shuriken* of the Shirai ryu.

Shirai Toru: A sword master of the Tenshi itto ryu. Toward the end of his life he founded the Tenshin den hyoho.

Shishido Baiken: According to the *Nitenki,* Shishido was an adept of the art of the *kusari gama.* Baiken is a name invented by the novelist Yoshikawa Eiji. Today, in Japan, this name seems to have come to be considered an actual historical personage.

Shogun: The title of the chief of all the feudal lords of Japan and all its warriors. The full title is *sei-i-tai shogun.* This position was granted by the emperor. The first shogun was named in 794.

Shoho: The Shoho period (1644–1648).

So Doshin: Founder of the art of *shorinji kenpo* in the twentieth century.

Soken: The Buddhist name of Hatano Jirozaemon.

Sugimura Hyoma (eighteenth century): A Shinto priest and sword adept of the Onko chishin ryu, one of the branches of the School of Musashi.

Sukesada: A sword smith who lived in the late sixteenth and early seventeenth centuries.

Sumiyoshi: A shrine located in the Sumiyoshi neighborhood of Osaka.

Tachibana Hokin: An adept of the School of Musashi. He was the fourth-lineage successor of the branch derived from Terao Magonojo. He wrote a series of accounts of events in Musashi's life entitled *Tanji Hokin hikki*.

Tahara Hisamitsu: Musashi's older brother, according to the theory of Harada Mukashi. (17)

Tahara Iesada: Musashi's father, according to the theory of Harada Mukashi. (17)

Tajimanokami: Yagyu Tajimanokami Munenori. *See* Yagyu Munenori.

Takada Matabei: An adept of the lance of the Hozoin ryu, a vassal of Ogasawara. He fought Musashi around 1634 in Kokura.

Takano Sazaburo (1862–1950): One of the most important kendo masters of the twentieth century.

Takayanagi Mitsutoshi: A contemporary author.

Takehito: The ideogram for "Takehito" can also be read as Muni. Takemura Yoemon: One of Musashi's three adoptive sons, also known as Hirao Yoemon. Musashi conferred on him the leadership of the Enmei ryu, and he taught in the fief of Owari, where he acquired the rank of vassal.

Tanji Hokin: The pseudonym of Tachibana Hokin. *See* Tachibana Hokin.

Tasumi Masahisa: According to a controversial hypothesis, Musashi's father-in-law.

Tenryuji: A Buddhist temple.

Tenshin shinyo ryu: A school of jujutsu whose lineage goes back to the eighth century. Kano Jigoro studied the katas (standardized sequences) of this school before founding his school of judo.

Tensho: The Tensho period (1573–1592).

Terao Magonojo (seventeenth century): Succeeded Musashi as the head of the Hyoho niten ichi ryu. He was the recipient of the *Gorin no sho,* Musashi's most important written work. With his younger brother Motomenosuke, he directed the main school that arose from Musashi's teaching.

Terao Motomenosuke (seventeenth century): The younger brother of Terao Magonojo. He received from Musashi the *Hyoho sanju go kajo*. With his brother Magonojo, he was the head of the main school that arose from Musashi's teaching.

Terao Sama: A member of the Terao clan. He was an Owari vassal and a native of the region of Sakushu where Musashi spent his childhood.

Tochigi: A prefecture located north of Tokyo in the Kanto region.

Toda Seigen: A sword master of the Chujo ryu who used a short sword *(kodachi)*. One of his students was Kanemaki Jisai. *See also* Kanemaki Jisai.

Tokugawa: A family that held the position of shogun from 1603 to 1867.

Tomari: A shrine in the Banshu region (Hyogo prefecture), of which—according to Harada Mukashi (17)—Musashi was a native.

Tonegawa: The river Tone, located between Chiba and Ibaraki prefectures.

Tori ryu: The school of swordsmanship of Miyamoto Munisai, Musashi's father.

Toyoda Kagefusa: The grandson of Toyoda Seigo; he completed the composition of the *Nitenki* in 1755.

Toyoda Seigo (eighteenth century): A sword adept of the School of Musashi and vassal of Lord Matsui. Author of the *Nitenki*, which he began in 1712.

Toyotomi: The name of a clan. In 1587 Toyotomi Hideyoshi (1536–1598) gained ascendancy over the feudal lords of Japan and took the supreme power. His second son, Hideyori (1593–1615), committed suicide in 1615 at the time of the battle of Osaka. The continuity of the Toyotomi clan was broken by the power of the Tokugawa regime.

Tsujikaze: An adept of the Yagyu ryu who was defeated by Musashi in Edo.

Tsukahara Bokuden (1489–1571): Born into a family of Shinto priests of the Kashima shrine, he received the martial arts teachings of his predecessors and founded the Shinto ryu.

Tsutsumi Hozan (fifteenth century): Twelfth disciple of the monk Jion of the Nen ryu, founder of the Hozan ryu of the *jitte*.

Ueda Umanosuke: A sword adept of the nineteenth century.

Ueno Izu (eighteenth century): An adept of the art of throwing needles, vassal of the Sendai fief.

Ueshiba Morihei (1882–1969): The originator of aikido. He was influenced by the teachings of the Daito ryu aiki jujutsu school of jujutsu, which he studied under the direction of Takeda Sokaku.

Ujii Magoshiro: A sword master of the Yagyu shin kage ryu and a Hosokawa vassal. In 1640 he fought Musashi in the presence of Lord Hosokawa. Musashi defeated him without striking a blow.

Ukita: Feudal lord of the sixteenth century.

Usaka: Town situated in the Echizen region.

Watanabe Koan (1582–1711): A warrior, vassal of the Tokugawas. Around 1630 he left his position as vassal and traveled in the various regions of Japan. He lived an exceptionally long time and was 127 years old when Lord Maeda of the fief of Kaga sent his vassal Sukiki Sannojo to undertake a series of interviews with him. These are related in a work entitled *Watanabe Koan taiwa*.

Yabunouchi senke: One of the principal schools of the tea ceremony.

Yagyu: The name of a fief.

Yagyu Jubei (1606–1650): Eldest son of Yagyu Munenori.

Yagyu Munenori (1571–1646): A sword master of the Yagyu shin kage ryu. He became sword master to the Tokugawa shogun.

Yagyu Muneyoshi (1529–1606): Father of Yagyu Munenori. He received the ultimate teaching of Kamiizumi Nobutsuna of the Shin kage ryu and founded the Yagyu shin kage ryu.

Yamada Jirokichi (late nineteenth and early twentieth centuries): A sword master of the Jiki shin kage ryu .

Yamamoto Gensuke (*also* Gennosuke): A sword master of the School of Musashi, successor of Terao Magonojo.

Yoshida Seiken: A contemporary author and adept of the sword.

Yoshikawa Eiji (1892–1962): A famous contemporary author. He wrote a long novel entitled *Miyamoto Musashi*.

Yoshiko: According to a controversial hypothesis, Musashi's mother-in-law.

Yoshioka Denshichiro: The younger brother of Yoshioka Seijuro; died fighting Musashi in 1604.

Yoshioka Kenpo: A sword master of the sixteenth century. According to legend, in his youth he fought Miyamoto Munisai in the presence of Shogun Ashikaga.

Yoshioka Matashichiro: The son of Yoshioka Seijuro; nominal head of the Yoshioka family at the time of its last three confrontations with Musashi. He was killed by Musashi.

Yoshioka Seijuro: The eldest son of Yoshioka Kenpo. He was defeated in a duel by Musashi in 1604 at Rendaino on the outskirts of Kyoto.

Yumeyo: One of the warrior names of Terao Magonojo.

Zeami (1363–1443): A master of Noh theater.

Terms

aikido: A martial art originated by Ueshiba Morihei in the twentieth century. *See also* Ueshiba Morihei.

aikuchi: Short sword without a hilt; a large knife.

ashi: Foot.

atari: Hit, blow.

bo: Staff.

bokken: Wooden sword.

bokuto: Wooden sword.

budo: A designation for the entire domain of the Japanese martial arts since the end of the nineteenth century.

bugei: Martial arts practiced by the Japanese warriors.

bujutsu: Martial arts practiced by the Japanese warriors.

buke: Warrior family, warrior class.

bunchin: A weight used to hold the paper in place in calligraphy or *sumi* ink painting.

bushi: Warrior.

daiji: Major issue, importance, essence.

daiku: Carpenter.

daimyojin: Reverential form of address for a deity.

denki: Anecdote, biography.

do: The way.

dojo: The place where the way is sought.

enso: Circular form, a circle that symbolizes in Buddhism a revelation or a profound insight.

eta: "Nonhuman" in the hierarchy of feudal social classes.

fu: Wind.

fukuro: Bag.

fukuro shinai: Bamboo sword wrapped in a long case.

gagaku: Noble classical music.

gedan: Low level.

gei: Art.

gekiken: A name used at the end of the Edo period and the beginning of the Meiji period to designate a practice of swordsmanship in which protective armor and bamboo swords were used.

genpuku: Rite of passage to the age of an adult for a warrior child. It generally took place between the ages of twelve and sixteen; a boy changed his name, his hair style, his mode of dress, and so on.

genzai: Present.

gorin: Five elements. See note 288 on page 437.

gunki: Military chronicle.

gyaku: Opposite, opposite side.

gyaku nito: The use of two swords in a reversed guard position; the swords are held in the opposite of the usual fashion, with the long sword in the left hand and the short sword in the right.

gyo: The primary sense of this term is "to walk," but in its Buddhist sense it designates any action, good or evil, as participating in the twelve principles of causality; it also refers to a practice aimed at attaining profound understanding.

hanatsu: To let go of, liberate.

happo ken: A throwing weapon in the form of an eight-pointed star.

hari: Needle.

heiho: *See* hyoho.

heimin: The common people.

hikki: Note, piece of writing.

himin: "Nonhuman" in the hierarchy of feudal social classes.

hiragana: Japanese phonetic writing.

hiryu: Flight of a dragon or a dragon in flight.

hiryu ken: A technique for throwing the short sword of the Onko chishin ryu.

hitotsu: One; only one.

ho: Law, method, principle.

hoka: Acrobat.

hokashi: Magician, acrobat.

hon: Root, essence, book.

hyogu: Military paraphernalia, weapons.

hyoho: Also pronounced *heiho;* designates the martial arts in general, including strategy.

hyoshi: Cadences.

iai: Art of drawing the sword.

ie: House.

iki: Breathing.

ippon: Singular victory.

ippon zeoi: A throw in jujutsu or judo in which one throws the adversary over one's shoulder by means of a hold on his arm.

isshin itto: A single mind, a single sword.

ite: Archer.

itsuku: To freeze or become fixed.

izu bari: A needle twelve centimeters long that is thrown as a weapon. The form of the needle and the technique for throwing it were developed by Ueno Izu. *See also* Ueno Izu.

jiki: Direct.

jiki tsu: Direct communication or understanding.

jikida: A technique of throwing the *shuriken* in which it is not made to turn.

jingu: Large Shinto shrine.

jinja: Shrine.

jitte: "Ten hands"; a weapon with ten hooks, and also a weapon with just one hook.

ju: Flexibility.

juji shuriken: A *shuriken* in the form of a cross with four points.

jujutsu: A bare-handed combat art developed by the Japanese warriors.

jumonji yari: A lance whose blade is in the form of a cross.

junshi: A suicide committed in order to follow one's master into death.

jutsu: Technique, art.

kabuto: Steel helmet.

kage: Shadow.

kaisha kenjutsu: The art of swordsmanship using protective armor.

kako: The past.

kama yari: A lance whose main blade has, on one side, a hook in the shape of the blade of a sickle.

kamae: Guard, guard position.

kami: God.

kan: Look.

kani: Crab.

kanji: Chinese ideogram.

karo: Principal vassal.

kata: Form, mold, prototype, standardized sequence of technique through which a martial art is transmitted or developed.

kataki: An enemy who has killed one's lord or a member of one's family.

kataki uchi: An act of vengeance against one who has killed one's lord or a member of one's family. During the Edo period, such acts of vengeance were encouraged and formed a part of the ethics of warriors; they were carried out on all social levels. They were prohibited in 1873, early in the Meiji period.

katana: Sword.

katsunin ken: The sword that gives life.

katsunin to: The sword that gives life.

katsu-totsu: An onomatopoeic expression reflecting cries or noises. See The Scroll of Water.

kaze: Wind.

kazoku: New nobles of the Meiji period.

kendo: Way of the sword, the modern practice of the art of the sword.

kendoka: Kendo practitioner.

kenjutsu: The art of swordsmanship.

kesa giri: Slash on an angle from the adversary's shoulder in the direction of his belly.

ki: Breath, vital energy.

ki ken tai: Integration of the vital energy, the sword, and the body in a strike in kendo; this integration constitutes the essential quality of the strike.

kiai: Bringing *ki* together by means of a cry or cries.

kinshi cho ohken: One of the secret techniques of the Itto ryu school.

kissaki: The point of the sword blade.

kizeme: Offensive utilizing *ki*.

koan: Phrase to be meditated on in Zen practice (simplified definition).

kodachi: Short sword, or the art of using it.

kokoro: Mind, thought.

koku: One koku equals 180 liters of rice (see note 1, page 362).

kosetsu to: "The sword that cuts down a tiger"; it is generally thought that this was the name of Sasaki Kojiro's favorite technique.

koshi: Pelvis, small of the back, hips.

kosho: Page.

kosu: Surpass, pass above.

kowakizashi: Small short sword.

ku: Emptiness, space, heaven, sky.

kuchi: Mouth, entry.

kuden: Oral transmission.

kuge: Noble class.

kurai: Level, the situation of things.

kuruma ken: Sword that turns like a wheel.

kusari gama: Sickle to which a chain with a steel weight on the end is attached.

maki: Scroll.

meika: Famous adepts.

metsuke: Way of looking.

mikiri: To cut through with a look, perceiving things with an incisive look.

mirai: Future.

mizudori: Water bird.

munen: Nonthought.

munen muso: Nonthought, a state of mind of emptiness.

musha shugyo: A journey for study and improvement in the martial arts.

myo: Excelling in a manner that is unfathomable by the human mind.

naginata: Weapon composed of a large blade and a long handle like that of a lance.

naka dachi: Sword of medium length, somewhere between that of the *tachi* (long sword) and the *wakizashi* (small sword).

nio zen: Zen meditation done standing.

niten: "Two heavens."

nito: "Two swords."

nuki uchi: To draw the sword and slash the adversary in a single motion.

oku: Depth.

omote: Surface, front.

omote gei: Superficial art, art that is shown to the public.

pinan: One of the standardized series of karate techniques developed by Itosu Anko.

randori: Judo combat exercise.

rikata: Discipline in which effectiveness is sought; a pragmatic method.

rokugu: Armor.

roppo: Six methods.

ryu: School, style.

ryusui: Flowing water.

sa do: The way of tea, the tea ceremony.

sakimori: Soldiers from the east of Japan sent to Kyushu to defend it against invasions by the Koreans and Chinese (eighth to tenth centuries).

sama: Expression of respect comparable to "sir" or "mister."

samurai: Warrior.

sanshin: Three minds, three intentions.

seiho: Method or technique of combat.

seme: An offensive.

senshi: Deceased master.

seppuku: Literally, "cutting the belly"; ritualized voluntary death.

setsunin ken: The sword that kills.

setsunin to: The sword that kills.

shaku: A *shaku* is 30.3 centimeters.

shike: The four families.

shin: That which possesses a strange power that governs the universe; superhuman spiritual being; the gods of Japanese mythology; the existence of a strange force unfathomable by humans; the spirit that inhabits the body.

shinai: Bamboo sword.

shizoku: Former warriors.

shoden: Short anecdotes, little stories.

shoji: Sliding door with a light wooden frame covered with paper.

shomen: Front; opposite or across from.

shorinji kenpo: A bare-handed combat art developed in Japan by So Doshin after the Second World War.

shuriken: Knife, sword, or other thrown weapon.

sodan: Collection of various anecdotes or stories.

sokui zuke: Sword technique that consists in making the blade of your sword stick to that of the adversary.

sumigane: Carpenter's tool—string soaked in India ink, ruler.

sumo: Traditional Japanese wrestling that was the basis for the physical education of Japanese warriors.

sun: A *sun* is 3.03 centimeters.

sunden: Vital point situated between the eyebrows.

tachi: Large sword.

tachi tsukai: Adept of the large sword.

tai yu: Substance and its function.

tameshi giri: Trial of slashing with a sword, a test of the quality of either the sword or the swordsman.

tanden: Field of cinnabar, the belly a few centimeters below the navel.

tanto: Large knife with a scabbard.

ten: Heaven, heavenly world.

teppo: Gun.

tokonoma: Architectural feature of the main room of a traditional Japanese house.

toku: Interest, virtue (*see* appendix 1).

totsu: See *katsu-totsu*.

tsu: Communication.

tsuba: Sword hilt.

tsubame gaeshi: Technique of slicing a swallow; favorite technique of Sasaki Kojiro.

tsuka: Sword handle.

tsukai: Expert, adept.

tsuki: To strike with the fist; to stab with a sword or a lance.

uchi: A strike.

udenuki: A string that is attached to the arm and to the hilt or the end of the handle of a sword to prevent it from falling during combat. A cloth or leather arm protector is also called an *udenuki*.

uke: Parry.

uko muko: Guardless guard.

ura: Behind, in relation to *omote* (front).

ura gei: Hidden art.

waki: Armpit, side.

wakizashi: Short or small sword.

ware: Me, I.

waza: Technique, art.

yari: Lance.

yin-yo: Yin and yang, positive and negative.

yoko men: Kendo technique, strike to the side of the head.

zazen: Literally, "sitting Zen"; meditation posture.

BIBLIOGRAPHY

IN THE REFERENCES below, Japanese authors are referred to by their family name followed by their given name or initial.

Editions of Texts Written by Miyamoto Musashi

1. Budho sho Kankokai (collective authorship). *Bujutsu sosho* (Collection of Texts on the Martial Arts). Tokyo: Jinbutsu orai sha, 1968. See item 1 under "General Works of the Martial Arts" below for an itemization of the texts in this collection.

2. Fukuhara Josen. *Miyamoto Musashi no tankyu* (Study in Depth of Miyamoto Musashi). Okayama, Japan: Miyamoto Musashi Kenshin Gorin no kai, 1978.

3. Imai Masayuki. *Niten ichi-ryu seiho.* Oita, Japan: M. Imai, 1987.

4. Kamata Shigeo. *Gorin-no-sho.* (Edited with commentary). Tokyo: Kodansha, 1986.

5. Kamiko Tadashi. *Gorin-no-sho.* (Edited with commentary). Tokyo: Tokuma shoten, 1963.

6. Mitsuhashi Kanichiro. *Kendo hiyo* (The Essential Secret of Kendo). (Editions with commentary of several texts by Miyamoto Musashi). Kyoto: Butokushi Hakkosho, 1901.

7. Miyamoto Musashi Kenshokai (collective authorship). *Shin Miyamoto Musashi ko* (A Further Study on Miyamoto Musashi). Tokyo: Miyamoto Musashi Kenshokai, 1977.

8. Nakanishi Seizo. *Miyamoto Musashi no shogai* (The Life of Miyamoto Musashi). Tokyo: Shin jinbutsu orai sha, 1975.

9. Ozawa Masao. *Miyamoto Musashi.* Tokyo: Yoshikawa Kobun kan, 1986.

10. Takayanagi Mitsutoshi. *Gorin-no-sho.* (Edited with commentary). Tokyo: Iwanami, 1942; rev. ed., 1969.

11. Terayama Danchu. *Gorin-no-sho: Miyamoto Musashi no waza to michi* (*Gorin no sho:* The Techniques and the Way of Miyamoto Musashi). (Edited with commentary). Tokyo: Kodansha, 1984.

12. Tominaga Kengo. *Shijitsu Miyamoto Musashi.* Tokyo: Hyakusen shobo, 1969.

13. Watanabe Ichiro. *Gorin-no-sho.* (Edited with commentary). Tokyo: Iwanami, 1985.

14. Yamada Jirokichi. *Kendo shugi* (Compilation of Kendo Transmissions). Collection of texts, 2 vols. Tokyo: Hitotsubashi kenyu kai, 1922. See item 14 under "General Works of the Martial Arts" below for an itemization of the texts in this collection.

Contemporary Works on the Life and Work of Musashi

15. Ezaki Shunpei. *Nihon kengo retsuden* (Writings on the Great Adepts of the Japanese Sword). Tokyo: Gendai kyoyo bunko, 1970.
16. Fukuhara Josen. *Miyamoto Iori no gisho* (The False Testimony of Miyamoto Iori). Okayama, Japan: Josen Fukuhara, 1984.
17. Harada Mukashi. *Shinsetsu Miyamoto Musashi* (The Truth about Miyamoto Musashi). Fukuoka: Ashi shobo, 1984.
18. Ishioka Hisao. *Hyoho sha no seikatsu* (The Life of the Warrior Adepts of the Sword). Tokyo: Yazankaku, 1981.
19. Morita Monjuro. *Kendo zen to kako no jutsu* (Kendo Zen and the Technique of the Past). Tokyo: Shimazu shobo, 1988.
20. ———. *Koshi to tanden de okonau kendo* (Kendo Based on the Small of the Back and the Tanden). Tokyo: Shimazu shobo, 1987.
21. Muneta Hiroshi. *Miyamoto Musashi*. Tokyo: Shin jinbutsu orai sha, 1976.
22. Nakanishi Seizo. *Miyamoto Musashi no saigo* (The Death of Miyamoto Musashi). Tokyo: Nihon Shuppan hoso kikaku, 1987.
23. Nakazato Kaizan. *Nihon bujutsu shinmyo ki* (Extraordinary Tales from the Japanese Martial Arts). Tokyo: Kawade-shobo, 1985.
24. Naramoto Tatsuya. *Gorin-no-sho nyumon* (Initiation into the *Gorin no sho*). Tokyo: Tokuma shoten, 1984.
25. Nippon Hoso Kyokai (collective authorship). *Miyamoto Musashi*. Tokyo: NHK, 1989.
26. Omori Sogen. *Ken to zen* (The Sword and Zen). Tokyo: Shunju-sha, 1973.
27. Okada Kazuo and Kato Hiroshi (editors of a work of collective authorship). *Miyamoto Musashi no subete* (Everything about Miyamoto Musashi). Tokyo: Shin jinbutsu orai sha, 1983.
28. Saotome Mitsugu. *Jitsuroku Miyamoto Musashi* (The Historical Truth about Miyamoto Musashi). Tokyo: PHP Bunko, 1989.
29. Shiba Ryotaro. *Nihon kenkyaku den* (The Story of the Adepts of the Japanese Sword). Vol. 2. Tokyo: Asahi shinbun-sha, 1982.
30. ———. *Shin setsu Miyamoto Musashi* (The Truth about Miyamoto Musashi). Tokyo: Asahi shinbun-sha, 1983.
31. Tobe Shinichiro. *Kosho Miyamoto Musashi* (Study of Miyamoto Musashi). Tokyo: Fukosha, 1984.

32. Watanuki Kiyoshi. *Nihon kengo hyakusen* (One Hundred Great Adepts of the Japanese Sword).Tokyo: Akita shoten, 1971.

33.Watanabe Ichiro, ed. *Budo no meicho* (Masterpieces of Budo). Tokyo:Tokyo copi, 1979.

34.Yamada Jirokichi. *Nihon kendo shi* (The History of theWay of the Sword in Japan). Tokyo: Hitotsubashi kenyu kai, 1922.

35. Yoshida Seiken. *Nito ryu o kataru* (Explanation of the School of Two Swords). Tokyo: Kyozaisha, 1941.

36.YoshidaYutaka, ed. *Budo hiden sho* (Secret Book of Budo).Tokyo:Tokuma shoten, 1973.

General Works on the Martial Arts

The first two works given below (numbers 1 and 14, cited in full in the first section above) are collections of ancient works. I indicate below their titles the main texts I consulted in them.

1. Budo sho Kankokai (collective authorship), *Bujutsu sosho* (Collection of Texts on the Martial Arts)

   a. Miyamoto Musashi. *Hyoho sanju-go-kajo* and *Enmei ryu kenpo sho*.Written in the seventeenth century.

   b. Hinatsu Shigetaka. *Honcho bugei shoden* (Little Tales of the Martial Arts in Japan).Written in 1715.

   c. AoyamaTakanao. *Shinsen bujutsu ryuso roku* (On the Founders of the School of the Martial Arts).Written in 1843.

   d. Itsusai Chozanshi. *Tengu geijutsu ron* (Discourse of the GodTengu on the Art of the Sword).Written in 1729.

   e. KotodaToshisada. *Ittosai sensei kenpo sho* (TheTeaching of Master Ittosai).Written in the seventeenth century.

   f. Minamoto Tokushu. *Gekiken sodan* (Treatise on Schools of Swordsmanship). Written in 1843. Minamoto Tokushu was a sword master and traveled about for more than ten years visiting different schools of swordsmanship.This work gives an account of the documents he collected.

   g. Hirayama Shiryu-gyozo. *Kensetsu* (Discourse on the Swords). Hirayama lived from 1759 to 1828 and was a master of the sword.

   h. Matsuura Seizan. *Joseishi kendan* (Joseishi's Philosophy of Swordsmanship). Written at the end of the eighteenth century.

   i. *Enmei ryu kenpo sho* (Writings on the SwordTechnique of the Enmei Ryu).

14.Yamada Jirokichi, *Kendo shugi* (Compilation of Kendo Transmissions)

a. Hinatsu Shigetaka. *Gajo shoden* (Text on the Traditions of the Various Schools of the Martial Arts). Written in the eighteenth century.

b. Kubota Seion. *Keijo ki* (On the Various Techniques of the Art of the Sword); *Kenpo yogaku denju* (Teaching the Sword to Beginners); *Kenpo chotan ron* (The Characteristics of Long and Short Swords); and *Kenpo ryakki* (The Main Outlines of the Techniques of Swordsmanship). Written at the beginning of the nineteenth century.

c. Miyamoto Musashi. *Gorin-no-sho* and *Hyoho-sanju-go-kajo.*

37. Domoto Akihiko. *Kendo kojutsu shi* (Collection of the Talks of Master Hakudo Nakayama on Kendo). Tokyo: Ski janal, 1988.

38. Hasegawa Junzo. *Kano Jigoro no kyoiku to shiso* (Education and Ideology According to Kano Jigoro). Tokyo: Meiji shoin, 1981.

39. Kato Jinpei. *Kano Jigoro* (A Study of Kano Jigoro). Tokyo: Shoyo shoten, 1964.

40. Katsube Mitake. *Bushido* (Dialogue between Tesshu Yamaoka and Katsu Kaishu). Tokyo: Kadokawa, 1971.

41. Mitsuhashi Shuzo. *Kendo.* Tokyo: Taishukan, 1972.

42. Mori Shohei. *Dai Nippon kendo shi* (The History of Japanese Kendo). Osaka: Kendo sho kankokai, 1934.

43. Nakayama Hakudo. *Kendo kowa* (Discourse on Kendo). Tokyo: Yushinkan dojo, 1937.

44. Naramoto Tatsuya. *Bushido no keifu* (Bushido Genealogies). Tokyo: Chuo koron, 1975.

45. Nitobe Inazo. *Bushido.* Tokyo: Iwanami, 1938.

46. Omori Sogen. *Sho to zen* (Calligraphy and Zen). Tokyo: Shunjusha, 1973.

47. ―――. *Zen no koso* (The Great Zen Monks). Tokyo: Shunjusha, 1979.

48. Ozawa Chikamitsu. *Ken shin itchi* (Sword and Mind Becoming One). Tokyo: Jutaku shinpo, 1978.

49. Sugimoto Sannojo. *Watanabe Koan taiwa* (Conversation with Watanabe Koan). Watanabe was a samurai who was born in 1582 and died in 1711 at the age of 129. When Watanabe was 127, on the command of Lord Kaga, Sugimoto collected and wrote down his stories as an expression of living history. Watanabe actually knew Musashi, whence the interest of this document.

50. Sasamori Junzo. *Itto-ryu-gokui* (The Supreme Teaching of the Itto Ryu). Tokyo: Reigakudo, 1986.

51. So Doshin. *Shorinji Kenpo.* Tokyo: Kobunsha, 1963.

52. Tokitsu Kenji. "Étude sur le rôle et les transformations de la culture traditionelle dans la societé contemporaire Japonaise" (Study on the Role and the Transformations of Traditional Culture in Contemporary Japanese Society). Third-cycle

doctorate thesis in sociology (director, G. Balandier), Université René Descartes, 1982.

53. ————. *La voie du karaté, pour une théorie des arts martiaux Japonais* (The Way of Karate: Toward a Theory of the Japanese Martial Arts). Paris: Éditions du Seuil, 1979.

54. Ueshiba Kisshomaru. *Aikido hiyo* (The Essence of Aikido). Tokyo: Tokyo shoten, 1972.

55. ————. *Aikido nyumon* (Initiation into Aikido). Tokyo: Kobunsha, 1972.

56. Yagyu Munenori. *Hyoho kadensho* (The Family Transmission of Hyoho). Tokyo: Iwanami, 1985. Written during the same period as the *Gorin no sho.*

57. Shiragami Ikkuken. Article on his school, the Shirai ryu. *Kendo Nippon* 8 (1978). Tokyo: Ski-journal, 1978.

Essays on Miyamoto Musashi

58. Naramoto Tatsuya. *Gorin-no-sho-nyumon.* Tokyo: Tokuma bunko, 1985.

59. Saotome Mitsugu. *Jitsoruku Miyamoto Musashi.* Tokyo: PHP bunko, 1989.

60. NHK (collective work). *Jitsuzo Miyamoto Musashi.* Tokyo: NHK, 1989.

Novel

61. Yoshikawa Eiji. *Miyamoto Musashi.* Tokyo: Kodansha, 1970.

62. ————. *La pierre et le sabre* (The Stone and the Sword), vol. 1; and *La parfaite lumiere* (Perfect Light), vol. 2 (the French translation of *Miyamoto Musashi,* immediately above). Paris: Éditions Balland, 1983. English translation: Eiji Yoshikawa. *Musashi.* New York: Harper and Row, 1981.

General Works on the History of Japan

63. Collective work. *Nihon no rekishi* (The History of Japan). 32 vols. Tokyo: Shogakukan, 1975.

64. Collective work. *Nihon no rekishi* (The History of Japan). 26 vols. Tokyo: Chuokoron, 1974.

65. Collective work. *Nihonshi no kiso chishiki* (Basic Facts of the History of Japan). Tokyo: Yuhikaku, 1974.

66. Collective work (Takayanagi M., director). *Dictionary of the History of Japan.* Tokyo: Kadokawa, 1982.

67. Kyokai. *Nihon ryoi ki* (Book of Strange Events of Japanese History). 3 vols. Tokyo: Kodansha, 1978. Written by the monk Kyokai in the eighth century.

68. Mishima Yukio. *Hagakure nyumon* (Initiation into the *Hagakure* [Book of the Samurai]). Tokyo: Kobunsha, 1967.

69. Mori Mikisaburo. *Na to haji no bunka* (The Culture of Honor and Shame). Tokyo: Kodansha, 1971.

70. Nakamura Kichiji. *Buke no rekishi* (The History of the *Bushi*). Tokyo: Iwanami, 1967.

71. Terada Toru. *Do no shiso* (The Ideology of Do). Tokyo: Sobunsha, 1978.

72. Tokutomi Soho. *Kinsei Nihon kokumin shi* (History of the Japanese Population in the Modern Period). 30 vols. Tokyo: Kodansha, 1982.

73. Yasuda Takashi. *Kata no Nihon bunka* (The Japanese Culture of Katas). Tokyo: Asahi Shinbun, 1984.

Before the Edo Period

74. Hayashiya Tatsusaburo. *Chusei geinoshi no kenkyu* (Study on the History of the Arts in the Middle Ages). Tokyo: Iwanami, 1960.

75. Miki Seiichiro. *Teppo to sono jisai* (The Introduction of the Gun and Its Epoch). Tokyo: Kyoikusha, 1981.

76. Owada Tetsuo. *Sengoku busho* (The Generals of the Period of Feudal Wars). Tokyo: Chuo koron, 1981.

77. Sakai Tadakutsu, ed. *Sekigahara kassen shimatsuki* (Writings on the Battle of Sekigahara). Tokyo: Kyoiku sha, 1991. Writings from the beginning of the seventeenth century.

78. Yamazaki Masakazu. *Muromachi ki* (Writings on the Muromachi Period). Tokyo: Asahi shinbun, 1974.

79. Yasuda Motohisa. *Bushi sekai no jomaku* (The Beginning of the World of the *Bushi*). Tokyo: Yoshikawa kobunsha, 1973.

80. Yoshida Yutaka, comp. and commentator. *Zohyo monogatari* (The History of the Soldiers of the Period of Feudal Wars). Tokyo: Kyoikusha, 1980.

81. Yuasa Jozan. *Jozan kidan* (The Writings of Jozan). Tokyo: Iwanami, 1939. Anecdotes and writings on the particular modes of behavior of the *bushi* of the sixteenth and seventeenth centuries.

Edo Period

82. Chiba Eiichiro. *Chiba Shusaku iko*. Tokyo: Taiiko to spotsu, 1982.

83. Collective work. "On the Individual and the Collective in the Edo Period." *Rekishi koron* (On History) 106 (1984). Tokyo: Yuzankaku.

84. Ezaki Junpei. *Yagyu Munenori*. Tokyo: Shakai shiso sa, 1971.

85. Hasegawa Shin, comp. *Nihon adauchi iso* (Strange Stories of Vengeance in Japan of the Edo Period). Tokyo: Chuo koron, 1974.

86. Hino Tatsuo. *Edojin to yutopia* (The Men of the Edo Period and Utopia). Tokyo: Asahi shinbun, 1977.

87. Imano Nobuo. *Edo no tabi* (The Edo Journey). Tokyo: Iwanami, 1986.

88. Inagaki Fumio. *Kosho Edo kibun* (Study on Strange Events in Edo). Tokyo: Kawade shobo, 1984.

89. Inagaki Shisei. *Adauchi o kosho suru* (Study on Japanese Acts of Vengeance). Tokyo: Obunsha, 1987.

90. Kitajima Masamoto. *Edo jidai* (The Edo Period). Tokyo: Iwanami, 1958.

91. Nakano Mitsutoshi. *Edo meibutsu hyoban ki* (Tourist Guide to Edo). Tokyo: Iwanami, 1985.

92. Nishiyama M. and Ogi S. *Edo sanbyaku nen* (The Three Hundred Years of the Edo Period). 3 vols. Tokyo: Kodansha, 1975.

93. Okubo Hikozaemon. *Mikawa monogatari* (The History of Mikawa: The Beginning of the Founding of the Tokugawa Shogunate). Tokyo: Kyoikusha, 1980.

94. Shimozawa Kan. *Shinsengumi ibun* (On the Shinsengumi [the Shogunate police]). Tokyo: Chuo koron, 1977.

95. Takayanagi Kaneyoshi. *Edo no kakyu bushi* (The Warriors from the Bottom of the Hierarchy during the Edo Period). Tokyo: Kashiwa shobo, 1980.

96. Tanizaki Junichiro, comp. and trans. *Bushuko hiwa* (Esoteric Anecdotes of the Bushu Region from the Edo Period). Tokyo: Chuo koron, 1984.

97. Watsuji Tetsuro. *Sakoku*. Tokyo: Chikuma shobo, 1963.

98. Yamamoto Jocho. *Hagakure* (Text Written behind the Bower Wall: Treatise on the Conduct of Warriors). Tokyo: Chuo koron, 1966.

Dictionaries

Reference Dictionaries

99. *Kokugo dai jiten*. Tokyo: Shogakukan, 1982.

100. *Kojien*. Tokyo: Iwanami, 1967.

Other Dictionaries

101. *Kokugo jiten*. Tokyo: Iwanami, 1963.

102. *Jigen*. Tokyo: Kadokawa, 1955.

103. *Shin kanwa chujiten*. Tokyo: Sanseido, 1967.

104. *Shokai kanwa dai jiten*. Tokyo: Fuzanbo, 1977.

105. *Kogo jiten*. Tokyo: Sanseido, 1962.

106. *Nihonshi jiten*. Tokyo: Kadokawa, 1982.

107. *Edogo no jiten*. Tokyo: Kodansha, 1979.

108. *Kanji no gogen.* Tokyo: Kadokawa, 1977.

109. *Koji to kotowaza no jiten.* Tokyo: Haga shoten, 1968.

Complementary Works

110. Fujiwara R. *Shinto-yoshin-ryu no rekishi to giho* (The History and Technique of the Shinto Yoshin Ryu). Tokyo: Sozo, 1983.

111. Gima S. and Fujiwara R. *Kindai karate-do no rekishi o kataru* (Conversation on the Modern History of the Karate Do). Tokyo: Besubol-magazin, 1986.

112. Hokama Tetsuhiro. *Okinawa karate-do no ayumi* (The Progress of the Karate Do in Okinawa). Naha, Japan: Minami P., 1984.

113. Kono Y. and Yoro T. *Kobujutsu no hakken* (Discovery of the Classical Japanese Martial Arts). Tokyo: Kobun sha, 1993.

114. Kuroda Tetsuzan. *Iai jutsu seigi* (Treatise on the Art of Iai). Saitama, Japan: Sojin sha, 1991.

115. ———. *Kenjutsu seigi* (Treatise on the Art of Kenjutsu). Saitama, Japan: Sojin sha, 1992.

116. Matsuda Ryuchi. *Chugoku bujutsu* (On the Chinese Martial Arts). Tokyo: Shin jinbutsu orai sha, 1975.

117. ———. *Chugoku bujutsu shi* (On the History of the Chinese Martial Arts). Tokyo: Shin jinbutsu orai sha, 1976.

118. ———. *Hiden Nihon jujutsu* (Secret Transmission of Japanese Jujutsu). Tokyo: Shin jinbutsu orai sha, 1978.

119. Nagamine Shoshin. *Okinawa no karate sumo meijin den* (The History of the Adepts of Karate and Sumo in Okinawa). Tokyo: Shin jinbutsu orai sha, 1986.

120. Onishi Hidetaka. *Yamada Jirokichi sensei no shogai* (The Life of Master Yamada Jirokichi). Tokyo: Hitotsubashi kenyu-kai, 1956.

121. Ono Kazufusa. *Kokoro no hyoho* (Strategy of the Mind: On the Yagyu Shin Kage Ryu of Today). Tokyo: Roppo-shuppan, 1982.

122. Ota Yoshimaro. *Kojiki monogatari* (The History of the Kojiki). Tokyo: Shakai shiso sha, 1971.

123. Collective work. *Shinsengumi taishi retsuden* (On the Members of the Shinsengumi [the Shogunate police]). Tokyo: Shin jinbutsu orai sha, 1972.

124. Jiguang Qi. *Ji xiao xin shu.* Taipei: Hualian, 1983. Sixteenth-century treatise on the Chinese martial arts.

125. Nango T. *Budo towa nanika* (What Is Budo?). Tokyo: Sanichi-shobo, 1977.

126. Gurvitch, G. *La vocation actuelle de la sociologie* (The Current Calling of Sociology). Paris: Éditions Presses Universitaires de France, 1969.

INDEX